Of Giants

MEDIEVAL CULTURES

SERIES EDITORS
Rita Copeland
Barbara A. Hanawalt
David Wallace

Sponsored by the Center for Medieval Studies
at the University of Minnesota

Volumes in the series study the diversity of medieval cultural histories and practices, including such interrelated issues as gender, class, and social hierarchies; race and ethnicity; geographical relations; definitions of political space; discourses of authority and dissent; educational institutions; canonical and noncanonical literatures; and technologies of textual and visual literacies.

For other books in the series, see p. 236

Of Giants

Sex, Monsters, and the Middle Ages

Jeffrey Jerome Cohen

Medieval Cultures
Volume 17

University of Minnesota Press
Minneapolis
London

An earlier version of chapter 3 appeared as "Decapitation and Coming of Age," in *The Arthurian Yearbook*, III (1993); reprinted with permission of *The Arthurian Yearbook*. A portion of chapter 4 originally appeared as "Diminishing Masculinity in Chaucer's *Tale of Sir Thopas*," in *Masculinities in Chaucer*, edited by Peter G. Beidler (Suffolk: Boydell & Brewer, 1998); reprinted with permission of Boydell & Brewer. A portion of chapter 5 originally appeared as "Gowther among the Dogs," in *Becoming Male in the Middle Ages*, edited by Jeffrey Jerome Cohen and Bonnie Wheeler (New York: Garland Publishing, Inc., 1997); copyright 1997 Garland Publishing, Inc., and reprinted with permission of Garland Publishing, Inc.

Published by the University of Minnesota Press
111 Third Avenue South, Suite 290
Minneapolis, MN 55401-2520
http://www.upress.umn.edu

Library of Congress Cataloging-in-Publication Data
Cohen, Jeffrey Jerome.
 Of giants : sex, monsters, and the Middle Ages / Jeffrey Jerome Cohen.
  p.   cm. — (Medieval cultures ; v. 17)
 Includes bibliographical references and index.
 ISBN 0-8166-3216-2 (hc). — ISBN 0-8166-3217-0 (pbk.)
 1. English literature — Middle English, 1100–1500 — History and criticism.   2. Giants in literature.   3. English literature — Old English, ca. 450–1100 — History and criticism.   4. Psychoanalysis and literature — England — History — To 1500.   5. Literature and folklore — England — History — To 1500.   6. Romances, English — History and criticism.   7. Difference (Psychology) in literature.
 8. Abnormalities, Human, in literature.   9. Monsters in literature.
 10. Sex in literature. I. Title. II. Series.
 PR275.G47C64   1999
 820.9'37 — dc21   98-53479

11 10 09 08 07 06 05 04 03 02 01 00 99   10 9 8 7 6 5 4 3 2 1

for Alexander Gabriel

Contents

✛

Acknowledgments

❖

One of the great pleasures of finishing a book is the opportunity it affords to reflect back upon the generosity of so many people who supported its writing.

The editorial and production staff at the University of Minnesota Press has been a pleasure to work with; I would especially like to thank William Murphy (who made this book possible), William Henry, Laura Westlund, Robin Moir, and Daniel Leary. Thomas Hahn has been a constant source of inspiration for more than ten years, and because of him I became a medievalist. Derek Pearsall guided me early in my career and helped set the trajectory for everything that followed. The original project from which this book traces its genealogy owes much to Larry Benson and Joseph Harris. Marjorie Garber and William Alfred were also generous in their support. Various chapters in numerous permutations have gained immeasurably from the comments and encouragement of Christopher Baswell, Peter Beidler, Kathleen Biddick, James P. Carley, Dick Chisholm, Susan Crane, Carol Everest, Steven Kruger, Lisa Ruch, William Sayers, Vance Smith, Lorraine K. Stock, and Bonnie Wheeler. Louise Fradenburg and Bob Stein were superb readers of the manuscript for the University of Minnesota Press; they helped me to improve the argument and avoid some errors (and any that remain are mine alone). Gayle Margherita also read the whole work in an earlier stage; I am grateful for her thorough commentary. My work is greatly indebted to the exciting intellectual community fostered by my colleagues in History and Literature at Harvard University, and the Department of English and Program in Human Sciences at George Washington University. I would especially like to thank Ines Azar, Janice Thaddeus, Daniel Donoghue, and Jeffrey Weinstock. Marshall Alcorn gave this project its psychoanalytic bent by drawing me into the Zizek Reading Group and the Association for the Psychoanalysis of Society and Culture, as well as by patiently helping me to keep my terms precise. Chris Sten ensured that I had the time and funding to pursue this project to completion. The members of the Program on Theory and Culture of the Institute for the Advanced Study of Culture (Debra Bergoffen, William Cohen, Jean-Paul Dumont, Sara Castro-Klaren, Rosemarie Thomson, Gail Weiss, and Stacy Wolf) have challenged me to think about embodiment in interdisciplinary terms. Martin Irvine and

Acknowledgments

Deb Everhart made sure that I never lacked the companionship of medievalists in Washington. Larry Kritzman and Michael Uebel encouraged the theoretical bent of my work. Bruce Venarde, in addition to being a superb teaching partner and friend, has constantly reminded me of theory's limits. I am happy to owe an unrepayable debt to Glenn Burger. Finally, this book could not have been written without the love and encouragement of a great many people, including Mark Cohen, my parents, and—more than anyone—Wendy Cohen.

The Intimate Stranger

The giant is represented through movement, through being in time....
In contrast to the still and perfect nature of the miniature, the gigantic
represents the order and disorder of historical forces.... And while our
daydream may be to animate the miniature, we admire the fall or the
death, the stopping, of the giant.

— Susan Stewart, *On Longing*, 86

Of the giant, Edmund Burke once wrote:

> It is impossible to suppose a giant the object of love. When we let
> our imaginations loose in romance, the ideas we naturally annex
> to that size are those of tyranny, cruelty, injustice, and every thing
> horrid and abominable. (*Enquiry into the Sublime and Beautiful*,
> 157–58)

His body an affront to natural proportion, the giant encodes an excess
that places him outside the realm of the human, outside the possibility
of desire. Yet a different cultural moment has enabled the same monster
who gives "satisfaction" only through his "defeat and death" (Burke, *Enquiry*, 158) to preside as a jolly green corporate emblem, assuring consumers that a certain brand of frozen vegetables is fresh and enticing. The
"double figure" of the giant arrives from the deep structure of myth.[1] In
the guise of Humbaba, he fought the hero Gilgamesh in ancient Babylon.
As the Nephilim, he embodied the transgression of divine laws governing
exogamy in the Hebrew Bible. Through the body of Ymir, he was transformed into the fabric of the earth in medieval Norse cosmography. Monstrously ancient, the giant Ysbaddaden threatened the fertility of Arthur's
court in Welsh legend. As the anarchic sons of Gaia, he defied Olympian
law and stormed the seat of the gods in the poetic imaginings and political allegories of the Greeks and Romans. Among his progeny are numbered Gargantua, the delightful grotesque invented by Rabelais to celebrate food, drink, and the pleasures of corporeality; Orgoglio, the puffed-up
personification of pride deflated by Redcrosse Knight in Spenser's *The
Faerie Queene*; Milton's mighty Satan; the Sleeping Giant, an anthropomorphized mountain in Kauai; the Brobdingnagians, a race who taught

Gulliver disheartening lessons about human nature; the Patagonians, imagined by early modern explorers to be the cannibalistic aborigines of the New World; the Lincoln Memorial in Washington, D.C., where the centerpiece statue yokes gigantism to a public spectacle of ideological authority; Paul Bunyan, the corporate mascot of a logging company who was manufactured as an "authentic" legend of the lumberjacks to increase paper sales; even that frustrated, hirsute Romeo of celluloid fame, King Kong. Mortal enemy and beloved companion, dead thing (stone statue, landscape) and vitality embodied, the giant is the crushing figure from whose gaze one flees in terror (Goya's magnificent *El Colosso*) and the mirthful monster in whose embrace one rediscovers a forgotten world of pleasure and consumption. This duality of the giant, this sublime dread crossed with an enjoyment that plants itself deep in the body, is mainly a medieval inheritance.

Throughout his long history in the England of the Middle Ages, the giant conjoined absolute otherness with reassuring familiarity. For the Anglo-Saxon homilists, for the twelfth- and thirteenth-century chroniclers of the island's early history, for the writers of romance and for Geoffrey Chaucer, the giant embodied a phenomenon that Lacanian psychoanalysis labels *extimité*, "external intimacy" or "intimate alterity."[2] The monster appears to be outside the human body, as the limit of its coherence; thus he threatens travelers and errant knights with dismemberment or anthropophagy, with the complete dissolution of their selfhood. But closer examination reveals that the monster is also fully within, a foundational figure; and so the giant is depicted as the builder of cities where people live and dream, the origin of the glory of empire, the base of heroism, an interior trauma that haunts subjectivity. The giant is humanity writ large, a text literally too big to ignore. Yet as my insistent use of the masculine pronoun in speaking of the monster suggests, he is also something smaller than a vast signifier of the complexities of constructing a "universal" category such as *homo*. The giant is a violently gendered body. While it is true that some medieval giants were female, especially in Norse tradition and in some of the crusader romances, these giants were then, as now, the exception.[3] A corpus caught within the process of its own coming into being, the giant is encountered in the performance of a masculinity as necessary as it is obscene. The giant's hybrid flesh is, however, not reducible to some pure state of male identity. Because he incorporates so much of the sensuous physicality with which medieval writers characterized women, and because his body functions as a disavowed point of origin, the giant shares more with the feminine, and specifically with the maternal, than his excessively male form might suggest. An ontologically *problematic* relationship between gender and embodiment will characterize the medieval giant in all of his identity-giving appearances.

"Of giants": the phrase itself is partial, a fragment intended to suggest that any capture of the monster into a complete epistemology is impossible. When placed inside a human frame of reference, the giant can be known only through synecdoche: a hand that grasps, a lake that has filled his footprint, a shoe or glove that dwarfs the human body by its side. To gaze on the giant as something more than a body in pieces requires the adoption of an inhuman, transcendent point of view; yet beside the full form of the giant, the human body dwindles to a featureless outline, like those charts in museums that depict a tiny silhouette of *Homo sapiens* below a fully realized *Tyrannosaurus rex*. To comprehend simultaneously both the body of the giant and the human body as complex, totalized wholes is a visual and epistemological impossibility. Either the human figure is reduced to a secretive miniature or the giant is fragmented beyond all comprehensibility. This unsettling oscillation between incommensurable frames is the essence of gigantism, the definition of *extimité*, a phenomenon that conjoins the intimacy of self-knowledge to a foundational alterity, an exorbitance as frightening as it is familiar.

The giant appears at that moment when the boundaries of the body are being culturally demarcated. In the England of the Middle Ages, he signifies those dangerous excesses of the flesh that the process of masculine embodiment produces in order to forbid; he functions at the same time to celebrate the pleasures of the body, to indulge in wine and food and sex. A historicist reading of the body would ordinarily condemn these dual significations as merely contradictory. How can the giant simultaneously prohibit indulgence (by his cannibalism, by his destructive consumption of every object and being that come close to his maw) and invite celebration (by offering to share his bounty of food, of sensuality)? How can the giant embody both the horror of rape and the delectation of erotic desire? How can the giant be at once the primal enemy of the human, and humanity's most constant companion? The key to this riddle lies in a psychoanalytically precise understanding of the nature of enjoyment (*jouissance*), which can as easily be sadistic, masochistic, and obscene as wholesome and delightful; and in the relation of enjoyment to the monster's simultaneous presence both within and outside human identity. I return here to the epigraph with which this introduction began: "The giant is represented through movement, through being in time" (Stewart, *On Longing*, 86). To gaze at the giant either through an exterior (gigantic) or interior (human, all too human) frame of knowledge is to fail to capture both categories in their fullness. Only in the constant movement between these two hermeneutics can the monster's nature be glimpsed. This "extimacy," this dual positionality as "intimate stranger," is a disturbing site that has much in common with the postmodern anti-identity term *queer*. Both indicate an abjected realm outside but entwined within, the "normal," the unambiguous, the culturally central—a surprising place, perhaps, to find so vast a body awaiting.

Inhuman History

Critical work on medieval monsters has concentrated primarily on what John Block Friedman called the "monstrous races," large groups of geographically distant wonders such as the pygmies and the cynocephali (dog-headed men), encountered by awestruck travelers at the margins of the world.[4] The monster in these appearances is simply "that which shows" (Isidore) or "that which warns" (Augustine), a morally and physically deformed creature arriving to demarcate the boundary beyond which lies the unintelligible, the inhuman.[5] The monster is definitionally a displacement: an exhibit, demonstrative of something other than itself. Unlike such culturally marginal but important figures as the transvestite, whom Marjorie Garber has argued must be looked *with* rather than *through*, it seems that the monster must become all transparence (*Vested Interests*, 11). As sheer representation, it follows that the monster should have no life outside of a constitutive cultural gaze, outside of its status as specular object.

Uncannily, however, the monster lives. Teratologists feel compelled to seek, in Stewart's words, "the fall or death, the stopping" of the monster. They seek to control its signification by caging its strange body in a freak show, filing its features away in an encyclopedia, reproducing its form in woodcuts so that it will not of itself reproduce.[6] Yet the monster escapes to reappear in some new guise, perhaps in some new world. The medieval giant counts among its lineal descendants such familiar popular culture figures as the wild man, Bigfoot (Sasquatch), and the Tibetan yeti. The *monstrum* demonstrates to its creators how little power they have to control their own progeny, textual as well as teratological. Despite the monster's semiotic slipperiness, analysis of medieval and early modern monsters has often assumed that they stand in stark opposition to the human, as "a measure of man" (one of Friedman's chapter titles), as an illustrative antithesis who proves through negative example the truth of civility (Hayden White), or as an impossibly distant body through which a repressed mind might dream its freedom (Jacques Le Goff).[7] Rather than repeat this bifurcating logic of exclusion, I explore in this book a limit case, a monster important because he cannot be fully banished from, or integrated into, those identity categories that his body constructs. The giant is at once a seemingly monolithic representation of otherness and a figure whose indomitable corporeality suggests the difficulty of being merely human in a world that demands the austere discipline of minute self-regulation.

In underscoring the giant's alterity, I am following Walter Stephens's conclusion in the only other monograph devoted specifically to giants,

Giants in Those Days: Folklore, Ancient History, and Nationalism—but,
as will become apparent in the course of this work, for wholly different
reasons. Stephens's main thesis concerns the interpretation history of
Rabelais, a subject about which Stephens writes brilliantly. Yet his estimation of the giant's cross-cultural signification in the Middle Ages is
too constraining for so enormous a figure. For Stephens, the word *giant*
is always to be written "with a capital *G*" because the term designates
an ontologically evil race of monsters generically distinct from humans.[8]
I will argue for the importance of the giant's *hybridity* upon his continued
popularity, usefulness, and appeal, at least in England; Stephens looks almost exclusively at medieval giants in their biblical and ecclesiastical purity.[9] Although Stephens is primarily concerned with the giants of France,
much of the material he surveys is of English provenance; my argument
is largely confined to the function of giants within a specifically English
national imaginary, but because the monster is as transnational as romance, the genre of his fullest realization, my study likewise draws on
important French material, much of which Stephens does not consider.

My conclusions are closer to a thesis about medieval wild men propounded in a more Freudian vein by Richard Bernheimer: such bodies are
excluded from the circle of the social but incorporate the secret interior
of "civilized" identity. Bernheimer suggests that the aggressive, hypersexual wild man is a nostalgic figure who embodies the abandoned pleasures
of the presocial, what Louise Olga Fradenburg calls the "mourned body
of freedom."[10] Because he was desired, this monster was over time transformed: an aphasic, violent cannibal in the early Middle Ages, the wild
man became by the early modern period an eloquent, pacifistic vegetar-
ian. No such progress narrative obtains for the medieval giant, in whose
body prohibition is always entwined with enjoyment, otherness with intimacy. I argue that if the giant is sometimes made to represent the masculine body's lost prehistory, that is precisely because he figures the dangerous instability of its present integrity. The giant reveals the limits of
selfhood, reveals that identity is intersubjective, ex-centric, suspended
across temporalities, as historically contingent as it is monstrously incomplete. If the giant is Other, then he is the Other as something "strange
to me, although . . . at the heart of me."[11]

I have argued elsewhere that every monster has its historical specificity: the vampires of Anne Rice are clearly different from those of Bram
Stoker, even if they are separated from each other by less than a century
and filiate from the same genealogical tree.[12] Although this book does
not ignore the determinative, localizing power of history, the giant necessarily spurs my interest in that currently unfashionable term, the *longue
durée*. Historicist inquiry has never been richer or more complex than
in contemporary medieval studies. The work of history-minded medievalists who are equally interested in medieval textuality—scholars such as
Lee Patterson and Caroline Walker Bynum—will surely endure as a high-

water mark of the discipline. Yet the limitation of an inquiry that mainly concerns itself with the interplay of text with immediate historical event is that it cannot account well for transhistorical phenomena, such as the enduring fascination exerted by monsters.[13] The giant is simply too large to be reduced to a narrative of historical causation. This book argues that the time is at hand for a return to a psychoanalytically informed cultural theory, a return that keeps the lessons of recent historicist methodology in mind while attempting to broaden its scope. Fradenburg has persuasively argued that "few contemporary analytical discourses...have given as rich an accounting as has psychoanalysis of how and why we desire our pasts—of how we constitute our pasts as past, as lost, in the production of an imperative to reclaim them" ("Be Not Far from Me," 45–46). The chapters that follow map through the English Middle Ages a history of desire that is the medieval desire for history, for the reclaiming of past that founds collective and individual identity.

Although many names familiar from the canon of contemporary theory appear in these pages, the methodology of critics such as the French theorist of subjectivity Jacques Lacan is filtered through the more recent, revisionary work of Slavoj Zizek and Charles Shepherdson, who insist that psychoanalysis is an indispensable tool for the understanding of ideology and culture. The mechanics of identity formation must be located within a larger matrix that includes, but is not limited to, historical determinism and transhistorical repetition, the particularities and the constants of subjectivization, and the cultural context of the process of embodiment. My methodology combines psychoanalysis with several schools of postmodern identity theory (including certain strains of gender and queer theory) that have sometimes been antagonistic to its praxis but can in fact press further its insights. I am particularly interested in the challenges to unified identity posed by Gilles Deleuze and Félix Guattari in their collaborative work, as well as the feminist reframing of their corpus by Elizabeth Grosz. This book also makes ample use of the discursive or constructivist theories of sexuality propounded by Michel Foucault and greatly expanded by Judith Butler, reading them into and against medieval conceptualizations of personhood and body.

"Subjectivity" and "embodiment" are my key terms throughout. Even if the former is most familiar from psychoanalysis, the latter from recent feminist theory, they should not be understood as separable halves of a unified dualism. Caroline Walker Bynum has recently demonstrated that the Middle Ages were not nearly as Platonistic or Manichaean as they have been made out to be. Her analysis of burial practices around 1300, for instance, reveals a continuity between "material body" and "person" that undercuts the doxa that medieval flesh and soul were always antagonistic binarisms (*Resurrection of the Body*, 325–26). Body, soul, and person were continuous, caught together in what gender theorists label a matrix of identity. Bynum writes that the literature of spiritual advice used matrimonial metaphors to stress "that body and soul are bound together by tenderness, even passion, into 'one flesh'; person is a psychosomatic unity" (332). This medieval insight seems to be one that contemporary identity theory is just learning. A recent book on the relationship between corporeality and identity poses a series of questions that, according to Bynum, medieval writers at various times have already answered:

> Can accounts of subjectivity and the psychical interior be adequately explained in terms of the body? Can depths, the interior, the subjective, and the private instead be seen in terms of surfaces, bodies, and material relations? Can the mind/body dualism be overcome using the concepts associated with the devalued term of the binary pair of mind and body?[14]

Throughout *Of Giants,* I read "subjectivity" as something that occurs only in, through, and upon bodies, and only in somatic terms; and "embodiment" as a corporeal process suspended in a psychical and social matrix. The body is a hybrid category, part cultural and part material, in which interior and exterior are always enfolded, always crossing into each other. The body *in abstracto* might be conceptualized as a Möbius strip, where any motion crosses constantly between inside and outside, undermining the utility of maintaining such frail distinctions. It makes sense, therefore, to speak of medieval subjectivity and embodiment as entangled, perhaps even inextricable processes, and to hold identity to be a cultural effect that results from a constant combinatory motion.

The first chapter of this book is the most psychoanalytic and lays a theoretical groundwork to be both refined and amplified as the book progresses. "The Ruins of Identity" examines the relationship between the extimacy of the giant and the construction of the category "human" in Anglo-Saxon culture. Although it is difficult to speak in large terms of such a long and varied era in insular history, the giant provides the tentative vocabulary toward a metalanguage for understanding a persistent cultural fascination that collects the period into a loose unity. Because Anglo-Saxon England was continuously faced with challenges to its integrity and self-definition, the hybrid body of the monster became a communal form for expressing anxieties about the limits and fragility of identity. Old English elegy, heroic poetry, and scriptural exegesis alike suggest that the giant gained a particular ascendancy as an embodiment of what it means to be human in a world where the body and subjectivity are under constant threat of dissolution, where history insists that every solid structure break into ruins. The giant is a foundational monster: from his body, the earth is fashioned and the world comes into being. At the same time, the giant menaces any architecture of meaning that humans erect, including language. The giant is at once abjected from human signification and installed deep within the structure of subjectivity, as both its limit and its history in eternal return.

The second chapter maps the installation of the giant at the heart of national identity, and his subsequent transformation into a monster who regulates the proper structure of gender within familial relations. When William the Conqueror annexed England to his possessions in Normandy, the newly installed aristocracy found themselves in the difficult position of having no usable past with which to solidify the authority of their reign. Geoffrey of Monmouth solved this crisis of identity by writing the *Historia Regum Britanniae (History of the Kings of Britain)*, a chronicle of the Trojan settlement of the land under Brutus that culminates in the glorious reign of Arthur. Like the British in Geoffrey's narrative, the colonizing Anglo-Normans traced their descent from the wandering heroes of Troy, so that his *Historia* furnished them with a legitimizing narrative. Brutus and Arthur overcome inimical giants and incorporate these monstrous bodies into the founding of the nation and the empire. These monsters became so central to the formation of a new *collective* ideology of identity that they were installed as statues in the center of Guildhall, where they remained until the Blitzkrieg, monsters at the heart of the nation.

Two hundred years after Geoffrey composed his text, the mechanics of gender inherent in its vision of history were explored in a new myth that posited an origin for his seemingly autogenic giants. The Greek princess Albina and her thirty sisters are exiled to uninhabited England when they refuse to become properly docile wives. In this new land, they attempt to found a gynecocracy but are rebuked when they learn the severe limits that their corporeality imposes on them. By the beginning of the fourteenth century, the giant has been successfully transformed from a limner of the coherence of the human to a monster who materializes the nation, the family, and the sexed and gendered bodies of which these structures are composed.

"The Body in Pieces," the third chapter, initiates the exploration of the function of the giant in the vernacular English romance tradition that occupies the rest of the book. In romance, the giant found his fullest, most complex realization. I am specifically interested in a subgenre that I label "identity romance," a loose confederation of texts that explore how the bodies of heroes are produced, sexed, and sanctified. In narratives as diverse as *Guy of Warwick, Bevis of Hampton, Lybeaus Desconus*, and *Octavian*, male identity or chivalric subjectivity is constructed through an encounter against the giant. By offering a spectacular, impossibly autonomous hero as a site saturated with desire, and by staging a triumph over the monster that relocates enjoyment to the interior of the chivalric corpus, romance aims to have a visceral effect on its audience, one that transforms subjectivities and offers a powerfully attractive formulation of masculine embodiment. Whereas the experience of corporeality is usually of a "body in pieces," of an identity that blurs into the world that surrounds it and upon which that identity depends, the fight against the giant in romance images a masculinity that is complete, self-sufficient, and produced through a strict regimen of interior regulation — an identity that would appeal both to the knightly bodies who were romance's generative audience and to an increasingly influential class of men whose power was directly tied to the circulation of capital and a burgeoning state bureaucracy. Through a central scene of decapitation and display that recurred with an almost machinic insistence throughout the long history of the genre, the giant is simultaneously disavowed and enjoyed, ensuring his longevity.

Even Geoffrey Chaucer, the "father of English poetry," was engaged in the cultural production of this monster. Fragment 7 of the *Canterbury Tales* has long been regarded as a miscellaneous gathering of narratives, but I argue that its organizing obsession is the instability of male sexuality. Two movements animate the fragment: flows of gigantism, associated with desire in its imagined "precultural" state, and ebbs of severe contraction, allied with the social inscription of the body as a reductive containment of this unbounded desire. "The Tale of Sir Thopas," the story offered by Chaucer the pilgrim to his fellow travelers, takes these movements to their extremes, reducing the terrifying giant of romance to the silly, three-headed Sir Olifaunt. By translating the familiar gigantomachia (battle against the giant) from romance into comedy, the sexual threat that the giant encodes dwindles to its vanishing point, just as Chaucer's possible rape of Cecily Chaumpaigne has been much diminished in the critical reading of Chaucer's corpus. This chapter makes use of some recent archival work by Christopher Cannon to argue that the giant not only was central to the romance notion of embodied subjectivity, but in Chaucer's case was intimately involved in his own self-figuration, and especially in the deployment of his sexuality.

The fifth chapter examines the dynamic relationship between the giant and two other monsters, the ethereal incubus and the dog-headed cynocephalus. Using the postmodern identity theories of Gilles Deleuze and Félix Guattari, I explore the resistance of medieval bodies to systemization, as well as their remarkable energy, motion, and contiguity. The underappreciated romance *Sir Gowther* insists that for a chivalric subject to be a proper man, he must first become an animal hybrid, a monster. Embodiment becomes a process of moving through a series of transitional identities that culminate in a masculinity so far removed from corporeality that it finally stands synonymous with sanctity. Gowther begins his life as if he were the typical giant of romance, committing every sin of the body from murder to rape; at his blessed death, he is abstracted into a disembodied, normalizing principle, a transfigurative saint. Along the way, his mutable, monstrous form suggests that the body is a construction whose skin is an insufficient boundary against the swirling world of desires, energies, intensities, and events by which it is surrounded, and to which it is connected by the strangest, most intimate bonds.

The last chapter examines texts such as *Sir Gawain and the Green Knight* that come late enough in the tradition of the giant to explore exactly how that monstrous body has been successively employed. Giants can be figures of sublime dread, immense forms whose gross corporeality menaces human bodies by declaring their fragility; they can also be monsters who invite celebration, who compel enjoyment, who replace anxiety with laughter. Comedy humanizes the giant, so that terrible figures like the Green Knight and the Carl of Carlisle are revealed to be underneath their giant's flesh ordinary men. The giant stands at the limit of identity because he reveals the impossibility of its self-sufficiency: embodiment is an intersubjective process, never complete because it is never self-contained within an autonomous form. Heroes such as Guillaume d'Orange and Bevis of Hampton adopt giants as squires or pages to teach these monsters that strict somatic discipline produces human contours; their lack of success suggests that the giant instructs the hero that a pure form of masculinity is as mythic as the giant's body. Finally, I argue that the extimacy of the giant has something in common with the identity term *queer*. It may be that knights in romance are most often tied to their enemy monsters by a bond of mutual hate, but Galehaut, the "son of the Beautiful Giantess," loves Lancelot so much that he dies for his *amis*. The complex relationship that entwines the monster in the formation of chivalric masculinity not only is saturated with homoerotic desire but also poses a final challenge to the stability of any normative system of identity. The giant, that foundational monster who produces the masculine corpus, is also its guarantee of failure, of its inability to vanquish forever the intimate stranger at its heart.

❖

The Ruins of Identity

The body doesn't lie.... Maps whose territories are named in languages which are no longer understood show where the passions are hidden.
— Kathy Acker, *In Memoriam to Identity*, 6

Foundational Moments

In the most celebrated essay in Anglo-Saxon studies, J. R. R. Tolkien liberated Old English literature from its monsters. The opinion of philologists such as W. P. Ker had long held sway: *Beowulf* was a poem valuable for the historical allusions that limn its periphery, worthless for the three battles against monsters that form its narrative heart. This fascination with grotesque bodies is the poem's "radical defect, a disproportion that puts the irrelevances in the centre."[1] In 1936 Tolkien delivered the Gollancz Memorial Lecture to the British Academy and challenged Ker's dismissive summation. "*Beowulf:* The Monsters and the Critics" argues that the cannibalistic giant Grendel, his vengeful mother, and the fiery dragon are beneath their lurid flesh ethical allegories. The dragon is "a personification of malice, greed, destruction" (17); Grendel is an adversary of the soul; the poem is about *pietas.* By translation from Old English into Latin, the monsters become "not an inexplicable blunder of taste" but "fundamentally allied to the underlying ideas of the poem, which give its lofty tone and high seriousness" (19).[2]

Beowulf had once been difficult to place, confusingly hybrid, *monstrous;* now it was a safely canonical object of New Critical, *humanistic* inquiry. Whereas Tolkien believed that the literary remnants of Anglo-Saxon culture may be studied in spite of its monsters, more recent critics have asserted that the corpus deserves critical analysis because of its monstrous content.[3] Writers and artists in early medieval England were fascinated by the grotesque and the marvelous. Their literature, historiography, manuscript illustration, and plastic arts reveal a cultural obsession with the malleability of the human form. *Wonders of the East,* a text with which *Beowulf* is bound in monstrous affiliation, is crammed with bodies transfigured and deformed. One magnificent illustration (British Library MS Cotton Tiberius Bv folio 83v) makes real the Donestre, a fabulous race described in the legends of Alexander. These strange crea-

1

tures embody a monstrosity that is both corporeal and linguistic. Because they know all human languages, the Donestre are able to hail foreigners with familiar speech, convincing them that they know their kinsmen and homeland. They then devour the body of their victims except for the head, over which they sit and weep.[4]

The illustration in Cotton Tiberius Bv consists of three successive scenes, read clockwise starting at the top. This Donestre is a fleshy, naked man with a lion's head. His curly mane sweeps the curve of his shoulder, and with a sad frown and huge, watery eyes, he commiserates with a traveler. The foreigner gesticulates widely, perhaps in the midst of relating some story about his distant home to his sympathetic auditor. The patient monster extends an enormous hand to touch the speaker, a reassuring gesture. Below and to the right is the next episode of the pictorial narrative: the Donestre, having heard enough, is busy devouring the traveler. His naked body is directly on top of the man, pinning him to the earth. The final scene, in the lower left corner, finds the Donestre looking melancholic. He holds his hands to furry ears, frowns miserably, and stares at the bodiless head of his victim, the only remnant of the gruesome feast.

When read chronologically, the Donestre's body undergoes a revealing transformation. At first more virile than bestial, the monster's animal head is fully anthropomorphized to give an empathetic look. His hands, calves, and chest bulge with muscles. His genitalia, painted a vibrant red, are prominently displayed. Compared to this hypermasculine body, the traveler's form is thin, stooped, ill proportioned. As the Donestre ingests his victim, he becomes more leonine: he is on all fours, as if he has just pounced; his nose and lips form a snout; his eyes suddenly lack whites. An oral, animal ecstasy characterizes the second scene as the monster—bare buttocks arched above the prone foreigner's hips—devours the man's erect arm. That this combination of violence, eroticism, and transgression is difficult to contain in the illustration is indicated by the Donestre's very human left foot, which steps out of the picture and into the frame—the only part of the illustration to violate the demarcative power of its border. The last segment of the tripartite story finds both bodies much reduced. The traveler has vanished, replaced by the peacefully oblivious head. The monster is an indistinct collection of curved lines that center around a trembling hand, a dark eye, and a tight frown.

The material incorporation of one body into the flesh of another, cannibalism condenses a fear of losing the boundary that circumscribes identity and produces discrete subjects. The illustration from *Wonders of the East* uses anthropophagy to explore selfhood's limits. Its polyglot and hybrid monster is a cultural, linguistic, sexual other who seems to be intimate (he knows you, he can talk about your relatives, he can share in your *mal du pays*) but in fact brutally converts an identity familiar and secure into an alien thing, into a subject estranged from its own body. In

2

Figure 1. Donestre with traveler. British Library MS Cotton Tiberius Bv folio 83v. Reprinted by permission of the British Library.

the last scene of the narrative, the traveler has been completely transformed. The severed head is an empty point of fascination that directs the viewer's gaze back to the alienating form in which the traveler is now contained, at the monster he has now become; he ponders what he once was from the outside, *as a foreigner.* The Donestre transubstantiates the man, making him realize through a somatic conversion that he was al-

3

ways already a stranger to himself, despite his attachment to—his self-identification by means of—*home*. The Donestre-traveler stares at the mute, lifeless head with such affective sadness because at this moment of plurality he sees the fragility of autonomous selfhood, how much of the world it excludes in its panic to remain selfsame, singular, stable.

The monster exposes the *extimité,* the "extimacy" or "intimate alterity" of identity: its inescapable self-estrangement, the restless presence at its center of everything it abjects in order to materialize and maintain its borders. To be fully human is to disavow the strange space that the inhuman, the monstrous, occupies within every speaking subject. To succeed on a mass scale, this disavowal requires two things: a degree of cultural uniformity and relative social calm. England in the centuries before the Norman Conquest was a heterogeneous collection of peoples who were constantly forced to examine who they were in relation to a shifting array of alterities. "Anglo-Saxon England" is a blanket term that hides more than it reveals. In a real sense, there were no Anglo-Saxons, only scattered groups of varied ancestry in growing alliances who were slowly building larger political units.[5] "England" existed as an ambiguous region of a large island and was very much in the process of being invented as a unifying geography, as a nation capable of transcending the differences among those bodies it collects beneath its name. The various Germanic peoples who sailed to England beginning in the fifth century were culturally diverse. As they settled the island they intermingled with the Celts (some Romanized, some not) and with each other. The Latin church colonized in successive waves, offering a European lingua franca to restructure their northern epistemological systems. In 835, the Vikings began their violent incursions, forcefully reminding the *gens Anglorum* of northern heuristics. Yet to speak of Latin, northern, and Celtic culture is to pretend that these were monolithic and discrete, when each was composed of often competing ideologies, dialects, mythologies—like "Anglo-Saxon England" itself. These various languages and discourses combined into fragmentary epistemes, as unstable and amalgamative as the many little kingdoms that formed and were absorbed into larger ones. The history of Anglo-Saxon England is a narrative of resistant hybridity, of small groups ingested into larger bodies without a full assimilation, without cultural homogeneity: thus the realms of Hwicce, Sussex, Kent, Lindsey, Surrey, Essex, East Anglia, Northumbria, Mercia, and Wessex were sutured over time into progressively larger kingdoms; but although they were eventually unified in political hegemony, these areas retained enough force of heterogeneity to remain dialect regions that persist to the present day.

Anglo-Saxon England is not so very different from the Donestre by whom it was fascinated: familiar and strange, hybrid rather than homogenous, an amalgamative body that absorbs difference without completely reducing or assimilating it. Because of its diversity and because of its permeable, perpetually transgressed borders, Anglo-Saxon England was relentlessly pondering what it means to be a warrior, a Christian, a hero, a saint, an outlaw, a king, a sexed and gendered being. If there is a generalization under which such a long and varied time period can be gathered without doing reductive violence to its expansiveness, it is simply that during the span of years now designated by the rubric "Anglo-Saxon England," the limits of identity were under ceaseless interrogation because they were confronted by almost constant challenge. It is not surprising, then, that the monster became a kind of cultural shorthand for the problems of identity construction, for the irreducible difference that lurks deep within the culture-bound self.

The Work of Giants

The mythology of the medieval European north, of which the literary remains of Anglo-Saxon England form a part, was fascinated by the giant.[6] When the various Germanic tribes that are now called the Anglo-Saxons arrived in the land now called England, they encountered towering structures of ancient stone that made them feel like small children as they stood beside them. They described this alien architecture as *enta geweorc,* "the work of giants." Some of these structures were the great monoliths, dolmens, and stone circles such as Stonehenge built by the mysterious pre-Celtic peoples, who have left no other trace of their sojourn. Other monumental edifices were built by the Romans during that period when the Eternal City could see all the way to the hinterland of Great Britain. The aqueducts and temples of Bath, for example, had written Roman civility across a resistant wilderness, transforming the Celts into imperial subjects and the land into the empire's dominion. But the memory of these builders (prehistoric and cloaked in mystery, Roman and clothed in history) had fragmented by the time the Angles, Saxons, and Jutes sailed in their war boats from Scandinavia, early in the fifth century. Since these Germanic tribes built their homes, sheep sheds, and mead halls exclusively from wood, stone in their sign system was associated with the primitive and the inert. Wood was a living substance to be carved and joined, the raw material of community; stone was recalcitrant and dead, good for etching runes but otherwise impossible to transform. Like their forebears, the Anglo-Saxons contrasted wood's modernity with the ancient, elemental harshness of stone. Men built with wood. Giants, the vanished race who had ruled the earth in its larger-than-life, Paleolithic days, were architects of stone.

The Bible only confirmed what their native mythology already told them, a story that the legends of the conquered Celts corroborated: humanity was a secondary race of creatures, belated, the gods' afterthought. Northern myth held that giants had been the first race to inscribe their identity into the earth's landscape, and that the human body was a continuation and reduction of that *figura*.[7] Gargantuan amalgams of appetite and strength, these giants were thought to live at civilization's periphery, often in a specially realized geography (Geirrodstown, Glasisvellir, Jotunheim). Creatures of the world's First Order, they were so close to nature that they were linked to meteorological phenomena—to the storms, lightning, fog, and blizzards that terrified northern explorers with their violent unpredictability. Unlike their counterparts in Latin tradition, Germanic giants could also at times be female; biblical, classical, and later medieval giants were relentlessly gendered masculine. The northern giants married freely with gods and men, as often representing a middle step between the human and the divine as an inferior genus between man and animal. The Aesir, the most powerful gods of the Norse pantheon, were descended from giants.[8] As elemental, perhaps autochthonous beings, giants were inextricable from the earth and stone they worked, so they gained an explanatory function as creators of landscape, ancient ruins, and mysterious architecture.

The Old English poem that most vividly captures this wistful genealogy of the giants' stone leavings is "The Wanderer."[9] The poem is spoken by a homeless exile (OE *anhaga*) who treks through a bleak, frozen landscape and meditates on the cruelty immanent in this world where the price of subjectivization is loss. Each morning he voices his sorrow as a way of coming to understand a painful history that haunts his present with spectral remembrances. This transformation of the past into poetic language enacts a fantasy of inhabiting it again as if it were a place, a blissful space-time before the trauma of separation irrupted. The Wanderer (*eardstapa*, "earth-walker") imagines that he is with his beloved lord once more, that his "gold-friend" (*gold-winne*) kisses and clasps him, that he lays his head to rest on his protector's lap, "swa he hwilum ær / on gear-dagum gief-stoles breac" [as he did once in days now lost, when he enjoyed the gift-stool] (43–44). He achieves in this gesture of conjoining a profound peace. *þegnscipe*, his homoerotic surrender to the word, agency, and body of his master, is absolute.

The dream breaks. The Wanderer awakens to find that he remains among hoarfrost and frigid waves. Seabirds perform their insensate rituals ("baþian brim-fuglas, brædon feþra," 47) while snow and hail swirl: a cold, inhuman world oblivious to the sorrow that wells within him. In this winterscape, "sorg biþ geniewod" [sorrow freshens] (50). This *sorg* of separation is written across the interior of his body, as a wound that scars his heart ("þonne beoþ þy hefigran heortan benna," 49); his ache for his beloved (*swæsne*), the dead lord, has not been reduced through a life spent wandering.

In early northern European culture, the mead hall (*meduheall*) was the center of community, the materialization into concrete public space of heroic group identity. By the time "The Wanderer" was written, probably in a monastery, this heroic age and its glorious halls were images from a history receding into myth. The elegy is doubly nostalgic. Quiet yearning for a vanished past is voiced once by the narrator of the poem, for whom that past is proximate, and secondarily by the writer(s) of the lines, for whom that past is almost wholly imaginary. "The Wanderer" asks what it is like to suffer the trauma of loss and discovers that what seemed a dissolution of wholeness is actually its reconfiguration into a diminished, bleak, and lonely state of autonomy. The text arrives at this insight by imagining an originary moment before the subject was alienated within the symbolic order that grants his meaning-in-being. Lacanian psychoanalysis, embedded in class- and time-specific ideals of familial structuration, dreams of an originary trauma that attends the separation from the mother, when the entrance into a paternal language occurs; the presymbolic bliss of "The Wanderer" is a bit queerer and resides in the complete union of two male bodies, materialized in the gesture of the embrace and lost through the violence of other men. Like Lacan, like "The Seafarer" (12–19), the elegy imagines a prehistory during which the subject could feel at home in his own body, at home in the world.

At home, or at hall. Architecture articulates identity: in the time of wholeness, in the time before loss and lack, the Wanderer resided with his lord in *sele-dreamas*, "hall-joys" (93). In the submissive tableau of being embraced, laying head upon lap, the Wanderer knew plenitude. The narrator rejoices not in his individuality (he is not even named) but in full contiguity; in the dependency of thane upon lord, he finds his full bliss. This primal enjoyment, frozen in time and frozen as place, is rendered possible through the hall, the structure that demarcates warm, communal Inside from frigid, solitary Exterior. Under the protective wood of the hall's steep gables, fires blaze and feasting resounds. Men drink and sing and exchange the gold rings that serve as material articulations of the system of relations that bind them like brothers, like circles of a closed chain. The exiled Wanderer is *sele-dreorig*: not homesick, but hall-sick (25).

Outside the hall, an inimical geography sprawls: ice-laden winds, tempest-troubled seas, dark promontories, the habitations of monsters. The danger of a happy hall is that one of these lone monsters will hear the sweet music that escapes from the windows, will rise from the dark mere, and will burst through the door like the giant cannibal Grendel and devour the place of home.

"Being Insists in Suffering"

You never look at me from the place from which I see you.
—Jacques Lacan, *The Four Fundamental Concepts of Psycho-Analysis*, 104

The door splinters at the giant's touch, and Grendel strides into the hall. The men still sleep. He seizes Hondscio, the nearest warrior, and guts him as he dreams. The giant rips the body to pieces, "bat ban-locan, blod edrum dranc, / synsnædum swealh" [bit into muscles, swilled blood from veins, tore off gobbets].[10] The giant eats the sleeper alive, everything, "fet ond folma" [even hands and feet]. The fear that animates this gory evisceration is that all that is rhetorically outside, incorporated into the body of the monster, will suddenly break through the fragile architecture of the hall, which is the fragile identity of the subject, and expose its surprised inhabitants to what has been abjected from their small world to make it livable.[11] Like the sleeping, peaceful, unspeaking Hondscio, the traumatized subject will be ingested, absorbed into that big Other seemingly beyond (but actually wholly within, because wholly created by) the symbolic order that it menaces.

In "The Wanderer," these monstrous anxieties cannot find expression in fleshly form. Instead they are written across the landscape, becoming no less potent for not having found a body to inhabit. The world itself comes to life. Anthropomorphized, it acts as one malevolent body (101–6). The cold ocean, the bitter winds, the bare trees, and the frozen hills all stir under the compulsion of a vaguely malevolent animism. Even the "rough hail" (*hreo haegl-farue*) has its inscrutable but inimical intentions ("norðan onsendeþ / hreo hægl-fære, hæleðum on andan," 104–5). What house or hall can stand when the very earth turns against it? Deep in sadness, the Wanderer turns to the stone ruins he sees before him and projects his story of persecution by a giant, unknowable Other onto this wreckage of an alien city, making his private history a palimpsest for History writ large. This big Other (Lacan's *grand autre*) is a fantastic, "personal" incorporation of the symbolic order by means of which the chaos of the world is organized into linguistic and epistemological coherence. As the desperate projection into place of a meaning in no way immanent there, this ghostly giant obscures the fact that meaning does not reside in any "there"—in any space, architecture, or geography—only in the structures by which it is organized, the monsters in which it is embodied.

The Wanderer's willful historiography occurs within a meditation upon homelessness. The motion that is his desire begins as a search for another hall in which to dwell, another lord under whom to serve, and culminates when his hopeless journey brings him to the ruins of an unknown city, broken stonework as cold as the bathing seabirds that conduct their animal rituals outside the realm of human meaning, of human feeling. A silent testament to the destructive inevitability of time, the windswept remains are described as "eald enta geweorc idlu stodon" [the old work of giants, standing abandoned] (87). For all of its stock character, the allusion fits tightly into the poem's obsession with unrecoverable loss. Associated with a race defined simultaneously by its terrible power and its ancient vanishing, the time-broken architecture becomes a living elegy. The Wanderer, alienated from his origin, projects this estrangement upon the ruins, estranging them from *human* origin.

Having given to the lifeless ruins a monstrous derivation, the Wanderer begins the process of rebuilding them, of anthropomorphizing their history to place in their center the warmth of human meaning. A barren landscape is imagined to encircle what it has shattered in defeat (85–93). At least four temporal frames intersect here: the distant past when the city was constructed out of stone by mythic giants; a nearer past when men lived and died; the bitter present of the Wanderer, whose melancholic state of mind is interjected into that past; and the timeless moment of the wise observer who moralizes on the remains. The city's giant builders are conflated with eulogized warriors who perished in a lost, bloody history; they in turn are linked with the recent plight of the *anhaga* (the solitary one, the homeless Wanderer), and his fate provokes a consideration of universal end. The poem is a condensed narrative of cycles of fall in which the passing of the giants, the Old Order of the world, is linked with the necessary passing of humanity. This somber dissolution is then doubled back into a monstrous prehistory for the city of man. The crumbling of the dwelling is like the banishment from Eden, or the devastating loss of the hall, or (to place the loss in the familial terms that the Wanderer would not have understood) the loss of the (m)other's body at the forced differentiation that entrance into the symbolic order demands. No place can ever be as certain, as paradisal, or as full as the imaginary left behind. To be human, the poem insists, is to be homeless. The primal dwelling has crumbled, and the world has crashed inside. This loss of a secure place to inhabit is constitutive of identity, of becoming a speaking subject (one who can voice elegy, one who can speak grief). Self-consciousness occurs once the mead hall is a ruin, when plenitude is a distant memory: "Eall is earfoþlice eorðan rice" [In the earth-realm all is crossed]. The price of subjectivity is to become eternally *anhaga, eardstapa*, a Wanderer.

Another poem from the Exeter Book, *The Ruin*, opens with a similar apostrophe to the time-blasted leavings of giants: "Wrætlic is þes wealstan, wyrde gebræcon; burgstede burston, brosnað enta geweorc" [Wondrous is this stone wall, smashed by Fate; the city is broken to pieces, the work of giants has crumbled]. Something of a ruin itself because of the poor condition of the manuscript, the poem describes what appears to be Roman remains through fragments of fallen stone and the ghostly presence of vanished inhabitants. As in Norse writings, the giants here suggest an alienating presence that predates humanity. In the uncertain past constructed by the sagas, the giants are encountered only in the waning of their race and are knowable in the author's present from the monstrous traces their bodies have etched into the landscape. Giants represent the unassimilated remnant of a past that, although it eludes the complete historical memory of the recorder, is integrally bound to the process of giving that history an identity. The vanished builders of *The Ruin* are also associated with a culture of idolatry (25), the sin of embodying in all too human form the gigantic might of the divine. The connection derives from the Book of Enoch, an apocryphal book of the Bible that seems to have exerted great influence on Anglo-Saxon gigantology (Kaske, "*Beowulf* and the Book of Enoch").

Enta geweorc (the work of giants) and its variants (*enta ærgeweorc, giganta geweorc*)[12] are somewhat formulaic descriptions, useful for completing a poetic half line quickly, but always something more than stock quotations. These phrases are fairly widespread in Old English literature, nearly always referring to ancient stone buildings or walls (*Andreas*, 1492; *Maxims*, 2.1; *Elene*, 30). A cognate phrase (*wrisilic gewerc*) even appears in Old Saxon. In *The Wanderer* and *The Ruin*, the elegiac resonance invoked through citation of the ancient giants fits perfectly the poems' cycle of loss and vanishing at the hands of fate (*wyrde*) and time. From a less literary viewpoint, stone ruins are logically *enta geweorc* not only because of the great size of the ruined architecture but also because of the elemental connection of giants with the earth and masonry in northern mythology.[13] Recent decades have produced theories that the Egyptian pyramids, pre-Columbian ruins, and geometric patterns in English wheat fields are the work of ancient aliens, carried from the margins of space in their chariots of the gods. The existential melancholy that drives such etiologic narratives arises because these more-than-human beings have abandoned humanity to itself, leaving enigmatic traces of a joyful proximity never to be regained.

Originary Fantasies

The giant must dwell in the fen, alone in the land.
—Cotton Gnomic Verses, 42–43

The giant builds the home (the ruins are *enta geweorc*, the work of giants), but the giant destroys the home, too: Grendel bursts the door from its hinges and devours the sleepers inside. Such is the vexing duality of the monster, especially in northern tradition. The giant is simultaneously the origin of the world and its greatest enemy. According to the surviving Norse cosmogonies, giants predate the material universe, which itself was fashioned from the corpse of the ur-giant Ymir:

Of Ymir's flesh the earth was shaped
   the barren hills his bones;
and of his skull the sky was shaped,
   of his body the briny sea. ("Vafþrúðismál," 21, in
   The Poetic Edda, 46)

The monster's body becomes the raw material of cosmogenesis. To read the giant into the landscape as creator of topography, builder of strange architecture, or (as in Vafþrúðismál) as the constitutive first matter of the earth is to partake of that philosophical category called the sublime, in which the (male) human body is projected across the land as its organizing principle. The landscape becomes corporeal as "the male individual makes over aspects of himself—particularly the bodily component he fears may be alienable, the phallus—to nature" and "one's words undergo translation into images" (Coates, *The Gorgon's Gaze*, 84). The giant, the human body introjected into the world, throws the land into tumult by smashing its mountains or making toys of its stones; or the giant erects huge and mysterious structures that dwarf human achievement, that threaten to overwhelm with their size and phallic power. The giant's spatial and temporal passing is registered only in the aftermath of the sublime, in the eerie ruins of his achievements, when his footprints have filled with water and become lakes—when words have returned to the observer, emotion can be harnessed, and speech can describe his path through the landscape, or through time. The earth and its altered features (mountains, bodies of water, the ruins of ancient cities) are the giant's story, a source of quiet wonder and contemplative sadness after sudden, cosmic fear.

This process of projecting a history upon the land is the mirror image of the process of identity formation outlined by the French psychoanalyst Jacques Lacan. In his originary essay "The Mirror Stage," Lacan established a new identity for psychoanalysis, reading the vast, fragmentary body of Freudian thought through Saussurian linguistics.[14] Lacan argues that the subject initially experiences itself as *un corps morcelé*, a body in pieces. By looking into a mirror or seeing itself mimicked in the actions of another, the subject receives its selfhood, a gestalt that confers a unity while radically estranging subjectivity from somaticity. Identity for Lacan is predicated upon a fundamental misrecognition (*méconnaissance*). The subject takes a specular, exterior image to be what it inside *is*. This misconstruction is a kind of teratogenesis: "The child, itself so recently born, gives birth to a monster: a statue, an automaton, a fabricated thing" (Bowie, *Lacan*, 26). This specular monster is anything but the giant. For the giant is a body that is always in pieces, since within a human frame, he can be perceived only synecdochically, never as a totality. The giant is the prehistory of the body, standing at that origin point before it metamorphoses from one kind of monster (*le corps morcelé*) to another (the "fabricated thing"): from monstrous birth to monstrous becoming. Lacan's originary nightmare never loses its power to haunt. A Boschian giant reappears in nightly visitations as *"imagos of the fragmented body."*[15] *Le stade du miroir* becomes the arena in which the subject is persecuted by the fragmentary body of the giant, the monstrous being that is undeniably both human and something Other (prehuman, posthuman).

11

Time, body, and place tumble together in Lacan's originary myth, leaving the self without a permanent architecture under which to find rest. The Wanderer best speaks this restless, radical alienation that is homelessness (*wræclast*, "the path of exile"):

> þeah-þe he mod-cearig
> geond lagu-lade   lange scolde
> hreran mid handum   hrim-cealde sæ,
> wadan wræc-lastas.   Wyrd biþ full aræd. (1–5)

> [Though he must traverse
> tracts of sea, sick at heart,
> —trouble with oars ice-cold waters,
> the ways of exile—Wierd [Fate] is set fast.]

Compare this Anglo-Saxon quest for a warm hall to Lacan's description of the subject's battle for a coherent "I." Embodiment occurs when an insubstantial image is materialized as the self. Because this image is exterior to the subject, a gap opens that cannot be bridged or filled, only temporarily allayed: the life of the *anhaga* who roams the "marshes and rubbish-tips" of the world in search of a "fortress, or stadium" or gabled hall in which to be at home. The Lacanian unconscious is a place, an imaginary geography in every way parallel to the wintry wastes and churning seas over which the Anglo-Saxon exile wanders.[16]

Lacan's creation myth is persuasive but, when read beside the giant-driven Norse cosmogony, lacks something. Vafþrúðismál suggests that constructing an identity for the subject and composing a history for the world are two versions of the same process. The giant is the fragmented body written across the landscape to provide *its* prehistory, its identity. The world coheres only after the body has been projected across its contours, arranging rivers, valleys, and mountains into a geography that gigantizes the somatic. Identity proceeds by both introjection (cannibalism) and projection (expulsion, abjection). The exterior delineates the body, while the body is written across the exterior. This doubled movement, this entwined and generative flux, ensures that identity and place are mutually constitutive. The *corps morcelé* of the land becomes the "alienated identity" of the map. Ymir becomes the earth, and even if his skull, corpse, and blood are recognizable in sky, soil, and water, it is because he cannot be gazed upon whole. To render the world an imaginary body makes it delusionarily coherent, just as to embody a subject in its specular image is to make that subject similarly an illusory, lacking whole: "We continually project the body into the world in order that its image might return to us" (Stewart, *On Longing*, 125).

This spectacular integrity is always temporary. The integral body (of the land, of the subject) is always about to become, once more, the body in pieces: a dream intervenes, and the giant reappears.

Homelessness

If the giant is simultaneously exterior *and* interior to embodiment, a fragmentary whole (*enta geweorc*) at the origin of human identity and a projection from its full form, then the home has already been invaded, and that timeless place of rest (the Wanderer's longed-for hall, Lacan's distant fortress) is neither pure nor safe. Perhaps there is no reason for Grendel to burst the door from its iron hinges and invade the warmth that the walls of Heorot enclose. Perhaps the giant is already there, at the foundation.

Gaston Bachelard succinctly speaks the name of "the chief benefit of the house": "The house protects the dreamer, the house allows one to dream in peace" (*Poetics of Space*, 6). His reverie over the integrative powers of this quintessential modern structure is rapturous, impossible, enticing. Like the Wanderer, Bachelard offers through his verbal conjuration a moment of repose for a world doomed to homelessness. The passage is worth lingering over:

> In the life of a man, the house thrusts aside contingencies, its councils of continuity are unceasing. Without it, man would be a dispersed being. It maintains him through the storms of the heavens and through those of life. It is body and soul.... Life begins well, it begins enclosed, protected, all warm in the bosom of the house. (6–7)

Bachelard's domestic reverie is suffused with nostalgia. He imagines a time when the subject was at peace, when the storms and tempests of the world did not "knock like a rifle-butt against the door," when the monster remained safely outside.[17] But nostalgia is always a yearning for a space-time that has never been. Nostalgia constructs a naive Other whose gaze we temporarily inhabit to look upon the scene for us so that we can believe in it, even though we know its paradisal simplicity to be impossible. The subject's relation to such temporal utopias is therefore "always divided, split between fascination and ironic distance: ironic distance toward its diegetic reality, fascination with its gaze."[18] The impervious Bachelardian house that "thrusts aside contingencies" is mythic, unreal, a Platonic form locked in heaven; in the true house, the vinyl-sided kind one finds by the million gridded across the suburban landscape, the storm has broken through the window, the giant is already within.

The door splinters at the giant's touch, and Grendel strides into the hall. In the Anglo-Saxon *heall*, the mighty structure that tames a formless wilderness into representability by establishing a structurating principle at its middle, the giant is already nearby, in some secret place (*healh*) not far from the threshold. Again, the problem of origins arises, the collapse into duality precipitated by the body of the monster, the hybrid nature of human identity. Which came first, the giant or the architecture he threatens? The safety of the primal dwelling, or the frightening presence of the Real, the monster or the tempest at the door? Do fantasies of buildings or embodiments that "thrust aside contingencies," whose "councils of continuity are unceasing," exist to protect humanity from becoming, like Hondscio, a "dispersed being"? Or does the monster's threat of fragmentation and ingestion intrude only after the strong walls of the hall have been erected, only after Grendel has heard drifting over his mere the maddeningly sweet, infuriatingly exclusive music of the hall?

Psychoanalysis offers another way of formulating the same question of origins and then suggests a resolution: Who came first, the Father of Prohibition or the Father of Enjoyment? These two paternal figures haunt the myth and history of the West because they arise from the same formal necessity, through the very process of symbolization. As origin incarnate, the two fathers suggest why in Anglo-Saxon England the monster is the necessary prehistory and intimate exterior of human identity. The Father of Prohibition initiates the law through the prohibition of incest and therefore stands at the mythic origin of culture. His primal "NO" hurls the child into language, the system that orders the wilderness of experience by taming it via the laws of syntax into coherent signification. The Father of Prohibition embodies the way in which, after the mirror stage has worked its optical magic, language estranges the subject from itself again. In the movement from the realm of visual phenomena (the Lacanian imaginary order) into verbal interaction with the laws of signification (the symbolic order), the subject becomes divided against itself by that same linguistic indoctrination that makes self-consciousness possible. Self-presence is predicated upon self-estrangement, just as words (signifiers) are phenomenologically distinct from the things they signify. The structures and strictures of language are *constitutive* of selfhood at the same time as they remain intimately *alien*.[19]

The Father of Enjoyment delights in being prior, and therefore exterior, to the law. This "primal father" of Freud's *Totem and Taboo* is the mythic and pre-Oedipal figure who must once have possessed the plenitude of enjoyment now barred the speaking subject. Yet this myth of origins is not so chronologically straightforward as it seems. These two paternal figures are ultimately one and the same. Freud's Father of Enjoyment does not know bodily limits and is therefore outside of the law (full enjoyment is his alone); but through his prohibitions, he differentiates the other members of the primitive horde, who then know themselves as sons, daughters, and wives only by virtue of the familial grammar he institutes and the access to enjoyment he withholds. These two fathers, Prohibition and Enjoyment, are as intertwined as speech and loss. "*Jouissance* is forbidden to him who speaks, as such":[20] if it is true that enjoyment is rendered impossible because of the estranging effect of language (that is, if it is true that the price of linguistic subjectivization is the barring of the full enjoyment symbolized by such fantasies of presymbolic bliss as the mother's body, the wanderer's hall, the dreamer's fortress, all those impossible visions of a lost, untroubled home), then the two fathers are part of the same retroactive fantasy by which the subject imagines a plenitude it never had in order to understand the *extimité* of its present selfhood.[21] The myth of the two fathers arises because if enjoyment is only *lost* rather than *impossible,* then the chance exists that it can be regained. In other words, the Father of Enjoyment is conjoined with the Father of Prohibition to confer "the form of a symbolic *interdiction*" upon a structural *impossibility* (no speaking subject can have unmediated access to *jouissance*).[22] The "problem of origins" arises as a formal effect of symbolization. The severe father who prohibits, and the obscene father who enjoys; the Bachelardian house, and the "storms of the heavens" that hurl themselves at its windows; the gabled hall that renders a frigid wilderness a cradled warmth, and the monster who shatters its primal unity: these visions of the world that teeter between "oceanic oneness" and a horrifying disaggregation are all versions of a retroactive fantasy by which the fragments of the past are sutured into a coherent, teleological history whose culmination is the homeless, self-estranged subject, the Wanderer. The fantasy materializes for the subject a continuous identity, a past that makes sense of the present's fragility. Further, by representing enjoyment as lost rather than impossible, the subject gains a future — if only a nomadic life spent searching for the hall or home where *jouissance* could be possessed again, where a giant has not yet risen from his distant mere in jealous hatred of communal songs.[23]

In the long postcolonial moment that occurred on the island as the Roman church extended the sphere of its epistemological hegemony, *Christianitas* was continuously promulgated as a unifying principle, as a point of identification strong enough to overcome the constituent differences that kept Anglo-Saxon England fragmentary, to effect a newly totalizing identity.[24] The two fathers become part of an ideological fantasy that covers over the radical alterity, the incommensurability, of the northern (pagan) and Latin (Christian) worldviews — a difference in symbolization so fundamental that it extends all the way to their foundational myths, their cosmogonies. Under the new regime of signs, the Father of Prohibition becomes the divinity who reconfigures the symbolic order through his resounding NO, the father who cuts off access to the riches of heaven by immuring behind strong walls what treasure it holds. The Father of Enjoyment, on the other hand, is he for whom enjoyment was once possible, the one prior to, or outside of, this foundational Law, celebrant of the flesh and the enemy of the divine. Conveniently, that figure is the giant in both traditions, and so this monster was a natural point at which to begin the translation of early northern myth into the exegetical *lingua Christianitatis.*[25] Within the new symbolization of the *ordo mundi* precipitated by the meeting of the Latin and northern cosmogonies, both Anglo-Saxon fathers became coincipient, mutually constitutive. Since God and the giants were entwined in a new moment of origin, both figured within a widespread cultural narrative of how the world received its primal ordering. In fact, whenever a problem of origins is approached in early medieval England, the giant lurks nearby, never far from the threshold of whatever architecture is being built to erect an interiority against a wilderness, to give a human form to history.

Late in the ninth century, King Alfred the Great reworked Boethius's sixth-century philosophical treatise *De Consolatione Philosophiae* (*The Consolation of Philosophy*) into Old English prose, the first of two English monarchs to translate the Latin work. His contemporaries may well have found the *consolatio* promised by the title as they read the work in its new vernacular edition. Medievalists are apt to value it more highly, however, for the insights contained in the numerous glosses to what Alfred considered difficult or obscure passages. For example, the somatic transformations worked by a sorceress in the *Odyssey* are connected in a short Boethian meter to inner morality and outward appearance. The Latin speaks obliquely of *dux Neritii* (Ulysses) and *pulchra dea solis edita semine* (Circe). In the course of explaining the second allusion, Alfred writes:

> þa wæs þær Apollines dohter Iobes [Jove's] suna; se Iob was hiora cyning, and licette þæt he sceolde bion se hehsta god; and þæt dysige folc him gelyfde, for þaðe he was cynecynnes; and hi nyston nænne oðerne god on þæne timan, buton hiora cyningas hi weorþodon for godas. þa sceolde þæs Iobes fæder bion eac god; þæs nama wæs Saturnus; and his suna swa ilce ælcne hi hæfdon for god. þa was hiora an se Apollinis þe we ær ymb spræcon. Þæs Apollines dohtor sceolde bion gydene, þære nama wæs Kirke.

> [At that time there was a daughter of Apollo, son of Jupiter; this Jupiter was their king and had pretended that he was the highest god; and that foolish people believed him, because he was of royal blood; and they knew no other god in that time, but worshiped their kings as divine. Thus Saturn, the father of Jupiter, had likewise to be a god, as well as each of his sons. One of these was Apollo, whom we just mentioned. This Apollo's daughter had to be a goddess; her name was Circe.][26]

The explanation does more than elucidate a difficult Latin phrase. It provides a myth of origin for the gods of classical antiquity. The pagan divinities are dismissed as prideful, all too human monarchs and their families, for whom deification is something of a fad: once the man named Jupiter succeeds in convincing his credulous subjects of his immortal blood, his father, sons, and even granddaughter insist upon their place in the new pantheon. The story validates *Christianitas* over pagan error while explaining to the curious how anthropomorphic pseudodivinities entered the world.

The linking of the deities of classical mythology to mortal or demonic impersonators is a commonplace in early theological writing. Justin Martyr in the *Apologia* and Augustine in *De civitate dei* were among the many patristic writers to reiterate the belief. Isidore of Seville summarized this exegetical tradition in his influential *Etymologiae* (8.xi), "De diis gentium":

> Those whom the pagans worship as gods were once human and lived among men, such as Isis in Egypt, Jupiter in Crete, and Faunus in Rome.... They were formerly mighty heroes [*viri fortes*], founders of cities; when they died, images were erected to honor them.... Persuaded by demons, posterity esteemed these men gods, and worshiped them.[27]

These deceiving *viri fortes* were first described by the church fathers as fallen angels; then, with a shift in the exegesis, they became powerful, evil men, often said to be descended from either fratricidal Cain or Noah's mocking son, Cham. In Anglo-Saxon England, the *viri fortes* became *gigantes*. Oliver Emerson argues that the early Christian writers precipitated this myth by building on the conflation of the giants of Genesis with the classical stormers of Olympus by the Jewish historian Josephus ("Legends of Cain," 905). No doubt this conjoining was enabled through the moralizing of the biblical giants already well under way by the time of the Jewish apocrypha. The Book of Wisdom characterizes these monsters as corporeal signifiers of overbearing pride, destroyed as a rebuke to that primal sin: "From the beginning when the proud giants perished, the hope of mankind escaped on a raft and ... bequeathed to the world a new breed of men" (14:6). The biblical passage underscores the giants' historicity: these monsters predate the flood, which was sent to cleanse the earth of the evils they embody. By simultaneously reading the body of the giants as allegory, however, the Book of Wisdom suggests a continuity with the giants of classical tradition, likewise condemned as monstrously prideful in their failed attempt to pile Ossa on Pelion to steal from the gods the immortal home of Olympus.[28]

After describing the demise of the giants, the passage from Wisdom explains how later in world history "tyrants" devised idols to deny the fact of the body's mortality (Wisd. 14:15–21). The story entwines loss (a father mourns his dead son with an image that others worship as a god), pride (despots [*tyranni*] thinking themselves greater than human order their statues venerated), the alluring power of the visual (the idols elicit awe because of their "ideal form," an artistically induced numinousness), and the reifying power of the law (the longer the idol is worshiped, the more natural such action appears, so that through repetition a reality is materialized for divinity). As in the Lacanian mirror stage, a jubilant image becomes a trap for the gaze, a lure that catches the unwary subject in an estranging identification—here, one that produces a false deity rather than an embodied ego.

In the Latin church, wicked men rather than inhuman monsters were invariably held to be those *tyranni* responsible for the sin of embodying divinity within human corporeality. For Anglo-Saxon writers, however, these primordial deceivers were always the giants.[29] The Book of Wisdom unites the giants and the "despotic princes" only by narrative proximity, but in early medieval England, the two episodes in salvation history (the destruction of the giants, the promulgation of idols) became conjoined into a newly hybrid foundational narrative that bridged classical, biblical, and northern traditions. The homilist Ælfric explicates this myth of origin in the "Passio Apostolorum Petri et Pauli," as an elucidation of why Peter should have called Jesus "son of the living God":

> [Petrus] cwæð "þæs lifigendan Godes," for twæminge ðæra leasra goda, ða ðe hæðene ðeoda, mid mislicum gedwylde bepæhte, wurðodon. Sume hi gelyfdon on deade entas, and him deorwurðlice anlicnyssa arærdon, and cwædon þæt hi godas wæron for ðære micelan strencðe e hi hæfdon; wæs ðeah lif swiðe manfullic and bysmurfull. (366)

> [Peter said "of the living God" to distinguish the lesser gods, who deceived the heathens with various heresies. Some believed in dead giants, and raised up precious images, and said that they were gods because of their great strength; nevertheless their lives were very sinful and unclean.]

The giants are an ancient, vanished race whose fossilized remains are not mysterious bones or odd topography but the lingering worship of their iniquity. The references to constructing idols and deifying the sun and moon that follow make it clear that Ælfric has both biblical and classical deities in mind. By describing the genesis of the false, mortal divinities of the Greeks and Romans (along with those of the Babylonians, Canaanites, and wayward Israelites), Ælfric is repeating a connection frequently made in Old English literature between the opprobrious giants of Christian tradition and the gods of classical mythology.

Etiologic myths linking biblical exegesis with Greek and Roman literature were a favorite of erudite Latin culture throughout the Middle Ages. Yet there is something distinctly Anglo-Saxon about this fascination with giants conjoined to the formation of alienated, human identities. In the course of one of the many homilies collected by Napier, a discourse on the early power of the devil over humanity leads to an excursus amounting to a full creation myth for the numerous gods of old:

Se deofles man rixað on middanearde, and swa lange he winð ongean god and godes þeowas; and he ahefð hine sylfne ofer ealle, þa ðe hæðene men cwædon, þæt godas beon sceoldan on hæðene wisan; swylc swa wæs Erculus se ent and Apollinis, þe hi mærne god leton; þor eac and Owðen, þe hæðene men heriað swiðe.

[The devil ruled men on earth, and he strove against God and God's people; and he raised himself over all, so that the heathens said that the gods were their heathen leaders; such a one was the giant Hercules and Apollo, who left the glorious God; Thor also and Odin, whom the heathens greatly praise.][30]

Apollo, the classical pantheon, and even the semidivine Greek hero Hercules are not the only divinities invented by megalomaniacal giants. Thor (þor) and Odin (Owðen), the most familiar gods of northern provenance, also become originary *entas*. Even after the Vanir and Aesir had been replaced by Christian monotheism, traditions of giants lingered. As erudite culture displaced the more indigenous, heathen tradition, this old order of giants became conflated with the vanished gods whom they had aided and battled so that both could then be denigrated as deceivers and impersonators, validating the superiority of *Christianitas* as a homogenous, erudite, right-thinking culture. The northern mythographic propensity to use giants in a drama of etiology was adapted to the formation of a new scholastic myth through which the Germanic cosmology could be restructured and subordinated beneath a new set of master signifiers.

The giants of the homilists are the ancient, primal, but *dead* Fathers of Enjoyment who committed every sin, including the institution of embodied divinity. The *deus pater* of Christian tradition is the second aspect of this originary paternal dyad: his Word is a speech act ("Let there be light, and there was light"), his prohibition the foundation of Law. Outside this regulation because he is its creator, this Father does not enjoy because he is likewise outside of sexuality (the origin of which is coincipient with the origin of law). The Father of Prohibition is autogenous, creating without the aid of female agency, without the aid of any kind of body at all. God guarantees the sanctity of the symbolic order by expelling the giants and the sins of their obscene enjoyment from its center.

The Book of Genesis relates that in the days after the banishment from Eden, several rebellious angels copulated with human women and engendered a *genus gigantum*: "Giants were on the earth in those days [*Entas wæron ofer eorþan on þam dagum*],[31] when the sons of God [angels] had intercourse with daughters of men and begot children [the giants] upon them" (Gen. 6:4). According to the dominant exegesis of this passage, God sent the Flood to cleanse these monsters and the stain of their sins from the earth. The eradication of the giant is contemporaneous with the establishment of the law that delineates exogamy and endogamy, for the giants are the organic realization of a primal miscegenation: angels

19

mix with humans, and the purely spiritual touches flesh. The giants arise and are destroyed to demonstrate that the word of the Father institutes and then controls sexuality. This instantiation of desire is the Oedipal moment: God the Father decrees through divine fiat the proper relations among sexed subjects, and the giants vanish. The Flood heralds the dawn of a new order, the postdiluvian age that extends to the present day, for humanity is as much descended from Noah and his wife as from Adam and Eve. Destruction becomes a kind of creation. The problems of origin are swept away by a world-purging deluge.

The same process of destructive birth or violent cleansing is enacted through the very Christianization that gives Anglo-Saxon England this new originary myth. The Oedipal Father of Christian tradition replaces the nonfamilial, nonautogenous, anthropomorphic deities of the Norse pantheon. Where once blurred boundaries and contiguity reigned, the church instituted a new model of relations based upon the almighty Father, who is originless and origin-incarnate. The pagan gods, who are no different from the giants (being descended from them, in both traditions), are made to vanish, rendered as good as dead. The giants perish with them, for who can withstand such an exegetical flood?

When Beowulf defeats Grendel's mother in her lair by means of a conveniently discovered "ealdsweord eotenisc" [old giants' sword] (1558), a weapon so large that it is, like the ruins that the Wanderer beholds, "giganta geweorc" [the work of giants] (1562), it is impossible to say exactly which tradition of giants is supposed to be responsible for having forged the blade. That this "enta ærgeweorc" [ancient work of giants] (1679) is also "wundorsmiþa geweorc" [wrought by wonder-smiths] (1681) points to an association with the giants of northern tradition, renowned for their skill as smiths. Yet Hrothgar sees that depicted on the hilt is "fyrngewinnes, syðþan flod ofsloh, / gifen geotende giganta cyn, / frecne geferdon" [that ancient strife, when the flood, the rushing sea, slew the giants, who suffered terribly] (1689–91). If the story depicted is that of the biblical deluge, sent by God to destroy the giants, who, then, made the sword? The same giants it depicts being destroyed? The death by water carved upon the weapon's hilt could also represent the flood caused by the letting of Ymir's blood by the Norse gods, an act that was supposed to have drowned all the remaining giants of the world except Bergelmir and his spouse. In either case, the originary relationship of metalsmith to depicted subject, and of these giants to Grendel and his mother, is impossible to disentangle.

This *ealdsweord eotenisc* serves well as an emblem for the impure identity of the Anglo-Saxon giants and their entanglement in narratives of *human* origin. In Latin tradition, in Norse mythology, and in psychoanalytic myth, the Fathers of Enjoyment vanish so that the reign of the Father of Prohibition can begin. The giant represents access to that lost enjoyment that *must* at one time have been possible, access to a lost sense of oneness with the world that explains a contemporary feeling of estrangement. That the giant is a monster suggests the danger that a return to *jouissance* represents to a symbolic order founded upon its impossibility, to a subjectivity made possible only through its occlusion. In the end, what matters is not from where the giants derived, but what origin they enable.

In both Christian and Germanic tradition, a flood destroys the giants. More importantly, in both traditions, *the giants return.* Despite the primordial catastrophe depicted on the sword's hilt, Grendel haunts his mere and prompts the men he besieges to revert to the worship of idols. The Hebrew Bible overflows with stories of postdiluvian giants: Og of Bashan, the aboriginal inhabitants of Canaan, David's mighty nemesis, Goliath. Only Noah and the contents of his ark were supposed to survive God's celestial wash cycle, and yet giants were still walking the earth after the divinity purged its dirtied landscape. Some theologians speculated that these monsters survived by climbing the tallest mountains and thrusting their nostrils above sea level for forty days and forty nights, or that one of them, Og, had simply ridden atop the roof of the ark. But the myth of the two fathers and its relation to the Anglo-Saxon giants suggests a very different conclusion. The giants endured because they have always already lurked at the threshold of the house of God, in the haunted *healh* against which his holy *heall* stands. His rule begins with a founding Word that simultaneously excludes the giants and makes them a structural necessity: no prohibition without mythic enjoyment, no God without monsters. To abject the giant and everything his body encodes from cultural meaning is to ensure that the monster will haunt the periphery that abjection constructs, because a signification based upon exclusion depends upon the continued presence (if only a presence in death) of the thing it exiles. When northern mythology met Christian epistemology, the resultant clash of meaning systems led to a new systemization of belief, one in which the giants and the instantiation of Christian divinity were coincipient, coconstitutive. The fate of the giants of the Bible was alloyed, like the metal of Beowulf's sword, to the fate of the giants of northern cosmogony: both became part of a symbolic structure that condensed around a new Father, a Christian father, one who could banish the giants with a flood and transport the enjoyment they embodied from the past into the future, as the promise of heaven.

The Letter Killeth

John Hunter, the father of British surgery, was just as happy to have the bones of the giant James Byrne as to study him alive. Similarly, Frederick I of Prussia, attempting to kidnap a giant named Zimmerman, smothered him in a coffin, yet was just as satisfied with his skeleton.
—Susan Stewart, *On Longing,* 111

21

If the symbolic order—the landscape through which the speaking subject treads "the paths of exile" in a doomed search for permanent place
of repose—is already a dead order, structured as much around the primal
absence of gods as the presence of a transcendent divinity who stands
outside as its guarantee of meaning, then why fear the giant? Perhaps
because he embodies a pronouncement heretical to voice: the system
through which subjects are formed and through which they gain their
self-consciousness is inhuman, monstrous, alive in death—like language
itself.[32] To master language is to be mastered by language, since language
is structured around prohibitions; it is also to be torn apart, made a collection of things with an autonomous existence quite separate from the
self that is supposed to unify them. Slavoj Zizek writes in a characteristically Hegelian mode of how "word is murder of a thing," how "the
word 'quarters' the thing, it tears it out of the embedment in its concrete
context, it treats its component parts as entities with an autonomous
existence" (*Enjoy Your Symptom*, 51). The entrance into the linguistic
system is thus also the Oedipal moment, when the father's NO precipitates a mutilating, exclusionary form of embodiment that renders the subject aware both of its fragility and its constitutive lack. To be Oedipalized,
to become a speaking subject, is both to be born (as a unified being) and
to die (be torn apart, become monstrous). Identity is constituted by the
tumbling together of both terms.

The giant lurks here, even at this entry into language.

In Dante's *Inferno*, as the narrator prepares to descend into the ninth
circle of hell, he sees in the distant fog what he believes are enormous
towers that encircle the vast pit of Malebolge. From his wise guide Vergil,
the narrator learns that these warding structures are living giants, buried
in the earth from the navel down. The fiercest of the monsters bellows
at hell's two tourists: "Rafel mahee amek zabi almit!" These enigmatic,
indecipherable sounds provoke Dante's guide to declare, "His very bab-
bling testifies the wrong / he did on earth: he is Nimrod, through whose
evil / mankind no longer speaks a common tongue" (31.76–78; trans.
John Ciardi, 260). Medieval exegesis held that the giant Nimrod had been
the architect of the Tower of Babel, "the first great collective effort of
pride against God," so that his punishment is the somatic reification of
his traditional sin (Walter Stephens, *Giants in Those Days*, 86). Nimrod
is even more deadly, transgressive, and anarchic than the classical giants
Ephialtes, Briareus, Tityos, Typhon, and Antaeus—the other infernal
"towers."

Genesis makes no reference to Nimrod's size, labeling him during his
brief appearance in an extended genealogy only a "mighty hunter before
the Lord," a grandson of Cham, and the founder of the kingdom of Babel,
in Shinar (Gen. 10:8–10). The Plains of Shinar are, by chance, the very
place where the Tower of Babel was constructed (Gen. 11:2), so that Nimrod eventually became its putative builder in various exegetical works,

both Jewish and Christian.[33] The Septuagint had used the Greek word for "giant" to describe Nimrod. Philo and Orosius followed, promulgating the idea. According to Stephens, Augustine "bequeathed to the Latin Middle Ages this idea that Nimrod was...a 'mighty hunter *against* the Lord' ('gigans uenator *contra* Dominum Deum')," mainly because of his use of a pre-Vulgate text drawn from the Septuagint (358). Further, even the word *venator* (hunter) amplified Nimrod's gigantism for Augustine, signifying "deceiver, oppressor, and murderer of the earth's animals."[34]

Nimrod's giant body becomes the transgressive architecture that he aspired to build, a living and speaking *enta geweorc*. The Tower of Babel is an affront to the house of God that would bring divinity down to earth. God's punishment against the tower's human builders is to render them wanderers who must circle the earth, speaking new languages that ensure they will never by one another be fully understood:

> Once upon a time all the world spoke a single language and used the same words. As men journeyed in the east, they came across a plain in the land of Shinar.... "Come," they said, "let us build ourselves a city and a tower with its top in the heavens, and make a name for ourselves; or we shall be dispersed all over the earth." Then the Lord came down to see the city and tower which mortal men had built, and he said, "Here they are, one people with a single language, and now they have started to do this; henceforward nothing they have a mind to do will be beyond their reach. Come, let us go down and confuse their speech, so that they will not understand what they say to one another." So the Lord dispersed them all over the earth.[35] (Gen. 11:1–9)

A community united by their transparent communication seeks a permanent (celestial) place of rest and is punished by confusion of tongues and perpetual motion. *Babel* ("gate of the gods," a city in which to dwell like an unmoving divinity) becomes *balal* ("to babble," to be compelled to search for steadfast meanings). Linguistically and geographically, the architects of Babel lose their home and become nomads; henceforth, no place of union will exist, no city, tower, or hall will stand.

Like the giant erector of the Aesir's citadel Asgarðr or the rebellious giants who in Greek myth piled Pelion on Ossa to attain Olympus, Nimrod is stopped just as his subversive architecture nears completion; the act is always memorialized in its incompletion, to testify to some final, monstrous inadequacy. According to James Dean, "Nimrod's name in medieval writings is synonymous with perversion, that is, with a turning away from old paths toward something novel, with a change for the worse."[36] Again at a point of origin and human identity the giant is lurking. Anglo-Saxon exegesis multiplied the authors of Nimrod's heaven-bent construction, attributing the tower not to one lone giant but to an entire race. The homily *De falsis deis* declares that "Nembroð and ða entas worhton þone wundorlican stypel æfter Noes flod" [Nimrod and the giants constructed a marvelous tower after Noah's Flood].[37] Ælfric's homily "For the Holy Day of Pentecost" gives a fuller account. He counterpoints the speaking in tongues awarded the apostles at Pentecost and the moment of linguistic unity it created with the expulsion into opaque signification embodied by the giants:

> Hit getimode æfter Noes flode,þæt entas woldon aræron ane burh, and ænne stypel swa heahne,þæt his hrof astige oð heofon. Êa wæs an gereord on eallum mancynne, and þæt weorc wæs begunnen ongean Godes willan. God eac forði hi tostencte, swaþæt he forgeaf ælcumðæra wyrhtena seltcuð gereord, and heora nan ne cuðe oðres spræce tocnawan. Hiða geswiconðære getimbrunge, and toferdon geond ealne middangeard; and wæron siððan swa fela gereord swað-æra wyrhtena wæs. (*Sermones Catholici*, 318)

> [It happened after Noah's Flood, that the giants wanted to erect a city and a tower so high that its roof would touch heaven. At that time all humanity had one language, and that work was undertaken against God's will. God therefore scattered them, so that each worker had his own language, and they did not comprehend each other's speech. Then they wandered away from their edifice, and dispersed throughout the earth; and there were then as many languages as there had been workers.]

The building of the tower is a parable of a second Fall: the one language in which signifier and signified were not separated by any gap gives way to a new, Saussurian linguistics in which words connect only randomly to things. The old language given by God loses its pure signifying power under the giant's influence, replaced by a gibberish that has to be reanalyzed as new languages to reachieve communication. *Rafel mahee amek zabi almit*: a chaotic system of arbitrary signification and linguistic difference reigns where unmediated understanding had once obtained. Radical estrangement becomes the fate of all who enter the symbolic by learning to speak. Their words are not them, are not anything, and yet the words themselves speak, make meanings articulated beyond intention or control. Language, which had been a bond of absolute union, ensures now only distance, removal, loss.

On Reaching the Giant's Home

The giant threatens the secure place of home, imagined as a stable core for identity as well as a geographical locus. In Norse myth, the monsters of Jotunheim so menace the god's heavenly abode of Asgarðr that a giant is tricked into immuring its towers and then is destroyed; this mythic association of giants and the building of primal architectures is kept alive in the Old English phrase *enta geweorc,* which transforms ancient human ruins into monstrous history. In classical myth, the primal sons of the earth uproot mountains and assail celestial Olympus, that *arduus aether* (high heaven) might be no safer than the earth (Ovid, *Metamorphoses,* 1.151–62). Jupiter strikes down the rebellious monsters with his divine thunderbolts, and from the scattered gore of the fallen giants, a newly monstrous birth arises, spawned of incest (the *gigantes* are the sons of that maternal earth whom they in death impregnate): not giants but men, "sons of blood" (cf. Hesiod, *Theogony,* 58). According to the Bible, giants are the progeny of humans and devils. They are likewise leaders in the revolt against divinity, the architects of the tower that would have taken heaven away from God. All three myths intertwine monsters, homelessness, and the barring of the subject from full enjoyment (in Christian terms, from union with the divine). Human identity and restless nomadism become inextricable.

Yet none of these myths quite capture the melancholic fascination of Anglo-Saxon England with the giant as figure both of origin and of loss. The monster's connection to human identity received its fullest consideration in the myths the Anglo-Saxons wove for themselves as they tried to make a hybrid past cohere, as they tried to discern why history had placed an intimate stranger at the heart of subjectivity. Grendel, the most famous monster of Old English literature, embodies this Anglo-Saxon fascination with *extimité* well. The giant intrudes into the narrative just as Hrothgar's scop is singing, Cædmon-like, of the creation of the world — a bright song that begins with the shaping of the earth (91–92) and ends at its populating (97–98), before the introduction of original sin. Hrothgar's warriors are by conjunction immediately brought into this antediluvian golden age ("Swa ða drihtguman dreamum lifdon" [So the men lived in joy], 99), until Grendel suddenly intervenes. The monster hates their music, a dynamic metaphor of their communal harmony; this enmity places him outside the realm of the social and aligns him with everything abjected from the warmth of Heorot in order to render it a livable world.

The parallel to the biblical advent of the giants and their promulgation of evil among humanity in the days before the Flood is subtle but unmistakable. Grendel is immediately linked with Cain, who is in turn the progenitor of the very giants of the Book of Enoch and of Genesis whose deeds Grendel is repeating: "Swylce gigantas þa wið Gode wunnon / lange þrage" [such giants that fought against God for a long time] (113–14).[38] Grendel exists in an uncanny (*unheimlich*) narrative temporality that is simultaneously before the deluge (in its biblical time frame) and after it (in its "historical" setting).[39] The attachment of northern monsters ("eotenas ond ylfe ond orcneas," 111) as Grendel's brethren in Cain's genealogy further complicates the temporal frame, merging these heterogeneous fragments of history into some uncertain, monstrous past that they suddenly share. This manifold history is quietly defined against the Christian present of the poet throughout the narrative. Its point of vanishing is the interlocked deaths of Beowulf and the dragon at the close of the work.

Grendel's relation to the *comitatus* of Heorot is one of illustrative antithesis.[40] He disperses the unity of the war band with an eruption of misdirected violence. He supplants Hrothgar as ruler of the hall through senseless, jealous slaughter. The maintenance of order in a warrior society is achieved only by the repression of those impulses Grendel embodies. Wergild, for example, the system that disallows blood vengeance when a legally binding sum of appeasing gold has been offered to a victim's family, works well at defusing violent action only so long as a people can be made to abide by its strictures. Grendel represents a cultural Other for whom conformity to societal dictates is an impossibility because those dictates are not comprehensible to him; he is at the same time a monsterized version of what a member of that very society can become when those dictates are rejected, when the authority of leaders or mores disintegrates and the subordination of the individual to hierarchy is lost. Grendel is another version of the *wræcca* or *anhaga*, as if the banished speaker of *The Wanderer* had turned in his exile not to elegiac poetry but to the dismemberment of that cultural body through which he came to be.[41]

If the Wanderer and Grendel are merely different figurations of the same symbolic role, another point of human origin has found a giant lurking both without and within. By way of conclusion, it is perhaps worth venturing to the home that the monster inhabits, to see what relation it bears to Heorot before its violation, to Bachelard's protective house or Lacan's distant fortress, to the Wanderer's eternally lost but incessantly beckoning hall. The *Beowulf* poet describes the submarine cave that Grendel and his mother share in horrifying terms: fen locked and frost bound, the lake that bubbles above the cave is overhung with dead trees that "clutch" as if alive. Its violent waters burn with mysterious fire, and "No man alive, though old and wise, knows the mere-bottom" (*Beowulf*, 1356–67). The giant's den is a terrifying locus of epistemological uncertainty. Of Grendel's descent, Hrothgar warns Beowulf, "no hie fæder cunnon, hwæþer him anig wæs ær acenned dyrnra gasta" [no one knows of his father, whether any was ever begotten for him among the dark shapes] (1355–57).[42] This inability to name a progenitor from which to trace descent condenses all the problems of origin the giant embodies. Although Grendel has no father to compel him through some primal prohibition to leave the body of his mother, this union could hardly be described as presymbolic bliss (*jouissance*). The giant dwells in a land that is an extension of the same signification system that distorts his monster's flesh: it is an inhuman realm that offers only dissolution and death.

26

Aeschere's lifeless head is dropped on the cliff by the mere, a mute testament to monstrosity that recalls the Donestre's desubjectifying cannibalism.

This monstrous realm is also a gendered place: here Beowulf meets, fights, and is almost crushed to death by a giantess, a protective *mother.* Grendel's devoted parent, supposedly less fierce than her son (1282–84), is in fact more terrible and figures within the poem's homosocial milieu the "vortex of summons and repulsion" that Julia Kristeva has called abjection (*Powers of Horror,* 1). In this horrifying, fascinating space, repulsion curves into desire, and everything thought to be "ejected beyond the scope of the possible, the tolerable" is revealed as residing deep within the architecture of selfhood. Kristeva allies abjection specifically with the maternal, with everything that the Wanderer's wished-for embrace excludes.[43] Grendel's unnamed mother, his companion on the paths of exile (1347–48), violently reinscribes into a masculinist account of heroic self-fashioning the bodies, origins, and possibilities that narrative excludes; it is a tribute to the complexities of the poem that it accomplishes this reinsertion by demonstrating that the abjected realm of the monster is also a roofed hall (*hrofsele*) "described in human, almost homey terms" (Orchard, *Pride and Prodigies,* 30) — just another version of Heorot — where Beowulf plays the role Grendel previously enacted. As the dragon will prove again later, the difference between foe (*feond*) and defender (*stearcheort,* "stouthearted one") is a question of perspective, with each term forming the secret interior of the other.[44]

Like Hrothgar in Heorot, Grendel's mother lives for fifty years undisturbed in her hall. Yet her habitation is at once *hrofsele* (roofed hall) and *niðsele* (hateful hall), both beautiful and frightening. This home, which is something less than Bachelard's integrative vision of domesticity, is worth comparing to a more modern version of Beowulf's descent into the mere, this time as described by a critic of the poem who determined to find in modern Scandinavia the exact topography of the Old English narrative:

> When we arrived at the lakeside, I found the grassy sward so inviting and the lake so blue and calm that while Randy went back alone for the car I dozed off in the sun, exactly...where Grendel and his mother were wont to roam. Even more disconcerting, or pleasing, depending on one's level of irony, a sanitarium with serene and well-kept grounds now stands "in the very place" where those two monsters used to rage and tear apart their victims for dinner. (Overing and Osborn, *Landscape of Desire,* 22)

In the daylight, the place of monsters is transformed. What was for Beowulf a "place between two deaths" where giants cannibalized their victims becomes a grassy hill that invites dreamy reminiscence. Grendel's lair is not so very different from the Wanderer's hall after all. This duality of signification characterizes what psychoanalysis labels the place of *das Ding,* "the real-traumatic kernel in the midst of symbolic order."[45] *Das Ding* is Freud's appropriately Germanic word for a "sublime object" that is as numinous and inviting as it is horribly alien; *das Ding* is both a longed-for home and the dwelling of the monster. This Thing that is an extimate trauma lurks at the center of subjectivity, ensuring that the process of becoming human is also the process of becoming monstrous: "As soon as brute, pre-symbolic reality is symbolized/historicized, it 'secretes' the . . . 'indigestible' place of the Thing" (Zizek, *Sublime Object,* 135). As Grendel and the Donestre demonstrate, the human body is quite *ingestible* — that is, human subjectivity and human embodiment are historicizable phenomena with a recoverable cultural specificity. What escapes this process of symbolizing the body of the past, however, is its monstrous component, its intimate alterity: there always remains within the subject something "more than itself," something that lurks like a familiar stranger at the threshold of the hall. *Das Ding* is the guarantee of the inadequacy of history, the reason it cannot fully explain the non-contradictory coincidence of what appear on their face to be antithetical extremes.

Beowulf celebrates the death of the giant; the *Liber monstrorum* (c. 650–750), composed by someone familiar with the *Beowulf* tradition, opens with a nostalgic reflection on the dwindling space of the monstrous in the modern world, then fills the gap opened by the triumph of the human (*humanum genus*) over *monstra* by offering a long catalog of unfailingly disturbing hybrid bodies, many of whom are giants.[46] Anglo-Saxon England knew well the inhuman presence that stands at both the origins and the ruins of identity and had the perfect term for this haunting: *enta geweorc,* the work of giants.

CHAPTER 2

Monstrous Origin
Body, Nation, Family

Mortui non vivent, gigantes resurgent.
[Let not the dead live, let not the giants rise again.]

—Isaiah 26:14

The Giants of Guildhall

For many centuries, Guildhall, London's center of civic governance, enclosed within the order of its architecture a pair of menacing giants. These intimate strangers at the heart of the nation were two immense statues erected before the mid–sixteenth century, perhaps as early as the reign of Henry V. The effigies have been given various names. Sometimes one was "Gogmagog" (the leader of a troop of giants in Geoffrey of Monmouth's *History of the Kings of Britain*), and the other "Corineus" (the man who defeated Gogmagog in a wrestling match, occasionally represented as giant sized himself); sometimes these figures were "Colbrand" and "Brandamore," giants from romance tradition; but ordinarily the name of Geoffrey's single giant, Gogmagog, was broken in two by reference back to the word's biblical derivation. The primal monsters Gog and Magog were held to be the first impediment to British colonization of the island, and their enchainment in Guildhall was a frighteningly public reminder of the monstrous past on which the nation was built. The giants were regularly featured in mayoral processions. Records indicate that they greeted Philip and Mary at their public entry into London in 1554 and hailed Elizabeth four years later as part of a ceremony preliminary to her coronation.[1] Such occasions served as political theater in which to repeat the legendary history of Britain, a performance that aimed to materialize royal power in the present through the invocation of a long and therefore authoritative genealogy.

Perhaps Henry V himself had these giants erected, to memorialize the heroic past of the nation he was striving to enlarge. Henry had a special fondness for conquered giants, an affection he no doubt learned from reading romance. In 1415, as the king entered London in triumph from his military campaigns in France, two giants were erected on London Bridge to offer an ax and the keys to the city (Fairholt, *Gog and Magog*, 27). The history that Henry cited through the enactment of the giants' sub-

29

GOGMAGOG,

THE GIANT IN GUILDHALL.

Figure 2. Neoclassical Gogmagog. From F. W. Fairholt, *Gog and Magog, the Giants in Guildhall*, published in 1859. Private collection; reprinted with permission.

mission was, by the early fifteenth century, already a venerable one. According to numerous chronicles based ultimately on *The History of the Kings of Britain*, the first inhabitants of Britain were a race of towering monsters. When a band of Trojan refugees led by Brutus, great-grandson of Aeneas, came ashore with dreams of colonization, the giants attacked and attempted to destroy them. The Trojan triumph over these bellicose monsters marks the birth of the British nation. By positioning giants to recognize him as conqueror as he entered London, Henry becomes a second Brutus. The present king's triumphal procession into the city suddenly filiates from the ancient hero's foundation of London as "New Troy," two similarly great events within a glorious and ongoing *Gründungsage*. By erecting statues of primordial giants in Guildhall, Henry could reincorporate the subdued monsters into the architecture of the nation, just as Brutus had once erected the structure of community atop their fallen bodies.

The Guildhall giants were destroyed when the Great Fire gutted their home and razed much of the surrounding city. Rebuilt in a neoclassical style in 1708, they persevered until the Blitzkrieg. London's Guildhall now stands empty of giants, but Great Britain would not exist without these monsters lurking at the depths of its past. This chapter traces the transformation of the giant during the postcolonial moment that occurred in England after the Norman invasion of 1066, and specifically within the crisis in historical continuity experienced in the wake of the conquest. From a strange presence at the heart of a conflicted cultural identity in Anglo-Saxon England, the giant became a monstrous body standing at the originary moment when a heterogeneous group of conquered Anglo-Saxons, ruling Anglo-Normans, and even some Celtic peoples began to imagine themselves a collective entity. This movement toward communal identity was brought about through the agency of the giant, a procession of heroes, and a cleric named Geoffrey who envisioned a singular history for them all.

Monster Nation

All the legends of giants are closely related to the relief of the locality where the story is told.
—Mikhail Bakhtin, *Rabelais and His World*, 342

The latest "research reference guide" on giants contains many eyebrow-raising paragraphs such as the following, which attempts to explain the origin of those giants (Hebrew *Nephilim*) who figure so mysteriously in the Bible:

Calculations by Bible chronologist James Usher indicate that God created Adam and Eve about 4004 B.C. But they were not the earth's

31

first people. That distinction, as Moses himself tells us, belonged to an *evolved* people called the Nephilim (i.e., the *fallen ones*). . . . Lucifer and the many angels loyal to him made their way into this material world and started playing around in the animals. . . . They probably derived their greatest fun and pleasure from matings. . . . In time, the world of the flesh began to exert such an irresistible pull upon them that they became permanent incarnations in the beasts. From these incarnations sprang the Nephilim. (Deloach, *Giants*, 213, 220)

Distinguishing between *created* beings such as Adam and Eve and *evolved* beings descended from primordial giants, Deloach has here achieved what few theologians would dare attempt: a complete resolution of the incommensurable accounts of human origin offered by Genesis and evolutionary biology. By reading evolution back through the biblical narrative and rendering it a theory of teratogenesis, he is able to make sense of what for others is a deadlock of symbolization.

The Bible gives Deloach a formal structure for thinking through the problem of creationism versus Darwinism, and ultimately a means of giving the past a coherence, a weight. Deloach's theory is in many ways quite medieval. Along with classical myth, the Bible could be described as the collective discursive unconscious of the West; its stories provided the palimpsests that medievals used in making real their own experience of history, of reality. Because giants figure in the biblical account of the origin of humanity, Deloach envisions that they must have played an important role in the modern version of that same myth, evolution; and so two incompatible versions of the past combine to materialize a coherent present. Likewise, when Geoffrey of Monmouth was constructing a past for early Britain, he imagined that similar giants must once have menaced the island, and so Brutus eradicates an enemy very like the biblical Nephilim exterminated under the command of Joshua. Because David fought a giant as the first step to assuming his identity as hero and king, so future heroes and future kings such as Arthur fight the same battle, triumph against the same monster, come of age through the same ritual of dismemberment. By secularizing the biblical narrative of David and Goliath, Geoffrey constructed in Arthur a vision of embodiment that equates self-determination with communal good, eliding the difference and potential incommensurability between group and personal identities. In doing so, Geoffrey bequeathed to romance a script so powerful and so essential to its own self-identity that the genre enacted it repeatedly, obsessively, for more than three hundred years.

Like most medieval clerics, Geoffrey equated the writing of history with the writing of story (the literal meaning of *historia*); medieval historiography is concerned with turning the past into a meaningful narrative, rather than with excavating some time-bound set of facts, and is therefore inherently presentist.[2] That is not to say that *historia* is mere fabulation. As he composed the *Historia Regum Britanniae (The History of the Kings of Britain)*, Geoffrey relied on the Bible, the work of earlier historians of Britain such as Gildas and Bede, classical literature such as the *Aeneid,* and scraps of Celtic myth to provide a structure inside which a new history could unfold and seem ancient, authoritative, and substantial. He asserted that he was translating *(transferre)* the *Historia* because he had "not been able to discover anything at all on the kings who lived here before the Incarnation of Christ, or indeed about Arthur and all those who followed on after the Incarnation" (51).[3] He then filled this epistemological gap by furnishing a cohesive narrative of the Trojan-descended British and the glorious nation that they engendered, especially under Arthur.

Yet there could be no Arthurian golden age without an anterior hero to lay the groundwork for nationhood. From the reign of Augustus in imperial Rome to late medieval historiography, an obsession with tracing patrilineage back to the heroes of fallen Troy flourished, so that the Trojans became an entire race of founding fathers. Invoking Trojan descent was an easy way to legitimate newly established regimes as well as to glorify existing orders by attaching to them long precedent and the weight of classical tradition *(translatio imperii).* French chroniclers were calling the royal blood *Trojanorum* as early as the seventh century, and Charles the Bald further popularized the myth with official sanction. Through Geoffrey's immortalizing of Brutus's cultural paternity, England dreamt of a Trojan origin of its own.[4] Robed in the typology of Moses, the great-grandson of Aeneas liberated a group of Trojans from Greek slavery and led them to Britain, *altera Troia* and, by means of a prophecy from Diana, a divinely promised land. According to the oracular vision that the goddess sends to Brutus, "Insula in occeano est, habitata gigantibus olim, / Nunc deserta quidem, gentibus apta tuis" [There lies an island in the sea, once occupied by giants. / Now it is empty and ready for your folk] (9, 65). The reference to the giants as extinct representatives of an earlier era recalls the Anglo-Saxon and Celtic traditions that the giants had once been in the land and were knowable in the present only from their stonework traces; the foggy Age of Giants, long passed, is resolving again into an Age of Man.[5] These words of the goddess, however, are not wholly accurate.[6] Geoffrey describes the arrival of the Trojans on the English shores: "At this time the island of Britain was called Albion. It was uninhabited except for a few giants [*exceptis paucis hominibus gigantibus*]" (72, 13). As in his introductory description of the island, Geoffrey follows Bede in representing Britain as a country of natural superfluity. Whereas the biblical Canaan was so fruitful that the land flowed with milk and honey, this secular promised island surfeits with wide forests and fertile rivers, *copia piscosorum.* The giants are part of this fantastic overabundance, vast signifiers of an untamed landscape that, fecund enough to sprout monstrous excess, poses a threat to the domesticating (*domos aedificare*) order that Brutus and his men embody. Yet despite their immensity, these giants are *paucis*, few in number. They are the remnant of a race encountered in its twilight, living artifacts of a prehistory ready to cede to a heroic era. As in the foundational narrative of the Book of Genesis, a time of giants is yielding to empire.[7]

The giants are uncivilized, a word that at its root means "noncitizens," *alieni*. They are wholly outside the coherence of Trojan language and law. In opposition to the colonizers, the giants lack any power of cultivation, being wildness itself. Thus the island is not truly occupied (*inhabitatam*) until Brutus orders, divides, and peoples it, until nature is rebuffed by human architecture and its superabundance tamed into tidy fields (*agros incipiunt colere*). Because the giants lack voice, skill, and a stronger than tribal social organization, they are marginalized, driven *ad cavernas montium* — to those stony heights where domestication cannot penetrate. Brutus, meanwhile, renames the land and establishes a new language that transforms the feral island into an orderly colony: "Brutus called the land Britain [*Britonia*] from his own name, and his companions he called Britains [*Britones*]." If the giants can speak, their voices are unrecorded. That place formerly called "Albion" (whatever it was, whatever it means) becomes "Britonia," and Brutus becomes eponymous.

The first Trojan encounter with the aboriginal giants has a clear biblical subtext. The spies sent by Moses to search Canaan discover dwelling there a race called the Anakim, towering giants in whose sight the invading Israelites say they seemed like small insects: "The land which we have seen devours its inhabitants. The people whom we beheld are tall of stature . . . in comparison to whom we seemed like locusts" (Num. 13:33–34). The inhabitants of Canaan are imagined as gigantic in order to convey the difficulty of the ensuing settlement. Just as the bounty of the country is great (*fluit lacte et melle*), so is its resistance to colonization (*sed cultores fortissimos habet*). The desirability of the land is signified by the surfeit of valuable commodities and the exaggerated proportions of its warding occupants. Envisioning the anterior culture as monsters (*ibi vidimus monstra*) justifies its displacement by making the act heroic.[8] This rationalization of displacement through the monsterization of anterior inhabitants is a process both very old and, throughout history, very useful.[9] Walter Stephens summarizes the raison d'être for these various groups of giants and their consequent signification when he writes that "such Giants embody the forces that resist expansion, conquest, cultivation, and domestication. Because they oppose the origin of a culture, they are envisioned as archaic, even autochthonic; they are an explanation of origins made by cultures that see themselves as invaders or latecomers" (*Giants in Those Days*, 72–73). The irony, of course, is that the Celtic ("British") peoples whose history Geoffrey is writing stand exactly in this aboriginal position to the Anglo-Saxons who "settled" the island — that is, in the preconquest account of English history, the Celts occupy the place of the Galfridian giants, the invading Germanic tribes that of the glorified British.[10]

Shortly after Brutus divides and names the New World that he claims, the settlers are besieged in the midst of a holy day observance by a war band of the remaining giants. The leader of these monsters is Gogmagog (or Goemagog). His composite name is lifted either from the Hebrew Bible, where it has no connection to giants, indicating a leader and his people; or, more likely, from the Book of Revelation, where Gog and Magog are nations led by the devil to war against the kingdom of God (Rev. 20:7–10). "Gogmagog" as "Gog et Magog" reminds once more of the biblical subtext to the secular history. If Geoffrey has the episode from Revelation in mind, then the tribe of giants has replaced the evil nations under Satan at the apocryphal last battle, and the Trojans act the part of the encampment of saints whom Gog and Magog attack. Satan is hurled to his destruction, just as Gogmagog is thrown off a cliff. The creation of a "new heaven and a new earth" that follows in the Bible is likewise secularized at the moment of the Trojan foundation.

In the Alexander romances, monsters named Gog and Magog guard the gates of Eden against human return. The island of Britain here simultaneously becomes New Troy, Canaan, and paradise. Rather than reworking in a programmatic way the biblical palimpsests of his story, Geoffrey is giving an incredible tale the weight of established authority through the circulation of familiar textual subcurrents. Different from simple allegory, suggestive typology of this sort is common in Bede and other early English historians. Geoffrey's radical break with this tradition is to apply typological historiography loosely to a relentlessly secular project.

The distortion of the giants' bodies is a physical signifier of a moral state. Gogmagog leads his savage troop against the Trojans in an attempted massacre as the colonizers observe the rites of a religious festival. After many Britons are killed, the men finally rally and slay all the attacking giants except for Gogmagog himself. This monster is made to wrestle with Brutus's *fidus Achates*, Corineus, who becomes the prototypical English giant slayer, especially in later, derivative literature.[11] The match ends with Gogmagog dashed into fragments, hurled by Corineus from a cliff onto sea rocks. Even if the giant's gross body is destroyed, he himself is immortalized as geography, as earth: the place of his death is called Gogmagog's Leap, *in presentem diem* (14). Through his destruction, Gogmagog attains a limited form of the eponymous power that Brutus and the Trojans originally precluded through their linguistic transformation of the island from Albion to Britain. Like the extimate monsters of Anglo-Saxon England, the giant is installed within the system of language at the very moment he is excluded.

"Gogmagog's Leap" affixes British history to a landscape of monstrous origins, a linguistic colonization that transforms the resistant earth and renders it *terram inhabitatam*. The bodies that existed outside the new order return in death as its structural support. Translated into the "crooked Greek" (*curuum Grecum*) of the Trojans, which Geoffrey asserts is the "modern" British tongue (*Cymraeg/Britannica*), the giants become bodiless names through which New Troy arranges the surrounding wilderness into a semblance of itself.[12]

Giants and the Invention of Empire

All culture is ultimately nothing but a compromise formation, a reaction to some terrifying, radically inhuman dimension proper to the human condition itself.

—Slavoj Zizek, *Looking Awry*, 37

Louise Fradenburg has persuasively argued that myths such as those that circulated around Arthur are "delections, not denials, of the natural body" that create their subject's immortality by entwining the continued experience of loss with the promise of return "so that desire for the legendary figure will make its way into the future" (*City, Marriage, Tournament*, 162–63). This enfolding of desire, loss, and eternal return is well illustrated by a medieval archaeological "discovery." In 1190 the bones of Arthur were found deep beneath the ground near Glastonbury Abbey, interred with a cross that proclaimed, "Here lies buried the renowned [*inclitus*] King Arthur in the Isle of Avalon" (Ashe, *Discovery of King Arthur*, 25–26). The royal corpse was exhumed and grandly enshrined in the Abbey church. The monks rejoiced because they now had in their possession a tourist attraction. Henry II likewise rejoiced because the Welsh could no longer claim that a living Arthur was about to return and lead them to their independence.

A long debate has raged over who had the the bones placed near the abbey to be conveniently discovered—the monks or Henry. No matter how they arrived in their "ancient" grave, however, the relics reveal how quickly the *Historia* had material effects on social reality. In creating a past, Geoffrey also shaped a future. The power of this "onceness and futurity" is embodied in Arthur. Brutus became through Geoffrey's account the founding father of Britain, but he and the giants that he conquers are described only to provide the heroic base on which the glory of King Arthur could be erected. The *Historia* culminates in the conflicted, ambiguous, but ultimately resplendent portrait of Britain's greatest king. Geoffrey's achievement was to bestow on the Middle Ages a monarchical body through which England dreamed its own prehistory and inhabited it as if it had always been home.[13]

The *Historia* predicates the birth of the nation on two symbolically charged encounters with giants. Brutus's founding of New Troy and his clearing away of the island's aboriginal monsters replays the biblical encounter with the *gigantes* of Canaan, whose wildness must be gentrified in order for Israel to find a stable identity, in order for its nomadic exile to cease. Both episodes write invasion as first settlement. The transfiguration was no doubt appealing to Geoffrey's Norman audience, a ruling class separated from their origin in conquest by less than four generations. Once the giants and the land they embody have been reduced through the Trojan colonization to passive *materia* awaiting a heroic imprint, Brutus gives birth to his nation. The Brutus episode enacts an agenda of national unity by dreaming an originary moment. Later in the *Historia,* Arthur raises this considerable ante by introducing a plan for world domination through the defeat of the Holy Roman Emperor, Lucius. Arthur's bid for universal political and cultural hegemony, portrayed as already having been accomplished in the heroic past, is an appealing wish-fulfillment fantasy of triumph fully inscribed within a causative historiography. According to the rules that Geoffrey in part adopts from his Celtic analogues, in part imports from his study of the Bible, and in part fashions in his own imagination, Arthur must prove himself not as *rex* but as *imperator* before ascending to the ultimate step of the heroic *cursus honorum* — before rising to that uncrowded zenith on which Alexander the Great and Charlemagne stand. In the mode of biblical David and Celtic Culhwch, this rite of heroic passage is signaled by Arthur's defeat of a menacing giant, the anthropophagous monster of Mont Saint Michel.

Just as Brutus's defeat of the aboriginal giants early in the *Historia* rationalizes expansionism at home, Arthur's battle against the giant on a continental mountaintop celebrates the forcible acquisition of territories abroad. The episode unites England with France before envisioning world domination, a fantasy of boundless empire that would have been powerfully attractive to an insular aristocracy that had not yet lost its dual holdings and Norman titles. Having set sail from Britain with his army, Arthur learns at Barfleur that "sceleratissimus inuisi nominis gigas" [the most odious of all giants] (118) has wandered into France from "certain regions of Spain," presumably a hint of Saracen provenance.[14] The giant inhabits Mont Saint Michel, a steep mountaintop and, in Geoffrey's day, a popular pilgrimage site where a new church was being planned.[15] The monster has abducted Helena, the niece of a duke, and fled to the precipice; those knights foolish enough to try to rescue his captive he eats while they are still half alive. The monster's sexual intentions in kidnapping Helena are obvious enough, but because the violation of a noblewoman is too indelicate for Geoffrey to include in his narration, Helena dies of fright, and the crime is displaced onto her nurse, an old woman whom the monster (and the text) finds easier to "befoul." The giant is described as possessed of a "filthy lust" and a "madness of bestial desire" (239), and in proof of his right to these titles, he holds the nurse prisoner on his sea-wrapped promontory, violating her elderly body through nightly forced intercourse. Her advanced age (*senectutem meam*), the cultural sign that her body is supposed to be outside the possibility of sexuality, only enlarges the impression of the giant's carnal voracity.

The monster's appetite is for "force and violence" (*vis et violentia*), erotic pleasure (*fedus coitus*), and vast quantities of disgusting foodstuffs (*tabum semesorum porcorum*). When Arthur encounters the giant, his huge face is "smeared with clotted blood" from half-cooked pigs he roasts but cannot wait to cook (239). The giant's body is one that knows neither limit nor control, only immediate sensual gratification. He dwells on his mountaintop, in isolation from the civil world, precisely because the desires to which his excessive form gives instant expression mark him as not quite human: men control their appetites (for *vis et violentia*, for *fedus coitus*), and that domination over their own bodies is what constitutes their humanity. Yet the sins that gigantism writes across the flesh also make the monster all too human. Men control their appetites *in theory*, but in reality, these appetites are always finding illicit expression, as even a quick glance at the records of the contemporary courts demonstrates. The reign of Henry I, during which Geoffrey composed the *Historia*, has been accurately described as "a series of revolts, burnings, assaults, cattle rustlings, hangings, dismemberments, abductions, fratricides, broken alliances, ethnic rivalries, gougings, and acts of mutilation and castration" (Curley, *Geoffrey of Monmouth*, 88)—and that was just in Wales.

The giant's form is unmistakably human, and male, but his vast size indicates that he fits neither of those categories well. Alone among the "singular" giants of medieval tradition, the monster of Mont Saint Michel has no proper name, even if he is *inuisi nominis*, "of detested name."[16] Perhaps the giant is so terrifying because he is a liminal body, partially human and partially other, a form suspended between categories who threatens through his unnamability to smash the distinctions on which categorization is based. He cooks his meat, but he eats it raw, too. He fights with a weapon, like a man, but that weapon is a crude club, suggesting archaism and savagery. The giant is not quite *Homo sapiens*, but uncannily manlike; not exactly an animal, but disturbingly feral. Nor does he occupy a stable middle ground between the two genera. The monster is intriguing beneath his repulsiveness because he challenges any easy attempt to stop or place him as he slides from one cultural meaning into the next. He is the male body writ large, but he must be killed because his spectacular form disturbingly suggests that there is something not fully human about that body, no matter what its actual size.

Geoffrey is sparing of rhetorical device, even of metaphor, throughout his writing. His analogical attempts to reify the unencounterable sound all the more strongly for the clearness of the air. When Arthur wounds the giant in the forehead, he charges madly, "uelut aper per uenabulum in uenatorem ita irruit per gladium in regem" [Just as a boar hurls itself at the huntsman, despite the latter's boar-spear, so the giant rushed against the King's sword] (118, 240). After a long and bloody fight, the giant noisily expires: "Uelut quercus uentorum uiribus eradicata cum maximo sonitu corruit]" [At this the evil creature gave one shriek and toppled to the ground with a mighty crash, like some oak torn from its roots by the fury of the wind] (118, 225). These epic similes recall the giant's elemental proximity to the violently natural; it is as if he were the embodied raw *materia* of the earth, or of history itself—horrifyingly protean, but through Arthur's piercing weapon fixed forever into place.

Arthur's decapitation of the giant's corpse and his command to exhibit the head to his troops transforms this monster into historical narrative, putting an end to his messy ambiguities, his threats to category construction. The display of the severed head is like the metamorphosis of menacing Gogmagog from monstrous body to bodiless name, from vigorous defiance to eternal arrest in the midst of a demonstrative action ("Gogmagog's Leap"). The giant of Mont Saint Michel likewise tumbles into the new signifying chain that Brutus and his men forged. The giant's body is transformed, mortified, beneath the new master signifier of British manifest destiny. Like Gogmagog, this giant's fate is to see his monstrous excess contained within a heroic story about the progress of a nation.

The triumph against the giant prefigures Arthur's victory against Lucius, the emperor of Rome, just as Arthur's shipboard dream had earlier prefigured both the fight against the monster and the fight against the emperor. Yet the battle with Lucius takes place in Burgundy, not Rome. Arthur never reaches the gates of the Eternal City as he intended, for news arrives shortly after his triumph that his nephew Mordred has allied himself with the Saxons and is already enjoying "forbidden sexual love" with the queen. Arthur does succeed in transforming his role from *rex* to *imperator*, but it is an achievement that ultimately proves fragile, conflicted, and costly. These doubts that limn the construction of Arthur's heroic integrity, however, never quite succeed in stealing from him the mantle of glory that the battle against the giant provides; it was up to the author of the Alliterative *Morte Arthure* to perform that unclothing. Even if Arthur ultimately fails in his quest to unite the Western world under British hegemony, the force of his desire ensures that this fantasy of conquest would live beyond the text in which it is contained.

Geoffrey's account of Arthur ends with a famously ambiguous death scene: "Arthur himself, our renowned King, was mortally wounded and was carried off to the Isle of Avalon, so that his wounds might be attended to" (261). At the same time as the fatal wounds are carved into the monarch's mortal frame, the possibility of their healing is announced. His body is carried off before it can be integrated into the fabric of history through proper obsequies and a definitive burial. At this moment when the king's material form vanishes, he becomes in Geoffrey's account *noster rex*, and this sudden gesture of alliance between past and present ensures that the monarch will survive his death. Arthur's destiny is to be the once and future king, just as Great Britain has throughout history styled itself the once and future empire.

Arthur materializes Britain. It did not exist as a continuous, corporate community until he was invented. Through filiation from the body of the king and the sublime nation that it represents, Britain received the seamless, heroic past that historians such as Henry of Huntingdon had long sought in the archive but failed to discover. Slavoj Zizek explains well this retroactivity of historical narration, this necessity of "bringing about" the past:

> As soon as we enter the symbolic order, the past is always present in the form of historical tradition and the meaning of these traces is not given; it changes continually with the transformations of the signifier's network. Every historical rupture, every advent of a new master-signifier, changes retroactively the meaning of all tradition, restructures the narration of the past, makes it readable in another, new way. . . . It is this elaboration which decides retroactively what they "will have been." (*Sublime Object of Ideology*, 56)

Despite the frantic search for a historical Arthur exemplified by Henry II and the Glastonbury monks, and which even now animates scholars like Geoffrey Ashe, the veridicality of the king's existence is ultimately beside the point. The effect precedes the cause, which is projected back into the past to organize from its disparate fragments a coherent story of origin. Through the agency of a fantasy that is both essential and identity giving, history becomes the precipitate of the present, a discourse that makes sense of a confusing and insufficient past by structuring it into a coherent body, rendering it solid.[17]

By positing a new master signifier ("Arthur") under which the scattered pieces of British antiquity could finally be materialized as discrete, continuous, and even glorious, the *Historia Regum Britanniae* marks the culmination of a "historical rupture" that retroactively changed "the narration of the past." This rupture was instigated in 1066, when the language of power abruptly shifted from English to French, and the men in control of the nation were suddenly strangers to its customs and culture. As a colonialist regime, this new aristocracy was still feeling the insecurity of displacing latecomers. Ninety years after the invasion, the acute crisis of the postcolonial moment had become the chronic anxiety of a regime that now felt itself intimately connected to the land it ruled, but still somehow alien, not quite at home, because it lacked a long history. Conveniently, the same king whom Geoffrey exalted as British could be admired by the reigning Anglo-Norman monarchy, who likewise claimed Trojan descent. Geoffrey of Monmouth is the true father of "Britain" as an *imaginable* community — and *Britain* is in turn the true father of *En-*

gland, which is in turn the true father of the empire. And so Susan Reynolds writes, "By the end of the thirteenth century, the English had taken over the Brutus story from the British so that Edward I could, paradoxically, use the supremacy of Brutus' eldest son over his brothers as an argument for English supremacy over all Britain."[18] The Geoffrey-Arthur complex ultimately was to become the authoritative origin of England—a source of *auctoritas* that romancers and historiographers alike could cite to provide for their own work a secure cultural place outside of mere fabulation.

An immediate objection that might be raised to my reading of Geoffrey's *Historia* and its tangible cultural effects is that it does not grant the narrative that problematic, subversive status argued by Valerie I. J. Flint and rearticulated by Lee Patterson.[19] As both critics make clear, the *Historia* is not an uncomplicated celebration of British superiority. Geoffrey's chronicle is replete with murders, sodomy, perfidy, and political ineptitude.[20] How, then, can the text be read as a powerful ideological fantasy that solidified a potent corporate identity? True, the *Historia* envisions a world where a parricide could become the founder of a nation (Brutus accidentally kills his father with a wayward arrow) and where a king whose paternity is far from unproblematic could become its greatest leader (Uther uses Merlin's magic to transform his body into a semblance of his enemy Gorlois, then impregnates the man's wife with Arthur). From these inauspicious episodes and from the narrative's long chronicling of a "monarchical history...riven with generational violence" and "internecine self-destruction," Patterson concludes that the *Historia* is "a myth of origins that deconstructs origin" (*Negotiating the Past*, 202). Yet the stains on the heroic bodies of Brutus and Arthur are not exactly shocking. William Rufus was killed by a wayward arrow while hunting in a forest, under circumstances far more unsavory than those between Brutus and his father; William the Conqueror was a bastard child, but that fact did little to stop the Norman assertion of his right to the English throne. Patterson himself writes that "Anglo-Norman supremacy was both challenged from below and, more seriously, subject to the fragmentations occasioned by its own inner dynamic."[21] A kind summation of Anglo-Norman rule would be to label it a chronicle of internecine strife—just like *The History of the Kings of Britain*. My point should already be clear: Geoffrey's *Historia* is already uncannily similar to pre-existent Anglo-Norman *historia*. Rather than deconstruct origins, it cites them in all their complexity, in order to reify the world "as it always has been."

An ideologically persuasive materialization of history is not one that flattens the fabric of the past into a seamless narrative of unambiguous foundational moments. Rather, an effective ideology grants history its contradictions, its impasses, its messiness, but is nonetheless able to transcend them through *enjoyment*—in Geoffrey's case, through a pleasure in both heroism and obscenity. If the narrativization of history resulted in a simple chronicle of heroic triumph, if it did not contain elements of what Flint and Patterson call "excess" (and what psychoanalysis would call *surplus*)—if it were not in its intimate interior *monstrous*—then it would not be efficacious, it would not function as a persuasive reality, it would offer little to enjoy. Contradiction, division, and polymorphous plurality do not deconstruct myths of origin. They are the foundation of such histories, an integral component of how they materialize the real.

The reception history of Geoffrey's *Historia* bears witness to this multifaceted response, especially in the commentary on the text that manuscript illustration conveys. An illuminated manuscript of the *Chronicles of Hainault* (Bibliothèque Royale Albert 1er, Brussels, MS 9243 f.49v) depicts Arthur's battle against the giant of Mont Saint Michel. The king is as vigorous and agile as his foe is dull and clumsy. The battle takes

Figure 3. Arthur battles the giant, observed by nurse. Bibliothèque Royale Albert 1er, Brussels, MS 9243 f.49v. Reprinted with permission.

place on a round island enclosed by upward-thrusting rocks. This tight circumscription of their field of action has the visual effect of isolating the two figures from the remainder of the busy scene: to the left, the raped nurse watches the action unfold; meanwhile the foreground is crowded with twenty-three soldiers on the mainland and four in a boat. Despite this brightly painted bustle of action, the king and the giant seem very much alone on their island, mutually excluded from the careful groupings of bodies elsewhere. The deep blue of their similar armor picks up the hues of the obscenely erect stones that surround them, stones that are mostly shaped like penises—suggesting a common, aggressively somatic masculinity at the base of their martial play.

An illustrated capital from a twelfth-century manuscript of the text (Douai, Bibliothèque Municipale, MS 880, f.66v) brings this undercutting further by depicting in its center Arthur's beheading of the same giant. The monster's immense corpse, knees pushed close to his chin, is crammed into the circumscribing mouth of an O. His huge club, in contrast, extends menacingly beyond the letter's frame. His dead fingers still clasp the weapon, and the tip of the armament is set with long rows of spikes. In one hand, Arthur grasps the giant's matted hair, pulling back the monster's head; with the other, he clasps his sword, which has already cut halfway through his defeated foe's neck. The blade of the king's weapon likewise extends out of the frame, where it neatly slices the word *gigas* in half at the same time as it severs the giant's head from his body (*corpus* is *textus*). The principle that structures this illustration seems to be nothing more than simple contrast. Arthur's visage is well proportioned and handsome: long, impeccably coifed hair; unblemished skin; a neatly trimmed beard that just outlines the curve of his face; a frown of concentration that picks up the graceful arching of his eyes, brow, chin, and nose. The giant's face is, in contrast, asymmetrical and ugly: huge mouth full of teeth, exaggerated nose, expansive forehead topped by unkempt hair, brows and cheeks that seem gouged in stone, sunken eyes, a hideous grin that persists even in death. Yet a telling feature hints that this depiction of the gigantomachia is aware of the complexities of Geoffrey's rendition. Arthur looks childlike in comparison to the giant. His small body is obscured by that of the monster, rising out from behind its knees, and the monarch must place his little foot on the giant's stomach or groin to get close enough to decapitate his foe. Arthur's crown is huge, about double the width of his head and almost twice its length. It balances precariously, as if it might either topple to the ground or simply fall past the king's ears and lie atop his shoulders. There is something too diminutive about this Arthur, so that the illustration suggests that his empire building is both a glorious nationalistic moment and an absurdly puerile game.

The History of the Kings of Britain could accommodate a complex response and elicit several layers of enjoyment. The *Historia* therefore sur-

Figure 4. Arthur beheads the giant of Mont Saint Michel. Bibliothèque Municipale de Douai, MS 880, f.66. Reprinted with permission.

vived some contemporary condemnation to become seminal and wildly popular. Copies proliferated quickly after the manuscript's first appearance in 1136. Widely paraphrased and translated, Geoffrey's text eventually eclipsed the histories of those who, like Giraldus Cambrensis and William of Newburgh, had been vociferous in denying its veracity.[22] Tatlock and Knight have argued that Geoffrey wrote to justify the rule of the Norman kings, and critics have repeatedly argued that his "translating" of *quendam britannici sermonis librum uetussimum* ("a certain very ancient book written in the British language") was an act of incipient nationalism, but the original purpose of the *Historia* is ultimately lost beneath its astonishing effect.[23]

Geoffrey's narrative voice is characterized by an earnest, matter-of-fact tone that can belie the ideological complexity of his historiography. Through suggestive typology and a sparsely adorned prose style, he imbued the founding of England with a resonance both biblical (the Vulgate was famous for its lack of rhetorical ornament) and historical (recalling the praxis of the popular Latin historians of Troy, Dares and Dictys). This deceptive simplicity continued to appeal to the later chronicle writers, but many were infuriated by Geoffrey's consequent lack of detail. His first lines on newly discovered Britain are indeed laconic: "Erat tunc nomen insule Albion que a nemine exceptis paucis hominibus gigantibus inhabitabatur" [At this time the island of Britain was called Albion. It was uninhabited, except for a few giants]. As in the opening of Bede's *Historia Ecclesiastica Gentis Anglorum,* the reader is left to wonder why Britain should formerly have been called by another name. If, as Geoffrey states, Brutus was the first settler, who could have bestowed upon the geography a pre-Trojan designation? Further, how did Gogmagog and his band arrive in the land? What is the connection between the naming of Albion and the aboriginal giants? Just as Geoffrey wondered why Bede and Gildas had not spoken of Britain's earliest history, later chroniclers began to question why Geoffrey had not commenced his narrative at the very beginning. In the early fourteenth century, all these questions were laid to rest as an origin was suddenly established for Geoffrey's origin.

Body, Woman, Monster

No biological, psychological, or economic fate determines the figure that the human female presents in society: it is civilization as a whole that produces this creature.

—Simone de Beauvoir, *The Second Sex,* 249

To give the coherence of history to a polymorphous antiquity is never an easy project, but Geoffrey's was an especially difficult task, for England's was an especially messy past. Before the Norman Conquest, the island had its moments of stable hegemony, such as Wessex under Alfred the Great, but Anglo-Saxon England is notable more for its discontinuities: Celtic peoples to be assimilated and displaced, heterogeneity among the colonizers to be overcome, Scandinavian raiders to be accommodated. The events of 1066 changed everything. New, French-speaking rulers demanded new visions of the "English" past while battling political fragmentation in the present. Geoffrey sutured these various pieces of insular identity into an ideologically persuasive alignment through embodiment within the *gesta* of historical heroes such as Arthur and Brutus. At the same time, he imagined a community with whom the Anglo-Norman rulers recognized an alliance, for both groups shared a Trojan origin that heralded a twinned, glorious destiny. Geoffrey created a past that could materialize out of discontinuity a unified vision of the political present. Under the new "originary" master signifier of Troy, the Anglo-Saxons were reduced from glorious ancestors to monsterized marauders. The Normans were transformed from aggressive colonizers to descendants of a sublime, legitimate, *classical* order. Affiliation and the retroactivity of historical narration ultimately allowed Geoffrey to solidify Anglo-Norman sovereignty by providing it with a foundation, by providing a prehistory that it could cite in order to keep its authority and power unquestionable, freely flowing.

This poetics of nation building is also a discourse of gender construction. Sexed bodies are materialized along with the past in which they figure. It is surprising, then, that women play so small a role in the lives of Brutus and Arthur. Brutus defeats the giants, divides the island, founds a city, institutes the law. Then Geoffrey adds, almost as an afterthought, that "in the meantime Brutus had consummated his marriage with his wife Ignoge" (75). Forced into marriage against her will, Ignoge had earlier been placed in Brutus's ship and promptly vanished from the narrative. She is reinserted into the text just when it seems Brutus is so busy with his founding of a nation that he could not possibly have a sex life, too. As the pluperfect tense of the verb indicates, Ignoge's belated second appearance is just as accurately a disappearance, for the marriage has already been consummated, and her body enters only to provide a source for children. Locrinus, Kamber, and Albanactus are given their proper descent, Brutus passes along his paternal power, the sons become famous, and Ignoge is never mentioned again.

The next woman to figure in the narrative is Gwendolen, daughter of Corineus. Although she rules Britain for fifteen years, she immediately abdicates the throne when her son is old enough to take her place. Several generations thereafter arrive the political complexities engendered by Leir's daughters. Cordelia is ultimately deposed by her nephews, indignant at their people's submission to the rule of a woman. Later in the *Historia*, Arthur's wife does not fare much better. Although Guinevere is given a role in her husband's plenary court, she graces the scene only to process to the Church of the Virgins and then to celebrate the feast segregated from the men ("for the Britons still observed the ancient custom of Troy, the men celebrating festive occasions with their fellow-men and the women eating separately with the other women," 229). In her next appearance, the queen is living adulterously with the traitor Mordred. Ultimately she will become a nun. This celibacy, it seems, is linked both to her promiscuity (as its fitting reversal) and to her barrenness (as its extension): Guinevere bears no children, ensuring that Arthur's reign is doomed, all the more glorious for its brevity and tragic loss.[24] Likewise, Arthur's mother Ygerna plays an insubstantial role in the narrative. She is tricked into sleeping with Uther, bears Arthur and Anna, and is wholly forgotten.

Maternal bodies are problematic sites of origin in Geoffrey's *Historia.* Ignoge is forcefully wed to a man she does not desire. Guinevere is as unfaithful as she is infertile. Ygerna bears Arthur innocently, but adulterously. Even Merlin is the son of a deceptive incubus. Perhaps this disavowal is a classical inheritance. Rhea Silvia bore the twins Romulus and Remus so that Rome could find its destiny, but those two sons and their mother were replaced by Aeneas, who abandoned Dido in the realm she founded so that he could build a masculine city of his own. The Trojans were a race of founding *fathers.* In early northern Europe, women could settle land and found dynasties.[25] Unlike Icelandic historiography, however, no secure place existed for women and mothers within the narratives of nation building connected to the Trojan diaspora.

The maternal body bears children, dies, and vanishes; the heroic body, fantastically self-sufficient, can bear nations and be forever remembered in the name of its colossal progeny.[26] Brutus is almost divine in his procreative power. He inseminates a virginal, superbly fecund land with his men, who erect in his honor a nation (*patria,* etymologically a father [*pater*] translated into the feminine, a fantastic composite of both genders). Geoffrey creates the illusion that Brutus begets Britain parthenogenetically. Although women must have been among the wandering Trojans, acknowledgment of their presence is strangely absent, at least until the belated mention of the already consummated relation with Ignoge, a woman reduced to pure body who has outlived her narrative utility at the very moment she appears.

An interest in the gendered mechanics of history building is not a concern that only modern readers bring to Geoffrey's text. Included in the early-fourteenth-century compendium of romance, pious tales, and historiography known as the Auchinleck manuscript (MS Advocates 19.2.1) is a bouncy contemporary account of England's past, *The Anonymous Riming Chronicle.*[27] The poem is written in four stress couplets full of clumsy repetition and clanging rhymes. Ending with a terse account of the death of Edward II ("At berkele dyed þe king / At glowcester is his biriing") and a prayer for Edward III, the chronicle's subject matter is better and more fully told elsewhere. All of these facts would seem to justify the intense inattention that the poem has attracted, except that the Auchinleck history begins with a curious explanation of how Britain received its original name.

An unnamed king of Greece had twenty fair daughters whom he married to various men of renown—"Noiþer to king nor to emperour," the narrator tells us, "all þai were maride wel" [Neither to king nor to emperor, but still they married well] (26–27). The eldest daughter, Albina, is incensed at the marital strictness of her new husband.[28] She convenes her sisters and announces that her spouse has "betreyd" her, circumscribing the limits of her speech by keeping her body under the constant surveillance of his punishing gaze. Humiliated that she cannot speak a single public word against him, she declares, "I shall be avenged!" [þerfor ichil awreken be] (65). Her sisters confide similar complaints and agree that their spouses are likewise unworthy to have wed women of so high a lineage. Albina decides that they will place knives beneath their pillows and, on an appointed night, stab to death their slumbering husbands. The princesses will then hide the corpses "in a foule diche" and afterward enjoy the status of "maisters" and "comandour" without masculine interference, "Eueriche man to don our wille" [every man to perform our will] (96). The youngest sister, however, repents of her actions and reveals to her husband the intended treachery of her siblings, an act she declares to be "oʒaines riʒt oʒaines lawe" [against right, against law]. The husband in turn warns their royal father, who decrees that his daughters shall be cast adrift in a vessel without oars, rudder, and sails. This ship of state emblematizes the realm they would have created through usurped rule, a state severed from the kind of patriarchal law that Brutus bestows on Britain to ensure that past and future cohere through patrilineage and precedent (*History of the Kings of Britain*, 74). This particular punishment is traditionally reserved for incestuous daughters and women who have given birth to monsters, anticipating the sisters' ultimate fate.

The wind buffets the ship, waves toss its frail bow, and for weeks the sisters weep together in its midst. Eventually they are transported to an unnamed, uninhabited island. Albina's first act on stepping ashore is to decree: "þis lond ichil sese to me / After mi name Albion / ʒe schullen it clepe euerichon" [I take this land as my own. Every one of you shall call it Albion, after my own name] (308–12). Now that Albina has, like Brutus in Geoffrey's *Historia*, given a name to the wild expanse of land, her sisters, like the arriving Trojans, set about building shelters. Whereas the first Britons immediately transformed a shapeless waste into cultivated fields and homes, the women forage for food in the wilderness and, like parodic Diana figures, set about capturing the "venisoun" that they crave. As the giant of Mont Saint Michel demonstrated, gluttony and lechery are always intertwined in the medieval imagination, two versions of a single drive to consumption. When the Greek princesses grow fat on the meat of the rough country, desire awakes and "after lecherie hem gun long" [they began to crave lechery] (334). They yearn for the company of men, for those bodies that they would have slain as they slept in the very beds where they might have enjoyed them. The inadequacy of Albina's dream of a self-sufficient matriarchy is written across her expanding flesh.[29]

Always willing to oblige, the devil appears and copulates with the women, just as in Greece he more figuratively "into [Albina's] hert aliʒt" (35). The princesses are impregnated by the infernal visitation, and this second expansion of their corporeality is yet another manifestation of their lack of proper limit. Their danger is their boundless dilation; it is also their downfall.[30] The sisters give birth to fierce giants, a third and supremely monstrous writing of their somaticity. Albina and her sisters are wholly replaced by — subsumed within — gross *corpora*, and their story abruptly ends. The tribe of giants rules the land for eight hundred years, until the arrival of Aeneas's great-grandson, who imposes on their primal chaos a new world order (343–49).

Capable of generating only half-formed and grotesquely excessive *monstra*, Albina and her sisters contrast in their insistent physicality to the fantastic body of Brutus, able to give birth to a nation without any mention of body at all. Albina becomes a misogynistic incorporation of disordered Nature, of the way in which the material world reproduces itself outside of human intention or control. At the time of her disappearance into the monstrous flesh of her children, she is the Real in all its inhuman, biological vitalism. Brutus, on the other hand, is a structurating principle that overcodes these obscenities of the flesh, of the merely material, and prevents through a symbolization into heroic order their generation of monstrousness. At the point of Brutus's arrival, *The Riming Chronicle* picks up the familiar story of the Trojan colonization derived from Geoffrey of Monmouth and Wace, as if Albina and her sisters had always belonged to English history. And suddenly, they do.

Various renditions of another popular chronicle, the *Prose Brut*, contain the only other widely available retelling of the Albina story in English, and here the tale appears as a prologue appended to the main Galfridian history.[31] Several changes are evident in comparison to the Auchinleck redaction of the Albina myth: the sisters are identified as the daughters of the "noble kyng and myghty" of Syria (*Surrye*), Diocletian; their number is increased to thirty-three; the king chastises them for their shrewishness after their besieged husbands complain to him; the youngest daughter does not reveal the plot, so that the murders are accomplished; and the devil with his airy body is directly linked with the tradition of the giant-spawning incubus. The excessive size of the sisters' bodies parallels their concupiscence ("þei tokyn flessh of diuers beestys, and bycomen wondir fatte, and so þei desirid mannes cumpanye and mannys kynde þat hem faylled," 18–20), and the gross giants that these ever expanding women bear are immediately linked to the foes of the arriving Trojans: "þei broughten forth Geauntes, of þe which on me called Gogmagog. . . . & þey dwellyd in Cauys & in hulles at here will, & had þe lond of Albyon as hem liked, vn-to þe tyme þat Brut Arryved" [They brought forth giants, one of which was called Gogmagog. . . . and they dwelled in caves and hills as they desired, and had all the land of Albion as pleased them, until the time when Brutus arrived] (26–32). The story ends with the explicit "Here endeth þe prolog of Albyon, þat þo was an Ile" [Here ends the prologue of Albion that was then [the name of] the island]. MS Trin. Coll. Dublin 490 had introduced the same version of the tale with "Her may a man hure how Engelande was ferst callede Albyon and through whome it hade the name." A monstrous, feminine origin has been provided for Geoffrey's orderly masculine one.

That the monstrous, the feminine, and the inchoate formlessness of nature were easy to conflate in the medieval imaginary is suggested by the ultimate fate of the giants Brutus conquers: by the time Caxton prints the legendary history of Britain, one of the giants will be named Albion—as if the land, the founding woman, and the monster were all one and the same, and all equally opposed to patriarchal imprintation. History receives a new foundational order, as does the nation. But so do some smaller structures on which history and national identity rely for their continuance.

The Familial Monster

The institution of new social orders has always gone hand in hand with the reinvention of foundation narratives.
—David A. Hedrich Hirsch, "Liberty, Equality, Monstrosity," 115

If the communal identity that Geoffrey provided for England was founded on the primal incorporation of a monster, this intimate but alien body nonetheless remains a *gendered* body. The ogre of Mont Saint Michel and Gogmagog are grossly male, embodying in gigantic form everything masculinity cannot be in order to delimit the constricted space of heroic manhood. The Albina myth suggests that this extimate other could just as easily be the feminine body, and more specifically the maternal, in all its pregnant and originary power. What does it mean for a nation to have a monsterized maternity immured at the heart of its own self-formation?

In the English versions of the Albina myth, the feminine and the maternal are interchangeable, as if biological function were the destiny of feminine identity. This simplified and excluded body returns to haunt the masculinist national fantasy of origins, only to be expelled. Banished, it finds its habitation in that marginal expanse where the other monsters that trouble sexuation and embodiment dwell, like Grendel and his mother in their fatherless mere. An early, perhaps "original" version of the Albina story (c. 1250–1334) composed in Anglo-Norman French suggests why these abjections and substitutions are performed. The maternal body vanishes so that a masculine order of pure language can be imagined. Within this incorporeal order, Brutus finds his mythic autogeny, his power to reify the nation that he names. Embodiment becomes indistinguishable from a linguistic structuration imposed on a resistant materiality. Language produces the masculine corpus, making it coherent; the feminine, the maternal, and the monstrous become at once its excluded remnant and its surplus, its excess. Sex and gender are imag-

50

ined in the Albina myth to have a singular moment of origin so that a specific formulation of what it means to be an embodied person can trace its authoritative genealogy to a determinative past.

Georgine Brereton edited under the title *Des grantz geanz* (*Of the Great Giants*) an Anglo-Norman version of the Albina myth found in MS BM Cotton Cleopatra D.ix. Both the Latin and English accounts may descend from a text similar to this one. Here the sisters' monstrousness is intimately connected to their fleshiness: their corporeality is their textuality. Of Albina's parents, the unnamed king and queen of Greece, the narrative proclaims: "Pere e mere furent granz, / Ausi devindrent les enfanz" [Father and mother were large, and so their children became likewise] (22–23). This definitional surplus immediately allies the women's bodies with the giant, so that their monstrous progeny are only the fullest organic realization of what they always already were. The sisters plot to murder their husbands because of their *orgoil* and *fierté* (36, 37). This "pride" and "arrogance" are the sins of gigantism. According to the Douce Bestiary, giants stand simply for *superbia*: "Giants signify proud men who wish to seem greater than they are."[32] The Book of Wisdom characterizes giants as symbols of overbearing pride, destroyed by the Flood as a rebuke to that primal vice (14:6). Pride is an inflationary sin, its effects written across the body. Albina and her sisters refuse to become wives because as daughters of a king, they believe they can decline the position of docile subject into which matrimony would place them: "Nule ne voleit aver mestre" [none were willing to have a master] (58). Biblical giants are likewise monstrous because of their prideful refusal to submit to a divine law that requires absolute subjection: "The ancient giants did not obtain pardon for their sins, and were destroyed trusting to their own strength [*confidentes suae virtuti*]."[33] Isidore of Seville combined both pride and presumptive overreaching in his gloss on the word *gigas*: "The giant represents a type of devil, who with haughty desire assaulted the summit of divine heights."[34] Isidore is speaking specifically of Nimrod, builder of that primal affront to God's celestial sovereignty, the Tower of Babel, an architectural structure in every way antithetical to the proper *domos* (houses) with which the Trojans reverently transform the British landscape.

The allegorical reading of the giant's transgressive body is also well expressed in the *Ovide Moralisé*, a text roughly contemporary with *Des grantz geanz*. Ovid's *Metamorphoses* describes the attempt by a group of giants to storm Olympus and steal heaven from the gods, an episode that was widely thought in Christian exegesis to be a classical version of the Nimrod story. The *Ovide Moralisé*, a long vernacular composition that summarizes and then allegorizes the Latin narrative, considers the "fable" of antiquity to contain essentially the same information as the divine history of the Bible reveals. Jupiter destroys "li jaiant qui furent jadis" [the giants who lived in those days] (1070), just as God the Father

51

smashes Nimrod's tower and scatters the builders ("'Babilon,' c'est 'confusion,'" 1179). Giants are glossed as bodies compounded of "Tout orgueil, toute felonnie, / Toute traïson, toute envie" [all pride, all felony, all treason, all envy], as monsters who through "mad presumption" thought themselves the superior to divine law (1191–95).[35] God has little to do with the relentlessly secular vision of history in which Albina intervenes, but replace his name with the master signifier of "nation," and the extent of her crimes against a masculinist notion of proper embodiment becomes clear. Albina and her sisters violate the "natural" order by refusing their position as docile subjects, as proper wives. Their actions are placed in monstrous affiliation with the sin of the giants at Babel, when the original, divinely instituted order was so dangerously challenged that God unleashed a disaster whose linguistic effects humans still daily feel.

The giants of the Albina myth are in every way continuous with the women who beget them. Yet giants in biblical and Galfridian tradition had been insistently gendered masculine. In positing an origin for the Brutonian moment of origin, the Albina myth enlarges the conception of the giant's identity. This expansion, however, corresponds to a shrinking or localizing of the monster's role. In Anglo-Saxon England, the gender of the giants was not of especially great concern. Their function in the cultural imaginary was to bestow a meaning on human identity, a category that did not necessarily (or at least did not always) universalize the male subject position. *The Wanderer* has its counterpart in "The Wife's Lament," an elegy where the declensional endings of the opening lines clearly indicate that the alienated speaker is a woman. Giants in Anglo-Saxon tradition could sometimes be female, as Alfred wrote in his gloss on Circe; giants in the related northern traditions were as often female as male. In the tradition of historical writing that Geoffrey initiated, however, the giants are excessively and exclusively male. No doubt Geoffrey was following his biblical models in this regard, but the sexual poetics of nation building in the twelfth century also demanded narratives about founding fathers and masculine struggle, since the English crown had so often pitted fathers, sons, and brothers against each other in a struggle for monarchical legitimacy. The Albina myth, in turn, harnessed the monster's identity-giving powers to explicate the balance between power and gender not in empire but in *marriage*. From a figure who haunts the origin of the human to a monster who stands at the establishment of the nation, the giant was transformed into a signifying body who founds a proper notion of family and matrimonial governance.

Before explicating the Albina myth's domestic thrust, it is worth contextualizing how its grand gestures inscribe family as an extension of national and salvation history. Just as the arrival of Brutus in the new world of Britain rewrites the biblical story of the arrival of the Israelites in Canaan, the Albina myth also has a biblical palimpsest, citing Genesis

6:4 and its strange reference to miscegenation between human women and fallen angels.[36] In the days before the Flood, Genesis states: "Moreover giants were upon the earth in those days: for afterwards the sons of God went in to the daughters of men, and they bore children, who are the mighty men of old, men of high renown." The interpretation history of this ambiguous verse is complex, centering on the meaning of *filii dei* (sons of God).[37] In "the earliest Christian phase," the sons of God are held to be fallen angels who copulate with mortal women, but in the "orthodox phase," they are as mortal as the woman they violate (Dean, "The World Grown Old," 560). Augustine established the orthodox interpretation by declaring that the *filii dei* were the offspring of Seth, who had been forbidden by Adam to intermarry with the descendants of Cain (the *filias hominum*).[38] Miscegenation between the two segregated genera was thus responsible for the birth of the giants, who become a fully human phenomenon.

Although the earlier interpretation of the passage had been officially refuted by Augustine, its narrative of illicit sex and monstrous progeny enjoyed a widespread popularity throughout the Middle Ages. The fallen angels in its recipe for monstrous births quickly became incubi, airy spirits who appear on earth to rape and impregnate women. Augustine had affirmed the physical existence of the incubus at the same time as he denied that any were involved in the Genesis narrative, lending validity to continued discussion of their supernatural role (Kiessling, *The Incubus in English Literature*, 12). Ralph Higden, following Peter Comestor in the *Polychronicon*, at first cites the Augustinian thesis ("Godes sones took men douȝteres, þat is to menynge, Seth his sones took Caym his douȝteres and gete geantis") but then adds: "And hit miȝhte be þat Incubus, suche fendes as lieþ by wommen in liknesse of men, made geantes be i-gete, in þe which geantes gretnesse of herte answereþ and acordeþ to þe hugeness of body" (Trevisa's translation, 2.5).[39] The Pearl Poet summarized this non-Augustinian account at length in *Cleanness* (269–73).

The Albina myth conjoins the biblical tradition of rapacious giants with Geoffrey's secular version and produces a smaller product through the combination, a history with familial interests behind its nationalistic gestures. The spirits who copulate with Albina and her sisters in *Des grantz geanz* are called *incubi, malfez*, and *deables*; their offspring are consequently horrifying to behold (*a regarder hidous*) and abnormally large. Incubi in medieval myth are, like giants, always male. They have no material body of their own but are nonetheless able to implant an organism (organization of being) within the bodies of the women they violate, causing the birth of a monster. Sexual mother, rapacious incubus, and infant monster are the vertices of an unholy family triangle that obscenely contrasts with the model medieval family of Virgin Mother, sexless Holy Spirit, and sinless divine Son. The Holy Family remains an incorporeal ideal by wholly eliminating sexuality and the body from its narrative of origins, but this second familial triangle violently reinscribes flesh and sex into bodily generation.

The Albina myth translates into monstrous form two conceptualizations of the biological origin of human life as medical science understood it in the Middle Ages. For medieval theorists of the body who followed Aristotle, the mother contributes formless bodily matter (*materia*) to the child, while the man imposes with his seed (*semen*) a structure that organizes this inert substance into a sexed and gendered being. The Aristotelian model is obviously another version of Brutus's mythology of nation building: the woman is the elemental matter from which offspring are produced, just as the land is the raw *materia* of nation. The influential treatises of the physician Galen, on the other hand, argued that both men and women contribute seed (and therefore structure) to their progeny.[40] The Galenic conceptualization of reproduction corresponds to the rejected model of origin that Albina represents. She and her sisters contribute as much to their progeny as their sexual partners. The conjoining of incubus and errant woman results in a new body that mixes the nature of both, the repudiating *monstrum*. This monstrous family invokes the domestic triangle of father, mother, and child to illustrate what happens when a body strays from its properly subordinate place in the regulative trigonometry of the idealized medieval household. Albina oversteps her (cultural, biological) place as submissive wife, and disaster ensues. Brutus must intervene and overwrite Galenic equality with Aristotelian masculinism: feminine bodies become as passive in the generation of progeny as they must be in the articulation of *familia*.

Geoffrey's *Historia* brought a fragmented political field into widespread coherence through an ideologically cohesive master signifier: Britain/England, the "Nation-Thing" as sublime object of ideological identification. Circulated almost two hundred years later, long after that cultural unity has been achieved, the Albina myth extends the same ideological intervention to a basic identity relationship by which the larger imagined community writes itself *in parvo*. Albina and her sisters refused their subject positions in marriage and attempted to erect a structure for human relationships in which femininity and the maternal were not dominated by, or absorbed into, masculine mastery. The sisters strove in Greece to bring about a world in which their agency would be absolute, where "none of them would be willing to have a master, nor be placed under anyone's duress, but always be mistress of her husband and of whatever he owned [*mestresce de sun seignur e quant q'il out*]" (58–61). Albina would destroy a culture that depends for its continuance on the replicative reinscription of the family, the miniature version of the patriarchal state.[41]

After retelling the Albina story, John Hardyng wrote that "women desyre of al thynges soveraynte, and to my concept, more in this land than any other, for they have it of the nature of the said sisters."[42] He could easily be quoting Chaucer's antimatrimonial nightmare, the Wife of Bath. The tale that the Wife tells begins, significantly, with incubi and threats of rape. Its hero is a knight who, in punishment for having casually violated a maiden, is compelled to discover what thing women most desire and determines that "wommen desiren to have sovereyntee" (3.1038). This prideful desire for mastery in marriage motivates the Wife of Bath herself. Her prologue to her tale chronicles long fights to gain absolute dominance over a succession of five husbands, whom she consecutively reduces to subordination. The Wife of Bath inhabits that same male fantasy space from which Albina derives, so that she can be invoked by Chaucer in the "Lenvoy a Bukton" as a monstrous warning of the woe that is in marriage. Both Albina and Alisoun of Bath teach husbands that governance in marriage is as authoritarian and severe as the autocratic governance of the state. Rather than argue that this aggressive dominance comes naturally to men, or that submissiveness is an affect of the feminine body, the Albina myth *naturalizes* the occurrence of both by showing how, through "historical necessity," such an ordering of gendered relations came to be established. The myth constructs aggressively constricted roles for husbands at the same time as it illustrates through negative *exemplum* the properly domestic boundaries of the ideal wife.

Nature, Culture, and Language

This not owning of one's words is there from the start, however, since speaking is always in some ways the speaking of a stranger through and as oneself, the melancholic reiteration of a language that one never chose.

— Judith Butler, *Bodies That Matter*, 242

In translating into English Wace's French translation of Geoffrey's Latin *Historia*, Robert Mannyng of Brunne was forced to admit that he was uncertain about the existence of giants. As he describes the monsters who await the arrival of Brutus in England, Mannyng observes that "Geant is more þan man / so says þe boke, for I ne kan" [A giant is bigger than a man—so says the book, but I don't know] (*The Chronicle*, 1751–52). They are "like men...in flesch & bone," he asserts, even if "in my tyme, I saw neuer non" (1753–54). Mannyng's understated incredulity is endearing, but at the same time as he casts some doubt about the existence of the monsters, he is happy to pass along official information about them to his readers. Most of all, he states, giants are characterized by their similitude: they present an exact if inflated replica of the masculine body (1755–56), a perfect simulacrum.

"Man" is used as if it were a universal category throughout Middle English writing, but in Mannyng's description of the giant, it retains its gendered specificty. His "membris" and "lymes" mark the giant as manlike, but also as male—as the description of Gogmagog and his monstrous crew that follows in the *Chronicle* makes clear. The giant as the magnified, insistently physical masculine corpus is Geoffrey of Monmouth's contribution to medieval gigantology, and although Mannyng might undercut the possibility that giants existed, he does not doubt their sex. Whereas Galfridian tradition chronicles only male giants battling for supremacy against male foes, however, the Anglo-Norman Albina myth repeatedly inserts feminine and maternal bodies, even after Albina and her sisters have vanished into biological function. Invoking the giants' primal associations with sexual violation, the narrative details their race's continuance by linking its monstrous life to the transgression of what Claude Lévi-Strauss has called the first patriarchal law, the incest prohibition. The male first generation of giants begets children upon their own mothers. A cycle of historical repetition through incest is then set into motion, in which "filz et filles" [sons and daughters] engender more monsters "par grant outrage"—sometimes on their mothers, sometimes on each other (434–36). The offspring of these unions likewise grow large, becoming a people "of immense body" (438–40). Until the arrival of Brutus, Albion exists as a hideously closed world of continuous sexual confusion that reenacts, relentlessly, the failure of the first family triangle established in the narrative. Signification and sexuation are conjoined in their monstrous impropriety.

Maud Ellmann has observed that "kinship laws, which govern the system of combinations in mating, correspond to linguistic laws governing the combinations of words in a sentence or letters in a word."[43] The antifamilial, antimatrimonial system that the women established is doubly incestuous, somatically and linguistically. Its monstrousness inheres in its "bad grammar" that at first will not culturally differentiate wives from husbands and then cannot separate mothers from children, brothers from sisters: "For without kinship nominations, no power is capable of instituting the order of preferences and taboos that bind and weave the yarn of lineage through succeeding generations."[44] Albina does in fact establish the order of human relations that she sought to materialize through a usurped speech act, only to learn that she is excluded by the language she invokes, that its power will monstrously transform her feminine body as it flings her back to the passive materiality from which she fled. Albion under Albina devolves into a realm of pure, undifferentiated nature. It awaits the imprint of a new, masculine language to materialize an order, to precipitate culture through some foundational prohibition, through some heroic fiat.

The organization of bodies into culture through the instigation of a kinship system is very like the ordering of the phenomenological world into reality that language accomplishes, or of the past into history that narrativization executes. All three of these performances are strongly gendered acts. Yet they do not receive their gendering before their effects on reality; rather, "gender" is produced through the very fantasies in which these systems ground themselves, and through the continued repetition of their "foundational" gestures. To assert male dominance within these structures, originary myths are invented that authorize an oppressive present through anchorage in a similar past. Lévi-Strauss bequeathed such a myth to anthropology when he wrote *The Elementary Structures of Kinship,* a work that equates "raw" nature with feminine bodies, and the legitimizing power of culture with the founding fathers who invent the incest prohibition (i.e., Law itself) and therefore also invent gender.[45] According to Lévi-Strauss, "man's sexual life" (the gender of the noun is important) is originally wild, "natural" (12). The incest prohibition, synonymous with the institution of a law that generates family relations, organizes this formless sexuality into a culturally legible norm; it allows the exchange of women between men, which in turn generates endogamy and exogamy, which in turn transform nature into culture (because an "absence of rules seems to provide the surest criterion for distinguishing a natural from a cultural process," 8). Culture here is the same as kinship systems; culture arrives at the same time as "relationless" bodies are hierarchized into families.

Lévi-Strauss writes in an Aristotelian vein. Men invent the laws regulating sexuality that distinguish the human from the animal; women are passively invested with meaning by these laws as their bodies trace paths of affiliation between the men who exchange them. Lacan reiterated this originary myth when he used Lévi-Strauss as his own foundation for a semiotics-inflected psychoanalysis: "The primordial Law is therefore that which in regulating marriage ties superimposes the kingdom of culture on that of nature abandoned to the law of mating.... This law, then, is revealed clearly enough as identical with an order of language" (*Écrits,* 66). The Albina myth is an early version of the same kind of originary narrative. It allows a masculinist logic to equate nature with femininity (a "mystery," because it is prelinguistic, and therefore also excessively corporeal), and culture and language with men (fully knowable, because they invent speech, and speech orders the world). The Albina myth, Lévi-Strauss's incest fantasy, and Lacan's dream of a wholly phallogocentric language are all moments in a long history by which the masculine gender is erected as a universal, and women are allied with the abjected, the marginal, the monstrous. If the world and the linguistic structures used to understand it inevitably and eternally took their origins in this way, men and women alike would be right to heed Luce Irigaray and despair of ever using language to construct a nonexclusive reality for all bodies, regardless of anatomy.[46] Fortunately, the Albina myth suggests a different fate for masculinist originary fantasies: a change in the structure of linguistic and cultural signification via some historical rupture that reconfigures the master signifiers, resigning old myths to the quiet loneliness of the archive, where they can teach but cease to harm.[47] No system of human meaning is ever complete, invulnerable, and impervious to history.

Like many medieval writers, Alain de Lille imagined in his "handbook" (*enchiridion*) on the laws of nature that the power of language over material reality, including sexuality, is absolute. A telling scene of *De planctu naturae* (*The Complaint of Nature*, c. 1165) describes Genius at his writing table:

> In his right hand he held a pen, close kin of the fragile papyrus, which never rested in its task of inscription. In his left hand he held the pelt of a dead animal, shorn clear of its fur of hair by the razor's bite. On this, with the help of his obedient pen, he endowed, with the life of their species, images of things that kept changing from the shadowy outline of a picture to the realism of their actual being. As these were laid to rest in the annihilation of death, he called others to life in a new birth and beginning.[48]

The (masculine) stylus, perfect vehicle of an unfailing language, inscribes the world on the stilled surface of the vellum—once a living body, now passive *materia*.[49] Likewise, the Anglo-Norman version of the Albina myth imagines an unchanging masculine order of pure language through which human identity and historical identity are solidified. Divorced from its own materiality, the male body becomes as impossibly airy, disembodied, and indestructible as a language that exists outside of time and change; the male body becomes synonymous with the frozen *verba et grammatica* that inscribe meaning on the body of the world, as well as on bodies in the world. Albina's naming of the land linguistically parallels Brutus's expressed desire for geographical immortality, his fathering of a country and a people through a name:

> Albine est mon propre noun,
> Dunt serra nomé Albion;
> Par unt de nous en ceo pais
> Rembrance serra tutdis. (ll.347–50)

> [Because my name is Albina, this land shall be called Albion; by this our eternal memory shall live in this country.]

Compare the same scene written in the masculine gender in the *Historia:*

> Denique Brutus de nomine suo insulam Britoniam appellat sociosque suos Britones. Uolebat enim ex diruatione nominis memoriam habere perpetuam. (13–14)

> [Brutus called the land Britain after himself. His intention was that his memory be made eternal through the derivation of the name.]

Albina invokes the reifying power of language, as if she were a hyper-masculine Trojan hero, not a monstrously transgressive Greek woman. She "repeats" in the past the same linguistic ritual that will render Brutus the generative parent of Britain. Fathering a nation (and its substructure and support, the family) is metaphorically possible without recourse to female agency; indeed, both rely on female passivity, on the provision of a "natural state" or formless materiality on which to impose structuration.[50] Albina's linguistic ordering of reality yields only monstrous forms: bodies that are at once male *and* female *and* incestuous, bodies that do not know their proper cultural place because they preexist the masculine "invention" of place. Brutus is able to repeat the same words, and by reference to a linguistic authority his by dint of the subject position from which he articulates his words, he produces a nationalistic matrix for the proper gendering of identities, a model for male dominance.

In Brutonian history, both the monsters and the feminine body vanish at this moment of origin, evacuated of meaning "in their own right" and installed into the progress narrative of history. Like those monumental statues in Guildhall, they commemorate a monstrous past that exists only to envalue an architecture of power in the present. This haunting presence-in-death is foregrounded by giving the giants an archaeological reality. The monsters are visible now, not only as huge petrified bones "qe hom puet trover / En mult des leus de la terre" [which a man can find in many places across the land] (443–56), but as earthworks and ruins. The narrative stresses that these remnants are, like Gogmagog's Leap in Geoffrey's *Historia*, still a part of the landscape of England. Past and present intersect and filiate. Brutus slaughters the giants upon his arrival in Britain, but he spares Gogmagog. This giant tells him the very tale that *Des grantz geanz* itself relates: the creation and lineage of the giants, how they came into the land, and why Britain should once have been called Albion. Brutus responds by ordering the history memorialized "so that others afterwards might know the marvel of this story" (543–44). Appropriately enough, historical narrativization is achieved through the mouth of a monster.

Medieval England is far from alone in imagining that its land was once ruled by a primordial matriarchy. The Albina myth partakes of a long tradition of fantasies of female sovereignty. One manuscript of *Guiron le Courtois*, a French grail quest romance that opens with a survey of English history, compares the Greek sisters directly to the archetypal gynecocracy of the West, the Amazons. Since the publication of Jacob Bachofen's *Das Mutterrecht* in 1861, many scholars have seen in the pervasive literary imaginings of primal matriarchies such as the Amazons an encoding of historical fact. Other critics have pointed out that these myths of female rule function instead to justify the subjugation of women "by providing a purportedly historical account of how this reality came about."[51] Such times and places in the Western imagination are primarily the creations of men, who imagine these inversions in order to validate their own dominant position. According to the classical myth, Theseus invades the Amazonian *mutterland*, and the rebuked matriarchs are transformed into properly subordinated wives. Similarly, Brutus and his men purge the land of its subhuman citizens in order to rewrite the wrongdoing of the Greek sisters. Along the way, they also establish a double *sovereyntee:* for the management of the nation, and for the management of the family. In both, the feminine body is conjoined with the monster, to vanish in a foundational act.

The story of Albina's colonization of England was wildly popular. Manuscript evidence suggests that the narrative was originally composed in Anglo-Norman, then quickly translated into English and then Latin. As Carley and Crick point out, vernacular texts were rarely rendered into Latin in the Middle Ages, so that "when it did occur, it represented an elevation of the text, its enshrinement in linguistic authority."[52] This translation into the language of Geoffrey's *Historia Regum Britanniae* also marks an elevation into history: from the early fourteenth century to the last surviving days of the giants in Guildhall, the maternal body and the monstrous with which it is intimately connected receive a foundational, structural positioning within the identity of the English *historia.* Albina and Gogmagog become mother and son.

Giants and Smaller Bodies

As Lewis Spence wrote his treatise *The Minor Traditions of British Mythology* shortly after the end of World War II, his mind was occupied by giants. Two chapters treat these monsters directly, and many others are haunted by them, since like the Anglo-Saxon homilists, he saw in their vast bodies an incarnation of the lost, original gods of England.

Spence's giants are the product of nostalgia, impossibly complete love objects that stand in for everything that perished during the conflagration of the war. On the possibility of a childhood without giants, he writes: "What a truly dreadful proposition! It is (or must one use the past-perfect?) from the giant that we received our earliest thrills" (58). Of the giants of Guildhall, the reified forms of the monsters whom Geoffrey of Monmouth enclosed at the heart of national identity, Spence is elegiac:

> It is sixty years since, on my earliest visit to London Town, I first stood, a gaping urchin, before the garishly bepainted effigies of Gog and Magog in Guildhall, which have since been destroyed by German thunderbolts.... Since I first beheld them, a lifetime ago, I have been haunted by the mystery surrounding them, and have made more than one effort to dissipate it. (59)

These giants represent for Spence the innocence that war is conventionally depicted as having robbed. He writes bittersweetly of London ap-

60

prentices ("unruly young blades") confined for their misdeeds beneath the giant statues, where they "might cogitate on the follies of riot and truancy" (60)—that is, learn from these Guildhall monsters the proper management of their bodies that is the sign of being an adult. These giants allow him to write his own childhood and coming of age using the same script that the nation followed in overcoming them in Galfridian history: from wild nature to a refinement that allows the scripting of nostalgic prehistory. Spence's melancholy arises because he has lost "by German thunderbolts" the tangibility of this object so dear to his selfhood. He is unaware that he has not in fact lost the giants at all, for he is building a subjectivity around the installation of their presence-in-absence, just as England materialized around the same.

Spence's meditation ends with a patriotic call for new giants to be constructed and placed once more at the heart of London, the heart of the nation: "But Gog and Magog, the ancient palladia of London and of the white cliffs of Britain, will . . . rise again, in all their quaint medieval grandeur, in another and equally royal Guildhall in the heart of our undefeated metropolis, the ancient and timeless 'Troynovant' " (61). Spence wants returned the history that England has always already had, and he fantasizes that Gog and Magog bear that gift. Geoffrey of Monmouth's triumph, then, was to erect a persuasive ideology of community through the body of the monster—so persuasive that it was still being invoked in the aftermath of a world war eight hundred years later. Spence suggests a reason why this imagined history should have instantly and irrevocably become fundamental. Not only does the giant stand at the origin of England in the *Historia* (and at the origin of the state *in parvo*, the properly managed family, in the Albina myth), but as Spence's image of boyhood wonder and unruly apprentices confined before Guildhall's "bizarre" bodies illustrates, the giant also enables that foundational moment when the male child steps into his adult gender role and learns the monstrous, public origin of the "private," masculine body.

❖

CHAPTER 3

The Body in Pieces
Identity and the Monstrous in Romance

The human being is this night, this empty nothing, that contains
everything in its simplicity—an unending wealth of presentations,
images. . . . Here shoots out a bloody head, there a white shape. . . . One
catches sight of this night when one looks human beings in the eye.
—G. W. F. Hegel, *Hegel's Recollection*, 7–8

Slashed Bodies

In the Sega video game Mortal Kombat, players triumph over their opponents through the martial arts, usually by kicking them to death. The victor's electronic avatar reaches into the prostrate enemy's body and rips out the spinal cord, to which the brain is still attached. He performs a brief victory dance, displaying the gruesome trophy, and then moves on to other conquests and adventures. The demographics for video games are revealing. Although their audience is diverse and cuts across race and gender lines, their most avid consumers are middle- and upper-class adolescent males, and it is for this group that these games are formulated. Why should male pubescents be so interested in dismemberment?

Carol Clover offers one possible answer: for the same reason that they enjoy consuming slasher films.[1] In this gory, visually obsessed genre, the human body is torn apart, objectified into trophies and fetishes, sometimes (as in *The Texas Chainsaw Massacre*) reconfigured into a piece of conceptual art. The trigonometry of identification in these films is complex, but it involves a movement from inhabiting the gaze of the killer ("a male in gender distress," 27) as he transforms whole persons into the Real of their material components—into a mess of blood, flesh, and bone. The point of identification shifts later in the film to "the Final Girl," the last survivor of the carnage and the embodiment of the "active investigative gaze." She heroically resists this process of desubjectification by asserting her inviolable integrity against the force of the monster's somatic deconstruction: "The moment at which the Final Girl is effectively phallicized is the moment that the plot halts and horror ceases. Day breaks, and the community returns to its normal order" (50). The Final Girl is a "congenial double" for the adolescent male spectator, who is himself perhaps a "male in gender distress," at that limen between the ambiguities of childhood and the constrictive demands of an adult gender identity; she is thus "a male surrogate in things oedipal, a homoerotic stand-in, the audience incorporate" (53). The slasher film is a masculinist discourse in which female bodies are coherent only when they signify (male) lack, or, as with the Final Girl, when they represent a triumph over that lack, when they encode for the audience the possibility of being an autonomous subject—a possibility realized only by ceasing to be feminine. Community order is restored at the same time as the *male* body's symbolic order is reestablished. The film ends when a certain formulation of subjective integrity can withstand the monster's threat to the body in which it is manifest.

An array of medieval artifacts, especially texts, reveal that a fascination with monsters, dismemberment, and the materiality of the body is not the invention of late-twentieth-century Hollywood. To find a medieval equivalent to the complex gender dynamics that Clover outlines, one need look no further than chivalric romance. The monster as it is known today—the monster of film, fine art, juvenilia, and popular culture—is directly descended from this culminating medieval genre. The power of attraction of romance, like that of the monster itself, runs deep. Combining history, myth, folklore, the classical heritage, popular culture, and even philosophy and theology into archetypal tales of heroism and desire, romance is perhaps more cultural mode than literary genre, as much a catalyst to cultural creation as cultural product. Knights self-appointed and royally anointed subscribed with a sometimes fanatic zeal to the dictates of a chivalry for which many of these works were exemplary vehicles—sometimes long after such behavioral codes had become divorced from their generating cultural moment.[2] The progeny of romance endure in almost every register of culture, from the modern survivals of the bourgeois sentimental novel (Harlequin Romances) to cinema high and low (Bergman, Spielberg, Lucas, Gilliam). And while dreaming of origins and lines of descent, why not add another child to the family tree: slasher films, with their obsessive gaze on the limits of the body, the smashing of its integrity, and the gendered process of its reconstruction.

The commercial success of both Mortal Kombat and *The Texas Chainsaw Massacre* depends on their ability to fascinate the gaze of their consumers, to elicit an identification with a body that is as insubstantial as it is imperiled (bodies in both genres are flat images composed only of the light they radiate from a screen). Romance likewise depended for its cultural success on a fantasy of the body in pieces coupled to a "final" identification with a wholly imaginary form of the ideal self. But whereas slasher films perform complete dismemberment for their intended audience, romance was content with decapitation.

Toward the History of a Gesture

The scene repeats itself.

In the forests of the Country of the Living, the young hero Gilgamesh battles the giant Humbaba ("evil"). Gilgamesh decapitates the monster's corpse, displays the head to the gathered gods, and is divinely transfigured.[3] Perseus slays Medusa and holds her serpented head aloft to announce his triumph over his surrogate father, Polydectes. Freud universalizes the same episode to stage a personal fantasy of triumph over fear of difference and misogynist loathing.[4] In *Culhwch ac Olwen,* a tale from the Welsh *Mabinogion,* Culhwch defeats the ancient Ysbaddaden Penkawr ("chief giant"), shaves and beheads him, sleeps with his daughter, and thereby asserts his identity as adult and as warrior.[5] Culhwch is an adolescent on whom his stepmother has imposed a *geis,* compelling him either to marry Olwen, the daughter of the king of the giants, or to be barred forever from a heterosexual identity (he will never be able to "touch the side of a woman"). The formal humiliation of the giant functions as a ceremonialized rejection of the sexual tyranny that he embodies, and a validation of the bodily enjoyment that Arthur (*pen teyrnedd yr ynys hon,* "chief of the princes of the island") oversees. Ysbaddaden's head is cut off and mounted on a spike, a bloody testament to the superior ethic of Arthur's version of leadership.[6] Culhwch's rite de passage is the communal slaying of the giant; accomplishing the feat gains for him both a wife and admission to the company of warriors from whom, like Chrétien de Troyes's Perceval, he has been raised in isolation.

Beowulf's victory over Grendel is not complete until he decapitates the monster. Having overcome the invader of Heorot, Beowulf tears the clawed arm from his opponent and displays the trophy on the roof for all to see. Grendel's mother appears, a reminder that Beowulf's monstrous business is unfinished, and snatches away the bloody limb. He follows her to a distant lair, discovers Grendel's body, and finally beheads it. When Beowulf drags the giant's head by its hair into the mead hall, he replaces the mounted arm with a new emblem, a more powerful lure to visual fascination; his audience is stunned by the trophy into silence (1647–50). Something so horrifying emanates from beneath the severed head's gory locks that the viewers' gaze becomes stuck, as if the dead object itself obscenely glares back. The inexpressible thrill of horror, a repulsion within an attraction: this fleshy remnant of Grendel functions as "a coagulated, stigmatized, signifying chain repelling signification with an excess of sticky enjoyment."[7] First the gaze of both the men and the women (*eorlum, idese*) is arrested on the "horrifying spectacle" (*wliteseon wrætlic*) of the head, an intriguing phrase that could just as easily apply to the narrativization of the scene itself (*wrætlic,* "artful, ornamental"; *wliteseon,* "beauty-sight"). Then Beowulf redirects the vision of the men (*weras*) in order to affix the monster's power of fascination to himself.

He renarrates the story of his defeat of the giant (1650–76), announcing the death of the solitary individualism that Grendel embodied. Having given the trauma a stable, gendered, heroic meaning, Beowulf allows Heorot to return to its normal order. Fascination is broken, the circuit of the gaze reconfigured. The ritualized display of the severed head is public theater within narrative theater. The highly charged exhibit validates the conservative, nostalgic ethos of the poem's imagined culture and unambiguously announces Beowulf's full status as hero, as the proper leader who realizes that identity exists only within the corporate hierarchy of community. Having accepted his symbolic mandate by conquering the giant, Beowulf can sail homeward to embrace his destiny as king.

In the Hebrew Bible, a shepherd boy defeats the menacing Goliath with a slingshot and uses the giant's own sword to decapitate the corpse. David exhibits the monstrous head to the gathered Philistine army, who flee in fear (1 Sam. 17:51). The gesture announces both a personal and a political coming of age, the birth of a heroic and a national identity.[8] The encounter between David and Goliath interprets the subsequent battle as a conflict both theological and nationalistic.[9] Goliath curses David by his gods (*maledixit Philistheus ad David in diis suis*), and the boy courageously replies, "You come to me with a sword, and with a spear, and with a shield, but I come to you in the name of the Lord" (1 Sam. 17:45). The battle is constructed to assert the potency of a singular name under the aegis of which a nation collects its identity — a name so powerful that in Hebrew it cannot even be written — over and against a scattered plurality of gods that will be revealed to have no signifying power. The humiliation of Goliath is a gleeful deconstruction of any identity that attempts to formulate itself outside the circle of Israelite law: a shepherd boy too young to wear armor, carrying a weapon that the giant can only bemoan as grossly insulting ("Am I a dog that you come to me with a staff?"), challenges a monster "six cubits and a span" (more than eleven feet) tall and defeats him with a well-placed blow from a slingshot. Chaucer underscored the episode's recurrent site of enjoyment, its delight in excess:

> O Golias, unmesurable of lengthe,
> Hou myghte David make thee so maat,
> So yong and of armure so desolaat?
> Hou dorste he looke upon thy dredful face?
> ("Man of Law's Tale," 934–47)

Goliath's fate at David's hands becomes the promised end of all giants, a dismemberment that transforms a remnant of his body into a potent sign of terror for use by the victor. In that dead fragment of the monster who embodied them, the frightened Philistines behold the sign of their rebuke, the collapse of their self-determination of meaning and its final enslavement below the Israelite master signifier of *nomen domini*. They scatter in terror — their lack of consistency the final proof of the solidity of Israelite group identity.

Battles against inimical giants that culminate in a decapitation uncannily recur in the myth, literature, and historiography of the West, like the repeated advent of a portentous dream. These scenes function formally as a rite of passage, inextricably linking the defeat of the monster to a political, sexual, social coming of age. The scene repeats itself because a new male generation is always engaging in the fight against the giant, struggling with the behavior codes that gender some actions and monsterize others. Such narratives are components of a larger cultural discourse of masculine maturation, intergenerational conflict, and differentiation, within which the gigantomachia and its emblematic decapitation and display construct a stable vision of adult masculinity. Romance is the medieval genre most self-invested in the invention of the mythically autonomous male subject, and so romance's vast topography is the most fecund site for an investigation of dismemberment, visual fascination, and embodiment.

Geoffrey of Monmouth's *History of the Kings of Britain* invented the matrix of gendered and monstrous "historical" bodies that enabled the birth of romance. The *Historia* contains a beheading scene so powerful that all the long romance tradition of decapitation scenes can be said to be an extended citation of its originary moment. Arthur has just defeated the giant of Mont Saint Michel, a monster who rapes innocent women (a maiden, an elderly nurse), murders knights and peasants, produces nothing, and devours all. Once he defeats his foe, Arthur orders Bedevere to decapitate the giant's corpse and present the head to a squire, "so that it might be carried to the camp for all to go and stare at." The men first gape at the severed head, but their attention quickly moves from the fragment of the giant whole to the warrior who fragmented the giant and remained whole: "All their men gathered to gape at it and praise the man who had freed the country from such a voracious monster" (241). Like Beowulf's exhibit of Grendel, this theatricalized display is composed of a twofold movement. First the gaze of the men is caught en masse (*cateruatim*) by the trophy, which radiates an uncanny power of visual fascination (*admirari*, "regard with wonder, gaze at passionately, desire"). This ocular glutinousness arises from a difficulty in exactly placing the grotesque emblem — like the giant himself, the severed head is (to return to Zizek's words) "a coagulated, stigmatized" point on the signifying chain that, although saturated with meaning, paradoxically *repels* signification because "an excess of sticky enjoyment" inheres there (*Looking Awry*, 151). The stupefying pleasure of the monstrous arises from its frightening ambiguity, which invites a fascinated *jouis-sense*, an obscene enjoyment in the contemplation of its dreadful signification. The horrifically thrilled, fixated gaze of the men must next be "bumped," made to

Figure 5. Arthur decapitates the "horrible Giaunt" of Mont Saint Michel. Lambeth Palace Library, MS 6 f.62v. Reprinted with permission of the Archbishop of Canterbury and the Trustees of Lambeth Palace Library.

stick on the one who presents this Medusa-like object for visual consumption. The monster's uncanny power is thus harnessed and attached to the hero's body. In the course of this transfer, an ideological message is imparted to the totem, integrating it into meaning and breaking the monster's spell. The watchers stare finally at Arthur, in the realization that the monster's powers have been incorporated and re-encoded by the king.[10] The giant's threat of anarchy (pure force [*vis*] without socialized direction), installed beneath the aegis of monarchy, becomes the king's power over individualism. Like the monstrous head of Grendel, the dead countenance of the giant announces that appetite and wrongful autonomy, the bases of the monster's evil, have been rebuked, and that *comitatus* or *societas* and its attendant control have been validated. The giant's vast, polysemous body is torn into a meaningful little fragment, reduced to a trophy.

The audience ingests the ideological meaning of the episode at the moment they open their mouths to praise the one "qui patriam a tanta ingluuie liberauerat" [who had freed the country from such a voracious monster] (119). Geoffrey's choice of terms is revealing. The Latin noun Thorpe blandly translates as "voracious monster" is *ingluvies,* literally "maw." The term is both metonymic and synechdochic. Perhaps the monster is being rendered here an allegory for gluttony. Such personification is fitting, since the giant embodies appetite of all kinds, enfleshing those sexual and sensual sins where a body does not know the limits of its contours. But there is more to the giant than simple, reductive allegory. As Michael Camille points out, in an era when reading meant transforming the visual (words on a vellum page) into the oral (speaking aloud their sound), ingestion and digestion were never far removed from making meaning of a text (*ruminatio*, "muscular mastication . . . that released the full flavour or meaning of the text").[11] Both were bodily functions; both are potential sites for monstrosity. Despite its containment within heroic signification, the head of the giant remains uncanny. It is a dead thing, yet it pulses with meaning, with life. Even as its gory flesh is made to encode a simple, glory-giving story about Arthur, a remnant of the giant's threat still lingers in its monstrous instability.

Unlike Arthur, the monster has no proper name, no definitive placement in the grammar of cultural meaning. He does not respect the privacy of other bodies in the world, even while insisting on his own supreme individualism; identity is not relational or communal for the giant, who alone in his mountain kingdom insists on his right to self-determination—a murderous version of Thoreau at Walden. *Ingluvies* as "maw" suggests something larger: cut to a fragment of its monstrousness and made to signify within Arthur's heroic narrative of proper masculine identity, where only exceptional bodies like that of a hero are allowed autonomy, the giant's severed head is still dangerous, a metaphoric "maw" or feral mouth that devours the gaze of the men who "stare" and "gape at it." The formal structure of the narrative may harness the giant's power of visual fascination on Arthur's behalf, but it cannot guarantee it will stick only there, for something about this anthropophagous mouth exceeds containment into a merely optical trigonometry.[12] The monster marks a point of origin (the body before its social containment) but also offers a Lacanian "trap for the gaze," a point of dangerous return.

Because the giant as *ingluvies* has affinities with medieval representations of the mouth of hell (usually depicted as a monstrous head swallowing damned souls), the display of the devouring maw resonates with a Christian air of triumph. That the enjoyment that clings to the monster's maw also has a specifically sexual dimension is perhaps suggested by the interchangeability of mouth and vagina in later fabliau tradition, a conflation of orifices well documented by E. Jane Burns: "The vagina that eats, sucks, swallows, opens and closes its mouth appears routinely as a *goule*, or gaping mouth."[13] In "La Veuve," a vagina is even described as *goulu Goliath*, a giant's mouth (Burns, *Bodytalk*, 54). In fact, *gula* (throat, glutton, mouth) and *Golias* were often connected by medieval etymologists, so that *mouth* becomes the synechdotal point of overlap between gigantic and feminine bodies.[14] As the Albina myth demonstrates, the corporeality and consumptive drive of the giant allies him with misogynist representation of medieval women. The defeat and beheading of the monster is therefore a violent moment of gender assertion, a triumph of desubstantiating ascesis (gendered masculine) over fleshly excess (gendered feminine). That this abjecting moment of becoming male also marks a potential point of future collapse is indicated by the monstrous impossibility of incorporating the *ingluvies* in all its gendered complexity into the mythically pure form of the hero.

In psychoanalytic terms, the severed head as nexus of visual fascination functions as a "sublime object," the vessel for a powerful symbolic message (about the limits of the body, about embodiment as a process of cultural control) as well as the container of a certain surplus, "a certain inert presence" (Zizek, *Sublime Object,* 71). The head fascinates those who gaze upon it, both inside and outside the text, because although a story about "normal" bodies attempts to evacuate the power from its dead countenance, some remnant of enjoyment (a term that includes the possibility of sadistic, masochistic, and obscene pleasure) continues to adhere, making it difficult to turn away — even once the signification of the episode within an "official" ideology has been made clear. The sins that gigantism collects are not easily banished from delectation. Even the gesture of their eradication pulses in its formal structure with their obscene presence, however "invisible"[15] such enjoyment may be to the optics of the gaze.

Against this collapse into monstrousness, the heroic name of Arthur in Geoffrey of Monmouth's text becomes a *point de capiton,* a "quilting point" where the contradictions that inevitably undergird any subject, any ideology, are temporarily allayed by finding embodiment in a "rigid" signifier.[16] Arthur is autonomous, his will and his desires are efficacious, but at the same time, his identity is radically contingent on his place in the community. The contradiction at the heart of heroic masculine embodiment is simply that the body gains its meaning at once from something innate, ontological, and "individual," so that the medieval hero is as autarkic as that other myth, the "self-determinate capitalist"; and identity is at the same time relational, "the gift of the community," the effect of a certain place occupied within the symbolic order (Marx: "One man is king only because other men stand in the relation of subjects to him").[17] Although Arthur is this system incarnate, he escapes the ideological impasse that forms its center. Arthur sutures a set of free-floating and potentially contradictory signifiers (community, hero, monster, empire) into a coherent, meaningful narrative. "Arthur" is a point of fantasy identification where a group as large as a nation can locate itself, as if group and individual identification were wholly commensurable. When the potential antinomy between communal and private identity is evaded through their mythic embodiment in the British monarch, Arthur receives the radiance that announces his own charismatic, overdetermined status in the symbolic order. Geoffrey dreams Arthur, and through this new body, a glorious past, a telos for the future, and a present identity are materialized for the British and the Anglo-Normans, and ultimately for England. At the same time, romance is precipitated out of historiography.

69

The narrative trajectory of romance will be determined by this uneasy balance between a *point de capiton* as a rigid designator of surface meaning (the hero's name as specific, constrictive formulation of masculine embodiment) and the monstrous stain of *jouissance* that lingers within the very thing that this signification appears to condemn. Such obscene enjoyment, however, is the key to the success of the larger ideological system in which this meaning is embedded. The hero's power of fascination derives from the impossibility of the complete evacuation of enjoyment, from the horrifying visual and somatic pleasure that the monster evokes and the hero steals, harnesses, transforms, but can never fully gentrify. The monstrous enjoyment that smears the formal structure of Galfridian and romance masculinity ensures that the contradictions that lay at its center will strengthen its cultural power, its *instance* (agency, insistence), by ensuring that it remains beneath its smooth surface an identity category in constant, ambivalent motion.[18] Psychoanalysis insists that persuasive ideologies work not because they squelch contradiction and subversive *jouissance* but because they make full use of their productive, disharmonious power.

Both Brutus's conquest of the aboriginal giants and Arthur's battle with the lone giant of Mont Saint Michel were quickly established as foundational moments in the history of England. The giant material and its song of expansionism were incorporated essentially unaltered into a growing tradition of chronicle histories. Layamon's *Brut*, Robert of Gloucester's *Metrical Chronicle*, and Robert Mannyng of Brunne's *The Story of England* vary little from their ultimate source in retelling the Trojan settlement and Arthur's victory over the Spanish giant. The *Historia Regum Britanniae* was established as consensual history, the beheading scene a *tableau vivant* compelled to repeat. The *Roman de Brut*, a metrical chronicle composed by the Jerseyman Wace under the command of Henry II, transformed Geoffrey's clerical Latin into the aristocratic vernacular of Norman French. From Wace, Geoffrey's Arthur passed directly into romance, first in France (Chrétien de Troyes) and then in England. Wace altered Geoffrey's giant story little but bestowed upon the monster his *nom propre*: Dinabuc. Wace's giant practices his pleasures against the folk of the countryside, destroying their houses, stealing their wives (*femes mener*), and carrying away their children (*porter enfanz*). The abducted maiden Helen is smothered beneath the monster's enormous body in a scene that conjoins corporeality to sexuality to distinguish both from an ethereal principle of identity that resides in neither (*l'aume*). The gross physicality of the giant is conveyed by an enormous compounding of synonymous adjectives ("trop fu ahoeges, trop fu granz, / trop laiz, trop gros et trop pesanz," 11409–10) that literally overwhelm the *tendre* maiden. The giant's masculinity is so invested in bodily performance that he crushes the soul from her body as he attempts his rape. Arthur, on the other hand, knows the limits of the flesh. Wace's king is more cunning in battle than Geoffrey's vigorous monarch, using his wits against the giant's lumbering corporeality. The giant is decapitated, and the head is brought to the camp, *pur faire a merveille mustrer* (11560). As the trophy is displayed to the army, the narrator asserts that no man had ever slain such a strong, misshapen, and visually enthralling monster.

David's defeat of Goliath and his severing of the monster's head announced the advent of a new epoch of Hebrew nationalism, a new golden age. Likewise, Arthur's dismemberment of the giant of Mont Saint Michel signals his political coming of age, his readiness to assume the heavy mantle of world-class heroism and be numbered among the Nine Worthies. That Arthur's chivalric progression should be depicted as political rather than personal (or that it should write the political through the personal) is necessitated by the genre in which his development is placed: the *Historia* and *Brut*, no matter how imaginative in their ambitious sweep, are presented as collective history, and their gestures are consequently grand. A genre of personal realization more than national exploit, romance generally has a more local scope, limited to the history of a single, exemplary male body. Geoffrey's *Historia* was transformed in the movement from chronicle history to historical romance. The gigantomachia lost some of its political resonance as it ceased to exert its power of fascination over cultural bodies and turned instead to entrapping the gaze of individual subjects. This switch in preoccupation from communal to "private" identities was easy enough to accomplish, for both identifications are necessary to give these narratives their force.

Coming of Age in Romance

As on an X-ray photograph, therefore, a patch of disquieting opacity lay at the center of the human heart. What is distinctive is the speed and tenacity with which that dark spot came to be identified, in Christian circles, with specifically sexual desires, with unavowed sexual stratagems, and, as we shall see, with the lingering power of sexual fantasy.
—Peter Brown, "Bodies and Minds," 481

The mid-fourteenth-century romance *Sir Eglamour of Artois*, although infrequently read by contemporary medievalists, was quite popular in its time. Four early manuscripts survive, including a version in the Thornton manuscript, and numerous new copies were produced by scribes and by printing presses until about 1570.[19] The eponymous protagonist is in love with Christabelle, the daughter of the earl of Artois, but this prohibitive father will not consent to their marriage until the young knight proves himself by accomplishing three tasks. The first paternal demand is the slaying of the giant Arrok and the hunting of one of his beautiful harts. Eglamour kills the required deer, then meets its owner in dreadful combat. The giant swings his mighty mace at the knight and misses; the weapon lodges itself so deep in the ground that Arrok cannot retrieve it.

71

The eager young knight then blinds his adversary with his sword. They continue to fight until the forty-five-foot monster collapses, and the victor cuts off his head. Eglamour conveys this totemic remnant to the earl of Artois's castle, where the head is spectacularly displayed:

> The contré come hym abowte,
> To see the hedd that was grete and stowte,
>   Soche a hedd sawe they never none.
> Before the erle he hyt bare,
> "Lo! lorde, y have byn thare,
>   And that bare ye wytnesse echon." (337–42)

[The people of the country crowded around him, to see the great and grim head: they had never seen such a head before. Eglamour carried it to the earl: "Lo! Lord, I have been there, and to that fact you must all bear witness."]

This public demonstration works like the optics of embodiment that underwrite Arthur's display of the giant's head in Geoffrey of Monmouth's *Historia*, but here the visual power of the scene receives even greater emphasis. The short stanza maps lines of sight that pass from the gathered spectators to the severed head to the hero, and finally to the earl. Artois becomes an unwilling part of this staged spectacle, reduced from grandly inflexible dictator of impossible tasks to one among many admirers who stare at the head with wonder. The narrative gaze finally centers on, and is transfixed by, the young Eglamour, the new locus of power and agency. This pronouncement is seconded by the poet himself: "Thys ys the furste fytt of thys / That we have undurtane" [Thus ends the first fit of the work we have undertaken] (344–45), as if the physical inscription of the romance and the production of Eglamour's heroic body were one and the same activity.

The narration culminates in the beheading of the giant and the public display of the gory trophy. Giants always die in this severe manner. So firmly established was decapitation as the giant's fate that when Gustave Doré was illustrating an edition of *Les Aventures du Baron de Munchhausen*, he depicted giants in battle desperately holding their heads to their shoulders, in anticipation of their promised end (Pallister, "Giants," 310–11). Two hundred years after the completion of Geoffrey's *Historia Regum Britanniae*, the unknown author of the *Short English Metrical Chronicle* retold the defeat by Corineus of the giant Gogmagog at the dawn of British history, transforming the monster's fate in accordance with the rules of romance that Geoffrey's celebration of Arthur helped construct. In the *Historia*, Corineus hurls his monstrous adversary from a cliff into the rocky sea, where his body is "dashed to a thousand fragments" and the waters are stained by his blood (trans. Thorpe, 73). In the *Chronicle*, Gogmagog ends his life rather more spectacularly: "Wiþ a swerd þat wald wele bide / þe geauntes heued he gan ofsmite" [with a sword that always served well, [Corineus] chopped off the giant's head] (A 433–36, p. 55). The head is hung on a chain and exhibited in Cornwall. Rescued from loss in the forgetful sea, the bodily remnant of the monster is transformed into an enduring trophy that announces Corineus's permanent place in insular history. In the *Historia*, it was enough that a name ("Gogmagog's Leap") preserve the monstrous trace, but here the fragmented *materia* of the body becomes the *textus* on which *historia* is indelibly inscribed.

The hero must fight a giant. Such was the assumption of the romancers, as well as the audience's "horizon of expectation."[20] As Thomas Chestre was adapting Marie de France's *Lai de Lanval* into the romance *Sir Launfel*, he added a battle of the knight against the monstrous Sir Valentine of Lumbardye, for no other reason than Chestre seems to have thought a gigantomachia a prerequisite for the development of a proper identity narrative. In adapting the romance *Lybeaus Desconus* from its French original (some version of *Le Bel inconnu*), its author for the same reason deliberately misconstrued Malgiers li Gris, a human knight in black arms, as Maugys the thirty-foot giant, boar headed and "blacke as pyche" (Lambeth MS, 1296–1312). Likewise, when Chaucer set out to burlesque the genre in his "Tale of Sir Thopas," he centered his comic revision around the young knight's encounter with a giant, the wonderfully named Sir Olifaunt. Almost all of the "identity romances" feature these belligerent monsters: in addition to *Lybeaus Desconus* and *Launfel*, battles against giants are central to *Le Chevalier au lion*, *Gui de Warewic* and *Guy of Warwick*, *Boeve de Haumtone* and *Bevis of Hampton*, *Sir Degaré*, *King Horn*, *Sir Eglamour of Artois*, *Sir Gawain and the Green Knight*, *Sir Gawain and the Carl of Carlisle*, *Huon of Bordeux*, *Octavian*, *Perceval of Galles*, *Tristrem*, and *Torrent of Portyngale*.

Following the structure received from the David and Goliath story, the display of the conquered giant's head is often in its simplest terms part of the rite de passage from boyhood to manhood, from mistakes and potential ambiguity into the certainties of a stable masculinity. This narrative coming of age imbricates the personal and the political, the public with the private.[21] Such initiation rites are meant to ensure, through their successful completion, the adoption of a culture's conventionally male behaviors within its sex/gender system. The giant's destruction serves an enabling function in the text: it is perhaps the penultimate task in a series, allowing the knight to accomplish next the feat that will provoke public recognition of his true identity as hero, as a man powerfully aligned with the text's construction of masculinity. In *Le Chevalier au lion*, Yvain's destruction of the lustful giant Harpin de la Montagne precedes the freeing of Lunete, and overcoming the two diabolically engendered *géants* at the castle of Pesme-Aventure leads to the duel with Gawain that will reveal Yvain's hidden identity and unite him permanently with his wife, Laudine. In *Sir Gawain and the Carl of Carlisle*, severing the head of the giant brings about Gawain's marriage to the carl's daughter and the reunion of the Round Table. The death of the two giants in *Lybeaus Desconus* results in freedom for the captive maiden Violet and the eventual realization of Fair Unknown's identity as Gingelein, son of Gawain. This rite of passage is clearly a moment of sexual realization, as the liberation of the captive women indicates; yet at the same time, it signals a necessary sexual repression, as the hero demonstrates his interior control against the giant's exorbitant appetite.

The Middle English romance *Lybeaus Desconus* contains the most pedestrian and therefore the most straightforwardly illustrative use of the identity-giving gigantomachia. The romance was quite popular, surviving in six manuscripts, and describes how Gawain's bastard son learned the truth of his paternity. Raised by his mother in Perceval-like isolation, a young man arrives at Arthur's court ignorant even of his proper name. Arthur dubs him Lybeaus Desconus, "Fair Unknown," since his handsome form marks him as a youth of great promise. Because the romance body writes interior meaning as corporeality, physical beauty and moral worth are always indistinguishable, just as monstrousness is equally a somatic and ethical state. When a maiden arrives at court seeking help from Arthur, the newly minted knight swears his assistance, and they set off together. Late one night, the maiden's dwarf observes a wicked fire burning in the distance and pleads with Lybeaus to flee. The knight instead mounts his horse, gallops to the blaze, and encounters two "grysly" giants. One of these monsters is black and clutches to his bosom a woman he has kidnapped from a nearby castle; the other, who is red, hungrily turns a "wylde bore" over the flames. The giant's captive is about to be raped. Lybeaus rushes at the black monster and with his sword pierces his heart. The red giant then attacks, first with the spitted boar, then with an improvised club. Lybeaus suffers damage to his armor but succeeds in slicing away the giant's hand. The head quickly follows. After allowing the rescued maiden, Violet, to tell her story (a narrative reaffirmation of the romance compulsion to sexual restraint), Lybeaus cuts off the second giant's head and sends both to Arthur, so that "in courte ffast roose / Syr Lybeos Dysconeus noble loose / And all his gentill fame" [Quickly then in court the noble reputation of Sir Lybeaus arose, along with his noble fame] (Lambeth Palace 306 version, 714–16).

The fight against the giant is lifted almost directly from Geoffrey and Wace (the desolate setting, the fire, the roasting boar, the abduction and rape), but *Lybeaus Desconus* brings the episode to a new extreme: not only does the number of giants double (one for each kind of appetite), but the hero who fights them does not even know who has fathered him, what proper name designates his own body. The defeat of the chromatic monsters and the display of their heads at court is an important step toward the recovery of that name—or, better, toward the full coincidence of Lybeaus Desconus's body with the signification that the proper name "Gingelein, son of Gawain" encodes. Identification and differentiation structure the gigantomachia, and heroic embodiment is its outcome. The circulation of the severed heads publicly traces the widening gyre of Lybeaus's enlarged identity.

Just as the Lacanian mirror stage in the impossibility of its full success is its own guarantee that "Boschian monsters" will continue to haunt the embodied subject, fights against giants in romance are never a final victory. Having slain the giant Arrok, the guardian of the great hart demanded by the earl of Artois, Eglamour must next defeat the monster's brother Maras. This giant is intent on abducting the maiden Organata, and the knight dismembers him to prove that his sexuality is more tightly bounded the monster's. Immediately after Lybeaus has finally proven himself to his beloved Arthur and been inducted into the fellowship of the Round Table, he sets off from the court again in search of new adventures—as if to prove Carolyn Dinshaw's Auerbachian thesis that knighthood, like gender identity, is performative: "The behavior that makes a knight is intensely rule-governed; it proceeds either as a game or in the form of a game—tournaments, quests, courtship" ("A Kiss Is Just a Kiss," 213).[22] Repetition compulsion: the knight who, like Yvain, settles down with a wife in a comfortable castle ceases to be the protagonist of his narrative; the story ends when the performance of his identity finds a stable, stagnant resting place. Not surprisingly, the first episode of this second stage to Lybeaus's chivalric career is a battle against a *geaunt*, this time the dreaded Maugys. In a liminal, sublime place called in one manuscript the "Ylle d'Ore" ("Isle of Gold," Cotton 1269) and in another the "Jle Dolour" ("Sad Isle," Lambeth 1331), Lybeaus utters a speech that cites Arthur's battle at Mont Saint Michel and David's encounter with Goliath (1323–28). A reference to a falling oak tree is stolen from Geoffrey of Monmouth's epic simile in the *Historia*, and a delight in proportional contrast is taken from medieval treatments of the "child David" narrative. Lybeaus positions himself as both Galfridian hero and Christian *nanus contra gigantem*. The gigantomachia proceeds in the usual way: the monster verbally probes the knight's identity ("Tell me whate arte thowe!" 1343); Lybeaus asserts himself in return ("Kynge Arthure made me knyght / . . . thow deuyll black!" 1348–50); the performance is marked as public ("lordis and ladyes" gather "For-to se that syght"); the battle has theologic undertones ("Crysten knyght" versus an infidel who relies on the Saracen god "Turmagaunte"); the giant kills the knight's horse (he "dasshid oute the brayne") so that both fight on foot; the two bodies bleed as they are torn by wounds. After a long struggle, the monster is beheaded, and the remnant is ritually displayed: "He bare the hede in-to the towne; / With fayre processyoune / The folk come hym agayne" [He bore the head into the town with a fair procession. The folk came

75

out to meet him] (1458–60). *Lybeaus Desconus* provides the essence of the romance gigantomachia. One scene even rewrites an episode from *Guy of Warwick*, perhaps the single most important insular rendition of the romance battle against the giant. Lybeaus requests a temporary halt to the fighting so that he can have a drink of water from a nearby river. The giant agrees but attacks the knight the moment he steps out of his protective armor. Lybeaus, like Guy, takes the opportunity to give Maugys an impromptu baptism, and the battle wages on. The episode is formulaic, its repetition of traditional structures reverent.[23]

If the exhibition of the severed head is called public, like the decapitation by ax stroke after which the executioner holds high the severed part and announces, "Behold the head of a traitor!"[24] then we might rightly wonder who the observing public is, and what lesson they are supposed to learn from the display. Besides its frame audience of those within the narrative who watch and comment on the events, romance has its historical audience, its reading and listening public. Although reconstructing a listenership for the genre is notoriously difficult, it is generally conceded that at least one of its earliest addressees was the *juvenes*, the landless knights who were a perpetual worry to the medieval courts.[25] Clerical literature on the disruptive activities of this warrior class is fairly extensive. Peter of Blois, court chaplain to the same king who oversaw Wace's translation of Geoffrey's *Historia*, complained in a letter to Archdeacon John that "they plunder and despoil the poor servants of Christ, and, what is worse, they oppress mercilessly the wretched and satiate [*impleant*] with the pain of others their own forbidden pleasures [*illicitos appetitus*] and unnatural desires [*extraordinarias voluptates*]." The verb *implere* covers a range of somatic significations that includes "to fill one's desire," "to fatten, to make fleshy," and "to impregnate." These are the sins of gigantism, associated not just with a social disorder written in corporeal terms but specifically with the central bodily focus of the monster's consumptive drive, the mouth:

> Today the order of knighthood (*ordo militum*) consists of not keeping order (*ordinem non tenere*). For he who most pollutes his mouth with filthy words (*cujus os majore verborum spurcitia polluitur*), who swears most abominably, who fears God the least . . . that man is today considered the bravest and most renowned among the knights. . . . They are enfeebled by gluttony.[26]

No wonder, then, that the late-thirteenth-century *Dialogue de Placides et Timéo* connects the founding of chivalry with the biblical giant Nimrod, denying essential difference between knights and their antagonists to discredit chivalry as an ethical stance. Despairing of ever asserting the kind of control over knighthood that Bernard of Clairvaux had once dreamed, the clerical author wrote that from their monstrous founding father, knights have learned the skills of homicide, extortion, and unprovoked violence. The "heroic" code exists, he complained, only to justify their satisfying their every desire *par forche et par soutieuté et par couvoitise.*[27] The giant is the prehistory of the chivalric body, a monstrous origin that the romance gigantomachia publicly disavows, and that contemporaneous clerical writing reinscribes as the past and present of martial masculinity.

The line between gigantism and knighthood is thin and frequently trespassed. Nowhere is this dangerous porousness better illustrated than in Chrétien de Troyes's late-twelfth-century romance *Le Chevalier au lion* (*Yvain*), which contains one of the earliest depictions of the gigantomachia. The monstrous Harpin de la Montagne (Harpin of the Mountain) has besieged a hapless lord, desiring both his material possessions and his beautiful daughter. Two of the lord's sons have been murdered, and the giant intends to slay the other four, unless a champion can be found to defeat him. When the giant arrives at the lord's castle with his kidnapped sons in chains, he shouts that he intends to give the nobleman's daughter to his lackeys [garçonaille] to be their whore [jaelise] so that they—"all covered with lice and naked" [poeilleus et nu]—could shame her repeatedly (ed. and trans. Kibler, 4115–26). Harpin's threat is a double menace to the continuance of the aristocracy: the destruction of a family's sons, the lifeblood of patrilineal culture, and the grossly magnified public corruption of the daughter's virginity, destroying her open-market value as marrigeable commodity. Yvain's consenting to fight the giant on the lord's behalf sets into motion a clash of bifurcated representations, one of aristocratic and one of monstrous masculinity. Harpin battles against Yvain with a club, the stock weapon of the romance giant and an unrefined armament bluntly opposed to proper knighthood's keen-edged sword. Yvain, following a secular version of Saint Paul's dictum, is dressed in the armor of chivalric faith and sustains no bloody wounds, while the giant trusts to sheer might and is engored. When Yvain's pet lion leaps at the giant, he attempts to squash both the animal and its master with his club but falls short. Yvain seizes the opportunity to sever Harpin's head from his shoulders.

In the copious body of Harpin de la Montagne is condensed the sexual perversity (sexual expression *is* sexual perversion in the romances), anarchic violence, disregard for authority and its world-ordering hierarchies, and the gross, boundary-breaking appetite that characterize the giant of romance. He is similar in these traits to the giant in Wace's *Brut*, Dinabuc, who in turn is based on Geoffrey of Monmouth's giant of Mont Saint Michel. And yet there is much about him that is eerily different from those giants familiar from the chronicle traditions, something disconcertingly more human. Claude Lecouteux, in his essay "Harpin de la Montagne," declares roundly that "un géant n'a pas de valets" [A giant does not have valets] 221), and he argues that Harpin's household of servants renders him a seigneur rather than a monster. Lecouteux interprets Harpin allegorically, as a parvenu who has purchased a seigneury and usurped the title of chevalier (225). The Harpin episode becomes a tale of class conflict in which the giant represents the threat perceived by the nobility from the growing wealth and power of the boorish bourgeoisie.

Lecouteux finds Harpin to be too human and therefore in need of explanation. He is disturbed by the fact that Harpin rides a horse, even though numerous giants of romance both own and ride such steeds. He refuses to see the romance giant as anything but something Other—except in Harpin's case. Yet *all* giants at their base are human representations, despite their haunting alterity; from this admixture springs their power. Giants arise from human populations, the offspring of demonic couplings with women; or they are monsterized Saracens, who for all their disturbing distortions were recognized as essentially human. Vast differences separate Harpin from Spenser's insubstantial Orgoglio. Chrétien's giant is not a vehicle for pure allegory; he is part of something larger, something that is at once harder to ascertain and yet more firmly anchored in the historical real. Lecouteux is right in one thing, however. Harpin is a knight, just like Yvain. Both *géant* and chevalier live by force; their superiority is connected to their physical strength, and their life is defined by their relationship to other bodies within a hierarchy that gives them meaning. The knight is necessary to preserve order, and yet he poses an immense danger if he himself cannot be adequately controlled by the systems of power that have produced him. That the temptation within fighting classes was to live a life of sensual gratification and to express even in times of peace that combative aggressiveness in which they had been trained is amply attested to by ecclesiastical writers who, like Peter of Blois, recorded their fear and distrust of the warrior class. Chivalry was promulgated as a way of living one's life to try to prevent it from being lived in any other way. It was a vitally necessary delineation of acceptable social conduct, a control mechanism masquerading as a code of ethics. Chivalry prevents the knight from becoming the giant that he always, in a way, already is.[28]

Even Peter of Blois realized the relation of desire that unites the idealized representations of romance to the imperfect masculine bodies its behavorial code would tranform. Peter described his less-than-heroic knights as enraptured by depictions (*imaginaria visione*) of battles that they never in reality would have the heart to join.[29] Medievalists have long recognized that romance has an ideological function. Its narratives were promulgated in part to propagate the idealized masculinities clustered under the term "chivalry," in order to engender properly docile subjects. Although mainly a literary and historical fantasy, the chivalric code was also intended as a system of social control. Lee Patterson has accurately observed that knighthood was not simply a vocation that young men elected, but "their very mode of being, an ideological conditioning that precludes critical self-reflection because it wholly conditions self-construction."[30] Maurice Keen labels "literary influence, direct and indirect," on chivalry-as-behavior "powerful,"[31] and Joachim Bumke observes that

> the courtly ideal of knighthood was also meant as an appeal to live up to it. The poetic descriptions...wanted also to influence social practices. Whether they succeeded in doing so is difficult to determine. We can indicate, however, those spheres of real life where the idealized demands were used as practical guidelines. That was the case especially in the education of young noblemen. (*Courtly Culture*, 312)

Romance was a literature that created a mode of being, transubstantiating social reality. Tournaments, the arena for the public performance of chivalric subjectivity, were profoundly altered by romance representation. Once a dirty, vicious, and mainly private combat where knights killed each other for material gain, tournaments were transformed through the agency of romance into a public theater of good conduct, extravagant gesture, and bodily control.[32] As a result, those games that were once outlawed as dangerous to the public order became a spectacle useful, even essential, for a monarch to materialize his power over his subjects by performing a well-regulated, microcosmic vision of macrocosmic harmony.

Since the romance authors believed that they could have a formative, even transfigurative effect on their audiences, it seems natural to speak of the genre as a culturally engaged practice, connected in its genesis to containment, corporeal governance, and the construction of sexual identity. The bodily control (heterosexual monogamy, channeling of aggression) and respect for patriarchy that the romances envision was meant to ensure smoother societal functioning by redirecting the forces of violent male conflict. The audience of young knights are intended to admire and emulate the romance hero, to desire the same self-realization that he desires. The hero's textual coming of age serves as an idealized model for the male audience's own straight and narrow passage to adulthood. Overcoming, defining, asserting, and promulgating are all built in to the same ritual and its gestures, a complex of structures that give a social meaning to desire, and a heroic embodiment to the chivalric subject.

Beheading scenes are at once a prod to the adoption of properly aligned behaviors and a vicarious journey to their attainment. The defeat of the monster inscribes the romance compulsion to restraint, especially to sexual restraint, and the spoils of battle valorize a heterosexuality that is nearly celibate; at the same time, the fragmentation of the giant usually leads to inclusion among the homosociety of mentors, the fraternity of the Round Table. As Bruno Bettelheim points out of initiation rites generally, they are structured in such a way that "afterward, each person must settle down permanently to the single behavior assigned to his sex" (*Symbolic Wounds*, 62). A textual side effect of this method of straightened, narrowed definition *against* is the monsterization of feminine sexuality, with its other possibilities and allures. The bifurcating process of assertion explains in part the repeated linking of women with monsters and monstrous appetite in the medieval West.

Cannibal Poetics and Somatic Morphogenesis

Hannibal Lecter, the sadist/mastermind psychiatrist from Thomas Harris' serial-killer novels (The Red Dragon, Silence of the Lambs), *is the closest mass culture can get to the figure of the Lacanian analyst.*
— Slavoj Zizek, *Enjoy Your Symptom*, 67

The conclusion of Geoffrey of Monmouth's *Historia* stages what would now be called a postcolonial moment. The invading Saxons are triumphantly converting the island into their permanent dominion. The glory days of the British are vanishing to a heroic past and a prophesied, distant future. King Cadwallo has been stranded on the island of Guernsey, and his enemy Edwin has managed to keep him from his realm. A storm has destroyed many of his men, and now the king becomes "so filled with grief and anger" that he refuses to eat. His nephew Brian discovers that his lord longs for wild game and sets off with his bow. Finding nothing in the woods with which to nourish his sick uncle, young Brian carves a chunk of flesh from his own thigh: "He made a spit, cooked the meat, and took it to the King, pretending it was venison." Cadwallo savors the sweet taste and regains his health, the wind picks up, and the British army escapes the island to do battle against the Saxons (*History of the Kings of Britain*, 272–73). Christ so loved the world that he sacrificed his own body for its redemption; Brian so loves his king that he offers himself in a secular Eucharist, lovingly nourishing an ancient social structure with his youthful flesh.

The medieval *corpus* is frequently the body in peril. Its integrity is under constant threat not just by the law of the prevailing regime (the public spectacle of the criminal body: floggings, hangings, burnings, brandings) but also by exorbitant enemies, real and imagined (Saracens who circumcise their captives against their will, monsters such as the Donestre who dismember hapless travelers to foreign lands).[33] These fragmented bodies no doubt encode all kinds of anxieties about the limits and fragility of self-identity, especially when this fear is displaced to the unknown margins of the world; such anxiety is especially true for the numerous stories that circulated about cannibalism. As the intrepid explorer Sir John Mandeville is making his way through distant terra incognita, he encounters an island of thirty-foot giants who wade into the surrounding waters whenever a ship passes, snatching two men in each hand and "etynge hem goynge all raw & quyk" [eating them on the run, all raw and living] (ed. P. Hamelius, 190/5–6). Yet the anthropophagy in the Cadwallo-Brian episode is of a different order. The sacrifice of the boy's flesh is admirable rather than anxiety provoking. Brian suffers no lingering effects from slicing a steak from his thigh. Shortly thereafter, he is infiltrating the Saxon court, where he is repeatedly victorious in battle. By making a gift to the monarch of his own substance, Brian transcends the merely corporeal and becomes a hero. Kings may sometimes be cannibals in medieval representation—and occasionally, like Richard I, they devour human bodies knowingly and with gusto.[34] Ordinarily, however, that role is fulfilled via negative example by a monster, such as the giant, whose desire to consume or destroy the bodies of his victims illustrates some truth of identity within the text. Cadwallo as cannibal transforms the meaning of anthropophagy through a blissful rejuvenation. At the same time, the monarch unwittingly plays the role of Mandeville's "geauntes" or Dinabuc at Mont Saint Michel, suggesting that the functions of king (as incarnation of a legitimate system of power and identity) and giant (as its antithesis) are often two entwined supports of the same systemization of masculine embodiment.

The giant appears in romance because the *instance* (agency, insistence) of the monster precipitates full heroic identity, and he recurs because he threatens constantly to ingest this thing he helps to produce. Since he signifies desire prior to its full social coding, appetite before (or read back from) its limit, the giant teaches the medieval *juvenis* how to become a man, a process that biologically and culturally transfigures the flesh. The giant is enmeshed in the romance process of embodiment as a haunting, originary point as well as a constant, intimately strange limit to its selfhood, troubling the chivalric subject as a reminder of his contingency, his fragility, his gigantism.

"They wear the mask of Lancelot and of Tristan. It is an amazing self-deception."[35] The words belong to Johan Huizinga, whose *Waning of the Middle Ages* was among the first works to theorize medieval chivalry. These words could as easily have been written by Lacan, to describe the *méconnaissance* that allows bodies to occupy some pre-given position within the symbolic or discursive world of human meaning and identity, and to read their selfhood back from that mask or armor.[36] Lacan's description of the subject's lifelong battle for a coherent "I" could not have been written had romance been a less culturally formative genre, for his narrative owes everything to its conventions:

> The formation of the *I* is symbolized in dreams by a fortress, or a stadium—its inner arena and enclosure, surrounded by marshes and rubbish-tips, dividing into two opposed fields of contest where the subject flounders in quest of the lofty, remote inner castle. ("Mirror Stage," *Écrits*, 5)

In this fantasy, the "lofty, remote inner castle" will protect the subject's selfhood by immuring it at last behind strong walls, banishing forever the drive to follow "mobile desires," replacing their trajectory of *becoming* with the immobile certitude of simply *being*. All heroes, having defeated the giant who embodies the multiple desires that could cause a coherent body to disaggregate, end their lives in these placidly transcendent places. Such is the powerfully attractive promise of the genre. That this retirement to a castle in the suburbs should be the familiar ending of both medieval romance and twentieth-century psychoanalytic theories of identity formation is hardly surprising, since romance precipitates a "chivalric subject" not so very different from that troubled, divided, contradictory, alienated, but somehow supremely self-confident figure now called the capitalist individual.

The autonomous individual so dear to mercantile mythology and romance heroism alike is always in danger of being cannibalized, absorbed back into the system that grants it a subjectivity along with the illusion of independence. In Geoffrey's story about Cadwallo and Brian, the heroic youth offers his body so that the regulatory ideal that the king embodies might be sustained. The episode writes across the flesh a process on which all martial cultures depend: in order for battles to be fought and won, young men must be made willing to sacrifice their own bodies to ensure the endurance of the structure of power that their activity undergirds. Medieval political theory was obsessed with the metaphorical correspondence between the individual body and the social corpus, so that John of Salisbury could write in his *Policratus* (1159) that "the state [*res publica*] is a body [*corpus quoddam*]," its head is the prince [*princeps*], and each member of the commonwealth is a member of the body; the warrior class [*officales et milites*], for example, are the hands.[37] When the social hierarchy is readable as a corporeal order, the imposition of that structuration is, of necessity, a cannibal poetics.

The fight against the giant in romance furthers this correspondence between social bodies that ingest in order to regulate and the well-ordered "private" bodies that are the outcome of this systemization. The knight defeats in the giant those nonteleological desires that, when read back through the cultural matrix of chivalry, represent every vice that must be evacuated to construct both the orderly Socius and the properly gendered hero. The social body as gigantic and amalgamative corpus and the giant as gross and anthropophagous body are not so very different. To keep the Socius and its giant other distinct, a contradictory myth must be promulgated. According to this corporeal ideology, any part of the social body (the hands, for example) is *both* a controlled member of the balanced whole (the hands wield the sword only as the head directs) and at the same time a miniaturized version of that whole, a microcosmic body that moves through a world of infinite possibility, without any constraint except the "self-chosen" regulation that produces the autonomous subject. This internally discongruous body is the product of a regulatory regime, having fully internalized both the prohibitions and the contradictions that are its precondition. The impossibly split subject is at once *un corps morcelé*, a fragment of a greater body (the *ordo militum* as the hands of the social corpus) and an individuated whole (the chivalric hero whose will is efficacious, who exists quite apart from social determination or constraint). Another way of putting it: the chivalric subject is a "form of selfhood insistently, even exclusively public" that "ignored the merely personal or individual"; it is also a mode of embodiment and subjectivization obsessed with "personal worth," so that "chivalry tended to privatize all historical action" (Patterson, *Chaucer and the Subject of History*, 168, 175). Patterson concentrates his analysis on the first component of the chivalric subject, knighthood as public form; similarly, Susan Crane argues that "the term *hero*, with its implications of isolating uniqueness and autonomy, is not fully appropriate to [romance's] strongly interdependent identities" (*Gender and Romance*, 28). Even if "identity is finally in the gift of the community" (29), even if identity (as Marx, Lacan, Crane, and Patterson insist) is *public, contextual,* and *relational,* nonetheless romance and chivalry refuse to speak that knowledge. Their subjects depend on their communities for their selfhood, but they perform their heroism as if they were unconstrained, as if their individuality were self-determined, as if their movement through the world were the freely willed choice to live their lives exactly in the way they are socially constructed to exemplarize them. Chivalry is a mode of being that hinges on a fantastic originary moment when a "spontaneous" decision to self-regulation was made by its adherents. Knights and heroes choose the chivalric life not because they already owe their identities to it (even if they always do) but rather because, in order for it to be a culturally useful act, the assumption of the armor of chivalry must be represented as already having been chosen, and therefore necessary to insistently perform.

The chivalric hero represents a kind of hypermasculinity, an exaggerated and idealized version of maleness that is promulgated with a social intention: ordinary men of the middle and upper classes are to measure themselves against the impossible standard that the hero embodies and from this conditioned inadequacy strive to fight harder and control themselves better. No human body can actually occupy the impossible space of knighthood's inhuman ideals, and so these same bodies can be compelled to repeat its theatrical rituals through the promise of the possibility of one day coinciding with the permanence that chivalry's fictive models offer. The chivalric subject continues to perform chivalry as a way of continually producing himself. Danger occurs only when the lure to desire is not strong enough to keep the bodily performance in motion.

The cultural regulation upon which a discipline such as chivalry insists is not, as it may at first appear, the antithesis of "freedom." Rather, the *possibility* (rather than the *actuality*) of choice is the best catalyst to self-regulation, as the infinite multiplication of choice and consequent dwindling of possibilities in late-twentieth-century consumer society suggest. The subject interpellated by chivalry—the subject who recognizes himself as the addressee of this class-based ideology—cannot really choose *not* to live up to knighthood's performative demands: willful nonalignment dooms him to cultural illegibility, to the monster's accursed share. Chivalric freedom is the liberty to fashion oneself into the very thing one is already caught in the process of becoming, of what one is already being socially produced as. The ultimate incommensurability of these two modes of being, public and private, is submerged so effectively beneath the hypnotic glimmer of chivalric selfhood that this very contradiction in its continued vanishing beneath that spectacular surface is what ensured chivalry's longevity.[38] Chivalry works as an ideological system because it is able to submerge its foundational contradictions beneath a powerful visual lure (its own theatricality) at the same time as it offers a disavowed remnant of obscene enjoyment, clinging to the body of the monster (the "maw" [*ingluvies*] that offers an approach toward some "forbidden domain," of "meaning permeated with enjoyment, a Lacanian *jouis-sense*").[39]

Chivalry imagines a world where perfect self-fashioning is synonymous with historical necessity. By becoming the best possible knight, the romance hero ensures that everyone lives in the best possible world. His every action, no matter how secret and selfish, is public and altruistic. What the chivalric hero and the free-market capitalist share is this same intrinsic contradiction: both perform under the sign of autonomous individuality, of efficacious self-will, while coming into being through a system that allows them an identity only through their constrained relation to an externally imposed economy of desires—an economy inscribed into their very flesh, at the processes of their embodiment. Both modes of subjectivity are inherently individualistic. Autonomy is allowed only to an exceptional few (the successful capitalist, the victorious hero), and through a deterministic theology ("market forces," "heroic destiny") denied wholly to those outside its possibility (laborers, "monsters"—in both cases, a class distinction obtains). And yet this selfishness is inscribed through the logic of aristocratic mandate or trickle-down economics as a universal good.

The fight against the giant stages this subjectivating moment in romance. Its successful outcome is the simultaneously docile and heroic, integral and split chivalric subject. The defeat of the giant is a social fantasy of the triumph of corporeal order (in all of its various meanings) written as a personal drama, a vindication of the tight channeling of multiple somatic drives into a socially beneficial expression of masculinity. It is not enough simply to kill the giant, however; the aberrant body must be decapitated, *fully rebuked.* Of the head, Isidore of Seville wrote:

The first part of the body is the head, and it received this name, *caput*, because all the feelings and nerves [*sensus omnes et nervi*] have their origin there [*initium capiunt*] and because all the wellsprings of strength emanate from it.[40]

The head is the seat of the soul, the biological and allegorical ruler of the lower limbs. In its absence, the body (social or personal) is *acephalic*, undifferentiated. At the moment when the giant's head is displayed and the ritual of defeat enacted, the hero announces that masculinity has been restored to its proper somatic order. The *corps morcelé* as represented through the *membra disjecta* of the giant is rejected for the tightly regulated, hierarchized social body that the hero embodies in its small form. The staged rejection is visually powerful enough to make its witnesses look past its provisionality, the impossibility of its permanence: the decapitation ritual as Geoffrey of Monmouth formulated it, the infinitely repeating trap for the gaze. This is Freud's family romance, but here as written by the father, with a father's wished-for ending. The possibility of rebellion is itself sentenced to death, and the good son joins the body of patriarchs. The story is set to repeat.

Bodies and Pleasures

The body is also directly involved in a political field; power relations have an immediate hold upon it; they invest it, mark it, train it, torture it, force it to carry out tasks, to perform ceremonies, to emit signs. . . . The body becomes a useful force only if it is both a productive and a subjected body.

—Michel Foucault, *Discipline and Punish*

In the Christian iconography of the Middle Ages, the *nanus contra gigantem* ("youth against the giant") topos originated in the David and Goliath story is frequently repeated as a foundational religious moment that prefigures the defeat of Satan by Christ.[41] Goliath therefore became the quintessential wicked giant. Allegorized into a type for the devil, reviled for a wide spectrum of crimes never hinted at in the short biblical episode, he was by the time of the patristic commentators an embodiment of all that is unacceptable to Christian identity. His body a vast compendium of the deadly sins, overdetermined and wickedly fascinating, Goliath was—not surprisingly—quickly assimilated into the romance tradition of gigantism. In an illustration from the Visconti Hours, he grasps not the expected sword of the biblical narrative but a club, the inevitable weapon of the giant of medieval romance. Indeed, so powerful was romance as an epistemological phenomenon, as a way of organizing reality, that it transformed the narrativization of the biblical episode from which it took one of its origins. The vernacular rendition of world history known as the *Cursor Mundi*, despite the harsh condemnation of romance with which it begins, depicts the David and Goliath episode only through that disavowed genre's conventions. Whereas the Bible offers no physical description of Goliath, the giant of the *Cursor Mundi* is huge and ugly. Close attention is paid to the various enjoyments he embodies: he eats seven sheep every time he dines (gluttony); he is begotten "in fule hordom" (lechery); he swears by "Mahun" as if he were a Saracen (blasphemy, the sin of the mouth that lacks control). When David is dressed in Saul's armor, he cannot move even a step; the battle is preceded by an elaborate flyting; close attention is paid to the breaking of the giant's body (verbal and somatic sadism). The culminating moment of the narrative occurs when David presents the severed head to Saul, announcing his resolute identity against the king's own prohibitive desires (*Cursor Mundi*, Cotton MS version, ed. Richard Morris, 7439–7592).

Just how much was at stake in controlling the signification of the giant and the enjoyment that he figures can be glimpsed outside the chivalric milieu in the case of the Goliards, who took their name from a mythical "bishop" or "mentor" whom they named Golias, Latin for "Goliath."[42] Gregory, in his important exegesis of Job, had emphasized the fallen nature of the giants, heavily buttressing his argument with a pastiche of scriptural quotation.[43] His allegorical conception of the monsters as types for prideful men was frequently reiterated throughout the Middle Ages, eliminating the need for too much worry about the giant's real, historical presence as recorded in the Bible, the landscape, and secular history. The Goliards, however, would have none of this patristic seriousness. Their namesake had been made to embody everything that *Christianitas* abjects from its center to construct itself as a transtemporal, transgeographical collective entity. Because of his perverse associations, his alignment with the pleasures of the "private" body, Goliath also became the vehicle of an elaborate communal fantasy. The self-designated Goliardic Order was composed primarily of bored university students (studying, of course, to become clerics), now applying some of their inculcated Latin composition skills to inventing verses that praised love, food, and drink; some went further and extolled lust, gluttony, and drunkenness. In true schoolboy fashion, they wrote elaborate parodies of the sober ecclesiastical hymns and ceremonies. The hymn "Deus sit propitius huic peccatori" ("God have mercy on this sinner") became "Deus sit propitius huic potatori" ("God have mercy on this sot"). Rules requiring indulgence of all kinds were invented for the Goliards, but the order's existence continued to be more a wistful fiction than an actual brotherhood. The orthodox church eventually grew nervous at the challenge to its own version of what the bodies of giants signify, and at the celebration of these forbidden enjoyments. Anonymous works such as the *Apocalypse of Golias* suddenly appeared, in which the mythical bishop confessed his sins and condemned his evil ways. Golias was simultaneously acknowledged to exist and reinvented. This newly produced version of the giant supplanted the carnival vision of the Goliards: rebellion silenced by its own words, as the category "Goliard" is produced to make inhabiting that category impossible. The valence of Golias was quickly and successfully changed back to the negative, a silencing as effective as any beheading scene could be.[44]

The Goliards began to appear in the twelfth century, at about the same time that the first romances were being written. This imagined community might best be considered the clerical counterpart to the romance obsession with giants. Goliath's body may have been evacuated of the possibility of enjoyment, but romance ensured that some sticky residue of pleasure would continue to adhere to its giants, no matter how many times it staged their demise. Indeed, that very death in its insistent repetition enlivened that very *jouissance* it condemned to fragmentation.

Given that they are meant to act as catalysts to "real-world" identification, beheading scenes fail unless they can offer a site of *enjoyment* and *investment*, perform a ritual that *fascinates* and *traps* the gaze, and finally *redirect that desire through a particular mode of embodiment*. For the fight against the giant to perform its cultural work, it must become saturated with desire. So popular did these monstrous encounters become that the episodes often took on a life of their own. Guy of Warwick, for example, fights two giants in the course of the long romance that bears his name; each of these battles was eventually excerpted and circulated as a separate work. Guy spends the first part of the romance inventing himself as a worldly hero, a process he is ultimately not very good at: his worst mistake is to kill the son of the earl Florentine, a rash act that leaves the shadow of the grieving father hanging over much of the story.[45] In the conversion narrative that follows Guy's culminating defeat of the dragon, Guy speaks the wrongs he has committed as he sought the glory of secular heroism: "I haue many a man slane, / Abbeys brente and cytees tane . . . / I haue done mekyll schame" [I have slain many men, burnt many abbeys, seized cities. . . . I have done much shame] (7162–64, 7177–78).[46] Manslaughter, trespass, pillaging: these are the sins of gigantism. In the second movement of the romance, Guy forsakes this tainted identity by purging monstrousness from his body. He sets off for Jerusalem to become a martial saint, the next transfigurative plateau of heroic selfhood. This change in the hero's identity is conveyed by a change in meter, from couplets to tail-rhyme, as if the *textus* of the romance and the corpus of its hero were the same.[47]

In the Holy Land, Guy battles the "blake sarzine" [black Saracen] Amourant, a giant. Guy fights on behalf of a father whose youthful son has committed a crime very similar to the one Guy himself committed, and who will be put to death unless a champion redeems him. Guy agrees to engage Amourant to exorcise the ghost of the earl Florentine, last seen grieving over "hys sone, that was dedde" by Guy's hand.[48] Amourant is a monster from Egypt, the exotic East, who seems "as it were a fende, /

þat comen were out of helle" (62.11–12). This giant is described as a kind of visual blot, impossible to look at long enough to describe well:

> For ȝif he loked on þe wiþ wrake
> Sternliche wiþ his eyȝen blake,
>   So grim he is of siȝt,
> Wastow neuer so bold in al þe teime,
> þatow durst batayl of him nim,
>   No hold oȝaines him fiȝt. (76.7–11)

[For if he looked on you with anger, sternly with his black eyes, so grim he is to see that no matter how bold you have been in the past, you won't dare wage battle on him, nor fight against him.]

Amourant wears armor against Guy, carries the civilized weapons of lance and sword rather than a club, and even rides a horse. This giant is rather closer to the human than his Galfridian forefather on Mont Saint Michel; he stands, after all, only four feet taller than ordinary men, not the usual English estimation of thirty feet in toto. Yet for all his proximity to humanity, his Herculean sword has been bathed in hellfire (99.1), and he is frequently referred to as a "glouton," a good translation of Geoffrey's *ingluvies* that invokes his giant's nature as a creature of orality and appetite. The culminating scene of the battle occurs when Guy, who has been fighting incognito, announces his true identity to the giant and then dismembers him. The head Guy carries to King Triamour, on whose behalf he has been engaged. The monarch then sends the trophy to the sultan whose army had been attacking his lands. The circuit of the severed head traces the path of masculine indebtedness in the romance, inscribing Guy at the top of the new hierarchy. The fight against Amourant is Guy's religious rite de passage, the signal that his transformation from mundane to sanctified heroism is complete. His glorious triumph over the monster enables the liberation and vindication of his captive friends, as well as the conversion of the Muslims for whom he fought (87.4–88.12).

The amalgamative dilations of Guy's selfhood continue when he returns to England. In a culminating third movement to the symphony of his identity, he becomes a national hero.[49] This political coming of age is much like Arthur's transformation atop Mont Saint Michel. The bellicose Norseman Anlaf of Denmark has invaded the island and brought with him the African giant Colbrond "stout & grim" (235.7–10). Guy agrees to champion the king and engages against the monster, who arrives at the battlefield pulling a cart piled high with arms ("þe Inglisse for to quelle," 255.10), tokens of his superabundant Anglophobic aggression. Just as the battle between the Philistines and Israelites was enacted in narrative miniature by the encounter of Goliath and David, here the war between the opposing Danish and English forces is condensed into a formalized duel between Colbrond and Guy. Although the audience's expectation of the outcome is not defeated, the battle is prolonged and delivers serious wounds to both parties before the giant is dismembered and beheaded in the usual way. The head, a Gorgon's remnant of the defeated giant, terrifies the invading Danes and sends them fleeing from the land, leaving England safe for nationhood.

Colbrond, like the aboriginal giants of Geoffrey's *Historia,* was successfully used for nationalistic ends in a series of appropriations. Guy's triumph over the giant had occurred, after all, during the reign of Athelstan, the hero of the Battle of Brunanburg; when absorbed into the chronicle tradition, the battle against Colbrond smoothed over the differences between Anglo-Saxon England and its now fully integrated Norman conquerors, narrativizing as continuous a history marked by disjunction. Likewise, Guy's adventures originally seem to have had nothing to do with the earls of Warwick, but after he was invented, this house "adopted" him as heroic ancestor and instigated a centuries-long project of reifying his history (Fewster, *Traditionality and Genre,* 106–7). Local topography was transformed into a landscape baptized by romance as places such as "Guy's Cliff" sprung into being to parallel the "Gogmagog's Leap" of Geoffrey's history.[50] Guy's existence was made material, and his memory was perpetuated by the display of his armor and other relics at Warwick Castle, where they can still be admired.[51] That Guy was supposed to be renowned eventually made him so, especially as the influence of the house of Warwick waxed under the Beauchamps. The ultimate construction of Guy's heroism, however, is coterminous with the assertion of *communal* English cultural supremacy, with the promulgation of nationalism. Heroic attention is fastened at the end of the story on what one late-nineteenth-century scholar was still calling Guy's "proud claim to English fatherhood" (Morrill, *Speculum Gy,* xiii).

The battle against Colbrond enjoyed tremendous popularity and was repeatedly extracted from its encasing romance. The circulation of the episode illustrates well the cultural demand for repetitions of the gigantomachia. In 1338 the minstrel Herebertus sang a piece entitled the "canticum Colbrondi" ("song of Colbrond") in the hall of St. Swithin's (L. Loomis, *Medieval Romance,* 131). Gerard of Cornwall translated the battle into Latin prose, which Lydgate later transformed into a stanzaic poem of his own. A painting of the gigantomachia once adorned the north transept of Winchester cathedral.[52] In the Percy Folio manuscript, the battle sequence forms a stanzaic poem, *Guy and Colbrand,* which amplifies the gigantomachia to 636 fast-moving lines.[53] This retelling absorbs all of the detail of the Guy and Amourant fight, including Guy's generosity to that giant when he thirsted during battle, enlarging the significance of the encounter. Here, too, Guy beheads the giant with an ax rather than a sword, as if he were the giant-slicing hero of *Sir Gawain and Green Knight* or *Sir Gawain and the Carl of Carlisle.*

By the fourteenth century, the battle of Guy and Colbrond had been fully absorbed into historical tradition as a foundational episode in English history. Guy's birth into national heroism in his fight against the giant Colbrond was interpreted as the moment when England assumed its full national identity, and this formulation of insular history held sway until late in the Renaissance (L. Loomis, *Medieval Romance,* 127). Thus the *Anonymous Short English Metrical Chronicle,* bound in the Auchinleck manuscript with the earliest English version of *Guy,* declares that in Athelstan's time, Guy of Warwick "for Engelond dude batail / With a geaunt gret" [for England did battle against a huge giant] (596–97). This little fragment of English history powerfully condenses a burgeoning nationalistic pride into a cameo miniature: Guy fights the giant Colbrond, and English destiny unfolds — a historiographic picture worth a thousand romance words. The list of chroniclers who describe Guy's gigantomachia is immense: Robert Mannyng of Brunne, Hearne, Knighton, Rudborne, Hardyng, Rous, Fabyan, Grafton, Stow, Dugdale, Holinshed. These authors generally began their histories with a discussion of Gogmagog (or Albion, as he was sometimes called after being confused with the myth of Albin's settlement), and so Guy's battle with Colbrond gained the same historical importance as Brutus's defeat of the island's native monsters. England comes of age with the monsters it invents.

Slasher films and video games may owe their genesis to the leisured adolescent males of the late twentieth century, but these young men are certainly not their sole consumers. Likewise, the *juvenes* who caused so much trouble at the courts during the twelfth and thirteenth centuries may have been a catalyst to the promulgation of romance, but the genre claimed a wide readership that cut across gender and class lines. These changes in audience became especially evident during the fourteenth century. The nobility steadily lost economic hegemony as the mercantile class expanded its ranks and influence; political power, meanwhile, continued to be solidified in the crown. Susan Crane argues that these two forces prodded the aristocracy to adopt an identity predicated on cultural rather than military superiority: "The prestige of a complex courtly ethos seemed to replace the barony's eroded economic and political power with cultural power" (*Insular Romance,* 176). As a result, royal control was further facilitated, and "the higher strata of commoners" found terrain they could share with the nobility: "England's fluid social categories permitted the literature and history of courtly ideals to reach beyond the barony itself" (177). Chivalry began to exist outside its generative martial context, inviting into its folds men upon whose bodies the aristocracy did not rely for wartime protection and expansion. Edward III and his successors began to knight powerful merchants, so that romance quickly found new consumers. Romance was transformed from a socially progressive genre aimed at promulgating a new mode of embodiment to a culturally conservative form; its popularity only increased.

We are already in a position to speculate what exactly in these narratives should make them so widely attractive. First, the chivalrous hero is a powerful formulation of an "autonomous" subjectivity that would appeal to both aristocrats and merchants, especially in his suturing of heroic individuality to manifest destiny to create a body radiant enough to outshine, at least temporarily, the contradictions of its genesis. Second, romance is a discourse of desire that offers a parade of libidinal objects with which to connect; it is a genre that works through the creating and sustaining of all kinds of pleasure, from joy-in-(making)-meaning (*jouis-sense*) to obscene enjoyment; and finally, through that enjoyment, romance promulgates a construction of masculinity that is so culturally persuasive because, like Geoffrey's invention of Arthur, it retroactively bestows upon a new kind of embodiment the secure weight of long history.

Identity romances such as *Guy of Warwick, Bevis of Hampton, Perceval of Galles*, and *Lybeaus Desconus* continued to be copied, read, and enjoyed for several hundred years after they were first composed. Clearly, then, an argument that ties the cultural use and meaning of these narratives solely to the moment of their genesis is inadequate, for very often a particular romance survives in a version a century or more older than its putative original. Often these romances endure in great collections along with other examples of the genre, suggesting a widespread taste for romance in its various permutations; British Museum MS Cotton Caligula A. 2 contains, for example, *Lybeaus Desconus, Eglamour, Octavian, Launfal, Emaré, The Siege of Jerusalem, Le Chevalier Assigné,* and *Isumbras*.[54] Sometimes the other texts that are bound into the same codex as these romances are suggestive. *Lybeaus Desconus*, that "primal" narrative of identity formation and chivalric embodiment, is frequently the companion to treatises on the body: explications of humoral theory, medical prescriptions.[55] Frequently, too, the romances appear together with a range of other materials that defy attempts at logical characterization: the celebrated Auchinleck manuscript resists a determining principle of organization and in its very copiousness announces that the audience for all kinds of medieval texts was wide and overlapping—whoever commissioned the magnificently diverse compendium clearly enjoyed pious tracts and chronicle history as much as the exploits of chivalric heroes. The chivalric subject is perhaps best thought of as part of a collected array of identities that might inhabit a single body, a subjectivity no less copious, contradictory, and complex than what is currently labeled "postmodern."

This brief foray into manuscript provenance is a perhaps too abbreviated way of declaring that even though romance may have been tied in its genesis to a specific moment in the history of chivalric embodiment, romance endured because it was able to offer a formulation of identity with wide appeal: its hypermasculine heroes, saturated with desire, offer readers and auditors a powerfully attractive vision in which individuality is conflated with the common good. The body as organized through the fight against the giant and through the performative arena of *aventure* is a wholly imaginary body, and therefore all the more alluring—not only for chivalric subjects in the making, whose bodies must be brought under social control, but also for newly active mercantile and political identities, to give them a history with which to identify, to solidify for them a past. Ad Putter provides the most sophisticated recent interpretation of this hybrid audience, tracing it back to Chrétien de Troyes and locating its acme in *Sir Gawain and the Green Knight*. He observes that "Chrétien's patrons should therefore not be confused with the noblemen increasingly threatened by the rise of the state and money. They were in fact those from whom the threat emanated" (*"Sir Gawain and the Green Knight" and French Arthurian Romance*, 190). Jill Mann has argued at some length that a fusion of chivalric and mercantile identities occurred in London at least by the late fourteenth century ("Price and Value in *Sir Gawain and the Green Knight*," 298–318). The seventy-five-year period before and after 1400 saw a significant and revealing shift in vernacular English manuscript production. A steady trickle of texts scattered across the countryside (the Harley lyrics [BL MS Harley 2253] at Ludlow, *William of Palerne* [Cambridge, King's College MS 13] at Gloucester, *Sir Gawain and the Green Knight* [BL MS Cotton Nero A.x] in Cheshire) was transformed, circa 1390 to 1410, into a concentrated outpouring of "routine commercial production" centered in London.[56] No doubt a primary reason for this explosion of texts was the cultural ascendancy of a class of men whose power was directly tied to the circulation of capital and a burgeoning state bureaucracy—a class that had always been interested in romance.

Edwards and Pearsall have argued that this remarkable increase is due primarily to "the mature English writing of Chaucer and Gower (and, in a slightly different context, Langland)"; there also occurred a profound change in potential "paying customers" for such works, "customers themselves representative of a wider range of the literate public than the traditional court-based literary culture" ("Manuscripts," 258). Something rather snobbish no doubt lies behind the labeling of Chaucer, Gower, and Langland as "mature," for the effect is to consign romance to an era of English immaturity, as that rite de passage that allowed its literature to come of age as a corpus of work. It is clear that the popularity of the romances continued unabated throughout this period. It is also clear that Chaucer would not be Chaucer had he not incorporated the romance mode into the center of his praxis as writer.[57] Yet since romance imagines itself a catalyst to the metamorphosis into the solidity of a full identity, its placement as a prequel to "adult" English literary identity seems not only appropriate but inevitable.

Romance is the patriarchal myth par excellence. It begins by inventing the chivalric subject and thrives by ennobling a figure not so very different from the bugbears of the Marxists, the capitalist individual and the professional politician for whom all things are possible via their bustle of activity across a landscape that exists only to offer up its riches and rewards. Romance imagines a history for the world and for "private" bodies within that world. At the same time as it constructs a powerful vision of male subjectivity and embodiment, it also gives rise to vernacular English literature—that little slice of medieval writing that contemporary medievalists must overestimate because it is the sine qua non of modern literature and modern man, in all the universalist, relentlessly, violently gendered senses of those terms.

How the World Is Made Solid

In its broadest terms, this chapter has examined three modes for materializing reality. Geoffrey of Monmouth's citational praxis exemplifies the first, which could be labeled *symbolic:* here reality takes on its weight discursively, through the world of language and the law. Symbolic materialization describes the ways in which history collects the past into a tangible coherence by arranging it beneath some master signifier or by "quilting" it through a stable *point de capiton.* Once the fragmentation of the past is sutured, at least temporarily, by the agency of this authoritative sign, the present becomes knowable, and history is precipitated as a coherent whole. Judith Butler has argued at some length that bodies are materialized through a similar process of morphogenesis (although her model is more Derridean than psychoanalytic). Once the heroic corpus is established within the discursive practices of a "regulatory regime," other bodies can be measured against it, can "cite" its power: chivalry becomes a method of somatic regulation, an ethic for both the production and the care of the self.

To keep the Lacanian analogy going, the second mode of rendering solid the world could be labeled *imaginary*—not insubstantial, but based on a logic of *images.* Identification in romance works through imaginary reification: at the mirror stage enacted by the gigantomachia, the chivalric subject is invited to identify with the idealized form of the hero's body. The giant, *le corps morcelé,* the prehistory of the body, is abjected for an illusory coherence that promises transcendence from the merely corporeal. By defeating the giant, the subject assumes his full embodiment as autonomous subject—a vision of masculinity powerful because it ignores the severe constraints that inhere in its genesis. Imaginary materialization is wholly optical, based on a trigonometry of the gaze. The subject identifies with an exterior image that is saturated with desire, and he organizes his selfhood according to a spectacular *manque* (want, lack).

The last mode is also the most dangerous: *real* materialization, synonymous with *enjoyment* in its varied forms. Slavoj Zizek's substantial contribution to the theorization of ideology demonstrates that no effective meaning system is reducible simply to its own structure. Something always remains outside of signification itself, and this leftover is the Lacanian Real—the Thing that is foreclosed from discourse, its surplus. Jacques-Alain Miller described the Real as *extimité* (Shepherdson's "intimate alterity"), for although it seems exterior, it smears the formal structure of the symbolic network with its obscene presence—its pleasures, delights, and destructions. Strictly speaking, the real materializes itself, as an effect of symbolization; but the double-edged enjoyment that the real offers becomes enmeshed in both symbolic and imaginary identification, ensuring that these orders knot resistantly together. The monster is the "little piece of the real" that symbolization exudes: it is everything culturally suppressed in order for "culture" to come into being. At the same time as the monster's presence is disruptive, it is also necessary: the head of the giant with its obscenely gaping maw traps the gaze by exciting the body to perverse enjoyment. This little bit of *jouissance,* as terrifying as it is thrilling, is immediately reincorporated by the hero's body. The monster's power over enjoyment then becomes subordinated beneath the hero's disciplinary prohibition. The paradox is this: the hero triumphs over his body out of control, his body as magnified through the giant, *and this act of renunciation is itself enjoyable,* "enjoyment itself is a kind of surplus produced by renunciation."[58] The production of the chivalric subject depends on this paradoxical surplus, this little bit of the monster that settles deep inside the hero's body every time he is vanquished.

Romance materializes history; romance materializes bodies. Warwick did not exist as an earldom until 1088, long after the time Guy of Warwick was supposed to have been glorifying the name. The Anglo-Norman and Middle English versions of his biography are clearly fiction. Yet in 1271 or 1272, a son named Guy was born to William Beauchamp, earl of Warwick. Tradition dictates that elder sons be named only after ancestors in order to preserve familial continuity; thus the Beauchamps alternated between two names, Thomas and William.[59] Designating an heir "Guy, earl of Warwick" bestows a reality upon the romance as much as the romance bestows a reality upon the particular body born under its *nom propre.* Seventy years later, another Thomas Beauchamp named his three children Guy, Thomas, and Reynbron; "Guy" cites a grandfather as well as the romance hero; "Thomas" is literally the name of the father and reifies a continuous family history just as well as "Guy" does; "Reynbron" is the name of Guy's son in the romance and further expands the reality that the romance is even here constructing.[60] At the same time as these "actual" bodies incorporate "virtual" Guy into living history, material remains of the hero are being gathered: the inheritance of his armor can be traced in the family wills; tapestries, seals, and statuary depict his exploits as well as literature does; "around the middle of the fifteenth century a precise contemporary topography was being mapped out to correspond to the details of the romance" (Fewster, *Traditionality and Genre*, 114). Guy's fight against Colbrond is being re-worked in a growing number of chronicle histories of England. Indeed, England as a nation is being materialized through the body of Guy, whose "proud claim to English fatherhood" (Morrill, *Speculum Gy*, xiii) retroactively confers upon history a manifest destiny.

CHAPTER 4

The Giant of Self-Figuration

Diminishing Masculinity in Chaucer's "Tale of Sir Thopas"

We walk through ourselves, meeting robbers, giants, old men, young
men, wives, widows, brothers-in-love, but always meeting ourselves.
— Freud, "The Uncanny," 42

The Body of Romance

Caroline Walker Bynum has argued that the years around 1300 saw a widely renewed cultural fascination with the fragmentation of the human form, with the body in pieces.[1] First in Italy and then elsewhere in Europe, autopsies were performed to determine legal cause of demise, transforming dead flesh into living narratives; soon thereafter, dissection of cadavers was included in medical school curricula. Saints' bodies were more frequently divided at their deaths. Sacred hands, fingers, hearts, and hair were enclosed in reliquaries shaped like the bodily fragments that they displayed. The corpses of candidates for sanctification were torn open to search for signs of holiness sealed inside the viscera: the "wound of love" in the heart, precious stones encased in the organs. Royal corpses were routinely eviscerated, boiled, and divided in Germany; Pope Boniface VIII condemned the *mos teutonicus* in 1299, but the practice continued unabated. Lepers were increasingly looked upon as morally reprehensible, mainly because their bodies were caught in the process of disaggregation. Juridical torture was revived in England around 1300, and bodily mutilation was being practiced more frequently as a punishment for serious crimes. At about the same time, romance was gaining a particular ascendancy in Middle English.[2]

Romance is obsessed with the spectacle of the body. Dismemberment, sexual violation, torture, and somatic metamorphosis are all quotidian in the world that the genre makes solid. As with the body, so with the identity produced through its flesh: "Despite the dominance of a hierarchized conception of gender difference, romance also represents gender contrarily as unstable, open to question, and in danger of collapse" (Susan Crane, *Gender and Romance,* 13). Its violence, its fascination with the materiality of the body and the fragility of the self, and its conjoining of sex with death ensured that romance would exert an uncanny power of fascination on its audience. Romance also, I have argued, had a transformative effect on the subjectivity of its readers and auditors, an effect discernible at the level of embodiment. I would like to widen that claim a little and insist that this relation between corpus and *textus* figures just as prominently in the authorship of romance as it does in its reception.

When Geoffrey Chaucer was composing his *Canterbury Tales* in the late fourteenth century, romance was mature enough to invite parody, and culturally pervasive enough to be an inescapable influence on the production of vernacular texts. Chaucer clearly had the romance body in mind as he wrote his magnum opus. Five of his narratives are wholly situated within the genre, and many others make use of its conventions. Chaucer, however, owed more to the romance imaginary than a structure and source for his tales. Identity romance and its central gigantomachia were essential to his inscription of his own "historical" body, to his construction of himself as a sexual, masculine subject. The giant was for Chaucer something more than an intimate stranger: this monster was the vehicle in "The Tale of Sir Thopas" for his own self-figuration.

Male Bodies Large and Small in Fragment 7

Bodily contours and morphology are not merely implicated in an irreducible tension between the psychic and the material but are that tension.

— Judith Butler, *Bodies That Matter*, 66

Fragment 7 of *The Canterbury Tales* sutures into a single narrative six stories that have usually struck critics as thematically unconnected.[3] The bridges between these tales are especially rich and overflow with commentary from the Host, Harry Bailly, a "semely man" who "of manhood hym lakked right naught."[4] Taken together, these moments in the "roadside drama" suggest that one of the obsessions of fragment 7 is the gendering of male bodies. After "The Shipman's Tale," Harry jokes about the effusive virility of monks; after "The Prioress's Tale," he pokes fun at Chaucer the pilgrim, reducing him to an "elvyssh" freak. He invites the poet to tell the next story, then interrupts the performance to condemn "The Tale of Sir Thopas" as mere "dogerel." The Host is less bellicose after Chaucer provides a second narrative, the didactic "Tale of Melibee," in which the good wife Prudence instructs her husband in proper male reticence after his enemies beat her and murder their daughter. Never a man of restraint himself, Harry adds an epilogue in which the function of wives becomes to chide their husbands to acts of aggression against other men, mainly by calling them nasty names ("milksop" "coward ape"). The Host next ridicules the Monk, announcing that his vigorous, expansive body is wasted in the cloister. Harry insists that the religious orders have drained the world of its most robustly masculine citizens, leaving laymen who are mere "shrympes" and "wrecched ympes" to carry on the work of its population (7.4752–53).

Like Chaucer's "Tale of Sir Thopas," "The Monk's Tale" is also angrily interrupted. The Knight complains that its unremitting focus on the tragic fall of great men is simply too depressing; perhaps it also hits too close to home. The Host seconds this objection, and the Monk refuses to speak further. Harry then belittles the Nun's Priest for riding a "foul and lene" horse, and requests that he provide the next story. After this last teller relates a mock-epic fabliau in which the rooster Chauntecleer escapes a menacing fox, the Host brings the fragment to a close by praising the ridiculous vision of masculinity that the heroic cock embodies. The Nun's Priest himself should be just like that manly fowl, Harry insists, with "seven tymes seventene" concubine hens to service his virile needs (7.4251).

Male bodies of all kinds tumble along these dialogic bridges that connect the six tales: celibate, hypersexual, overly physical, otherworldly, diminutive, childlike, henpecked, hen serviced, ludic, and ludicrous. Yet the final vision of masculinity that fragment 7 offers is of a rooster proudly strutting through his barnyard harem, and a priest no one calls by his proper name—even Harry addresses him as "Sire Nonnes Preest," as if he lacked an identity outside his belonging to the Prioress. This body becomes the ironic, final, but far from stable site of masculinity in the series of tales. The Host pronounces a benediction upon its "breche, and every stoon" [breeches and both testicles] (7.4245).

The exaggerations and reductions of masculinity so evident in the bridges also occur, albeit more subtly, in the tales that they connect. Masculinity in fragment 7 is best described as *an economy of flows*: male sexuality diminishes and expands throughout as if it were a liquid (or humor) of which a particular body can possess too much or too little, sometimes in alternation. The fragment opens with a story about how capital can overcode and transform anything, even sex (coitus and gold coins become interchangeable in "The Shipman's Tale"), then constricts into the tiny narrative of the "litel clergeon," murdered by the vastly monstrous Jews and hurled into a latrine ("The Prioress's Tale").[5] After the stunned or pious silence that follows this reverent story of multiple dismemberments, Chaucer's own body is inserted, suddenly and unexpectedly, by the Host. Harry Bailey notices Chaucer the pilgrim, apparently for the first time, and exclaims, "What man artow?" [What man are you?] (7.695) The question resonates with undecidability, and the Host doesn't help much as he describes a Chaucer who is oddly expansive and amusingly "litel." "He in the waast is shape as wel as I!" exclaims Harry, remarking on the poet's rotundity; yet there is something dwarfish about this body, too: "This were a popet in an arm t'enbrace" [This is a doll to hug] (701). Despite this duality, the Host's rhetoric ultimately constructs a Chaucer eerily similar to the Prioress's "litel clergeon": innocent, otherworldly ("He semeth elvyssh," 703), asexual ("unto no wight dooth he daliaunce," 704), diminutive. The author offers himself here as a love object, a cuddly doll to fondle. There is something small and consequently endearing about this Chaucer, the narrator of "The Tale of Sir Thopas."

Indeed, there is something small and consequently endearing about "The Tale of Sir Thopas" itself. The eponymous hero is a bumbling little champion with an adorable name (*thopas* is the Middle English spelling for "topaz" and, as Skeat proclaimed, "an excellent title for such a gem of a knight").[6] Sir Olifaunt, a three-headed giant and the knight's monstrous antagonist, better fits a nursery rhyme than a chivalric romance. The tale's love interest, the Queen of the Fairies, is sweetly and remotely impossible rather than present and alluringly physical. The wildernesses that Thopas traverses are full of bucks and hares rather than the expected lions and bears. The "fair forest" that the knight "priketh thurgh" is aromatic with licorice, cloves, and nutmeg "to putte in ale," more an herb garden than trackless expanse. The "fer contree" of its hero's birth is proximate, bourgeois Flanders. "Thopas" is a story that keeps trickling into smaller portions. Fit 1 has 18 stanzas, fit 2 has 9, fit 3 has 4.5—each section is exactly one-half the length of the preceding one.[7] Meanwhile, the poem's layout in the two most important manuscripts of *The Canterbury Tales,* Ellesmere and Hengwrt, accentuates this dwindling effect by breaking each stanza across the page into consecutively smaller portions, so that the words appear to trickle away to nothing toward the folio's edge.[8] At the point at which the tale cannot become any smaller (because the ratio of fit lengths is 4:2:1), the Host interrupts the whole performance and condemns it as a reprehensibly meager poetic achievement rather than a charmingly diminutive one. Harry declares to Chaucer, "Thy drasty rymyng is nat worth a toord!" [Your crappy rhyming is not worth a turd!] (990). The doubled reference to excrement ("drasty" is from OE *draestig,* Latin *feculentus*) reduces what seemed a balanced, miniature world into one without proper limit, like a body that had seemed perfect in its delicately miniature scale but ends up being infantile, a body without control, a body that soils itself.

Harry Bailey's interjection marks a second point of enlargement in fragment 7. The "litel thyng in prose" that follows is the weightily pedagogical "Tale of Melibee." Perhaps, as Lee Patterson has argued, "Melibee" is an example of children's literature, like Chaucer's *Treatise on the Astrolabe.*[9] Yet this pastiche of quotations from classical and biblical sources is as alarmingly expansive as "Thopas" is wonderfully reductive. "Melibee" is followed by another gigantic work, the infinitely dilating tragic history of "The Monk's Tale." The Host will have to intervene again before the Monk's spiral of proverbs, anecdotes, citations, and *exempla* can be stopped in its boundless expatiation, for both "Melibee" and "The Monk's Tale" are narrative structures without any formal constraint or generic limit—each could go on forever. The childlike fascination that the miniature world of "Thopas" embodies is not, however, easily forgotten. Fragment 7 concludes with the diminutive "tragedy" of "The Nun's Priest's Tale," where the English Rising—the eruption of the traumatic Real of history in 1381—is shrunken into a delightful barnyard escapade.[10]

The six narratives of fragment 7 and their dramatic bridges explore how masculinity represents itself as something bigger than life, like a giant, a *universal*. Yet masculinity in reality, in practice, turns out to be a phenomenon of little things: merchant bodies, elvish authors, tiny clergeons, infantilized knights, self-inflated monks, farmhouse fowls. This chapter explores the first contraction of the fragment, especially as it reaches a near-vanishing point in "The Tale of Sir Thopas," the midpoint and fulcrum of the series. Masculinity shrinks, I will argue, to divorce gender from the dangers of sexuality. The male body is diminished in "Thopas" to keep it safe from the possibility of sex.

The Incredible Shrinking Knight

If you mention a giant in the text, see that it is the giant Goliath. And by that alone, which cost you almost nothing, you have a grand note.
—Cervantes, *Don Quixote*, 28

Desire in fragment 7 is allied with gigantism. "The Shipman's Tale" suggests that desire preexists any of the cultural forms it takes and requires a social coding before it can be entwined in gender or sex, or attached to other kinds of "goals." Many of the introductory lines are written for a woman to declare: "The sely housbonde algate he moot paye, / He moot us clothe, and he moot us arraye" [The silly husband must always pay. He must clothe us, he must costume us richly] (11–12). Either Chaucer was not a very careful reviser, or else the Shipman is cross-dressed or transgendered (even if he is impersonating a woman, briefly, for rhetorical effect).[11] The possibility of a transgendered (or *unanchored*) Shipman is perhaps unthinkable in late-fourteenth-century England, but that is beside the point: the effect of this authorial slip or carelessness or intentional provocation is to have a man's body speaking with a woman's voice as the fragment opens. Bodies, genders, and desires do not for a moment align.

"The Shipman's Tale" is radical in its dissociations. Not only is there no necessary correlation between gender and sex, but no necessity binds desire to *human* bodies at all. The narrative explores two indistinguishable economies of flows, of sex and of capital. They are not separable: the more money the merchant has, the more virile his body becomes. The circuit of capital through the tale traces the flow of sexual gratification. Monetary debt becomes marital debt, and prostitution becomes marriage itself, translated into economic language. By the end of the tale, all sexual relations are shown also to be relations of capital, gender identity is inscribed as a market before a bedroom performance, and matrimony becomes a legally sanctioned form of sex-capital transfer. It is not so much that monetary exchange becomes sexualized (as if sexuality were "naturally" invested only in *bodies*); rather, desire is revealed to be primal, and its object-causes (sex acts, gold coins) secondary. Money does not replace sex; the two simply become encoded as interchangeable sites within the system of distribution where desire circulates in socially determined but essentially arbitrary directions. As the French theorists of identity Deleuze and Guattari say: "Desire does not take as its object persons or things, but the entire surroundings that it traverses . . . an always nomadic and migrant desire, characterized first of all by its 'gigantism.' "[12] Desire knows no boundary, not even that of singular identities or bodies: "We always make love with worlds" (*Anti-Oedipus*, 294).[13]

If desire is associated with gigantism in *The Canterbury Tales,* the surprising Chaucerian corollary is that masculinity is inscribed as diminutive, as a shrinking away from large-scale investment of the social field. The Prioress's "litel clergeon" partially makes this point, with his innocent monomania. His boyish body is represented as too young and uncomplex to have its desire fixed on anything but a hymn about the Virgin Mother, on some Latin words that his uncomprehending mouth is trained to repeat, even in death. This process of miniaturization continues in the prologue and tale that follow. Sir Thopas and Chaucer in his own self-presentation embody diminishing masculinity in its attenuating extreme.

When Harry demands that Chaucer tell the Canterbury pilgrims a "tale of myrthe" to counteract the harrowing reductiveness of "The Prioress's Tale," the poet responds with "The Tale of Sir Thopas," an affectionate burlesque of the Middle English heroic romances. Sir Thopas is a miniature figure, as much a "popet" as the tale's narrator. His face is as pure as "payndemain" [white bread], his lips are red as roses, his complexion is ruddy as scarlet dye, and he has a "semely" nose. His clothing is detailed at similar length: his shoes are of Cordovan leather, his laced tights are brown, his costly robe is silk and gold. These stanzas are not so much like the *effictiones* of romance, those long narrative catalogs that describe a (feminine) body by breaking it into beautiful fragments (eyes like the sparkling sun, cheeks like rubies, and so forth); rather, the effect is of dressing up a doll in bright clothing.

The tight poetic control of these lines, which construct a sumptuary vision of their subject's exterior, is immediately translated into an interior, somatic control that characterizes Thopas in his relation to his body:

Ful many a mayde bright in bour,
They moorne for hym paramour,
  Whan hem were bet to slepe.
But he was chaast and no lechour,
And sweete as is the brembul flour. (742–46)

[Many maids in their bright bowers pined for him as a lover, when they were better off sleeping. For he was chaste and no lecher, and sweet as a bramble-rose.]

Although many women pine for his love, this chaste knight will have nothing to do with them. The overall impression is of tender oblivious-ness, of a body too innocent to know even what part it plays in the so-cial circuit—much like the Prioress's "litel clergeon," who seems unable to imagine that the Jews whose street he passes along each day might dis-like his constant pious hymning.

Lee Patterson has perceptively written about the rhetoric of diminu-tion in "Thopas" that "at every turn Chaucer stresses the youthfulness of his hero": his body is small, his favorite sports are "typical boyish pursuits," his fight against the giant is a "comic reversal" of David's battle against Goliath ("What Man Artow?" 129). Indeed, Thopas's dimin-utive size is best emphasized through the encounter with his spatial oppo-site, Olifaunt ("Elephant"), whose very name suggests vastness.[14] Some-thing more than comic whimsy dictates that Thopas face this monster. An encounter with a giant is the sine qua non of identity romance. David's battle against Goliath was the palimpsest for most of these bat-tles, and Laura Hibbard Loomis suggests that Chaucer knew the romance-inflected version of the biblical story in the *Cursor Mundi* (c. 1300–1325), a popular and lively vernacular retelling of biblical history ("Sir Thopas and David and Goliath," 311–13). Similar fights against a giant occur in *Sir Eglamour, Guy of Warwick*, and *Lybeaus Desconus*—ro-mances with which Chaucer seems to have been intimately familiar, as verbal and thematic resonances in "Thopas" demonstrate.[15]

The giant functions within the romance imaginary as a monstrous embodiment of sexual violence and unauthorized aggression; the giant enfleshes the set of all object-goals forbidden and abjected in order to materialize the chivalric subject. A cultural body on which the codes that produce a safely gendered identity have failed to adhere, this mon-ster conservatively demonstrates what masculinity must *not* be in order to regulate what form sanctioned gender identity will take. In medieval romance, the hero defeats his monstrous double in a battle whose out-come announces that the knight has learned to channel the multiple drives that traverse the body, rendering a multiplicity of desire (only the dangers of which the giant enfleshes) into a unitary being. Chivalric self-hood is an identity produced through severe cultural constraint, because the goal of romance is the formation of docile or socially constrained subjects.[16]

The adventure against the giant is constructed around a set of topoi that reappear with surprising consistency. The hero hears that a giant has abducted a maiden, and the hero decides to rescue her. The giant is a cultural other, usually a Muslim. The monster swears by the Saracen god Termagaunt, which conveniently rhymes with giant (*geaunt*) in both Middle English and French. The giant wields a club, and his first blow misses. The giant kills the hero's horse. The hero defeats the monster and decapitates him and then publicly displays the severed head in a ritual that announces to the world that he has conquered his own dark impulses. Unlike the giant, the young hero's body knows boundaries, and this beheading scene inscribes them, firmly and spectacularly. The gigantomachia maps the movement from gigantism of desire to libido in its socially sanctioned, Oedipalized, *miniaturized* circulation.

"Sir Thopas" burlesques all of the topoi of this primal scene of romance. After Thopas decides that he will love *"an* elf-queene" (as if there were a world of elf-queens to choose from, as if a hero could simply elect to be in love with one), he rides into the "contree of Fairye," a perilous place that "neither wyf nor childe" would dare seek. Sir Olifaunt commands Thopas to leave immediately with the resonant phrase "prike out of myn haunt."[17] The giant's use of *prike* resounds with good humor, for it is Sir Thopas's favorite verb. Early in the tale, when he first rides out from home, "he priketh thurgh a fair forest" (754) and "priketh north and est" (757); a little later, as he falls into "love-longynge," he "pryked as he were wood" (774), his horse tires of "prikynge" (775), and the knight himself becomes so weary "for prikyng" (779) that he tumbles into the soft grass and dreams of his beloved elf-queen.[18] Like Thopas and his horse, *prike* has been comically exhausted from overuse, and the giant's choice of words announces that this monster is safely part of the text's comedy of verbal play.

Olifaunt swears by "Termagaunt," just as he should. But whereas Amourant (*Guy of Warwick*), Grander's brother (*Bevis of Hampton*), and Maugis (*Lybeaus Desconus*) pose serious peril to the heroes of these narratives, and in fact carve bloody wounds deep into the bodies of their adversaries, Olifaunt never quite manages to menace. He announces that should Thopas not depart Fairyland immediately, he will slay his steed with a mace, as if the worst fate awaiting the knight were the inconvenience of having to walk home. Brave warrior that he is, Thopas replies in kind:

The child seyde, "Also moote I thee,
Tomorwe wol I meete with thee,
   Whan I have myn armoure." (817–19)

"Sorry, I don't have my armor right now—I'll come back tomorrow" really doesn't cut it as a performance of heroic masculinity. That Sir Thopas should be identified here simply as "the child," the word by which Olifaunt refers to his adversary—as if the text and the giant were positioned at the same point of narratival view, looking down on little Thopas—indicates that this word, too, is being overused to underscore its comic resonance.

The giant's vow to crush Thopas's horse seems silly, and in the context of the tale it is just that. But like the oath by demonic Termagaunt, the threat is lifted directly from the gigantomachia of romance. Giants in *Bevis of Hampton, Eglamour, Guy of Warwick, Lybeaus Desconus,* and *Torrent of Portyngale* kill their adversary's steed, an act calculated to undermine the hero's chivalric identity by reducing him to unmounted combat or even wrestling. Warhorses were extremely expensive in the Middle Ages and therefore functioned as important markers of social class. The possession of a horse is integral to knighthood, setting these class-obsessed men apart from the mere foot soldiers in their service. Possession of a well-trained mount was so entwined with aristocratic identity that following the example of Alexander the Great, horses usually bore significant names. A horse under the complete control of its rider was the public signifier of a knight's well-disciplined body. The French term for knight (*chevalier*), the base of the English word *chivalry,* is etymologically dependent on the word *horse* (*cheval*): *pas de cheval, pas de chevalier.*

The dismemberment of the knight's mount by the giant elicits anxiety about the fate of the hero's body, which is under a similar threat of disaggregation. The death of the hero's steed elicits what might be called a narrative stare: the audience is forced to linger for a few moments over the bloody sight so that the visualized body in pieces exerts its full force as a blow to subjective integrity. Thus in *Guy of Warwick* Amoraunt chops the head from Guy's steed: "þe sadel bowe he clef atvo, / þe stedes nek he dede also, / Wiþ his grimli brond" [The bow of the saddle he cut in half, along with the steed's neck, with his grim sword] (Auchinleck 101.1–3). The giant's weapon falls with such excessive force that it lodges in the ground, and Guy tumbles to the earth beside his fractured mount. Bevis's horse Trenchefis is likewise slain in combat against a giant, and the hero's words reveal that he knows the message sent through the body of the horse is directed toward its rider's own chivalric integrity (1881–93). In fury, Bevis cuts into the giant's flesh and is wounded in return when the monster hurls a piercing dart. After a long battle, Bevis finally beheads his adversary and overcomes the giant's menace to the stability of his being.

Olifaunt's weapon, a mace, is also de rigueur. The giant of insular romance nearly always attacks with a mace or club, its brutal and crushing force a blunt contrast to a sword's neatly slicing, morally demarcative blade. The variations on this weapon run from elaborate iron armaments to branches ripped from trees; in all cases, it is an unrefined, unchivalric instrument. Alagolafre in *The Sowdon of Babylon* fights with a "clog of an Oke.... That was wele bound with stele" (2919). The giant of Mont Saint Michel in the Alliterative *Morte Arthure* bears a club "all of clene iron" (1105). The gigantic brother of the sultan in *Perceval of Galles* wields a weapon described in more detail than he himself is, an "iryn clobe" that

> wheyed reghte wele
> þat a freke myght it fele:
> The hede was of harde stele,
>   Twelue stone weghte.
> þer was iryn in the wande
> Ten stone of the lande. (2021–26)

[weighed so much that it could knock down a monster: the head was of hard steel, twelve stones' weight. There was iron in the pole, ten stones worth.]

Perceval is forced to explain to his adversary that the danger of carrying a big stick is that it may be too difficult to wield. The club used by Grander's brother in *Sir Bevis* excels in length, for that weapon is twenty feet long (1883). Needless to say, that giant also has some trouble using the club effectively. Armor that signifies the moral strength of the identity that it encloses, a sword whose keen edge cleanly demarcates right from wrong as it slices to pieces the monster's body: the knight and his chivalric accoutrements always triumph over the atavistic, unchanneled, "naked" force represented by the unamored giant and his crushing club. Olifaunt and Thopas cite these conventions of the romance giganto-machia, but every citation is deflation, a merciless reduction.

Geoffrey of Monmouth labeled the giant of Mont Saint Michel with the synecdochical term *ingluvies,* literally "maw," figuratively "voracious monster." Giants in Middle English romance are often called *gloutons,* for they resemble the personified sin of Gluttony: with their gross, ingestive corporeality, they threaten to devour any identity produced through a disciplinary regime, any body materialized through the rigor of Christian self-control. Thopas's threat to strike the giant through his "mawe" (823) is wholly appropriate; his intention to commit this act of bravery with a "launcegay" (a parade or costume lance, a prop) is not. As Thopas draws back from the monster "ful faste," intent on returning home, the giant pelts him with stones. These are not the deadly missiles hurled at passing ships by the Homeric cyclops, but rocks shot from a "staf-slynge" (slingshot): David and Goliath in reverse, with Thopas as the retreating giant.[19]

After some extended "prykyng over hill and dale," the knight "with sydes small" arrives at town. When he narrates his aventure against the monster to his "myrie men," Olifaunt suddenly sprouts two more heads (842). Either the narrator of the romance is not very observant and has failed to convey a vital signifier of the giant's monstrousness earlier, or else the knight's little tale is growing in the telling. Thopas next commands his minstrels and "geestours" to recite romances while he arms himself, suggesting for a moment that the genre's presentation of exemplary heroes and their exploits is a metaphoric armor in which chivalric subjects dress themselves as kind of self-fashioning. Yet Thopas quickly undermines the whole equation by specifying that he will hear stories of "popes and of cardinales / And eek of love-likynge"—as if ecclesiastical celibacy and lovesickness were not mutually exclusive, as if both equally belonged to chivalric subjectivity.

The arming scene is long (six stanzas of a nine-stanza fit) and fragrant (a full six lines describe the various spices Thopas mixes into his wine). As the knight's naked, white "leere" ("flesh") is clothed, the effect is again ridiculously doll-like, so that when Thopas suddenly swears an oath upon "ale and breed" that the giant will die, the only worse thing that could happen is a loss of poetic control. The stanza immediately ends with an inane filler line ("Bityde what bityde!" 874), the second fit soon terminates, and the third movement tries desperately to get started but devolves into a slough of chivalric comparisons from which Thopas never escapes. The heroes Horn, Ypotis, Bevis, Guy, Lybeaus, "Pleyndamour," and Perceval are cited in rapid succession. Overwhelmed by these exemplary bodies beside which Thopas can seem only ridiculously diminutive, the poem trickles to an end. Harry Bailly breaks in, shouting: "Namoore of this, for Goddes dignitee!" (919).

The poem's last, revealing line is the simple and unfinished "Til on a day" (918). The phrase gestures toward a future at which Thopas cannot possibly arrive. What logically arrives next in the narrative would be the postponed battle against the giant, an encounter unthinkable for this knight. The gigantomachia in romance is always a sexually charged episode. The stakes are usually the body of a maiden, and the outcome of the fight is the knight's indoctrination into proper sexuality. The "chaast" and innocent body of Thopas is characterized throughout the tale by a relentless narrative protection from the mere *possibility* of sex, and so a fight against the giant is finally unthinkable.

Sex and Giants

What is, in fact, lost in this idealized miniaturization of the body is sexuality and hence the danger of power.
—Susan Stewart, *On Longing*, 124

"The Signification of the Phallus," an important essay by Jacques Lacan that proposes a poststructuralist methodology for theorizing the mechanics of gender identification, argues that the two possible positions within the symbolic order, masculine and feminine, correspond to "having" or "being" the phallus, the master signifier erected to stop the sliding of gender's semiotic chain. Lacan's explication of these terms is typically vatic and culminates in a rather strange assertion by which occupying a space in the symbolic order vis-à-vis "having the phallus" becomes a way of simultaneously gaining and losing a reality for one's identity:

> This is brought about by the intervention of a "to seem" that re-places the "to have," in order to protect it on the one side, and to mask its lack in the other, and which has the effect of projecting in their entirety the ideal or typical manifestations of the behavior of each sex, including the act of copulation itself, into the comedy. (*Écrits*, 289)

Lacan's difficult sentence ends with a magically transformative word that changes retroactively the meaning of everything that precedes. Heterosexual identification and the sexed roles that it dictates—roles that culminate in "the act of copulation itself"—are reduced by Lacan's last noun to a *comedy*. The term should no doubt be read in its Shakespearean sense, a series of ludicrous errors (mistakes, wanderings) that culminates in the stability of marriage (the proper social form governing the signification of the sex act).

What's so funny about heterosexuality? Much truth surely lies behind Lacan's characterization of its ridiculously normative power, as anyone who has ever identified as heterosexual will attest. But by reducing gender ideals to a comedic role, the "act of copulation" becomes something not to be taken too seriously. Again, there is no doubt some truth to this line of thinking, but it ultimately offers a partial and irresponsible view of human sexuality. If the performance of a sexed identity is a comedy, it is also at the same time a tragedy (dangerously invoking forces that could destroy a whole social architecture), a history (a drama whose script carries along with it the heavy weight of the past), and—as the Middle Ages knew well—a romance (a narrative that is marvelous, monstrous, larger than life). In medieval romance, the "act of copulation" is enmeshed in a complicated matrix of desire: masochistic (Lancelot's desire for Guenevere is eviscerative, fascinated by pain), ennobling (Orfeo so loves Heurodis that his identity as king depends more on his role as husband than as leader of a nation), incestuous (Gregorius, the offspring of brother-sister incest, loves his mother so much that he marries her), homoerotic (the passion of Amis for Amilun runs so deep that he murders his own children and washes his friend's diseased body with their blood). No doubt it is other things, too.

By describing the process of sexuation as a projection into comedy, Lacan diminishes sex, making it difficult to think it through in terms other than dismissive laughter. His extraordinarily masculinist conception of identification then becomes rhetorically easier to advance, and less open to critique.[20] "The Tale of Sir Thopas" similarly reduces heterosexual identity into a comedic set of roles. Chaucer's translation of gender performance from romance into comedy extends, to use Lacan's words, from the "typical manifestations of the behavior of each sex" to "the act of copulation itself." The encounter with Sir Olifaunt in "Thopas" is exemplary of what gets lost in the Chaucerian translation. The episode contains nearly all the topoi connected with the romance gigantomachia; every component of the fight is carefully elaborated in order to render it harmless, ridiculous. Yet an important subtraction fundamentally transforms the romance formula. Wholly missing from the adventure against the giant is any kind of sexual menace.

Indeed, sexuality is strangely absent throughout the narrative, as the very impossibility as love object that "an elf-queene" (788), with its "insouciant" indefinite article, underlines.[21] Those medieval narratives in which a fairy mistress has captured the heart of the hero explore the incommensurability of knighthood (a performance of masculinity that is relentlessly public) with love (represented in these stories as "durne loue," a secret, private bond between the fairy and her lover).[22] In Marie de France's lai *Lanval*, the hero must swear to keep the identity of his fay beloved secret; rebuffed for her seductive advances, Guenevere accuses Lanval of sodomy with his men, so removed from a public sexuality does he seem (*Lanval*, 277–92). In Thomas Chestre's *Sir Launfal*, the fairy mistress commands the hero "alle wemen for me forsake" (317); as a result, she does not exist for the court until she literally exposes herself, an announcement that unites Launfal with his heterosexuality at the expense of Dame Tryamour's power as fairy.[23]

In *Lanval, Launfal,* and *Thomas of Erceldoune*, the fairy mistress has a physical presence in the narrative, and the knight she takes as lover joyfully consummates the relationship. Thopas is content to encounter his queen in a dream. She never speaks or even appears in the text, outside of what Thopas and the giant relate on her behalf. Thopas's stainless, abstemious body has been previously remarked. He enters the story without a "lemman" for whom to perform his deeds of arms, happily oblivious to the world of sexuality. The scores of wakeful women who "moorne for hym paramour" (743) are better off catching up on their missed sleep (744) because like Chaucer the pilgrim, Thopas "unto no wight dooth . . . daliaunce" (704). What little action the romance offers is set into motion when Thopas awakens to sexual feeling in his dream about an elf-queen, but it is difficult to take his "love-longynge" seriously. One could hardly imagine Guenevere attempting to seduce Thopas and then accusing him of sodomy with his knightly friends; the possibility of any kind of fleshly desire is never attached to his diminutive body, and so the quest for a fairy mistress is appropriately ludic. Even the gem for which Thopas is named is noted in the lapidaries for its power against that most carnal of sins, lust.[24] I would not go as far as Lee Patterson and argue that Thopas is actually a boy playing at being a knight,[25] but Thopas is certainly developmentally arrested—childlike and therefore asexual. Children in the Middle Ages were represented as innocent of erotic feeling. The encyclopedist Bartholomaeus Anglicus, for example, asserted that "children before the age of fourteen are incapable of sexual intercourse" and that the Latin word for boy, *puer,* was etymologically connected to *puritas.*[26] If "Sir Thopas is all Don Quixote in little" (as Richard Hurd famously observed in 1765), this "little" leaves out much and renders even the giant a diminished figure.[27]

Chaucer's reductive poetics drain romance of its libidinal force, transforming the genre from an exercise in the excitation of desire to a comic demonstration of the body's innocuous innocence.[28] The David and Goliath story, diminished to a children's fable, is no doubt Chaucer's primary citational reference as he describes Thopas fleeing the shower of stones hurled at him by the belligerent Olifaunt. Another, previously unremarked analogue for this narrative moment occurs in Geoffrey of Monmouth's *History of the Kings of Britain,* when the giant of Mont Saint Michel kidnaps a maiden and carries her to his demesnes:

> This giant had snatched Helena . . . and had fled with her to the top of what is now called the Mont Saint Michel. The knights of that district had pursued the giant, but they had been able to do nothing against him. It made no difference whether they attacked him by sea or by land, for he either sank their ships with huge rocks or else killed them with a variety of weapons. Those whom he captured, and they were quite a few, he ate while they were still half alive. (238)

The encounter with Olifaunt absurdly repeats this nameless giant's horrifying intrusion. Both abduct a woman and keep her against her will; both are pursued to their lair by a would-be rescuer; both defeat approaching knights by hurling rocks. In "The Tale of Sir Thopas," however, every possibility of a menacing volatility is systematically drained from the narrative. Desire in romance is represented as dangerous because it is bigger than the human body: exorbitant, inhuman in its full expression, capable of sweeping up the whole of the world in the excitation of its obscene enjoyments. Desire in Chaucer's burlesque is laughable, a less than human thing, a ridiculously small part of a microcosmos in which bodies and desires are always something less than meets the eye.

Romance logic dictates that the monster's body ought to display just the opposite of Thopas's meticulous self-regulation. That Olifaunt has abducted the elf-queen and holds her in his lair suggests that he is the traditional giant of romance, intent on demonstrating his lack of so-

109

matic control on his unwilling "lemman." The expectation is quickly defeated, however, as Olifaunt reveals that he keeps the elf-queen in a happy, musical place: "Heere is the queene of Fayerye, / With harpe and pipe and symphonye" (814–15). The symphonic accompaniment to the queen's abduction effectively dismisses the possibility of a dark, sexual intention behind the kidnapping.

Or does it? The absurdly pleasant conditions under which the queen is held deserve contextualization. Giants usually inhabit the periphery of civilization: grim, haunted landscapes full of dark skies, dense trees, and infernal flames. Chaucer's audience, avid readers of romance, would carry all these expectations when such a monster is invoked. Olifaunt's melodious dwelling should be compared to the horrible crag to which the giant of Mont Saint Michel drags Helen in Geoffrey of Monmouth's *Historia*, a text that profoundly influenced the reception of medieval giants. Robert Mannyng of Brunne completed an English translation in 1338.[29] Here, as in Wace, the marauding giant is named Dinabroke, who seizes Helen "to do hir schame" (11856). Arthur's knight Bedevere is the first to reach the giant's lair, a gloomy mountaintop on which a mysterious fire blazes. Hearing a "grete pleint" that causes his heart to quiver, he believes the monster to be nearby. The cry comes from a woman who sits "nere all naked" atop a new grave, the tomb in which Helen's corpse is interred. The contiguity of the two women's bodies is repeatedly stressed, especially through the fact that this mournful woman was once Helen's wet nurse: "At souke I gaf hir of my pap, / I nourisshed hir of my breste" (11958–59). The nurse identifies herself as an extension of Helen's own "flesch . . . so faire" (11962), so that the fate of Duke Hoel's niece is essentially her own. This intersubjectivity allows the terrible recounting of the giant's crime to proceed from the victim's point of view. The switch from the diffident, masculine voice of the bodiless narrator to the fully embodied feminine is rhetorically effective in that it forces the audience to identify, like its teller, with the violated body.

According to the nurse, the giant appeared suddenly, kidnapped them both, and carried them to the isolated crag. He immediately attempted to rape Helen ("Heleyn he wild haf forlayn," 11969), but he was so gross that he crushed the life from her flesh; she dies in his terrible embrace (11971–74). This "schamly" demise is bad enough, but the giant then fills his "lichorie" on the distraught nurse. Worse, he keeps the frightened woman prisoner by the grave, making frequent nocturnal visits to repeat the rape. She cries to Bedevere that the very best for which she can hope is death.

As the heinous Dinabroke demonstrates, giants are rapists in the double sense of the word: they abduct innocent women, and they threaten these captives with sexual violation. This aggressive sexuality is a parental inheritance. According to both biblical exegesis and popular tradition, giants are engendered upon women by the demons or incubi who ravish them. Giants receive this sexual violence genetically: giants literally embody rape. Ideally, the young hero fights this monster to free the woman he holds in his castle or cave. The rescued damsel then becomes the victor's bride, and the anacoluthon of rape vanishes into the proper grammar of marriage. But as Geoffrey of Monmouth's *History of the Kings of Britain* illustrates, and as Wace and Robert Mannyng reaffirm, sometimes the *foedus coitus* occurs before the hero can prevent the act.

The horrifying spectacle of the woman's violated body haunts romance. Menaced and abducted women become, after Geoffrey's *Historia*, a constant feature of the gigantomachia. The Saracen monster Amourant in *Guy of Warwick* wants Guy's head for his "leman"; the giant Araganour of *Octovian* wages war to ensure that a sultan's daughter becomes his own possession. The unnamed giant in *Sir Bevis of Hampton* who smashes the life from the hero's horse keeps a woman captive in his tower, as does the treacherous Angolafer in *Huon of Bordeaux*. The giant who dwells "in the Grekes see" (79) in *Torrent of Portyngale* keeps five young nobles and a princess immured in his gem-encrusted fortress. Chrétien's grotesque creation, Harpin de la Montagne, reduces a provincial lord to ruin in his bellicose attempts to gain the lord's daughter; by the time Yvain destroys him, the giant is intent on transforming the maiden into a whore to service his retinue of a thousand verminous (i.e., laboring-class) *vileins*. Violette, rescued by Lybeaus Desconus in the romance that bears his name, is similarly a young woman abducted from a noble household by a giant; the monster is in the midst of raping her when the hero fortuitously bursts upon the scene. *Lybeaus Desconus* is also a narrative to which "The Tale of Sir Thopas" has a special affinity. The silly and unfashionable description of Thopas's facial hair ("his berd was lyk saffroun, / That to his girdel raughte adoun," 730–31) derives from two lines describing the dwarf who guides Lybeaus to the libidinous giant ("Hys berd was yelow as ony wax, / To hys girdell henge the plex," 127–28).

The giant's threat of sexual violation dwindles as "The Tale of Sir Thopas" shrinks. A similar diminishing of masculinity as reduction of a potentially dangerous sexuality also animates the prologue to the tale, where Chaucer the narrator becomes by rhetorical and thematic contiguity connected both to the presexual "litel clergeon" of "The Prioress's Tale" and to Sir Thopas himself.[30] Recall Harry's words to Chaucer, which construct a body completely exterior to the social circle of the Canterbury pilgrims ("unto no wight dooth he daliaunce," 704). Diffident, submissive, and self-excluding, this "litel" Chaucer cannot meet the eyes of those who look on him but stares constantly at the ground (697). The poet positions himself as object of the gaze rather than its point of issuance, a nonsensical position for an observant narrator to occupy. The Host summarizes this strange but apparently harmless being with the sentence, "This were a popet in an arm t'enbrace / For any womman, smal and fair of face" (382). Chaucer is a perfectly safe love object, a kind

111

of toy or a tiny child that any woman can scoop up and hug, a poet "in an arm t'enbrace." Chaucer the pilgrim is just as doll-like as Sir Thopas. To arrive at this miniaturization, sexuality has been subtracted from both men's bodies.

Reduction and the Historical Real

In 1381, in immediate reaction to an onerous poll tax, violence erupted in Essex and then at Kent. The cathedral at Canterbury was stormed, the archbishop's quarters sacked. On June 11 and 12, a former roof tiler named Wat Tyler led an armed multitude into London, seizing control of the streets. Once the gates of the city were thrown open, scores of Flemings were beaten to death, apparently because they were seen as an economic threat to English prosperity. The contemporary chronicler Jean Froissart described the revolt in apocalyptic terms:

> There occurred in England great disasters and uprisings of the common people, on account of which the country was almost ruined beyond recovery. Never was any land or realm in such great danger as England at that time. . . . [The rebels] drew in all the people from the villages they went near, and they passed by like a tornado, leveling and gutting the houses of lawyers and judges. . . . If their plans had succeeded, they would have destroyed all the nobility of England; and afterwards, in other nations, all the common people would have rebelled. (*Chronicles*, 211, 214, 215).

Contemporary writers who witnessed these events had no easier a time interpreting them than medievalists do. Sometimes the Rising was represented as the incoherent actions of inarticulate men;[31] but this placement of the disturbance outside signification is hardly satisfactory to a medieval mind intent on tracing the underlying, perhaps divine sense behind the chaos of the world. Walsingham described the rebellion within a biblical frame, transforming events into rather inconsistent moral *exempla*.[32] The first book of John Gower's *Vox Clamatis* depicted the rebels as hybrid freaks, beasts in men's bodies. This program of monsterization makes sense of the rebels' actions by placing them outside the realm of the rational and the normal, so that the Rising becomes, paradoxically, a conservative valorization of the integrity of the present cultural system.

The English Rising is a historical trauma, an event so fundamentally challenging to a society's symbolic system that no easy way exists to integrate it into meaning. Inarticulateness, exemplarity, and monstrousness are three cultural rhetorics that attempted to give the rebellion a stable signification, but that each was able to offer at best only a temporary narrative suturing suggests that the events themselves are too powerfully overdetermined to be reduced to a single or permanent signification. Given the traumatic force of 1381, critics of Chaucer have long been puzzled that the Rising is almost completely ignored in his works. "The Nun's Priest's Tale" shrinks the trauma of history by diminishing the revolt into a barnyard chase. It would be wrong to conclude from this miniaturization, however, that this social upheaval simply did not concern Chaucer. The storming of London was its bloodiest episode, and the rebels burst into the city by passing directly under his home atop Aldgate. Paul Strohm finds in "The Nun's Priest's Tale" a "literary supersaturation" calculated to ensure the diminishing of any "troubling social implications" that would naturally arise when the rebellion is mentioned, so that the "reference to Jack Straw's incitement to kill the Flemings is placed on the same plane of reference as the songs of mermaids in the sea, Boethius' love of music, the deeds of Lancelot, the Pharoah's baker, the sorrowing ladies of Troy" (*Social Chaucer*, 165). The explosive volatility of the event—armed men streaming through the city gates, blood and corpses on the London streets, the *ordo mundi* dissolving in riot—is reduced to a literary allusion. In his recent biography of Chaucer, Derek Pearsall asserts that this very "lessening of risk" is characteristic of the poet's praxis whenever he transforms history into literature, so that "political and social conflict" are routinely converted into mere "material for anecdotal humor, private and personal confrontations, and literary games" (*The Life of Geoffrey Chaucer*, 147). The English Rising of 1381 shrinks so that its dangerous significance as a fundamental challenge to the prevailing social order recedes. Diminution is a characteristically Chaucerian way of avoiding the real of history.

The miniaturization of sexuality in "The Tale of Sir Thopas" ought likewise to sound a warning bell that something traumatic is being reduced to avoid the fullness—the *gigantism*—of its potential signification. That event is perhaps the very possibility of rape that has, until a recent article by Christopher Cannon, been much diminished in Chaucer criticism. Is it too much to suggest that the *foedus coitus* that has vanished from the encounter with the giant in "The Tale of Sir Thopas" has its counterpart in the *de raptu meo* of Cecily Chaumpaigne? Diminishing masculinity is perhaps a way of avoiding a traumatic encounter with the historical real of May 1, 1380.[33] A release bearing this date was brought by Cecily Chaumpaigne into the Chancery of Richard II and there enrolled on the close rolls.[34] The document discharged Geoffrey Chaucer from "omnimodas acciones tam de raptu meo tam de aliqua alia re vel causa" [all manner of actions such as they relate to my rape [*de rapto meo*] or any other thing or cause].[35] The release had been witnessed three days earlier by some of the most powerful members of the king's court: William Beauchamp, chamberlain of the king's household; Richard Morel of the Grocer's Company, Chaucer's neighbor; William Neville, knight of the king's chamber and admiral of the northern fleet; John Clanvowe, poet and member of the king's household; John Philipot, alderman, member of Parliament, and former mayor of London. The document is obviously of supreme importance, but its exact meaning has long puzzled scholars. Its problematic relationship to three other legal records does not help much, but these two additional releases and a subsequent acknowledgment of debt apparently trace ten pounds, a vast sum of money, as it circulates from Chaucer to two intermediaries to Cecily Chaumpaigne, probably as a payment for her proceedings at Chancery.[36]

Chaumpaigne's deed of release is a legally binding promise not to bring the charge of *raptus* against Chaucer and speaks nothing about the truth-value such a charge would have. Little is known, moreover, about its bearer, other than the scant details provided by the archival record. Cecily Chaumpaigne was the daughter of the late William Chaumpaigne and his wife, Agnes. She may have been the stepdaughter of Alice Perres, "the former king's mistress, now in disgrace," who had done many favors for Chaucer (Howard, *Chaucer*, 318). Donald Howard speculated either that Chaucer "raped or seduced the stepdaughter of an old friend," or that Chaumpaigne may have been attempting revenge or blackmail:

> Human nature being what it is, neither meaning is out of the question. Stepdaughters and stepmothers are often on bad terms. Cecily's stepmother was a famous courtesan with few scruples and an excellent head for business; if they were on good terms, Cecily may have learned a trick or two from her stepmother. (*Chaucer*, 319)

Revenge or blackmail completely removes Chaucer from the ugly possibility of *raptus* by blaming Chaumpaigne (always called by her first name by Howard, a strange mark of intimacy) and her stepmother: either Cecily had sex with Chaucer to spite her stepmother, whom she would "naturally" dislike and want to spite (by being raped?!), or else Perres had indoctrinated her stepdaughter well into the evil ways of feminine scheming. No matter which explanation obtains, Chaucer becomes the victim of an alliance between two women, his body the innocent intermediary in a message sent from one to the other. Another ameliorating scholarly fantasy names Chaumpaigne the mother of Chaucer's son Lewis, for whom the poet wrote his one undeniable piece of children's literature, *The Treatise on the Astrolabe* (Howard, 320).

For a long time, the argument that *raptus* meant "abduction" and carried no sexual connotations was widely circulated, but Cannon's meticulous contextualization of the word through reference to other legal documents demonstrates that "*raptus* was reserved for describing forced coitus" (87). The impossibility of verification has usually been accepted within Chaucer criticism as an invitation to dismissal. If Chaucerians have attempted to diminish the trauma of rape in their subject of study, they are only following Chaucer's own praxis. Ever since F. J. Furnivall discovered the release in 1873, critics have taken their lead from "The

Tale of Sir Thopas," its prologue, and the "Envoy to Scogan," accepting Chaucer's own discursive construction of a Geoffrey whose body announces that he is exterior to the world of sexuality. On May 7, 1380, a memorandum of the Chaumpaigne release was recorded in the *coram rege* rolls. Even though this second registration of the release has only recently been discovered, these records of the Court of King's Bench would have been the most likely place where a copy of the document would be read during Chaucer's lifetime (Cannon, "*Raptus*," 93). Here the concise *de raptu meo* of the first recording of the release becomes the verbose "de feloniiis transgressionibus compotis debitis quam aliis accionibus quibuscumque" [concerning felonies, trespasses, accounts, debts and any other actions whatsoever] (90). "The Nun's Priest's Tale" demonstrates that diminution via what Strohm calls "supersaturation" is Chaucer's immediate rhetorical strategy against the irruption of trauma. The explosion of the single phrase into a giant *amplificatio* of legalese conveys very little meaning despite its expansiveness.[37] Rape, actual or possible, vanishes from Chaucer's life narrative, engulfed by a wide Latin expanse. As in the movement from the romance to comedy in "Thopas," much is lost in the transformation.

We cannot know whether Chaucer committed rape, but we can see in the possibility, in the accusation, the precipitation of a trauma that haunts his work. Through a close reading of the short poem "Adam Scriveyn," Carolyn Dinshaw demonstrates that Chaucer "represents himself as the victim of scribal rape," a positioning of himself as feminine that recurs throughout his opus (*Chaucer's Sexual Poetics*, 10). Elaine Tuttle Hansen argues that in Chaucer's work, "even the most egregious cases of rape are normalized and trivialized" (*Chaucer and the Fictions of Gender*, 262). The writing of rape is obviously connected to Chaucer's writing of his narratives, and to the writing of his own body. The casual sex crime that begins "The Wife of Bath's Tale" suggests this connection as easily as "Adam Scriveyn" and the Chaumpaigne releases do. But what are we to make of a work such as "Thopas," where the possibility of rape seems to vanish as a consequence of the tale's *reductio ad nihilum* of sexuality?

Sexuality shrinks almost to its vanishing point in "Thopas," but it does not fully disappear. Perhaps it would be more accurate to say that "Thopas" marks a point of collapse where gigantism and diminution become so intertwined they cannot be extricated. That Chaucer's body is simultaneously plump and tiny is suggestive. The narrator is both harmless and "elvyssh," a word with an undercurrent of sexual menace. In the romance *Sir Orfeo*, for example, the queen is abducted by a male fairy very like the rapinous incubi of romance legend, the fathers of giants—and so the giant in *Sir Gawain and the Green Knight* is "an aluish mon" (681). The Wife of Bath likewise conflates male elves, faeries, and incubi and connects all three to a long history of rape.[38] This "elvyssh" body then connects to the "childe" Thopas, placing both in "a puckish relation to 'the little people'" (Gaylord, "'Miracle' of *Sir Thopas*, 68). The language of "The Tale of Sir Thopas" becomes charged with an erotic undercurrent that surfaces in double entendre and sexual innuendo.[39]

The shrinking of masculinity into the inoffensive, childlike, asexual forms of fragment 7, especially in "The Tale of Sir Thopas," postpones but perhaps cannot completely avoid the encounter with the giant. Because this monster is rape incarnate, Sir Olifaunt is contained, diminished, by a pervasive rhetoric of desexualization. Yet to cite the giant even in a burlesque of romance is to activate a powerful chain of resonance, a whole horizon of expectation that the audience brings to the genre — if only to have those expectations raised in defeat. The possibility of rape haunts "The Tale of Sir Thopas" in the act of its forced banishment. The giant as rapist reinscribes the very body out of control that "The Tale of Sir Thopas" tries frantically to exclude. Sir Thopas is named after a precious stone, a highly unusual appellation in romance. Indeed, the only other name in all of romance tradition that bears some similarity is "Amourant." This title is adopted by Owein, squire to Amiloun, as he accompanies his leprous master into exile in *Amis and Amiloun*, where it suggests something like "[steadfast] lover," in imitation of the names of the romance's protagonists.[40] Amourant is also the name of the wicked giant famously defeated by Guy of Warwick in the romance that was, with *Lybeaus Desconus*, undoubtedly Chaucer's primary source for "The Tale of Sir Thopas."[41] Amourant is an especially nasty giant, perfidious in the extreme. Everything in this monster rages against the heroic body represented in Guy; he wants nothing more than to tear open his opponent, to reveal to the world the merely physical stuff from which heroism is composed. Guy, on the other hand, opposes Amourant's gross corporeality with a faith in metaphysicals: he fights for religion and is as interested in the transformative powers of baptism as of beheading.

Or at least he says he is while performing an identity every bit as physical as the giant's. As the battle between Guy and the giant wages on, each delivering gory blows to the body of the other, Amourant reveals that he fights to gain the hand of the sultan's daughter, the "miriest may on mold" (122.9), whom he describes as his "leman" (126.8).[42] The giant aims not for chivalric glory but for the pleasures of the body; he battles to obtain the very thing that Dinabroke took by force. The name "Amourant" in *Guy of Warwick* could again mean something like "lover," surely an ironic resonance in this narrative. It is a word that also means "emerald." This giant, among the most infamous in romance tradition, is named after a gem. Just like Sir Thopas.

"Emeraude" is the very noun used to describe the "litel clergeon" of "The Prioress's Tale," a small body that has much in common with the bodies of Thopas and Chaucer. When all of these identities are connected to the familiar giant of romance, the dangers that their diminished physicalities hide become more obvious. The innocent boy causes a massacre

116

via his relentless repetition of an expanse of Latin words that hold no direct meaning for him. His steadfast obliviousness is his guarantee that the bodily violence so impossible to attach to him will erupt elsewhere in the "litel" world he inhabits. Geoffrey the pilgrim and Thopas the diminutive knight likewise seem a great deal less precious than they at first appeared. Violence, specifically sexual violence, is the absent presence that haunts both diminutive bodies.

The defeat of the giant is a powerful textual moment that announces that the knight's tightly controlled body has no tincture of monstrousness. The ritual of defeat culminates in a decapitation scene when, as in *Guy of Warwick*, the severed head of the giant delivers a powerful message about the proper construction of the hero's masculinity. "The Tale of Sir Thopas" cannot stage such a triumph. Its insistent reduction of sex ensures that Thopas will never progress much beyond the miniature identity with which he enters the story. Thopas cannot triumph over the giant, cannot enact the chivalric ritual of decapitation, cannot exorcise the phantom of rape: unique in all of romance, Olifaunt has three heads, making the idea of a beheading scene laughably comic, and finally impracticable. The transformation of Cecily Chaumpaigne's original release to the diminished-expanded version of three days later suggests why. The impossibility of mastery arises in "Sir Thopas" and its prologue because the giant is already within: an interior trauma, a *kernkomplex* at the heart of Chaucer's self-figuration.

Trauma and Small Bodies

The English Rising, the social body out of control, was ultimately defeated by a child. Richard invited the rioting crowds to a meeting at Mile End, a large field outside London, where he vowed to grant their requests so long as they promised to return home. The scheme worked, dispersing the multitude and reducing the rebels' power to a controllable size. Richard was eleven when he was crowned king, and fifteen by the time he stood before the assembled malcontents: a version of the David and Goliath story in which masculinity is strongly asserted even in a "litel" body. Chaucer's diminished self in *The Canterbury Tales* clearly has a wider cultural context, for the events of 1381 occurred just as he began work on his magnum opus. No doubt Richard at Mile End was still fresh in his mind as he composed fragment 7, with its fascinated stare at bodies large and small in their relation to the performance of masculinity.

Richard's example of a diminutive body that dispersed through its steadfastness a gigantic moment of trauma no doubt offered a powerful historical model of how various social bodies could be brought back into harmony, of how an irruption of the real could be dissolved via assertive symbolization. Chaucer, I am suggesting, used this archetype to

117

devise a rhetoric to contain a trauma of a wholly different order. "Personal" traumas are never very distant from social ones. If I may be permitted one last, grand gesture in closing, I will suggest that the fight against the giant in Chaucer's "Tale of Sir Thopas" never takes place because England in the late Middle Ages was always haunted by the violence it committed against women's bodies. We will never know whether Chaucer raped Cecily Chaumpaigne (and that helpless lack of a firm epistemological footing is always a component of trauma, which exists outside all questions of veridicality). Nonetheless, what can be said with certainty is that the crimes against female bodies that romance describes (sometimes to celebrate, more often to protest) and that Chaucer diminished were undeniably real. The male body can be vastly comedic; fragment 7 of *The Canterbury Tales* is proof enough of that. But the same male body is also a source of great cultural danger, as the figure of the giant — and the giant of self-figuration — reveal.

CHAPTER 5

The Body Hybrid

Giants, Dog-Men, and Becoming Inhuman

The Church has always burned sorcerers, or reintegrated anchorites into the toned-down images of a series of saints whose only remaining relation to animals is strangely familiar, domestic.
—Gilles Deleuze and Félix Guattari, *A Thousand Plateaus*, 248

Canicular Days

In an intriguing short story, Vladimir Slepian writes of a man who decides to become a dog.[1] One limb, one organ at a time, he transforms himself, mapping the affects of the canine body across a human form in the strangest kind of diagramming. Dogs are quadrupedal, and so he ties shoes to hands and feet. When his new paws prevent him from lacing the fourth shoe, he uses his mouth, which becomes a dog's clever snout. His metamorphosis almost succeeds, but then he comes to the tail and can find no somatic analogue. For him to involve his sexual organ in this wild fit of becoming would tear him completely from the cultural meaning system that he has begun to flee; who would he be, if the signs of his identity were not readable from his anatomy? In the end, he chooses being a man over becoming something other, something freakish or monstrous. A "psychoanalytic drift" descends, and he is flooded with childhood memories—"all the clichés about the tail, the mother" (*A Thousand Plateaus*, 259). Suddenly it becomes clear what human limit he was attempting to flee: "Oedipus, phallocentrism, molar personhood itself" (Brian Massumi, *User's Guide*, 94). The man's becoming-dog fails, perhaps because he maps his escape across a body already too constrained: no freedom animates the household dog. Canine bodies, like human bodies, receive their meaning-in-being only to the extent to which they are Oedipalized, made to signify within a geometry of familial relations.

What would success have been like? Massumi offers one vision: "Having superposed human and canine affects" onto a mongrel form, Slepian's man-dog must resist the psychoanalytic temptation to retreat back into the stasis of a "molar identity," man *or* dog. As a body enraptured by an unstable, nonteleological process of transformation, he could "keep moving toward the great dissipative outside stretching uncertainly on the wild side of the welcome mat," never looking back as he sets out on a singular, quadrupedal "path of freakish becoming" (*User's Guide*, 95). The image is silly, of course, but that mirth arises simply from the fact that we lack a language sufficiently imprecise to conceptualize what this restless, posthuman hybrid might be like. The medieval imagination suggests a more serious possibility: a cynocephalus, an exotic body where human and canine affects are permanently at play. Like Massumi's vision, this monster with a dog's head and a man's powerful body is difficult to place because it violates categories; unlike Massumi's happy monster, however, the cynocephalus resolutely refuses dismissive laughter. Because he embodied fears about the fragility of Christian identity in the face of the Saracen threat, the medieval cynocephalus was a viscerally disturbing figure, very like the giant. In romance, both monsters produce an absolute limit for proper male embodiment and so could be combined into a triple hybrid, an animal-headed *geaunt* with a vast, hypermasculine body.

Saint Christopher, a giant as well as a cynocephalus, commenced his life as a monster and at his death was transfigured into an icon, endlessly painted on medieval town walls to bless passing travelers.[2] The Hereford mappamundi, that grand reduction of the world's sprawling geography into a single visual system, places two dog-headed figures labeled *gigantes* not far from Babylon, where their fellow giant Nimrod built the Tower of Babel. The monsters are depicted with raised snouts, apparently barking in joy. Each touches the hip or belly of the other's naked body, and their slender, extended arms form a sensuous bridge between their monstrous forms. The Hereford giants guard the gates of paradise against human return.[3] Herein lies the paradox of the medieval monster. For all the "cosmic terror" they inspire, the giant and the cynocephalus are twinned bodies beyond which lies not the utter dissolution of selfhood, but just the opposite: immortality, the gift of an identity that is unending and immutable, the reward of heaven itself.

Sir Gowther, a rapacious murderer born of a demon, raised as a giant, and revered as a saint, could have taught Slepian's failed cynocephalus that.

Enfances

It is the dog that makes us human.

—Marjorie Garber, *Dog Love*

It may seem strange to begin this chapter with an anecdote about a man intent on becoming man's best friend. But readers of the Middle English verse romance *Sir Gowther* will already recognize in the vignette a familiar story.[4] Gowther gains his adult identity through a similar process of transformation, mapping the potentialities of his unsocialized self across the grid of the canine bodies with which he shares food and place. Romance is a resolutely hybrid genre, and *Sir Gowther* takes this hybridity to an extreme. Its protagonist never fights the traditional giant, because his monstrous body already contains that enemy. The trajectory of the narrative postulates an originary gigantism for the masculine corpus, introjecting everything other romances write as exterior to the hero's body, and then plunges Gowther so deep into monstrousness that he will emerge purified, sanctified. This odd but wonderful little romance plots through the wilds of identity a monstrous route to becoming male in the Middle Ages.

Gowther's life does not begin well. His mother and father, the duke and duchess of "Estryke," have been wedded for ten childless years. The text holds the duke as much at fault for the lack of an heir as his wife ("He chylde non geyt ne sche non bare," 50), but he blames only her: "Y tro thou be sum baryn, / Hit is gud that we twyn; / Y do bot wast my tyme on the" [I believe that you're barren, so it would be good for us to part. I'm wasting my time on you] (53–55). In the duke's masculinist rhetoric, culpability falls on the maternal body, which is destined to become a disavowed site of origin in *Sir Gowther*. Yet the father's body does not fare much better. No son exists to carry into the future the family name ("Eireles mon owre londys bee," 56), the "paternal metaphor" condensed in the ducal title. This impersonal title is the only signifier of identity attached to the duke and duchess of Estryke, who *both* remain without personal names throughout the narrative.

Aristocratic familial history is germane to the "ancestral romances" (*Guy of Warwick, Bevis of Hampton*): such stories detail the foundational moments of provincial aristocracies to trace the phantasmatic power of family names. "Fair Unknown" romances (*Perceval of Galles, Lybeaus Desconus*) enact the same narrative without invoking the illusory "real" of particularized history. Jacques Lacan's psychoanalytic notion of "the Name of the Father" (*nom du père*) is useful in describing the textual mechanics of both genres: these identity romances often trace how young men mature into their proper name through a series of adventures—and, "as it turns out," the adult identity into which they wander exactly coincides with a family name that may have been hidden from them until that point.[5] Even when (or especially when) romance heroes do not know who their father is, their movement into adulthood is dictated nonetheless by the ghostly agency that the Name of the Father embodies in its narrative determinacy.

Sir Gowther is neither ancestral nor Fair Unknown romance but plays with the conventions of both to create a hybrid kind of identity narrative. The Name of the Father, that ghost that passes like Hamlet's father to each son and whispers, "Remember me," will stop appearing when the (nameless) duke of Estryke dies, for he has no son to compel with its impossible charge to historical repetition. The duke of Estryke despairs and breaks apart his family. His wife, however, finds a way to reconfigure the circuit of that name, by invoking a "real" phantasm, an incubus, as well as a larger history than the local one of ancestral romance.[6] The duchess prays to "God and Maré mylde" that, through some miracle, she will have a child, "on what maner scho ne roghth" [she didn't care how] (63). She wanders into the orchard and encounters a man resembling her husband who seeks her love. He leads her to a tree and "With hur is wyll he wroghtth" (69):

> When he had is wylle all don,
> A felturd fende he start up son,
>   And stode and hur beheld.
> He seyd, "Y have geyton a chylde on the
> That in is yothe full wylde schall bee." (70–74)

[When he had worked his will on her, he leapt up, a hairy fiend, and stood and looked upon her. He said, "I have engendered a child on you who, in his youth, will be very wild."]

She runs from the garden, terrified at this supernatural revelation — terrified that her desires have been simultaneously spoken and made real.

But she is not so frightened that she cannot see an advantage in the impregnation. The duchess informs her husband that an angel has descended from bright heaven to declare that they will conceive a child that very night (80–81). The tableau wickedly repeats in secular, imaginary history a foundational moment in salvation history. The duchess speaks as if she were Mary after the Annunciation, declaring the impending arrival of a miraculous birth through the agency of some bodiless Holy Spirit. The duke believes his wife, for his desires have likewise been realized; "he pleyd hym with that ladé" all night, unaware that a "fende" has already "bownden" with her (91–92). Joseph lost his paternal imperative to God; the duke loses his to a demon.

The baby is born and christened Gowther — christened *in nomine patris*, just as the romance is constructed around the search for a father's name under which to be. The evil deeds Gowther commits while still a youth cause the duke to sicken and die within a single line: no possibility of inheriting any identity-giving history from someone who has been, all along, a nonentity. Of Gowther's "biological" father we know little, other than that he was the same evil fiend who begot Merlin (95). A prologue in the British Library (MS Royal 17.B.43) version of the story yields some additional prehistory. Foul fiends, the text declares, once roamed the earth, passing themselves off as men in order to have sexual intercourse "with ladies free" (6–7):

> A selcowgth thyng that is to here:
> A fende to nyeght wemen nere,
>   And makyd hom with chyld,
> Tho kynde of men wher thei hit tane
> (For of homselfe had thei never nan). (13–17)

[It is a strange thing to hear: A fiend would lie with women, and engender a child on them, through the men's forms [or semen] they had taken (for of themselves they have none).]

The creature described here is the incubus, a monster with a complex medieval genealogy. Incubi would temporarily reside in illusory male forms to work their sexual crimes, engendering monstrous offspring on unsuspecting women before reverting to their disembodied state. Patristic exegesis connected these airy demons to the fallen angels and the birth of giants, tracing their history to an ambiguous passage in the Vulgate Genesis (6:4) in which giants arise when "sons of God" (*filii Dei*) copulate with "daughters of men" (*filiae hominum*). According to a tradition dismissed by Augustine but influential throughout the Middle Ages, the sons of God were fallen angels, the daughters of men mortals, and the offspring of this illicit mingling of the purely spiritual and overly physical were the giants, the most wicked and pervasive race of monsters in the Bible—and in romance.[7] Giants are almost always described as the sons of fiends. In *Torrent of Portyngale*, for example, "There ys a gyant of gret renowne... / He was get of the dewell of hell, / as his moder on slepe lay" [There is a giant of great fame who was begotten of a devil from hell upon his mother as she slept] (921–26). Incubi, raped women, and giants form the vertices of a monstrous family triangle with a long and unholy history.

From the Annunciation, we have moved back to those iniquitous days preceding the Flood. But we also recede into a specifically English history, into a version of what in chapter 2 was called the Albina myth. According to this popular prehistory of England, the island was settled by women who were impregnated by bodiless demons and gave birth to giants. Unlike the mother in *Robert le diable* who vows her son to the devil at conception, the duchess in *Sir Gowther* is replaying a particularly English scene that wholly transforms the French romance on which *Gowther* is based, giving it a "local habitation" along with a new name. History repeats: the intercourse of fiend and errant daughters of men in biblical history becomes the intercourse of fiend and transgressive princesses in national history, which in turn becomes the intercourse of fiend and disconsolate wife in the familial space of romance.[8] Even if these successive repetitions threaten to become a funnel that trickles out smaller versions of the same story, Gowther is nonetheless something of a giant. Like the monstrous progeny of the biblical and English chronicle traditions, Gowther grows at a prodigious rate: "In a twelmond more he wex / Then odur chylder in syvon or sex" [In a year he grew bigger than other children do in six or seven] (142–43).

His exceptional corporeality is the product of the flow of violence that nourishes him as much as the breast milk with which it mingles. His father arranges for him to have the best wives of the country as his wet nurses, and Gowther vampirically "sowked hom so thei lost ther lyvys" (110). In the first year of his life, he drains nine nurses of milk and life. The duchess is then forced to take over the feeding of this little monster:

> His modur fell a fowle unhappe;
> Apon a day bad hym tho pappe,
>   He snaffulld to it soo,
> He rofe tho hed fro tho brest;
> Scho fell backeward and cald a prest. (124–29)

[His mother suffered a foul misfortune. Upon a day she tried to breast-feed him. He sucked at it so hard, he tore the nipple from breast. She fell backwards and called for a priest.]

The physical violence that attends every attempt at nurture demonstrates that no place exists for him within the feminine, domestic spaces represented by the parade of nurses and his mother; even the maternal breast is torn to pieces. Gowther, from infancy, resists familialism.[9] Nor does his behavior improve much as he grows older. By the time he is fifteen, he is wielding a "fachon," a sword with a curved blade that signifies both his uncontrolled aggression (he and the sword are never parted) and his alterity (the falchion is an Eastern weapon, suggestive of Saracens, heathendom, and infernal origin). His father knights him, then dies of grief; his mother flees to a fortress where she immures herself against his energetic evil.

Gowther, now a "duke of greyt renown," passes his days happily abusing churchmen, hunting, and chasing mendicant friars. "Erly and late, lowde and styll, / He wold wyrke is fadur wyll" (172–73): like the young Jesus discovered preaching in the temple, Gowther must be about his father's business, only he has no idea who his father is, even as his actions inscribe him under that paternal name ("fiend"). In one bout of wickedness, he and his men rape a group of nuns who have issued in procession from their convent to beg mercy. He then locks the women in their church and burns them alive. The catalog of crime also includes spoiling virgins so that they cannot marry, violating wives and then slaying their husbands, forcing friars to leap off cliffs, hanging parsons on hooks, slaying priests, and igniting hermits and widows (190–201).

If chivalry is the code that regulates the proper construction of masculinity within the domain of haut bourgeois and aristocratic relations (and is simultaneously a fiction and an effective cultural intervention into gender codification), then Gowther embodies everything that the code excludes. Just as the *gigantes* (Nephilim) issue from the primal rape narrated in Genesis, just as Gogmagog and his bellicose companions are the vast progeny of the ravishing of Albina and her sisters, so Gowther is the grossly physical product of the duchess's encounter with an incorporeal incubus. Engendered of a demon and *filia hominum*, Gowther is the stereotyped giant of romance, the masculine body out of control whose abnormal size signifies rampant appetite, both somatic and social. The giant enfleshes everything Freud labeled "pre-Oedipal." His is the body unimpressed by social coding, a playground of unchanneled forces (aggression, orality, desire, and drive without boundary) that explode outward in monstrous excess.

The postmodern theorists of identity Gilles Deleuze and Félix Guattari have argued that the organizing principle of Western embodiment is the Oedipal construct ("Oedipus"), the primary structuration through which desire in its "molecular" multiplicity is regulated into the pure, "molar" forms of sexed bodies.[10] In classical psychoanalysis, submission to Oedipus means recognition of the dictative power of the father (Freud's "Oedipus complex"), or of the transcendental principle that the father ineptly embodies, beyond choice or control (Lacan's "Name of the Father"). In the theater of psychoanalysis, the Oedipal drama is a critical success when the denouement is acceptance of one's place within an identity matrix mapped across a triangle of familial relations. Oedipus is a productive prohibition whose outcome is a "global person," an "ego," an "individual."[11] The equation for Oedipus might be written as 3 + 1: the three members of the family triangle, plus a master signifier, a principle outside the structuration that acts as guarantor of its transcendent truth (*Anti-Oedipus*, 73). The Oedipalized subject that is the equation's resultant is a predictable distribution of forces and affects across a culturally coherent body. This embodied subject can then be exactly placed on a social grid by reference to filiation.

Oedipus works rather differently as a constitutive principle in the Middle Ages, depending on the particular culture employing its organizational power (and sometimes, of course, it does not obtain at all).[12] In identity romance, the moment of Oedipalization usually occurs during the fight against the giant. The young hero defeats his monstrous double, rendering a volatile multiplicity of possibility into a unitary, regularized being. Oedipus in identity romance is not predicated on rivalry with the father for the affection of the mother, with all its various displacements; it perhaps takes Freud's claustrophobic domestic interiors to enact that family drama. Romance geographies are wider, the cast of characters more numerous and less quotidian, but the Name of the Father becomes their cartographer all the same. The young hero learns what expression the historical, sexual, social forces at work on his body are to take and willingly steps into that sanctioned role: Yvain becomes master of his castle, settling down after long errantry to become both husband and lord. The romance ideal of masculinity involves a single heterosexual object choice (the requisite loving wife) coupled to an unambiguous situation within the grid of homosocial relations (ideally, as lord or king, the dominant position a final representational validation of the worth of the attainer). Oedipus ensures that in the imaginary but culturally effective space of romance, bodies particularly prone to troublemaking are brought under social ("familial") control — even if that family is the celibate family of the Holy Church.

The Names of the Father

As Jesse Helms has made clear, difference, in our culture, is obscenity. And it is this with which postmodern theory must contend.
—Douglas Crimp, "The Boys in My Bedroom"

What happens, though, when the restraints of Oedipus fail to produce a sufficiently docile, sufficiently pure body? Miri Rubin aptly describes medieval bodies as sites of "fear, conduits of joy, objects of shame, victims of pain" that were "lived in the knowledge of their vulnerability," of their lack of a transcendant principle of order ("The Body, Whole and Vulnerable, in Fifteenth Century England," 26). The "unbounded" body, porous and threatening, was the object of legal, ecclesiastical, and medical interventions but was never fully captured by their pervasive "ordering stategies." From the point of view of the power structures whose interplay composes a society or culture, this resistant and impure body is unstable, dangerous, perhaps monstrous. But the monster could itself be an "ordering strategy": by encoding what one must not become, it demonstrates what, in the gaze of its terrifying face, one is compelled to be.

Despite his wicked ways, Gowther possesses this insight. When an elderly earl accuses him of being the son of a fiend, he is horrified (210). He imprisons the man, gallops to the fortress where his mother is hiding, and demands to know the truth of his paternity. "Who was my fadur?" becomes the central question of the text, which now works with a machinic efficiency toward its resolution. The first reply to Gowther's demand is situational: the duchess states simply that he was fathered by the duke "that dyed last" (223). Gowther is not satisfied and repeats his query. This time the answer is historical, as the duchess invites her son to witness through her narrative the primal scene of his own biological and metaphysical formation:

Son, sython Y schall tho sothe say:
In owre orcharde apon a day,
    A fende gat the thare;
As lyke my lorde as he myght be,
Undurneyth a cheston tre. (226–30)

[Son, since I must tell you the truth: In our orchard one day, a fiend begot you. He looked as much like my lord as might be, underneath a chestnut tree.]

The scene of the no longer immaculate conception is detailed, with Gowther as its onlooker. The sexual relation, stripped of its mythology (no courtly love here, no rhetoric of the symbolic to clothe the naked real of the act) reduces Gowther to a genital outcome. This brief but disturbing account functions similarly to the psychoanalytic drama of a *pornographic* moment.[13] The sexual act, Slavoj Zizek argues, works narratively as "an intrusion of the real undermining the consistency of [the] diegetic reality" (111). The love stories that structure identity romances are built around an approach toward, as well as a swerving away from, the "unattainable/forbidden object" of desire; to go too far, to attain this structurating impossibility, instantly debases it: "Instead of the sublime Thing, we are stuck with vulgar, groaning fornication" (110). The orchard scene that opened the romance repeats precisely in order to push the narrative "too far," to expose the vulgarity of Gowther's conception as the vulgarity of *all* conception. Despite its revelatory power, however, the moment of origin remains indecipherable: Was it rape? Was it desired? A rape-in-desire? How does one judge such an event? How does one represent the real of the sexual relation? The seamlessness of the Symbolic (the discursive system that structures culture) is momentarily tattered by an intrusion of the Real (the utterly material, that which resists representation in language). Gowther is faced suddenly with the elemental nonsensicality of his coming into being. Through his mother's testimony, he witnesses the act in all its corporeality, and now he must find a way to symbolize that encounter, to sublimate its trauma into a meaning system not reducible to a "mere" biology of sex.

A theological reading of the passage must stress that Gowther has just been faced with the stark reality of his *human* birth into Original Sin, the fallen state of humankind.[14] The fiend is not really any different from the duke; indeed, a fiend attends upon every sexual relation. If the "kynde of men" that the incubus steals (12) refers to man's semen rather than man's shape, then the fiend is a disembodied delivery system, the sexual act in effect but not in a particular body; the "material imprint" interjected into the *materia* of the maternal body is still the real of the father. Another way of putting it: the fiend *is* the duke, or at least the "father in reality" (the father in his corporeality, as a sexual and fallible body), as opposed to the pure and incorporeal function of paternity (as "metaphor," as *nom du père*). "Who was my fadur?" After the situational and historical responses that Gowther's mother provides, the only answer that now remains to the riddle of masculine identity is a purely transcendent one that can leave behind the soiled physicality of this originary moment. All that is solid must melt into air: through transcendence lies the only possibility of escape.[15]

Gowther enjoins his mother to make confession, promises to do likewise, and departs quickly for Rome. He prays to "God that Maré bare" and "God and Maré hynde": his new family will be the Holy Family, and he will gain entrance through audience with the pope, Father of the Church. The bishop of Rome commands Gowther to "Lye down the fachon" (286), and the knight refuses; the sword is too much a part of his identity, a materialization into extrapsychical space of what he inside *is*. But the next papal commandment Gowther obeys without hesitation: "Wherser thou travellys be northe or soth, / Thou eyt no meyt bot that thou revus of howndus mothe, / Cum thy body within" [Wheresoever you travel, north or south, you must eat only what meat you snatch from dogs' mouths, nothing else may come into your body] (292–94). Gowther's body is to be completely closed to social exchange: his food predigested, his mouth an organ that receives and ingests rather than reacts and interacts through language. To become fully embedded within the Symbolic (that is, to become a Name divorced from the corporeality a name might signify), Gowther's body must become a passive object, a still surface upon which will be inscribed new codes of conduct and a new organization.

To be a man, Gowther is going to have to become a dog.

Transitional Bodies

All knowledge, the totality of all questions and answers, is contained in the dog.

— Franz Kafka, "Investigations of a Dog"

In acceptance of his penance, Gowther kneels before the throne of the pope, his first gesture of submission. In Rome he eats meat only from the mouths of dogs, wholly obedient to his vow; then he wanders from the Eternal City and arrives in "anodur far cuntre" (305). A greyhound delivers a loaf of bread for each of three days. When on the fourth morning the dog fails to appear, Gowther discovers the castle of a mighty emperor. Trumpets resound on the high wall, knights process into the main chamber, and Gowther follows as if he were that vanished greyhound, crawling beneath a table and silently sitting down (328–30). The steward, quick to enter the drama of resemblance, threatens to beat Gowther with a stick, like the dog he has become. Yet the penitential knight retains a strange dignity even as he maps the trajectory of his becoming through a domestic, shaggy body: the canine with which he will form an alliance, his point of departure to becoming something other than the son of a fiend, will not be any household pet, but the special favorite of the castle's master. Gowther seats himself under the high table, where the emperor recognizes that some higher calling may compel this man-dog, perhaps even a penance (343–44). He has Gowther provided with meat and bread from his own board and watches curiously as this foreigner who inserts himself at the court's center refuses to eat. When the emperor sees the speechless man snatch a bone from a "spanyell," he provides the hounds with extra food so that Gowther can share in the secondary feast. "Among tho howndys thus was he fed" (364), and at night he is led to a "lytyll chambur" ringed with curtains. He quickly becomes a court favorite, and they name him Hob.

The episode is structurally similar to the plot of Marie de France's lay *Bisclavret*, the protagonist of which becomes the favorite knight of the king by spending many months as his favorite hunting hound. A knight who also happens to be a werewolf is trapped permanently in canine shape after his fearful wife steals his clothing. His king comes across the wolf-man in the forest and refrains from killing him when he makes gestures of submission. He adopts the metamorphic knight as a pet, not realizing that the beast was formerly one of his men. Bisclavret endears himself to his master, sleeping in his chamber at night and passing the day at his feet. In quadrupedal form, he sees his wife for the treacherous woman she is and realizes the superiority of the bond that ties him to the king over that which had joined him to his spouse. By learning to be a proper dog (that is, by submitting with an absolute love to his allotted place within the masculine hierarchy), Bisclavret learns to be a proper man. *Nom* to *nom propre: bisclavret*, the Breton noun for "werewolf," becomes Bisclavret, the hero's proper name. In Marie's narrative, an antinomy exists between male-male and male-female bonds. Bisclavret is rewarded with his "true" body only after he takes his revenge on his traitorous spouse by biting off her nose to expose her crime. The wife, not the werewolf, is the monster: rather than lycanthropy being transmitted to successive generations, the wife's noselessness is passed along congenitally to her female children.

Gowther's body receives a "domesticating" (or, better, "familializing") imprint similar to Bisclavret's. He is the very thing that Anglo-Saxon England could not imagine: the household giant, as if Grendel had entered Heorot and been inducted into homosociality. Gowther is trained into the functional symbolic of the court just as a canine or infantile body is made to internalize the regulatory mechanisms that, through habit and repetition, render it coherent, legible, selfsame. For both Bisclavret and Gowther, a wild, molecular identity is constrained through a mapping across an animal body, receiving its molar being only after this interstitial (transitional, transferential) form has been successfully passed through.[16] In both cases, the liminal canine body has as much to do with the anthropomorphization of dogs as the becoming-animal of humans. Dogs are readily incorporated within human meaning systems because their bodies have been bred to be easy to imprint: we like dogs as household pets to the extent to that they act as if human, as if a simultaneously exaggerated and diminutive version of ourselves. Dogs are easy to Oedipalize.[17] Docility and a love for the disciplinary regime that requires an absolute submission are the canine affects that Bisclavret and Gowther become dog in order to instate. Rather than fight a giant to confront Oedipus, these monstrous knights are Oedipalized more slowly, through a grammar of transformation that will fix the undisciplined and metamorphic multiplicity of their bodies, their interior gigantism, into the stasis of a singular and externalized identity.

Gowther and the hound, like Bisclavret and the wolf, enter into a masochistic relation. He seems simply to be imitating the dog but in fact is engaged in a more complex process of intersubjective embodiment. To return to Deleuze and Guattari's terminology, the instinctive forces that animate the human body are being overcoded by transmitted forces. Deleuze and Guattari provide the example of a masochist who transfigures himself through a similar somatic mapping into a horse. Why a horse?

> Horses are trained: humans impose upon the horse's instinctive forces transmitted forces that regulate the former, select, dominate, overcode them. The masochist transmits an inversion of signs: the horse transmits its transmitted forces to him, so that the masochist's innate forces will in turn be tamed. (*A Thousand Plateaus*, 155–56).

And so with the dog: all the forces that are transmitted through the canine body rebound to overcode the human. An interstitial monster springs temporarily into being: a dog-man, a cynocephalus, a werewolf. But once the overcoding "takes," the body passes out of its freakish hybridity to be inscribed more fully than ever into the secure space of the human.

Gowther's becoming-dog ultimately follows a rather different trajectory from Bisclavret's, or at least a geometrically more complicated one. A trigonometry unites not only Gowther and the animals under the table but also the knight and the emperor's daughter, who is likewise mute ("was too soo dompe as hee," 372). Her body is the next mediating "partial object" that will pull him closer to a full identity. Conjoined by their mutual affect (silence), Gowther and the princess use the canine bodies as the bridge across which they communicate, beginning a new diagram that allows Gowther to leave these docile animals for new transitions. When the princess observes that he takes his nourishment only from dogs' mouths, she reacts with kindness. She calls two fine greyhounds to her side, washes clean their mouths with wine, places a loaf of bread in one and some meat in the other, and sends the pair to Gowther, who devours the food eagerly. The dogs become transitional, rather than restrictive, forms, and through the princess's intercession, Gowther begins the final process of transubstantiation. For the first time, Gowther's own corporeality is inserted into the text through a vigorous exclamation: "That doghty of body and bon" [That man hearty in flesh and bone] (447). No coincidence, then, that the bread, wine, and "flesch" she sends to him have their analogues in the Eucharist, where "lofe"

and "wyn" become a body, the "flesch" and blood of Christ. By directing the flow of his desire to the princess (who acts the intercessional
part of Mary), Gowther will be brought at last out from among the dogs
and into the Holy Family.

But first Gowther's desire must alight upon the princess as object, for
without the connection of desire, he cannot be pulled by a new investment of force from his place beneath the table. This process is initiated
through mimesis. No sooner does Gowther first see the emperor's daughter than she is constituted as object-cause of desire through the gaze of
another: a "sawdyn" (sultan) of great might declares he shall wage war
against the emperor "dey and nyghtt" until the princess is given to him
(376–84). The emperor refuses with the resonant phrase "Y wyll not, be
Cryst wonde, / Gyffe hor to no hethon hownde!" [I will not, by the
wounds of Christ, give her to any heathen hound!] (388–89). The declaration demarcates Gowther's third relational body, connected to him both
by its rhetorical contiguity to the dogs he imitates ("hethon hownde!")
and by its fascination with the emperor's daughter (dumb, like him; object of the gaze, like him). This third body will break the closed circuit
of his identity diagramming. Gowther is connected to the animal and
feminine bodies by relationships of becoming and movement; this new
enemy will teach him the necessities of abjection as differentiation, as
entrance into stable being. The sultan takes the place of the giant that
Gowther no longer can embody.

The Hounds of War

In his unpublished seminar on identity, Lacan writes of his dog Justine,
named after the heroine of the Marquis de Sade's novel. He apologizes in
advance, "I have no sadistic intention towards her."
—Renata Salecl, "Love Me, Love My Dog"

Paulus Deaconus insisted in the *Historia Langobardorum* that the Lombards were masters of tactical disinformation. Before engaging an enemy
in combat, they spread the rumor that a troop of cynocephali waited in
their camp as allies, ready to do merciless battle against any opponent.
These exotic dog-headed men, well known from medieval accounts of
the monstrous races, were often depicted in manuscript illustrations as
anthropophagous or as giants. The Lombards made full use of this monstrous mythology and insisted that their dog soldiers, eager imbibers of
human blood, were growing thirsty:

They spread the rumor among the enemy that these men wage war
obstinately, drink human blood, and quaff their own gore if they
cannot reach the foe. And to give faith to this assertion, the Langobards spread their tents wide and kindle a great many fires in their

camps. (*History of the Langobards,* trans. William Dudley Foulke, 1.11.20)

In the face of such intimidating foes, the credulous enemy would ordinarily beat a hasty retreat (20).

The rumor worked so effectively because cynocephali were familiar throughout the later Middle Ages as culturally expedient forms in which to embody the enemies of Christendom, especially Muslims.[18] Through this monstrous enfleshment, a whole array of anxiety-producing alterities could be simplified into spectacularly inhuman text and bone. *Chansons de geste, historiae,* romances, and manuscript illustrations depict Islamic men as dog-headed warriors ready to dismember Christian bodies. Such hybrid forms encode two competing but not contradictory affects: these Others are threateningly feral, but also responsive to domestication at the hands of an evangelical master. The Saracen cynocephalus incorporates a dual Christian impulse, bellicose and missionary. Above the central door to the Church of the Madeleine at Vézelay, a magnificent tympanum illustrates the Mission of the Apostles, the moment after Pentecost when they began their conversion of the pagan world. One panel is filled by energetic cynocephali whose sleek heads top supple, muscular bodies. The figures, simultaneously grotesque and enticing, await the arrival of the apostolic Word that will render them more human.[19] Considering that Bernard preached the second crusade at Vézelay in 1145 and that the church lay on the pilgrimage road to Jerusalem, the contribution of the piece to an ongoing program of Muslim monsterization is clear. That this process of cultural embodiment activates not only anxiety (about one's own body, about one's own identity) but also *desire* (to possess the foreign body, to tame and control its monstrousness in order to hold it close) has less often been remarked.

A similar but less spectacular technology of monsterization propels the representation of Islam in England, where the "Saracen threat" never encroached and therefore was always in danger of seeming fantastic and remote.[20] According to the popular romance *Kyng Alisaunder,* for example, the army of Darius had a contingent of houndlike men who could not speak, only bark in rage: "His men ne couþen speke ne grede, / Bot als houndes grenne and berken" [his men could not speak or shout, but like hounds bared their teeth and barked].[21] These warriors are doubly robbed of the power to be coherent: their speech is mere barking, their bodies are hybrid, subhuman, and therefore nonsensical. The monsters are also given a biblical descent from Cain, who by killing his brother was the first to prove that the body is a fragile and impermanent house. A similar scene appears in *Richard Coer de Lion,* a romance replete with metaphorical cynocephali.[22] The swarming heathens are transformed into a landscape of blood and corpses by Richard's divinely sanctioned War Machine:

And manye off þe heþene houndes
Wiþ here teeþ gnowȝ þe groundes.
By þe blood vpon þe gras
Men myte see where Richard was! (5115–18)

[And many of the heathen hounds
With their teeth gnawed upon the ground.
By the blood upon the grass,
Men could tell where Richard was!]

The reduction here is extreme, and deadly: Muslims to Saracens to dogs to inert bodily *materia* that exists only to proclaim a message about Richard's patriotic excess.

Even before the First Crusade, continental and insular sources imaged pagans as monsters. By the late fourteenth century, the depiction had been rendered culturally attractive for a set of reasons wholly different from those motivating early chansons and chronicle. Urgent compulsion was replaced by dreamy nostalgia. For all the abortive attempts at revival, true crusading spirit belonged to a distant past, when Christendom could be envisioned as a corporate identity capable of transcending the petty limits of the merely national. The cynocephalus, as a result, became in England part of a cultural fantasy of a time when enemies were easy to distinguish and glorious to defeat. The dog-man's monstrous body, despite its difficult hybridity, offered an unambiguous invitation "written in the flesh" to conquer and domesticate him into Occidental masculinity. Protracted, messy nearby wars in Ireland, Spain, and especially France spurred the English romancers to dream of a time when self-identity was easy to assert, because the enemy was wholly Other (dark skin, incomprehensible language, pagan culture) and therefore an unproblematic body to define oneself against.

The *Song of Roland* (c. 1100) could confidently declare: "Paiens unt tort e Chrestiens unt dreit" [Pagans are wrong, Christians are right]. Such propagandistic formulas, effective because of their idiotic reductiveness, are not so easily pronounced when a nation's wars oppose Christian to Christian and are proximate enough to leave their economic underpinnings visible. In the *Confessio Amantis* (c. 1386), John Gower considered the morality of killing for one's faith and pronounced its wrongfulness (3.2485). Yet the wide appeal of romance resides in its monomaniacal refusal to admit that identity is more complex than a simple abjection of difference from a consistent core of chivalric selfhood. Romance solves the problem of the present's intractability by constructing a lost past when Christian right and pagan wrong were rendered obvious through cleanly oppositional modes of embodiment. Nostalgically or anachronistically, Gowther's body suggests the physical and sexual vigor of the Vézelay tympanum's cynocephali, in their early Crusade-inflected depiction; in the face of the Muslim sultan, he will also come to embody the martial prowess of the dog-man, in its aspect of Western imperialist fantasy. Like the ancient cynocephali whom the wandering apostles converted in distant lands, Gowther temporarily inhabits these strange bodies to dream wistfully an absolute commensurability between essence and embodiment—between the purity of the soul and the mutable aesthetics of its fleshly house.

The cynocephalus is monstrous because of its hybridity. Human and canine affects freely play across its species-mingling flesh, marking it as alien. Miscegenation made corporeal, he has no secure place in a Christian identity structure generated around a technology of exclusion. A category violator, the monster must be marginalized to keep the system pure. Both the monster and the Christian male receive their identity only as the separation is enacted and do not exist as coherent entities before this movement. This is perhaps a too condensed way of stating what Judith Butler has argued at some length, that the "exclusionary matrix by which subjects are formed thus requires the simultaneous production of a domain of abject beings...who form the constitutive outside to the domain of the subject" (*Bodies That Matter*, 3). Trapped in a dialectic of disidentification against the monster, the chivalric subject places himself in constant proximity to that abjected remainder: the monster's (continued) existence, even if in the "zone of uninhabitability," is the condition without which the romance hero cannot come into being, and in whose absence he cannot know himself. Boundaries that are reified through abjection are inevitably weak because they exist only as materialized through their *constant* reiteration. Even when the rituals of exclusion are obsessively repeated in a frantic attempt to preserve self-autonomy, a little bit of the repudiated Other is always found staining the "domain of the subject." The proximity of the monster is a formal necessity to keep in motion the identity-giving process of its continued exclusion. Hence the paradox of persecution, which mounts in fury as the number of its possible remaining victims dwindles. The object-cause of the persecutor's hate becomes ever more present even as the "actual," living embodiments of that disavowed identity are destroyed. No matter how ruthlessly exterminated, the monster, the Jew, the witch, the heretic, and the sodomite return to haunt the Middle Ages—sometimes most powerfully once they have been completely eliminated as *physical* bodies.

This necessity of monstrous return was counteracted by a powerful cultural fantasy of complete somatic and psychological conversion. In its most extreme version, a desire for the introjection of the Other was realized through a cannibal logic that wickedly rewrites the Eucharist, as in *Richard Coer de Lion*. This romance's heroic king enjoys devouring Saracen flesh, at one point declaring, "þer is no fflesch so norysschant / Vnto an Ynglyssche Cristen-man /.../ As is þe flesshe of a Sarezyn"

[There is no flesh so nourishing to an English Christian as Saracen flesh] (3548–49, 3552).[23] Other conversion narratives incorporated the monstrous into the Christian body metaphorically, in order to humanize it to the point at which it could no longer threaten to reappear *as* monster. St. Christopher illustrates this recuperative tendency well. The *Legenda Aurea* describes Christopher as a Canaanite giant; in the *Acta Sanctorum*, he is a cynocephalus (*corpus hominis caput autem canis*).[24] As the *gigantes* of the Hereford map of the world demonstrate, these are two monsters whose mythology was always miscegenating, so that they are perhaps best conceptualized as bodies in constant overlap.[25] Originally named Reprobus ("Condemned"), Christopher seeks to serve the mightiest ruler of the world. After a king, an emperor, and the devil disappoint him, he decides on Christ. A hermit explains to the befuddled giant certain somatic limits that produce the proper Christian, such as fasting, but these injunctions to control fall on uncomprehending ears. Finally Reprobus is awarded his new name ("Christ-bearer") when he carries Jesus across a river and, as a result, is finally converted:

> Having learned his lesson, [he] humbly devotes his life to Christian service. He preaches the Gospel, but is especially an *athleta dei fortissima* who does battle against the armies of paganism. He is baptized by Saint Babylus at Antioch, when his appearance changes and his skin becomes white as milk. (White, *Dog-Man*, 35)

Walter Stephens summarizes the hagiographic narrative in a précis that could as easily have been written about Gowther:

> Every aspect of this conversion is calculated to present Christopher as a typical specimen of the Old Testament Giants, who were distinguished by their pride, their earthboundness or slavery to appetite.... Despite his desire to please, Christopher is literally unable to fast, or to understand explanations of prayer. As a Giant, he can understand power relations, and express his recognition of authority, only in terms of physical force. (*Giants in Those Days*, 48)

Christopher dies a martyr at the hands of the emperor Decius and is transformed into popular giant figures painted on the outer walls of cities that bless the bodies of passing travelers, preventing *mala mors*, unshriven death. From monstrosity to sanctity in a few easy steps: *gigantes* at the gates of paradise.

Gowther is very much like Christopher—giant, saint, and cynocephalus. He occupies a series of liminal, monstrous identities in order to convert them to something transcendent, like an icon that stands outside the merely physical world and blesses from on high the bodies left behind. A series of miracles occurs as the sign from God that he is triangu-

135

lating his passage from monstrous hybridity to saintly singularity well. When the sultan first attacks the emperor's lands, Gowther retreats to his chamber and prays for all the material signifiers of knighthood (weapons, armor, a horse): "He had no ner is preyr made, / Bot hors and armur bothe he hade, / Stode at his chambur dor" [He had no sooner said his prayer than he had both horse and armor, waiting at his chamber door] (406–8). These are the first words he has spoken since undergoing his penance, and the utterance has the potency of a speech act. That which he names is instantly materialized: signifier and signified are united. The scene rewrites his mother's frantic, wrongful prayer in the orchard, which likewise made real the thing it spoke. By rejecting both the maternal and the monstrous, by enduring a desubstantiating, disciplinary suffering that announces his triumph over the mere corporeality with which these two rejected origins are aligned, Gowther is close to being his name.

Nor is he any less effective in the aggressively physical arena of the battlefield. With his beloved falchion, he bursts enemy heads (422), spills blood and brains (426), and decapitates scores of heathens. Having ensured that the emperor's men will carry the day, Gowther returns home, where his horse and black armor vanish. He enters the hall where the emperor's men are celebrating their victory and promptly seats himself "too small raches betwene" [between two small hunting dogs] (441). No one knows the identity of the mysterious Black Knight but the princess, and she cannot speak her knowledge.

The sultan repeats his assault the next day, and this time Gowther is dressed by God in red armaments. Again he dismembers Saracens by the dozen, but this time it is his enemy who is "blake" ("black"): Gowther is moving through an alchemical process, becoming refined, his impurities removed. His slicing of the sultan's men into little bits has an analogue earlier in the poem, when on the day of his wedding, the duke of Estryke cracked men's skulls ("mony a cron con crake," 45) during a nuptial tournament. Gowther's violence is similar ("Mony a crone con he stere," 422), but sanctioned in ways that his father's could not be. Gowther's aggression is not for celebration. The self-effacing space of the battlefield substitutes for the performative arena of the tournament.[26] Gowther is most strongly himself when he learns the power of masochism: in self-denial is his self-assertion. The falchion that was the symbol of his unrestrained violence now becomes the visual signal of his proper control, the weapon by which those bodies antithetical to Gowther's new ethos are torn into pieces. This psychomachia on the battlefield is enacted in miniature on Gowther's body, with real effects: he suffers. After the customary dinner among the hounds, the battered knight retreats to his chamber to rest his wounds and meditate on the sins of the flesh that their painful materiality signifies.

The alembic process of Gowther's transformation is completed on the third day, when he charges into combat dressed in white. Gowther is as pure as the alimental milk that he once drained from his wet nurses along with their lives, only no trace of the monster now remains. The emperor thinks that multiple mysterious knights have been coming to his aid (520), and in a way he is correct: these are multiple Gowthers in that they are "Gowther under process," Gowther the fiend and Gowther the giant becoming Gowther the savior through a series of transubstantiations that culminate in this final version. Just as white is not a single color so much as the spectrum of all possible colors, Gowther as the white knight is the product of a long combinatory equation whose alchemical outcome is an elemental hero who has passed through a multiplicity of difference to become the sanctioned One. The battlefield Gowther is the continuation and culmination of all these other Gowthers. A wonderfully inept conjunction of images (598–606) imbues one of the martial passages with a special effectiveness: from a vigorous scene of Gowther smashing enemies on the battlefield with his beloved falchion, we are transported through a sudden textual shift to a timeless reminder of his adherence to the pope's commands (as if, for example, Gowther might hunger for a snack in the midst of the fight and survey the field for any dogs trotting about with food). It might seem as if there are two Gowthers (one on the field, one adhering to the papal injunctions back in the hall), but the rhetorical disjunction of the images also suggests that the narrative's manifold past is here moving its multiplicity toward a final unity.

Gowther Triumphant

The body is a most peculiar "thing," for it is never quite reducible to being merely a thing; nor does it ever quite manage to rise above the status of thing.

—Elizabeth Grosz, *Volatile Bodies: Toward a Corporeal Feminism*, xi

When the sultan succeeds in capturing the emperor, Gowther rides to his liege's rescue and stages a version of the familiar romance beheading scene. The sequence of events (623–30) is extraordinary in its toppling domino effect. Gowther strikes off the head of his enemy, overcoming and vanquishing the very thing he once was, renouncing monstrousness forever. In the exultation that this liberatory feat provokes, he is reminded all the more forcefully of his corporeality: even as he praises God for constructing his body from the raw materials of flesh and bone, even at the triumphant moment when he experiences a transcendence from the fleshliness of that frame, his body is transfixed through the shoulder by an enemy spear. The somatic chain reaction culminates in the princess for the first time finding her voice, a visceral response to the visible sign of Gowther's vulnerability — and to his being fixed, metaphorically and literally, in place.

The princess's fall into the signifying chain has its price. She tumbles from the window of her tower and lies dead. When the pope arrives to pronounce her obsequies, a miracle occurs: "Scho raxeld hur and rase" in order to speak "wyse" words to Gowther (652). The message she delivers is straight from God, who declares through her that the mute knight who still sits among the dogs is forgiven all his sins; that he may now speak without fear; that Gowther should eat, drink, and "make mery"; and that he is numbered among the chosen of heaven (656–60). To her father, she announces Gowther's true identity as the knight who fought as his polychromatic ally for three glorious days. The pope consecrates these proceedings by declaring to Gowther, "Now art thou Goddus chyld" (668), no longer a "warlocke wyld" [wild devil] (669). With the assent of these two new earthly fathers (the pope, the emperor), Gowther marries the princess and becomes heir to the land. Gowther is inscribed beneath a new family Name, a mightier one: emperor, rather than duke.

But Gowther is not yet ready to remain in place. He journeys back to Estryke and marries his mother to the old earl who precipitated his metamorphic journey. He finds something satisfying in returning the country to the normalcy of the family triad. Simple domestic bliss is not, however, the interest of this romance. Indeed, this return to the maternal only prepares for a second and final renunciation of it. Gowther memorializes and expiates his early sins by building an abbey where monks will pray "unto the wordus end" for the nuns he victimized. Nuns to monks: as the maternal vanished, so does the feminine. The narrative now moves toward the eternal, the immutable, the transcendent, as Gowther assumes his full identity as "Goddus chyld." Full of remorse as he recalls the crimes of his youth, Gowther can escape the return of the romance's triply enfolded past (biblical, national, familial) only by finding a way to stand outside of its mutability.

Gowther journeys "hom" to the demesnes he rules as emperor and spends his life performing good works. The princess is never mentioned again after the marriage. Nor is the existence of an heir: the body disappears as a textual concern in preparation for a final transfiguration out of all corporeality. Gowther dies, is buried in the abbey he constructed, and is worshiped as "a varré corsent parfett," a true saint (721). Pilgrims seek his shrine and are rewarded with divine metamorphoses of their disfigured bodies. The blind see, the mute speak, hunchbacks are straightened. Sanctified after a long journey through a series of transitional bodies, Gowther has come to signify a transformative, corrective, normalizing principle. Gowther in triumph is Gowther abstracted, the hero who becomes an incorporeal Name under which miracles are performed: from inhuman origins to superhuman transfiguration, an inhuman end.

"Who was my fadur?" Gowther has at long last found his purely transcendent answer to the riddle of paternity. God is his father. This simple fact guarantees Gowther's legitimacy, the truth of his identity, by allowing his body to be placed outside of the chains of filiation that would otherwise delimit him as the son of a fiend, the son of a nameless duke, the son of an all too human father, rather than of an abstract principle that looks down on him from heaven and smiles. Once the question has been answered, once Gowther's restless desire is transubstantiated into the unmoving tranquillity of blessedness, the narrative ends.[27] The British Library manuscript of the romance rightly ends with the phrase *explicit vita sancti,* "here ends the saint's life." From the perpetual motion of desire in identity romance, we move through multiple transformations into a still eternity of hagiography.[28]

The "transcendent principle" is the same as the "master signifier" that ensures the truth-value of Oedipus. In the equation 3 + 1, it is the exterior One that allows belief in the interior structure. This disembodied principle as it works its transfigurations on Gowther is equated with the Holy Spirit: "For he is inspyryd with tho Holy Gost, / That was tho cursod knyght" [For he who once was a cursed knight is inspired with the Holy Ghost] (731–32). Perhaps this inspiration allows us to see why the mother and the princess vanish so suddenly from the text. Gowther is Oedipalized into the celibate family of the church, where the place of the feminine body in the triangle has been usurped by a pure and mysterious spirit. The Holy Trinity of familialism is supplanted by the Holy Trinity of Father, Son, and sexless disembodied Principle. Gowther submits to this sacred trigonometry by learning to disavow the merely physical, aligned in the beginning and then in the end with the maternal and the feminine. His reward is to be rendered not a hero but a saint.

As Opposed to What?

Bodies are not defined by their genus or species, by their organs and functions, but by what they can do, by the affects of which they are capable—in passion as well as action.
—Gilles Deleuze and Claire Parnet, *Dialogues,* 60

We may as well reformulate Sedgwick's famous question about nationalisms and sexualities and demand, "Oedipus, as opposed to what?"[29] I am not arguing that Gowther had any choice within this long process of Oedipalization. After all, even if such things as unfettered choice and pure intentionality do exist, he is a discursive representation of a subject that does not see outside of his own generative text (a fact that perhaps makes him more human, not less). Oedipus was probably the same structural inevitability in England circa 1400 as it is in the United States circa 2000, but as this chapter demonstrates, its phantasmatic workings were at once very different and equally complex. By tracing the genealogy of Oedipal configuration, and mapping its effects across the body of Gowther, I have argued that gender is fixed and that bodies are sexed in culturally specific ways. Freud and Lacan depict the unconscious as a classical theater whose secret dramas are played out unknowingly by actors who keep repeating the same roles before dying and leaving them to understudies. This model is in many ways deeply Christian (especially in Lacan's formulation) and fits well with medieval ideas such as the sacred Trinity because it derives in part from them.[30] But I would like to suggest that sexuality and embodiment in the Middle Ages are far more complicated than they often are made out to be. Before it hardens into the armor of his final identity, Gowther's plastic body illustrates well two of the most remarkable assertions of Deleuze and Guattari: that the body is a site of multiplicity, process, and becoming ("a discontinuous, nontotalized series of processes, organs, flows, energies, corporeal substances and incorporeal events, intensities, and durations");[31] and that the unconscious is not a theater but a factory (Gowther's body is the site of endless production that grinds to a halt only at the imposed limit of saintliness, at the transubstantial death that is the reward for a successful embrace of transcendentals). The ahistorical, saintly, "psychoanalytic" body roughly corresponds to the reductionist model of a gender identity explicable merely by reference to a sexual anatomy; this is the static ideal already frozen into manuscript illustration and displayed on the dissection tables of the late-medieval coroners and medical schools. The particular, performative, "Deleuzian" body has much in common with the medieval body-in-motion, the Galenic body as compendium of organs, humors, and external phenomena: a Rube Goldberg machine through which chugs blood, semen, choler, biles, phlegm; a collection of assemblages that react in different ways to flows of heat and cold and pleasure; a construction whose skin is an insufficient boundary against the world of swirling zodiacal stimuli to which it is intimately connected.[32] Gowther before Oedipus can only be represented as a monster, because romance is ultimately a normalizing genre; but Gowther as monster, as a playground of somatic signification, is a site as intriguing in its multidirectionality as it is frightening in its gigantic excess.

. The body is not private. It is never really owned by an "individual" who inhabits it like an insubstantial soul in a temporary, physical prison. True, the Middle Ages might describe the body *in abstracto* with these carceral and merely binaristic terms, but romance demonstrates that the body in performance is something rather different from its abstract, theological ideal. Despite the universal history that *Sir Gowther* cites (St. Christopher, Saracen cynocephali, the giants and incubi of Genesis), Gowther's hybrid body is, in the end, a particularly English form. In the Albina myth, England had its own patriotic narrative of savage giants converted into the raw material of national identity. Gowther provides a miniaturized version of the same story. In the liminal figure of the cynocephalus, a more embarrassing national myth finds its anxious embodiment. According to legend, English men were supposed to have sprouted

140

doglike tails after Augustine of Canterbury cursed them for insulting him as he attempted to Christianize the land in 597. Thus in romances such as *Richard Coer de Lion,* the nasty French taunt their English foes with humiliating epithets such as "taylardes" and "tailed dogs."[33] *Sir Gowther* rescues the degraded, national, "cynocephalic" body by first rendering it a personal one and then forcing that multivalent site to ally itself with the canine forms to slough off the monstrous taint forever. That the narrative ends by transmuting its hero into a figure who stands wholly outside of temporality, physicality, and the material body is the logical culmination of this communal fantasy of embodiment as escape.

CHAPTER 6

⊹

Exorbitance

Only in the embrace is the other's body known as one's own, in parts.
—Susan Stewart, *On Longing*, 115

The Amazing Colossal Man

The 1950s were a decade of monsters: giant spiders, giant ants, giant bees, giant praying mantises, giant alien fungi, and of course, plain old giants. No other period in recent memory has been so obsessed with constructing, deconstructing, and reconfiguring the category "monster," with employing the label for nationalistic, capitalistic, misogynistic, and culturally imperialistic ends. One of the most memorable giants of the time was Glenn Manning (Glen Langan), otherwise known as *The Amazing Colossal Man* (1957, Columbia TriStar). Manning's sad story begins when he is exposed to radiation during the testing of a nuclear bomb. His hair falls out, giving him that retro-futuristic look of which the fifties were so fond, and then his body suddenly starts to enlarge. Both he and the expandable loincloth that the army specially designs for him grow at a fantastic rate, until he reaches a towering (amazing and colossal) sixty feet of height. After some touching moments in which he bewails the loss of his humanity, synonymous in the film with a quiet existence as paterfamilias, Manning rapidly becomes insane. When he rampages against the institutions that construct him as monster (the military, the family, the period's suburban dreams), he is hunted down and slain. The Amazing Colossal Man dies in a spectacular fall from the fifties' favorite monument to human progress over wild nature, the Hoover Dam.

Or, at least, the audience thinks he dies. When the movie turned out to be a drive-in smash, Glenn Manning returned in *War of the Colossal Beast* (1958, Columbia TriStar). The tumble from the dam has disfigured and desubjectivized the monster. No longer played by the same actor, crazed and unintelligible, the Amazing Colossal Man has ceased to be a man at all; he is inhuman, wholly animal. Suspended no more between categories, easily labeled and easily dismissed, he dies a second time in this uninteresting sequel, never to return.

For all its B-grade science and campy excess, *The Amazing Colossal Man* is an intriguing popular culture meditation on the construction of

142

masculinity in the late 1950s. What happens, the film asks, when a man outgrows the restrictive paradigms of daily living that have produced him as a docile subject? What happens when the aggressive and erotic drives that are supposed to undergo sublimation (at least according to the Freudian model then dominant) are instead expressed in all their elemental purity? The movie could not raise these questions unless it first constructed entwined visions of masculinity and monstrousness to be interrogated. Manning enters the narrative as the typical 1950s male: a husband and father, respectful of authority, happy in his social place. His becoming a giant amounts to a discovery of the truth of what he always already was, beneath the suburban miniaturization of his life. The giant's monstrosity is his insistent, exorbitant exhibition of what he is supposed to repress; the fantasy he embodies is that such "primal" wildness is somehow related to a purely natural state, to the lives of (male, aggressive) animals.[1]

Despite the rampage with which the film closes, it is more comic than tragic. With his fantastic stretch diaper, limbs that do not know their own strength, and subjectivity never at home in the awkward figure it occupies, the giant of *The Amazing Colossal Man* suggests that there is something quite humorous about the dangerous body of the giant, and about the process of masculine embodiment within which the giant is always caught. *The Amazing Colossal Man* demonstrates that the "cosmic terror" that the medieval giant inspires in its romance audience is only a fragment of a larger story.

The Green Knight's Gift

The other is there only to be reappropriated, recaptured, and destroyed as other. Even the exclusion is not an exclusion.
—Hélène Cixous, *The Newly Born Woman*, 71

The giants of the Bible and of Geoffrey of Monmouth's *Historia Regum Britanniae* are united in their wickedness. They exist only to be displaced, encoding in their gross flesh everything that is inimical to the divine or to the heroic. The frightening giant of nursery tales preserves this negative valence. "Jack and the Beanstalk," had it been written in the idiom of a loftier genre, is essentially the same story as "Guy and Colbrond" or David and Goliath. Yet twentieth-century audiences are more likely to think of the giant's body as jolly and green than they are to remember from their childhood his fiercer incarnations. The giant has clearly undergone a slow but radical shift, transformed from an incestuous breaker of every human law (the Albina myth) to a modern corporate emblem who assures consumers that frozen vegetables of a certain brand are fresh and enticing. The same monster who tried to prevent Brutus's men from taming his wild island into farms and houses, who violently attacked the encroachment of "progress," suddenly declares that it is good to eat spinach from plastic bags and aluminum cans.

Before the giant could be so completely domesticated, he had to be more fully humanized. Whereas Anglo-Saxon England tended, generally, to be fascinated with the *intimacy* of the giant, exploring the uncanny proximity between his monstrousness and the fallen state of being human in a difficult world, Geoffrey's *Historia* used a biblical palimpsest to emphasize the giant's *alterity*, so that the excesses of the monstrous body became a contrastive device for constructing the heroes Brutus and Arthur. The giant's *extimité* to the masculine corpus obtains in either case, but when monstrous difference gains an ascendancy over the sameness to which it is always conjoined, the monster terrifies more easily than he delights. Both horror and amusement are bodily excitations based on a complex interplay of enjoyment and identification, but for the monster to function as a comic or celebratory figure, he must dwindle into a more recognizably human form.

Sir Gawain and the Green Knight performs the fullest, most complex euhemerization of the giant, completely rewriting the gigantomachia at the heart of identity romance. Arriving late enough in the development of the genre to reflect thoughtfully back on its layers of sedimentation, *Sir Gawain* was composed toward the close of the fourteenth century, the autumn of romance. Yet the poem locates its action in romance's green season. The "fayre folk" of Camelot are still "in her first age" ("in the flower of their youth" [Tolkien, 55]. The romance situates itself as a prequel to the matter of Britain, set in the days before the betrayals that dismembered the court, in the days before the formation of an Arthurian identity. "Sumquat childgered" [rather boyish], Arthur cannot long sit still because of his "ʒonge blod" and "brayn wylde" [young blood and restless mind]. When the Green Knight bursts suddenly into the hall, he pretends that he cannot determine who is the king, declaring that "hit arn aboute on þis bench bot berdlez chylder" [There are only beardless children on these benches!] (280). By setting the action during the communal *enfances* of Camelot, the *Gawain* author wipes clean the accumulated history in which the court of Arthur had become embedded: there are no adulterous liaisons to explain, no incest or infidelity, no treason or sad deaths. Because all these calamities are yet to come, the poem works somewhat like Geoffrey of Monmouth's *Historia*, laying the narrative foundation for an Arthurian "present" by positing a formative anteriority.

The Green Knight plays the role of the traditional giant of romance, that catalyst to the formation of an adult identity, but with some important modification to that monstrous body. Grimly serious, he bursts into Camelot full of rebuke toward its lightheartedness. At the same time, however, the exuberance of the Yule festivities has its effect. This verdant intruder on the Christmas court has not arrived, as in *King Horn*, to announce national calamity; he is not encountered, as in *Yvain*, after long wandering to imperil identity and force its immediate assertion.[2] The Green Knight introduces not the deadly serious decapitation topos, familiar in its gory details from its insistent repetition in the English romances, but a beheading *gomen*, "game." A member of the court must strike an ax blow across the Green Knight's neck, and in return he will do the same in one year's time to whoever wields the ax against him. This strange conjoining of murderous threat to holiday game has a somatic parallel in the uneasy hybridity of the challenger's body. Although the Green Knight may be a monster ("Half etayn in erde I hope þat he were"), he is also a man ("Bot mon most I algate mynn hym to bene").[3] The poem simultaneously invokes and undercuts the disturbing mythology of the giant. Suspended between the categories "mon" and "etayn," the Green Knight's function is to interrogate exactly where the difference between these modes of being resides.

Gawain hefts the ax, the head rolls across the floor, the corpse spurts blood. According to the dictates of the romance gigantomachia, the conquering hero should at this point transform the head into a public exhibit, delivering some powerful symbolic message about proper masculine embodiment; but the ritual is present only in its haunting absence.[4] The Green Knight retrieves the missing part himself and climbs back into the saddle of his horse. His severed head he holds aloft by its lovely (*louelych*) green locks, and as he turns the face toward the king's dais the eyelids lift and the mouth speaks: "Loke, Gawan, þou be grayþe to go as þou hettez!" [Look, Gawain, that you be as ready to come as you promised!] (448). The decapitated head—here as in *Beowulf* as beautiful as it is terrifying—opens its dead eyes to stare at the gathered audience, to transform *them* into the object of the gaze. This living, bodiless object is the very definition of *unheimlich*: "Dismembered limbs, a severed head, a hand cut off at the wrist, feet which dance by themselves—all these have something peculiarly uncanny about them" (Freud, "The Uncanny," 397). A visual sticking point that thrills the body with its gaping maw and paralyzing stare, the severed head is supposed to become part of a powerful message about the proper expression of embodied masculinity. Here the dead mouth (Geoffrey's *ingluvies*) literally speaks, but its words announce only that the true encounter with the monster is yet to come.

When the Green Knight disappears from the hall, his horse pounding fire from the stone, the king commands his servants to mount the abandoned ax on the wall, "þer all men for meruayl myȝt on hit loke" [where all men could stare at it as a marvel] (479). Arthur's command cites his own, similar injunction in the *History of the Kings of Britain*, where he orders that the head of the giant of Mont Saint Michel be displayed before his camp so that "all the men gathered to gape at it" (240). In *Sir Gawain and the Green Knight*, the instrument, rather than the head, becomes the fetish, a staging of the ridiculous absence of a point of visual fascination around which Arthur can solidify his heroism. Although inelegant in its execution, the manuscript illustration of the beheading scene captures the poem's reversals well. Gawain holds the ax between himself and the disembodied head's line of sight, and as a further precaution, he turns his face away. The insolent gaze of the giant is a monstrous force that both Gawain and his king are not prepared to internalize, to make their own. The giant himself enacts the display that Arthur, David, Culhwch, Lybeaus Desconus, and Guy of Warwick once performed, holding aloft the ocular reproof and compelling the gathered public to watch. The gesture announces that the court has not come of age, that the necessary rites of passage must yet occur, lest Camelot remain fixed in its limited "first age."

That "gathered public" is no longer simply the company of men. In the two hundred years that separate the birth of romance from the meditation on its significance that is *Sir Gawain and the Green Knight,* the *Männerbund* united by fraternal bonds and heroic endeavor has become a gathering of lords and ladies who vie in their Christmas games for kisses. According to Bertilak at the end of the poem, an important member of the intended audience has all along been Guenevere, whom the jealous Morgana had hoped to kill with fear. As recent critics have pointed out, the narrative is as motivated by women's desires as by the desires of men.[5] The prominent position of women in the story suggests that the relations among gender, sexuality, chivalry, and courtly behavior are being scrutinized, plumbed for their potential ambiguity: how are kissing games like beheading games? The world of the giant in Galfridian history is homosocial and frightening, but *Sir Gawain and the Green Knight* situates the encounter within a heterosexuality that is full of games, comedic, and undercut by violence.

The traditional romance frame of the *juvenis* wandering into adult identity is adopted after the Christmas intruder's abrupt exit. As knight errant, Gawain battles a wilderness of fierce foes, seeking the Green Knight in order to receive the return ax stroke to which he has promised to submit. In the dark woods far from court, he encounters the expected giant—but this monster is met in a diluted, plural form (718–23). These *etaynez* are the monsters that Gawain, like Eglamour or Perceval or Fair Unknown, is supposed to conquer in the wilds or on the battlefield to enable the triumph of his occluded identity. This encounter should be the moment when his mettle is tested and its composition revealed, when his somatic control exorcises the giant's corporeal excess, but this pack of giants are dwindled denizens in a long list of marvels, no more remarkable than bulls and bears and boars (*bullez and berez and borez*). Unlike the romances that *Sir Gawain and the Green Knight* cites in the development of its narrative, the locus of mastery will not be the vast, psychological landscape of the wilderness, where the giant seems to represent everything exterior to the law, but will be postponed instead for the familiar, domestic spaces of the court, where the giant is revealed as abiding at that law's secret interior.

When Gawain arrives at the castle of Bertilak, he believes that he has found a safe haven, a place where he can forget for a while the terrible urgency of his quest. Feasted and praised, wrapped in warm bedcovers and decked in fur robes, Gawain does not realize that the beheading game *is* a kissing game, that the woman of the manor who daily tempts him to carnal indulgence is conducting on her husband's behalf a version of the very test in which the traditional giant of romance assays the flesh and is rebuked. Lady Bertilak probes the armor of Gawain's Christian chivalric identity—which, as Carolyn Dinshaw points out, partakes of both gender identity and sexual identity ("A Kiss Is Just a Kiss," 211). Lady Bertilak attempts to discover at once how straight Gawain's construct of sexuality is, and how sufficiently narrow his gendered behaviors are. Both are measured first through his conduct toward women, but ultimately by his fidelity in keeping the promise of *commercium* that marks his relationship to Bertilak.[6] Possibilities of homosexuality and adultery are tantalizingly raised, as is the temptation to break the sanctified host-guest relationship, but Gawain remains fastidious in his bodily control. Every small kiss he wins from the lady he bestows on her husband.

Dinshaw has observed that the poem is "preoccupied with keeping things together, preoccupied, that is, with division and loss," so that the narrative is obsessed with knots and suturing ("A Kiss Is Just a Kiss," 215). That its bodies seem on the verge of becoming *corps morcelés* indicates a recognition of the fragility of selfhood, as the bedroom temptations are immediately linked to scenes of dismemberment and bodily disaggregation that culminate Bertilak's hunting. Specifically, this interior testing occurs in conjunction with a series of ominous animal beheadings. Deer are gutted and their heads and necks torn off ("Boþe þe hede and þe hals þay hwen of þenne," 1353). A boar is decapitated, its head mounted on a pike. This remarkable trophy is ceremoniously presented to Gawain:

> þenne hondeled þay þe hoge hed, þe hende mon hit praysed,
> And let lodly þerat þe lorde for to here.
> "Now, Gawayn," quoþ þe godmon, 'þis gomen is your awen."
> (1633–35)
>
> [Then they hefted the huge head, so that the courtly man [Gawain] praised it,
> And professed horror at it for the lord to hear.
> "Now, Gawain," said the master of the house, "this game is your own."]

This game is your own. Bertilak's words are chillingly accurate. The boar's head atop a pole would suggest at once to anyone familiar with romance convention the ceremonial display of the dismembered giant, for giants are often depicted with animal heads, including those of boars.[7] Presented with an emblem of his own threatened end, as if he were both that hunted animal and that ritually dismembered monster, there is little more that Gawain can do besides express his deep horror ("let lodly þerat," 1634), a bodily reaction to a bodily affront.

The first two hunting episodes rewrite in a more reflective vein the two giant battles in *Sir Eglamour of Artois*, a popular romance in which a young knight is forced by a forbidding father figure to accomplish three tasks in order to win his beloved and assume his proper sexuality.[8] Eglamour's first labor requires hunting a deer guarded by a giant, whom he defeats and beheads. The second demand is the hunting of a boar, likewise guarded by a giant whom he decapitates. Both episodes culminate in the public display of the severed head to the earl who withholds enjoyment (in the form of his daughter) from the knight; this "Father of Prohibition" is then forced to declare Eglamour's proper chivalric identity within the rules of the game that he has established and according to which Eglamour regulates his conduct. *Sir Gawain and the Green Knight* takes these simple displays of the defeated monster's remnant and reverses their origin: Bertilak, seemingly on the side of enjoyment but soon to be revealed as likewise a forbidding father figure, presents Gawain with trophies that twice predict the inescapable failing of the young knight's embodied masculinity. *Sir Eglamour* is rewritten so that the animals lose their heads at the hands of the man who plays the giant, suggesting that the giant and the father figure have always been allied in romance, twinned aspects of the same identity regime.[9] Giant, father, and young knight align in monstrous filiation.

On the third day of Gawain's temptation, Lady Bertilak ceases to offer him the body's pleasures, appealing instead to its instinct for survival. She presents him a green girdle to protect his life from the blow he must receive, and Gawain succumbs, the triumph of death over sex. At the same time that Gawain stumbles, however, the third stroke of the game provides a more favorable omen. The captured fox, his throat under perpetual attack by the dogs, is kept whole when he is flayed, and the complete skin is presented to the knight. The possibility of an escape from disaggregation is finally suggested, but not before the drawing of blood. Gawain does not yield to the indulgence in sensuality that the lady of the castle offers, and he therefore will avoid (in the masculinist logic of the poem) the stroke that threatened to unman him, to obviate his difference.

Or does he? Gawain believes that the beheading game tests something essential (he takes what one *has* to be what one *is*), rather than constructed (masculinity as a set of culturally determined and potentially transmutable behaviors, rather than an invariable, "natural" given). Romance assumes that gender is not simply genetic, that masculinity is adoptable, performable, transmutable. Gawain thinks that he is guarding his difference, but his choice is made at the risk of losing his differentiating behavior. The third day sees Gawain surrounded by ladies, dressed in a beautiful robe of ermine and a blue mantle that reaches to the ground. He greets the returning Bertilak with an embrace and three kisses, bestowed "as sauerly and sadly as he hem sette couþe" [With as much relish and vigor as he can plant on him] (1937). For the first time, Gawain's payment seems genuinely ambiguous, for here the mis-en-scène suddenly underscores the extent of the text's inversions. As Dinshaw has demonstrated, because Gawain's kiss is placed on Bertilak's lips "sauerly and sadly," the exchange becomes as erotic as ceremonial. In his luxuriant robe, standing with the women, Gawain is like the initiate in the coming-of-age rituals that van Gennep and Turner described, preliminarily dressed in the habiliments of another gender.[10] It would seem that no orthodox sequel is possible to this dangerous episode besides the formal adoption of straight masculinity, publicly and for all time.

The Green Knight, however, stages the second part of the beheading game in the most private of spaces, a desolate valley where the two men stand alone, abandoned even by Gawain's guide. On this New Year's Day, the Feast of the Circumcision, the ax is readied and descends three times, one for each of his days of temptation by Lady Bertilak.[11] When Gawain learns not to flinch as the weapon is lowered—learns, that is, to submit to the proper adoption of the Christian chivalric code that passes for an adult male identity—he is grazed along the neck, a "symbolic wound," in Bruno Bettelheim's formulation, integral to the rite de passage. This cut, this "nirt in þe nek" signifies his mastery of his proper gender, as well as mastery over its abjected other. Red blood splashes onto the white snow: wedding sheets, of sorts, announcing Gawain's passage from adolescent ambiguity to the acute delineations of the adult male world, where the pleasures of the body are absorbed into the pleasures of the body politic. The young knight has learned his place. His individuality enables him only to renounce the dangers of excess, of too much faith in the physical, private, and domestic—that is, in the feminine.

Bertilak started as the patriarchs' antithesis, the menacing giant, but becomes at its close the father himself.[12] In this poem of games and reversals, however, Morgana unmans Bertilak: he is reduced to her servant by his revelation that she was behind the *gomen,* and thus he is robbed of his power of agency.[13] Gawain realizes that he has been initiated into a manhood wholly dependent on those bodies it would define itself *against.* Gender becomes a melancholic process of embodiment that disavows both its origins and its continuities.[14] Freud wrote that "the character of the ego is a precipitate of abandoned object-cathexes and that it contains the history of those object-choices."[15] For the chivalric subject, this "prehistory" of loss means simultaneously abandoning and internalizing all that the monstrous and the feminine embody, resulting in perpetual interior conflict and a self-division that cannot be voiced. Gawain directs his anger at this discovery toward women generally, making of them monsters, conflating the categories in the traditional, dismissive way; hence Gawain's horrifyingly misogynistic screed when Bertilak reveals the origin of his mission (2416–28). Later, in a more reasoned moment, Gawain accepts blame for his failing and declares the green girdle an emblem of his personal shame, of the "faut and þe fayntyse" of his own "flesche crabbed" [the faultiness and frailty of his perverse flesh] (2435). This "token of vntrawþe" he will bear until his death and from it derive his newly sober signification in identity (2509–10).

In her persuasive reading of the poem that I have been relying on throughout my argument, Carolyn Dinshaw concludes that *Sir Gawain* is a normative text that circulated in order to circumscribe the desires of its audiences (see especially "Kiss," 222). Her thesis is consonant in this way to the argument I have previously advanced about the simultaneously productive and controlling power of romance more generally. Dinshaw is specifically interested in how the text renders unintelligible the possibility of homosexuality for its auditors:

> To a culture of heteronormativity, homosexual acts, involving no women and by nature nonprocreative, may have appeared especially likely in a situation where there were "hordes" of young men with relatively limited means. *SGGK* depicts an ideal feudal society (the Round Table in *its* "youth") that—however immanent homosexual relations might be—kept young men unmarried yet still heterosexually focused. ("Kiss," 222)

Although I wholeheartedly agree that romances are transubstantiating—that they journey through the world as catalysts to profound changes in the cultural process of embodiment, that they aim to fundamentally alter the experience of corporeality in their audience—I wonder if the poem can really be called heteronormative. I do not disagree with Dinshaw's thesis that homosexuality is constructed in the poem as *unthinkable*. My point is rather that *any* performance of sexuality is rendered impossible in the poem—homosexuality through nonexistence, and heterosexuality through incoherence and failure. Whereas Dinshaw argues that the text insists "solid hetero-identity" can easily survive its own "splitting apart" (217), that the text serves as a kind of "publicity campaign" for an all-encompassing heterosexuality, it seems to me that *Sir Gawain* is ultimately a contemplative, rather than active, romance. The pivotal moment in the text is not the public staging of a culturally coherent, persuasive formulation of straight masculine identity, but Gawain's realization of the high cost with which such an impossibly complete identity arrives and his inability to convey that knowledge to his own audience. By the end of the poem, Gawain's body no longer belongs within the mirthful celebration of life and sexuality that characterizes both courts: the kissing games that occur in the castles of Arthur *and* Bertilak figure heterosexuality as a joyful, innocent comedy of exchange, and Gawain renounces participation in that structure of enjoyment. He refuses Bertilak's injunction to celebrate the New Year by joining him and his wife in feast ("Make myry in my hous!" 2468). On Gawain's return to Camelot, he meets a court that is still celebrating the same pleasures with which the poem began, but he discovers that his melancholic transformation absolutely excludes him from their frivolity. Gawain makes a powerful and rhetorically ornate speech to his former companions that declares his intertwined knowledge and shame (2505–12). Repetition of demonstratives gives his words a sonority that conveys the poem's final switch from a playful to a serious mode: "þis is þe bende ... þis is þe laþe and þe losse ... þis is þe token" (2506–8). Ready to share with the youthful court his somber realization, to reveal to its young men and women his painful passage into a manhood marked by inadequacy and interiorized violence, Gawain is rebuffed. The court listens to his speech and then erupts into laughter (2514). They fail to comprehend both his revelatory wound and the significance of his belt. They resolve that they shall all wear—men and women alike—his emblematic green girdle. Displayed on so many, the "token" loses its new power to signify difference or differentiation, and so the poem ends exactly where it began: with the siege and assault on Troy. The last full line of *Sir Gawain and the Green Knight*, "After þe segge and þe asaute watz sesed at Troye" (2525), curves back to its opening, "Siþen þe sege and þe assaut watz sesed at Troye" (1), like a snake that pierces its fangs through its own tail to form a circle that denies the possibility of progress to history.

As the text closes in on itself and sets to repeat, Gawain drops out of its identity structure; he is henceforth "illegible" to the court, exterior to its circuit. Even if Gawain realizes that the place of the giant is deep in the heart of the masculine corpus, even if he learns that being a "proper" man violently depends on an array of alterities against which masculinity constructs itself while abjecting them to its secret interior, he cannot articulate this realization to the immature court. Gawain is not "more" heterosexual by the poem's end, and he has no pronouncement about the superiority of heteronormative cultural relations to impart; indeed, he renounces sexuality and social relations altogether and ends the poem individuated, utterly alone. If the romance aims to impart an important message about sexuality, it is one that the court simply does not comprehend: identity is not the mobile effect of a bodily performance, but the painful precipitate of its renunciation. *Sir Gawain and the Green Knight* is a romance of failure. If the court figures heterosexuality in its comic fullness, Gawain is a somber reminder of its tragic insufficiency, and perhaps of its final impossibility: heterosexuality exists only as a naive but dangerous series of games that Gawain learns finally to reject.

The retrograde temporality of *Sir Gawain and the Green Knight* functions rather like the regressive poetics of Chaucer's "Tale of Sir Thopas," imagining a childlike masculine body for Gawain to inhabit before his temptations. Whereas Chaucer's narrative miniaturizes the body's physicality in order to retreat from the trauma that haunts its formation, *Sir Gawain* reduces its hero's body (and only its hero's body) to a mythical state of innocence in order to examine the violent process of its sexuation. The poem argues that for the *juvenis* to progress to *homo*, he must accede to the process of abjection, of interiorizing hate and violence, especially toward women, but also toward oneself. *Sir Gawain and the Green Knight* contains the most complex meditation on beheading scenes and gender assertion in all of romance, as well as the most subtle and the saddest. By refusing to place the monster anywhere but at the core of chivalric identity, the narrative denies the easy resolution to identity conflict that constitutes the bodies of heroes such as Lybeaus Desconus. Indeed, the moral of the story is eerily postmodern: identity is finally a repeated process of mourning, the slow abandonment of every possibility of being otherwise.

Sir Gawain and the Green Knight intertwines joyful celebration (a better Christmas poem is difficult to imagine), horror (the intrusion of the Green Knight is the singlemost frightening incursion of a giant in romance), and melancholia (Gawain's *tristesse* as he returns to the court and fails to convey the importance of his revelation is palpable). The poem also has its enjoyably comic moments, such as Gawain, naked beneath the covers, trapped by Lady Bertilak in his bed; or Gawain and Bertilak locked in a sweet kiss. This comedy involves a body that is learning the limits of its own self-regulation, that is internalizing the practice of control. Because he threatens this discipline, the giant is ordinarily the catalyst to fear. But because he becomes in *Sir Gawain and the Green Knight* more fully human, more intimate in his alterity, the giant becomes a monster who invites a second response just as visceral: laughter.

The Cruelty of Laughter

The body is molded by a great many distinct regimes; it is broken down by the rhythms of work, rest, and holidays; it is poisoned by food or values, through eating habits or moral laws.
　　　　—Michel Foucault, "Nietzsche, Genealogy, History," 87

Sometime in the late fourteenth century, Geoffrey of Monmouth's giant of Mont Saint Michel was reinvented again, adding another version of the monster to the varied collection assembled by Wace, Laȝoman, and Robert Mannyng of Brunne. The giant of the Alliterative *Morte Arthure* is the culmination of this repetition-compulsion, the most troubling monster in all of romance. Arthur's most heroic battle is waged against this "masculine body out of control" who keeps a "kyrtill" fashioned from the beards of subjugated kings.[16] Arthur punishes his foe with a double dismemberment: castration (the giant is a rapist) and decapitation (the promised end of all giants). So far, nothing unusual. Giants always perish through the breaking of their bodies, a corporal and symbolic rebuke to the deviance that they incorporate. Yet Mont Saint Michel is, in the Alliterative *Morte Arthure*, the habitation of no ordinary giant. True, he receives the traditional narrative condemnation by encoding almost every negative attribute a monster is capable of embodying, especially in his boundless appetite and cultural alterity; but this reflexive rejection is subtly eroded by conflating him with Arthur, and by the text's investing a perverse enjoyment in the celebration of his atrocious excess. Like *Sir Gawain and the Green Knight*, the Alliterative *Morte Arthure* suggests that the defeat of the giant is not always a banishing, not always a transubstantiation of power with a reversal of its moral valence. In Arthur's case, monstrousness and heroism are states not wholly predicated on difference.[17]

Repeated phrases and gestures verbally link the two bodies, monarchical and monstrous. The giant is, like Arthur, a king. He controls fifteen realms, demanding as yearly tribute the beards of his vassal regents. This emasculating act of public shaving will be restaged by Arthur on the envoys of Lucius later in the poem. The "kyrtill" that the giant fashions from the kings' collected hair undermines the ideological purity of Arthur's vision of forcibly uniting disparate realms under British sovereignty, materializing Arthur's own ambition of empire into a costume with which to clothe a monstrous body. The giant's role as speculum of what Arthur might be (or become) is made evident by the cord of desire that binds the giant to the British king: he desires nothing more than to add Arthur's beard to this garment of forced subjugation. At the end of their long battle, the king and the giant are physically entwined to the point at which they can be separated only by death; Kay thinks it is Arthur who has been overcome.

Even after his defeat, the giant continues to have an ambiguous life within Arthur, and toward the end of the narrative, it becomes difficult to tell the "king's two bodies" apart.[18] Unlike the Green Knight, there is no redemptive return to humanity for Arthur, because his monstrousness is ideological, a product of the imperialistic political system he embodies, and not the result of some playful enchantment. Late in the campaign against Rome, long after he has destroyed Lucius, Arthur degenerates in his battles to self-aggrandizement and corrupt excuses for looting. The narrative lingers over an extended visualization of the devastation of war, undermining the endeavor that the British king has declared to be his culminating achievement:

Walles he welte down, wondyd knyghtez,
Towres he turnes and turmentez the pople;

Wroghte wedewes full wlonke, wrotherayle synges,
Ofte wery and wepe and wryngen theire handis,
And all he wastys with werre thare he awaye rydez—
Thaire welthes and theire wonnynges wandrethe he wroghte![19]

[He tore down walls, wounded knights, razed towers and tormented the people; he made nobles widows, who lament their fate, often curse and weep and wring their hands, and he wastes all with war, wherever he rides—their belongings and habitations he completely destroys!]

Read "the giant" instead of "Arthur" for the text's "he," and the description seems no less appropriate, so completely does the king become his own foe.

Because regnal and monstrous bodies ultimately coincide in the romance, Arthur is implicated in the crimes that the giant commits. The "tyraunt" of Mont Saint Michel has depopulated the countryside and destroyed all the male children, whom he has "caryede to þe cragge and clenly deworyde" [carried to the crag and completely devoured] (851). He is the monstrous king who commodifies his subjects, the nightmare father who ingests his children, the dragon who (as in Arthur's ominous dream) drowns the people he should protect. On the same day when Arthur arrives in Normandy, the giant abducts the duchess of Brittany to his mountain abode, "to lye by that lady aye whyls hir lyfe lastez" (855). These giant appetites of his extend to more than anthropophagy, and the duchess is reduced to nourishment.

Before Arthur reaches the mountaintop, he and his two men pass through a paradisal grove in which nightingales and thrushes pleasantly sing to the accompaniment of gurgling waters. The passage to the otherworld in romance is typically signaled by a movement through such a liminal area. The transitional place is here full of reindeer, flowers, and flowing streams—an eternal May, a *locus amoenus* that promises procreation but will give way, as Arthur progresses, to *foedus coitus* and death. Unlike Wace's version (the author's immediate source), Arthur leaves his companions Bedevere and Kay to await his return from the "pilgrimage." As in the Galfridian narrative, the solitariness of the quest underscores its personal nature for the king. From the vigorous scene of life, Arthur passes alone to the desolate crag on which two fires flare and a woman is weeping over a new grave. Beneath this mound, the duchess is buried, a victim to the sexual aggression coursing beneath the nightingale's song of idealized love.

The wailing woman is the duchess's foster mother, a widow, and to her is left the narration of the young woman's fate. According to Geoffrey and Wace, the duchess died before the giant could violate her; in this darker version, the rape is performed and vividly recounted. Its culmination is the tearing of her young body to the navel (989). The widow moves from elegizing her foster daughter to explaining the obsession of the giant with Arthur of Britain, not realizing that she is speaking to him. Giants are monsters of appetite, and the author of the *Morte Arthure* brings this sin of excess to such an extreme that its description becomes sickly comic in its disgusting superfluity. The foster mother describes a typical evening repast:

He sowppes all þis seson   with seuen knaue childre
Choppid in a chargour   of chalke-whytt syluer
With pekill and powdyre   of precious spycez,
And pyment full plenteuous   of Portyngale wynes. (1025–28)

[He regularly dines upon seven male children, chopped in a serving dish made of chalk-white silver, with spiced sauce and a sprinkling of precious spices, and plentiful honeyed wine from Portuguese vineyards.]

The giant of Mont Saint Michel is something of a gourmand. Another elaborately detailed connoisseur's feast occurred earlier in the narrative, only this extravagant dinner was staged as Arthur entertained the Roman ambassadors at the New Year:

Flesch fluriste of fermyson   with frumentee noble
Therto wylde to wale   and wynlyche bryddes,
Pacokes and plouers   in platers of golde,
Pygges of porke-de-spyne   þat pasturede neuer;
Sythen herons in hedoyne   hyled full faire,
Grett swannes full swythe   in silueryn chargeours,
Tartes of Turky,   taste whan þem lykys. (180–86)

[Venison fattened in the close season with noble frumenty [soup], as well as wild and goodly fowl in abundance, peacocks and plovers on gold platters, piglets of porcupine that had never grazed, then heron covered in fancy sauce, large swans next on silver serving dishes, Turkish tarts pleasing in taste.]

The list unwinds for twenty more lines, a canticle of excess so rich that the verse itself surfeits, ultimately repelled. The effect is intensified in the rhetorically similar description of the giant's meal, for here the recipe calls for the severed limbs of children, and the spitted roasts are attended by four maidens, doomed to the giant's bed that night, "his byddynge to wyrche" [his bidding to work] (1030). The spices used to prepare the giant's feast are just as exotic as those used by Arthur's cooks, but here they flavor torn humanity.

The juxtaposition of the two repasts retroactively transforms the significance of Arthurian consumption. In both, the food is eaten from silver "chargeours" (185, 1026), and both feature young, "ungrazed" meat (183, 1025). The one is a formal state dinner, cooked to regal order and served as public theater, a staged assertion of the controlling power of the monarch over the lesser kings who attend his tables. The other is a darker version of the same meal, in which this monarchical power is unmasked (or un-masqued) as originating in a violent system of force predicated on unwilling subjugation, which, if perfected, produces a despot among symbolic eunuchs, as well as graves and gullets full of innocent bodies. Both feasts explore the limits of the state-as-body metaphor familiar from classical and medieval political philosophy; both feasts, when paired with each other, suggest that if power is a corporeal system, it is also a cannibalistic one.

The unluckiest victims of this ideological structure are the women who roast the meat and die in bed, as well as the children who are no more human than pigs (the food of the giant in Geoffrey's version of the story, and Arthur's food in this retelling). Portrayed on the crags of this bleak mountain is a *tableau vivant* of the underside of the chivalric world, the disavowed bodies (of women, of children) that, in their return, undermine a sexuality that according to the chivalric myth is wholly spiritual. These violated women and victimized children insist that despite all its protestations to the contrary, chivalry cannot unhinge sex from body; desire may be portrayed as incorporeal and "pure," but such representations serve only to exclude the bodies on which its masculinity is actually practiced, through which it is produced, and as a consequence of which more disavowed bodies are engendered. This foundational absence is rendered so vividly present that the text once again surfeits, this time with calculated disgust. The spectacle of these victims arouses Arthur's anger, and he charges the giant, as if in an eruption of violence he could forget the victims of his own martial campaigns and avoid the self-interrogation with which the tableau assaults him.

Just as discomforting as the way in which the narrative entwines masculine and monstrous identity is the text's delectation of excess. Exorbitance is obsessively invested with enjoyment. The giant is described through a menagerie of animal similes that exceed all reasonable length, rendering any precise imagining of his body impossible for the audience; the giant remains a nontotalizable collection of metaphors, a body in pieces. His nightly feast is imbued with equal measures of disgust and delight as its gruesomely detailed description artfully unwinds. Rather than look away from the severed bodies that are being served to the giant, the narrative gaze lingers on their careful preparation, savoring each spice sprinkled on the roasting limbs. It would be difficult to describe the scene as comic, but in its insistent inappropriateness and in the prolonged anxiety that its staging elicits, a bodily reaction something *like* comedy is produced. The giant of Mont Saint Michel produces quiet but cruel laughter, a dismissive somatic reaction that disinvests readers and auditors of the obscene enjoyment that the narrative has forced them to share with the monster.

Because the giant is the male body writ large, and because there is always something both terrible and comic about large bodies, the giant of romance has always been associated with various kinds of laughter. This visceral reaction of a human body to an "inhuman" one (a reaction no doubt precipitated through the relief of disidentification) is as likely to be cruel as merry. Later in the Alliterative *Morte Arthure*, Arthur is cutting his way through the army of Lucius, the Roman emperor, leaving a trail of corpses and blood. His heroic attention is caught by a group of giants who are pounding his men with clubs. Arthur rides to his troops' rescue, charging the giant Golopas "who grieved him most" (2124). With a mighty swing, Arthur cuts away the giant's knees and taunts: "Come down . . . and karpe to thy ferys! / Thowe arte to hye by þe halfe" [Come down and speak to your peers! You are too tall by a half] (2126–27). He then strikes off the head (2129). Arthur's reconfiguration of the giant's body is disgustingly amusing, a site of both obscene enjoyment and *jouis-sense* ("joy in making meaning," here, in rendering the verbal corporeally). The giant clearly deserves what he gets, the king's witty words mask the pain of the bodily violence he commits, and so the episode is heroic. The slicing of Golopas down to human size is the excision of that which has inflated him — and, by metonymy, his commander Lucius — to grossness. The rebuke is at once symbolic and material. A similarly comic humiliation occurs in *Perceval of Galles*, where the hero admonishes a giant whose foot he has just severed to hop away and stop bothering him (2017–95)

Comedy that involves the body nearly always has an element of sadism, and this observation is as true of the grim humor of the battlefield and gallows as it is of slapstick. Not all the laughter that the giant elicits, however, is as mean-spirited as that in the Alliterative *Morte Arthure. The Sowdon of Babylon*, for example, incorporates a wide range of comedic responses to the giant bodies that populate it. Derived ultimately from the French chanson *Fierabras*, this fourteenth-century Middle English romance features two animal-headed Ethiopian giants of demonic origin. Alagolafre is a monster so intimidated by his master's order to prevent Richard of Normandy from crossing the bridge that the giant wards that he immediately wraps the entire structure with twenty-four chains. When Alagolafre is defeated in battle, a huge giantess named Barrok strides out from the nearby city of Mantrible to avenge her dying husband.[20] Wielding a scythe "large and kene," she wades through the men and mows the Christian army down ruthlessly, at least until Charlemagne dashes out her brains. The sudden appearance of the giantess is striking and perhaps suggests an ultimately northern influence, yet Alagolafre has more at home than a wife. Later in the romance, Richard comes upon the giant's two young children, seven months old and four feet tall.

The soldiers christen the youngsters Roland and Oliver, after their leaders, but deprived of their mother's milk, the two infants soon perish. Even though the binarism between the categories "human" and "monster" is suggestively undercut by envisioning a giant having both wife and family, granting him the possibility of a domestic life, the text quickly retreats to the orthodoxies of antagonistic dualism. The momentary entwining of the Christians with their pagan enemies is nonetheless a suggestive, evocative, and undeniably comic gesture. The humor derives from the noncoincidence of body and milieu: Saracen monsters who viciously attack Christian armies are not supposed to have loyal wives, sheltering houses, and cute "little" children who eagerly await their return.

Earlier in the *Sowdon of Babylon,* the giant Estragot invokes a similarly comedic response to a body that wanders away from its "natural" context, this time with gruesomely alarming results. Whereas Alagolafre had a leopard's head, Estragot has that of a boar. The animal attribute makes the monster subhuman, but his man's shape suspends him in that troubling space between categories, the place of the hybrid that Gowther knew so well. The meanings that the giant's dark skin signify are made evident in a narrative aside on his ancestry: "I trow, he were a develes sone, / Of Belsabubbis lyne" (356–57). Not only is the monster the son of an incubus, but he is an "Ethiopian," an imprecise ethno-geographical term in the Middle Ages that gestured vaguely toward African provenance. The medieval body makes little distinction between interior and exterior; any moral failing is signified through flesh, so that no deviation remains secret. The racialized giant therefore incorporates an ethical, as much as an ethnic, alterity.

Estragot's strength is so tremendous that he is able to smash the portals of Rome to pieces with his "myghty mace." His shattering of the gates of the *urbs aeterna* is a powerful image, contrasting the supposed solidity of the Latin tradition with that brute, barbaric physicality whose power to fragment it was supposed to have been tamed, like a gentrifying soul in the wilds of a body. The giant's intellectual powers are fortunately not quite so impressive as his corporeal prowess. He strides at once into the city, and the inhabitants immediately drop the portcullis. The giant's body is chopped in half, a fitting fate for a troubling composite. He crumbles to the ground and fills the air with harrowing cries until Mohammed takes his soul "to his blis" — the author's tongue-in-cheek locution for a quick descent to hell.

If it is true that all bodily comedy constructs a sadistic subject position for its enjoyer (think, for example, of Charlie Chaplin's sublime suffering behind his comedic veil in *Modern Times*), the giants in the Alliterative *Morte Arthure* and the *Sowdon of Babylon* suffer their ultimate fate as a logical extension of the investment of the audience in their suffering. The giants perish through a ritual dismemberment that stages a public rejection of all the monstrousness they incorporate. Can a medieval giant enjoy without punishment, without losing forever in a monotonous rebuke the integrity of its body? A romance written at about the same time as *Sir Gawain and the Green Knight* that functions as an "obscene double" to that poem's courtly refinement poses just this question.

Enjoy Your Monster

Enjoyment is primarily enjoyment in the signifier.... To imagine a possible gratification equals its actual gratification.
—Slavoj Zizek, *Enjoy Your Symptom*, 27–28

Sir Gawain and the Green Knight explores the lack of a firm boundary between manhood and monstrousness, abjecting the feminine to bring masculinity and the monster into coherent bodily alignment. The giant is not a force to be overcome and banished, as the gigantomachia of romance tradition insists, but rather an interior Other, foundational rather than antithetical to chivalric identity. This revelation of the fallen state of the masculine subject Gawain is unable to communicate to the frivolous court; the poem is ultimately about the impossibility of successfully incorporating the kind of heroism that the identity romances construct.

Although exceptional in its artistry, *Sir Gawain and the Green Knight* was not alone in exploring the continuity between chivalry and gigantism, those supposed opposites that keep coinciding. In a loose taxonomy of romance giants, the most intriguing genus is a group of enchanted giants rather similar to the Amazing Colossal Man of fifties filmdom. Like Glenn Manning, these giants move between the categories "man" and "monster" in order to demonstrate how the masculine corpus is produced from a prehistory of wildness that always threatens to become the body's future. Mainly a late, English addition to romance, enchanted giants are men who through some work of magic have been transformed in size and nature out of their humanity and into the gross flesh of gigantism. What few of these stories exist in English are interrelated and center around the redemptive power of Gawain's courtesy and are therefore analogues of *Sir Gawain and the Green Knight*.

The best example appears in a curious romance commonly entitled *Sir Gawain and the Carl of Carlisle*. Two versions survive: the 660-verse specimen of the Porkington manuscript, composed circa 1400 near Shropshire (the text on which I will mainly rely), and the much later Percy Folio version of about five hundred lines, probably composed in Lancashire between 1500 and 1550 (Severs, 59–61).[21] Neither manuscript reproduces its lost original in toto, but the complete story can be reconstructed through comparison—appropriate enough where giants are concerned, for who could ever know a body so immense at once, as an unruptured whole? As *Sir Gawain and the Carl of Carlisle* opens, Arthur is gathering a hunting party that amounts to a litany of illustrious knights lifted from popular romances: Lancelot, Percival, Launfal, Reinbrun (son of Guy of Warwick), "Syr lebyus dyskonus," and "syr ferr vnkowþe" (Libeaus Desconus *and* Fair Unknown). Bringing up the rear is Sir Ironside, of whom it is said, "Gyanttys & he wer euyr at were" [Giants and he were always at war] (77). In fact, each of the eponymous knights in the expedition has a significant encounter with a giant in the particular romance to which he gives his name. *Sir Gawain and the Carl of Carlisle,* like *Sir Gawain and the Green Knight,* explores at length what is at stake in this ubiquitous encounter between hero and monster.

Toward the end of the hunt, Gawain, Kay, and Bishop Baldwin are separated from the king's retinue when an impenetrable mist rises from the moor. On Kay's obnoxious insistence, the men try their luck at a nearby castle, despite the owner's reputation for fierce inhospitality. The seneschal's suggestion of immediate, violent subjugation of the Carl of Carlisle is counteracted by Gawain's determination to use "fayr wordys" to secure safe lodging. When Gawain "curtessly" requests admission of the porter, he is warned against entering with the declaration "My lorde can no corttyssye" [My lord does not know courtesy] (193), and a search for a stable signification for the term will occupy the remainder of the narrative.

A bull, a boar, a lion, and a bear spring to attack the knights as they enter the fortress. "Ly doun!" the carl shouts, "my whelpys four" (235), and the animals scurry beneath the table like frightened puppies. Controlled by a domesticizing command, these pets of the carl are both wild animals and tame beasts responsive to voice commands; they embody on his behalf his liminal position both as feral, "natural" body and as subject produced through law. He is at once a dangerous wild man and a lord who efficiently manages a large household. A self-proclaimed "gyannt" (390), the carl is huge and hirsute. A space of "ij tayllors ʒardes" divides his shoulders, and he is nine such yards in height.[22] An extended catalog of the carl's enormous bodily members (vast arms, "fyngyris" as large as legs, "moʒth moche") severs the corporeal pieces from a totalizing referentiality, heightening the impression of immensity and the anxiety of disaggregation that giants always invoke.

Although the carl is thoroughly rude, admonishing a politely bowing Gawain that "her no corttessy þu schalt have, / But carllys corttessy" [Here you shall have no courtesy but carl's courtesy!] (276–77), he nonetheless orders that wine be served his unwelcome guests. After rejecting a four-gallon cup as insufficient for him alone, a nine-gallon tub is produced for all to share. Wheareas in other romances such indulgence exists only to be gazed upon, condemned, and rebuked, the giant's delight in devouring is part of this text's celebration of the body and its pleasures. In Geoffrey of Monmouth's *Historia,* Arthur dismembers the giant of Mont Saint Michel as a rejection of his function as *ingluvies,* a maw that produces nothing and consumes all. The obscenity of the mouth is contrasted against a severe and desubstantiating optics, a regime of the gaze that harnesses some of the enjoyment staining the site it condemns in order to bring bodies into new alignments of meaning. Here, quite in contrast, the giant's "moȝth moche" is a point not just of fascination but of celebration, and so Gawain joins the giant in a hearty drink.

In *Sir Gawain and the Green Knight*, the young and flustered Gawain answers Bertilak's wife's invitation to casual adultery with "I be not now he þat ȝe of speken" [I am not now the person you are speaking about] (1242). The implication of his vastly comedic assertion is "I am not (yet) that Gawain about whom all those naughty romances were written." The particular joy of *Sir Gawain and the Green Knight* is to desexualize the knight's body by imagining its prehistory, before he came into his "adult" romance identity as a Casanova who populates the countryside with bastard children. In *Sir Gawain and the Carl of Carlisle*, the protagonist is already that lady's man, for he falls immediately in love with the carl's beautiful, normally proportioned wife. Later that evening, the giant commands Gawain to climb into bed with his spouse, and then to kiss her. Eager to be courteous, Gawain obeys without hesitation while the giant watches and approves. Gawain's "courtesy" eventually provokes him to respond with too much vigor: he is about to "donn þe preve[y fare]" [do the private thing] when the carl hastily interjects with "whoo ther! / þat game i the for-bede" [Whoa there! I forbid that game!] (467–68). For his unthinking compliance with the demands of the carl, Gawain is awarded the bed of the giant's daughter. With his host's benediction, they "play to-geydor all þis nyȝt" [play together all that night] (486).[23]

This unhesitating compliance with his repeated injunctions is mainly what the carl means by "courtesy." The word does and does not signify restraint. Gawain performs only the actions that the carl dictates, but the carl's commands are, paradoxically, imperatives to indulgence. Long ago, the carl vowed to dishonor the host-guest relationship, showing all visiting knights "carllys cortessy," an uncourtliness that culminates in murder. He buffets both Kay and the bishop to teach them "sum cortessye" (340) but never raises a hand to Sir Gawain, whose willingness to suspend judgment of unfamiliar rules while following them without hesitation ultimately redeems the carl. The most severe test of Gawain's compliance with the giant's inflexible, inscrutable demands occurs when he commands that the knight of the Round Table behead him. Gawain obeys, striking off the head with an ax, and the giant "stood up [as] a man."[24] Gawain accedes to the carl's demand, and the giant is transubstantiated into a figure very much like Gawain; they are even the same height. The carl explains that twenty years ago he promised to kill any visitor who did not do exactly as he required. He slew the many knights before Gawain who had failed to follow his dictates, and their gory remains he now repentantly reveals ("X fodir of ded menn bonys," 533). Gawain's extreme courtesy, synonymous with unthinking obedience, not only evokes the declaration "Nowe wulle i forsake my wyckyd lawys" [Now I will forsake my wicked laws] (541) but transforms the giant into a proper knight. The carl invites Arthur to a feast at Carlisle, publicly acknowledging the newly subordinate status that marks the giant's return from churl to earl, the double meaning of *carl*. The work concludes with Arthur's royal visit and the admission of the carl to the fellowship of the Round Table, the supreme circle of recondite heroic male identity. Gawain marries the former giant's daughter, and the story ends with a satisfying dual integration. Gawain is as much a part of the carl's world as the carl is of Gawain's. Monstrousness and masculinity peacefully coincide.

At the narrative's conclusion, the carl has lost the defining attributes of his gigantism. His incorporation into the Round Table is the true signifier of his restored humanity. Gone are the anarchic violence evident in his slaying of knights seeking shelter, the grossness of appetite suggested by the enormous drinking cup, the potential violation inherent in his possession of a human-size wife. His rough independence and marginal status yield to a centered position as Arthur's own knight, so that the metamorphosis from giant to man is the migration from margin to middle, from rural lord to urban vassal. And yet the drama of identification is far more complicated than its reductive ending suggests. Although the carl is bodily reconfigured from a grossly physical monster to a reduced, respectful knight, at the same time, Gawain is transformed in the course of the narrative into a giant. Gawain performs every demand his uncanny host enjoins upon him. He drinks from a huge vat; he flirts with a giant's wife and has sex with a giant's daughter; he cuts off the head of his host with an ax, an action he has every reason to believe will kill the carl. Gluttony, lust, homicide: these are the sins of gigantism, the ascendencies of the body forbidden by the chivalric code (because so frequently practiced by "actual" knights). Even as Gawain explicates "courtesy," the courtliness that is supposed to construct a proper chivalric subject, Gawain occupies the textual position of the monster.

The giant's numerous commands to Gawain can be summarized by a single imperative, "Enjoy!" Gawain is compelled to commit those actions that every chivalric subject is supposed to reject, in the identity romances, in order to produce a heroic selfhood. He seems to have a great deal of fun in doing so. Following Mikhail Bakhtin's influential practice, critics reflexively label narratives that overtly celebrate the body as "popular," usually in opposition to "official" codes that forbid such enjoyment. In the most recent edition of *Sir Gawain and the Carl of Carlisle*, Thomas Hahn writes that since "carl" is cognate to Old English "churl" ("someone of low estate, without rank or consequence"), then a " 'carl's castle' is therefore as much a contradiction in terms as 'popular chivalric romance,' and such a location could only exist inside this hybrid literary form" (81). The problem with this formulation is that it is difficult to discover a romance that is *not* a "hybrid literary form," a romance that is purebred and "official" rather than "popular" or (to use Bakhtin's term) *grotesque*. The body in romance may be produced through a disciplinary ascesis as severe as that in any hagiography; as *Sir Gowther* well illustrated, however, the romance body is at the same time a "body in the act of becoming. It is never finished, never completed; it is continually built, created, and builds and creates another body."[25] These are not two distinct bodies, the one impossibly closed to the world, the other "never clearly differentiated from the world, but... merged and fused with it" (339) — the one official and sober, the other "familiar and colloquial," a popular body born of "folk culture" that opposes the "cosmic terror" of the ruling regimes. What "popular" means in the late Middle Ages is not always easy to determine, but it is clearly not, as Bakhtin would have it, a pure term in an antithetical pair. *Sir Gawain and the Carl of Carlisle* suggests a more complex way of thinking about the body, its enjoyments, and their relation to authoritarian discourses.

Bakhtin's festive giants are seditious. They undermine official cosmography and signal the triumph of life over the mortifying power of the church and state. *The Carl of Carlisle* features an indulgent giant in the Bakhtinian tradition, and yet the romance is not exactly a subversive or culturally dangerous narrative. Gawain does not break the commandments of the law; he follows the law to its letter, to its extreme. Gawain operates not in a sphere of illicitness but in the arena of the law's "obscene double." The carl's "wyckyd lawys" are not exterior to chivalric masculinity but wholly contained within its identity system. Psychoanalysis insists that "the establishment of the symbolic law, the (systemic) totalization of a signifying structure, cannot take place without producing a remainder, an excess, a dimension of the real that marks the limit of formalization."[26] As the "remainder" that Lacan labeled *jouissance* (enjoyment), this excluded "product" or "excess" seems to be outside the law, as its disruption (Shepherdson, 47). In fact, it is wholly bound up within the structure of power through which it is produced. Enjoyment can be folded back into its generating system, which then uses its power of attraction and entrapment for its own perpetuation and expansion. A world of difference may seem to separate the "popular," with its compulsion to enjoyment, and the "official," with its austere discipline, but this antagonism turns out to be chimerical.

Charles Shepherdson argues that this conjoining of prohibition to an imperative to enjoyment is particular to the contemporary United States, so that "defiant freedom" and "carefree excess" become inextricably entwined within "the most obscene form of superego punishment": a compulsion to enjoy, to be happy and healthy, is conjoined with an unceasing imperative to guilt — "Don't eat too much, don't go out in the sun, don't drink or smoke, or you won't be able to enjoy yourself!" ("History and the Real," 45). The romance version of this same duality works in a

similar, if less obvious, way: the giant prohibits all kinds of bodily pleasures in order to materialize the chivalric subject, but at the same time,
the giant offers these pleasures to that subject as a means of furthering
adherence to the very law that "produces" (defines, regulates) these enjoyments. It is the supposed illicitness of these excesses that ensures that
any indulgence in them is strictly controlled and enacted only through
a superegoic imperative. Chivalry relies on its "obscene double" as a site
for indulgence that undergirds its own generative ascesis. As a technology of selfhood, it relies on the interpellation of the subject as split, conflicted, failed, and guilt ridden to keep the subjectivity of its adherents
"in motion," in process, under surveillance. Power depends on this splitting for its own continuance.

Bakhtin argued that laughter is revolutionary and always distinct from
"official and authoritarian" institutions: "Laughter...overcomes fear,
for it knows no inhibitions, no limitations. Its idiom is never used by
violence and authority" (*Rabelais and His World*, 90). Slavoj Zizek insists
on the reverse. In his Lacanian-inflected analyses of ideology, Zizek has
written at great length how the "stain of enjoyment" (embodied in romance, I have argued, by the giant) is essential to the proper functioning
of authoritarian structures. He insists that an apparatus of power does not
attempt to evacuate the body of its attachment to pleasure but rather
secretly shares in these enjoyments to further its control. When the law
and obscene enjoyment meet, he argues, there lurks "the uncanny mixture of imposed enjoyment and humiliating coercion; the agency of Power
which shouts severe orders, but simultaneously shares with us...ob-
scene laughter bearing witness to a deep solidarity" ("Re-visioning 'Lacanian' Social Criticism," 18). Zizek's words uncannily capture the force
of *The Carl of Carlisle*, where the giant becomes both the Father of Prohibition and the Father of Enjoyment. His severe law must be followed
to the letter, but at the same time, he shares the overflowing bounty of
food and sex and violence that, in adhering to his commands, Gawain as-
sents are the carl's alone to control. The giant is regulative and obscene
simultaneously, without contradiction. His inclusion in the Round Table
only reinstalls this conjoined function of power under the aegis of Arthurian kingship, under the watchful eye of a surveillant and centralized disciplinary regime. This consolidation results not in the persistent feeling
of paranoia with which Foucauldian panopticism has too often been
charged but with compelled celebration of the body's vitality: the chivalric subject is an impossibly complete subject, a self-regulating body that
enjoys.

The Carl of Carlisle does not accomplish anything radically new in
its inscription of the giant as a locus of shared or communal *jouissance*.
Anglo-Saxon ruminations on *enta gewoeorc* as a lost temporality when
joy (*dream*) was possible and Arthur's victory over the gluttonous monster of Mont Saint Michel both demonstrate that the giant has been a

164

site of enjoyment as long as England has been an imaginable community. The romance's achievement is to bring into the light that "obscene shadowy realm" ruled by the giant. No longer does the monster inhabit an impossibly lost time or a forbiddingly remote place; the carl is a monster who is also a provincial aristocrat, who already plays the game of courtliness through steadfast adherence to a set of rules. The giant is exposed as the foundation of an architecture of subjectivity that has always disavowed that very stain of *jouissance* on which it is constructed and by which it is maintained. He sternly forbids and happily compels enjoyment. Both functions are necessary to chivalric male embodiment, revealed as a sober progress narrative *and* an indulgent comedy.

A rich vein of humor courses through *Sir Gawain and the Carl of Carlisle*, stimulating the bodies of its audience to laughter and making its readers complicitous in its delectation. The proffering of the nine-gallon drinking tub, the well-placed buffets to the obnoxious Kay, and the offer of a night of "play" with the carl's daughter invoke the traditional association of giants with force and consumptive drive, but here their significance has shifted; necessary textual condemnation gives way to limited celebration in a comic atmosphere that will end with a wedding. About a hundred years after *Sir Gawain and the Carl of Carlisle* was composed, a romance that takes the comic grotesque to new limits appeared. The plot of *The Turk and Gawain* is rather difficult to follow owing to mutilation of the manuscript leaves, but it involves the mysterious Turk (like the carl, an enchanted knight) conducting Gawain to the Isle of Man. This island is in fact an Isle of Monsters: the king and all his court are "giants strong and stout / and uglie to looke upon."[27] When he demands an adventure of them, this "hideous rout" challenges Gawain to a game of tennis. That a martial competition should be tennis is incongruous enough, but Gawain plays men bigger than him "by the halfe," with a ball made of brass. As the nine giants line up for a match, they think how much they'd rather swing at Gawain's head than at the ball. A fireplace-lifting contest ensues. The adventures end successfully when the invisible Turk assists Gawain in toppling the king of the giants into a cauldron of handily placed molten lead.

The understated comic elements of *The Carl* have become, in the space of a hundred years, the (literally) overplayed humor of the parodic court of giants on the Isle of Man. The author of *The Turk and Gawain* had *The Carl* itself specifically in mind, or at least a very close analogue; indeed, the later redaction *The Carl of Carlisle* is found in the pages of the same collection as *The Turk*.[28] Both celebrate the pleasures of the body by conjoining the monstrous to festive enjoyment; both have analogues in the processional giants and holiday figures who are part of late medieval public spectacle.[29] Yet comic giants and the humor of the grotesque body that they display predate both these narratives. Laughter and giants have always coexisted in some monstrous form.

Sir Gawain and the Carl of Carlisle and *The Turk and Gawain* need not be seen as popular culture antitheses to the "disciplinary" identity romances. As the "obscene double" of these works, celebratory romances feed enjoyment back into the same structure of embodiment, a closed system that converts its own excess into more energy to strengthen its hold over bodies and desires. Not all *jouissance,* however, nor all the excesses of the body, can be reintegrated into the formal limits of the systemization from which they emanate. Power may be immanent, unseen, and everywhere; but not every potentiality of embodiment and subjectivization originates within an omnipresent, surveillant regime that produces bodies and pleasures only as a means of control. Obscene enjoyment is a psychoanalytic phenomenon with a certain ideological utility; yet enjoyment, like the Real itself, has an existence outside of all systematicity. The carl and the Turk suggest that there is more to the body than the narrow confines of the human frame. There is also laughter, and laughter is always an intersubjective experience that pushes at the limits of embodiment by exposing the body's partiality, its embeddedness in an energetic cosmos that figures not an absolute exterior but a boundary beyond which a distinction such as self/other no longer strictly obtains. Laughter can be cruelly induced, rendered a systematic effect, like the "ideological" laughter of the battlefield flyting. As Bakhtin realized but expressed in too constrained a formulation, it can also escape a particular body and form a circuit with a larger, unbounded world—and this escape ultimately marks the failure of "body" as a singular marker of category.

Rabelais before Rabelais

It is . . . not lack of cleanliness or health that causes abjection but what disturbs identity, system, order. What does not respect borders, positions, rules.

—Julia Kristeva, *Powers of Horror,* 4

Walter Stephens has argued that Rabelais invented the comic giant. The thesis of *Giants in Those Days* is that most of what has been written about medieval giants is "fundamentally wrong" (1). Contra Bakhtin, Stephens insists that no jolly or "carnivalesque" giants populated the Middle Ages. He writes of a "coherent transcultural logic" that produced the inhuman race of giants (99), monsters "of terrible and hostile alterity" (57) who were uniformly evil from the time of the Old Testament until Rabelais created Gargantua.

The giants of the Bible and of Galfridian chronicle are, without a doubt, irredeemable.[30] But wholly missing from *Giants in Those Days* is a consideration of the giants of English and French romance. As *Sir Gawain and the Green Knight* and *Gawain and the Carl of Carlisle* have demonstrated, the medieval giant is not a genus of creature wholly distinct from humankind. The giant's body figures not an alien corporeality but an intimate strangeness that *is* human embodiment. A little bit of the giant stains even the most controlled or self-contained of human bodies. As *Sir Gowther* demonstrated, the only way to escape the taint of gigantism is to escape corporeality. The giant of romance is not unremittingly wicked, and he does not merely terrify. Bakhtin, as it turns out, was at least partially correct: the medieval giant does contain in his grotesque flesh an invitation to carnival, a summons — and sometimes an imperative — to enjoyment.

The giants of the Middle Ages are neither as glum nor as monolithically evil as Stephens makes them out to be — even if giants, like other monsters, often seem unlikely figures for celebration. According to romance's poetics of representation, that which is foreign or culturally marginal was ordinarily demonized or exoticized out of all real existence. These categories therefore resist by their very nature any move from their malevolent periphery to a Western, civilized center. Yet early in the Charlemagne cycle, the very tradition that made monstrous caricatures of the Muslims by evacuating humanity from their demonized flesh, characters such as Fierabras appear. This ferocious alien is overcome by heroic Oliver, requests baptism, and becomes a valiant Christian fighter.[31] Otinel likewise joins the ranks of the Holy Roman Emperor's forces after a sudden conversion, this time precipitated by the alighting of the Holy Spirit in the shape of a dove on the Saracen's shoulder.[32] These integrations are complete and unquestioned. Otinel is even given the hand of Charlemagne's daughter, Belisent, in a secular benediction to his spiritual transformation. This missionary reflex, not to be confused with tolerance, extended even to the most pernicious and monstrous representation of the Muslim as cultural other, the giant.

A tradition of Old French epic that was popular and influential in England detailed the interactions of Guillaume d'Orange and his giant retainer. The *Chanson de Guillaume* and *Aliscans* both make reference to Rainoart (or Reynald), a Saracen giant who was transformed from denigrated kitchen slave to celebrated Christian knight.[33] A richly comic character, Rainoart is given his fullest treatment in *Aliscans*, the foremost poem of the Guillaume d'Orange cycle and the favorite chanson de geste of the twelfth century. The fifteenth son of a pagan emperor, Rainoart serves a degenerative decade and a half in the household of King Louis. Well regarded for his strength but unloved because of his gigantism, he is soiled literally by the filth of the kitchen and more figuratively by the socially inferior position of laborer. Although the young giant has a fair and beautiful body (3151), the chief cook has transformed its appearance by demeaning him: he shears Rainoart's hair and blackens him with ash ("his whole face had been smeared with charcoal"), perhaps the first instance of blackface in literature, for Rainoart is made by the cook to perform as if he were the excessively racialized face he bears.[34]

Rainoart is taunted by the household squires, who swat at him with brooms and read the text of his body only from its darkened surface. The attacks mount until in a fit of rage he gruesomely murders one of the boys, hurling the tormentor against a stone column. The squire hits the pillar so violently that "his sides break and his heart is shattered, and both his eyes fly out of his head and his brain pours out and scatters" (3181–82). The spectacle of this body in pieces announces to those watching the fight that an identity greater than what should be contained in the figure of a charcoal-sullied scullion lurks beneath the giant's skin. Unlike Estragot or Amourant, "black as pitch," Rainoart's racial alterity is artificial, the literal result of a smear campaign. Unlike these giants who declare that inner nature is readable through its exterior inscription, through skin pigmentation, Rainoart's body suggests that the deformity of difference is culturally constructed on a beautiful (because white) template.

Rainoart's monstrosity derives only in part from the uncontrolled violence that his understandable rage conveys. His gigantism also finds expression in a good-natured gluttony. In a typical episode, Rainoart kills a cook who cruelly prohibits him from a kitchen, then dines on geese roasted in garlic and a barrel of wine (232). He bursts into a refectory, devouring all the food and drink that the miserly clerics have hoarded within. When a monk tries to stop his illicit feasting, Rainoart hurls the man against a pillar so violently that both eyes fly out of his head (3696). This textual fascination with eyes that will not stay in their proper place — with a vision of the body so bent on enjoyment that the circumscribing gaze of the "official" structure of power is knocked out of orbit — indicates that the giant's love of wine and food is being celebrated rather than condemned. As in the romance gigantomachia, the disembodied optical trigonometry of a disciplinary regime is contrasted against an ingestive physicality associated with the giant's mouth. Here, however, the text sides with the pleasures of the body rather than the prohibitions of the gaze. After all, the giant's heart is in the right place. As Rainoart exits the refectory, he is met by a crowd of poor people who have gathered to beg. Rainoart brings them the bread that the monks had locked inside their house, and the people rejoice, and enjoy.

The giant's violence, strength, and appetite are the very traits that distinguish him as a site of raw potential to the visiting William. Aroused by the young man's fair figure beneath his besmirched skin, William decides to indoctrinate Rainoart into the ways of chivalry by teaching him how to channel his drives and prowess toward a set of goals. The process of the giant's education under William's tutelage creates a narrative space in which an underlying ideology of embodiment moves into the open through an extended explication. William and the other Christian knights gently instruct Rainoart in the care of the self, enjoining him to impose demarcating limits upon his body, allowing him to produce himself as chivalric subject. When the knight Bertrand is stranded on the battle-field in need of a horse, for example, Rainoart endeavors to capture one for him. The giant must train his arms to exert the proper amount of force when striking enemies with his club. The first three swings hit Sara-cens so hard that both they and their steeds are crushed uselessly into the ground. On the fourth attempt, the giant succeeds in controlling his *vis et violentia* just enough: he splits the rider in half while leaving the horse unscathed. Rainoart's body will hereafter strive for a harmonious balance between excess and sufficient violence, between monstrous and heroic force.

The battle of Aliscans is staged as a series of confrontations between Rainoart and the monsters he might have been. Baudus, fifteen feet tall, is the black-skinned and curly-haired African that the romance giant or-dinarily resembles; Haucebier taunts Rainoart for his ragged vestments and learns that clothes do not make the man (or giant) when the object of his ridicule destroys him; Desramé, Rainoart's father and the Saracen leader, discovers the limits of filial devotion when his son disavows and attempts to behead him. King Agrapars possesses burning red eyes, heel-length hair, and feral claws that signify that he is the traditional giant of romance; he disfigures Rainoart's body by gouging flesh from his face. This action is intended to make the Christian-acting giant more resemble the malformed Agrapars, to draw him back to his originary monstrosity. Rainoart smashes King Agrapars's spine with his club, declaring dramat-ically, "I absolve you of hatred" (6109). At the scene of battle, he leaves behind this crumpled semblance of the monster he might have become, rejected for all time. The slaying of his brothers Walegrope and Grishart ("who ate human flesh"), as well as his sister Flohart, forms only a foot-note to this culminating episode of self-assertion. In each encounter, the message is clear: Rainoart refuses filiation from the body of the monster, allying himself instead to William's masculine-heroic form.

The unbaptized giant becomes through William's mentoring a renowned and beloved Christian fighter, christened with the admiring title *Rain-oart au tinel* ("Rainoart of the Club").[35] Even the traditional, unchival-ric weapon of the giant is reconfigured out of its negative valence into a celebrated attribute of the hero. Rainoart leads his master's forces to victory over the pagans at Aliscans, the scene of William's humiliating defeat in the opening scenes of the chanson. He converts one of his fel-low giants, Baudus, to Christianity—an accomplishment made both ad-mirable and inevitable by the long narrative stare at the contours of that monster's grotesque alterity (7261–66). Unlike the King of Tars, whose pigmentation instantly changed from black to white as he was baptized, or Rainoart himself, whose dark color was washed away to reveal a fair countenance, the skin of Baudus is an indelible "ink" that no longer signifies anything about the body-text beneath it.[36] The achievement of *Aliscans* is to imagine that a body's form might signify nothing about that body's inherent meaning; signification is *not* written across the flesh for Baudus, a very unmedieval argument.

Rainoart's abundant physicality is repeatedly offered as an object-cause of desire. Women in the text invariably have the same reaction to the giant, a response that the romance itself inculcates in its audience: first they look away from the spectacle of his grossness in fear, but in the end, they stare at his energetic figure with love. The Christian knights react similarly, ultimately claiming the giant for an admired hero. Cultural evidence suggests that this embrace of the giant succeeded on an extratextual level as well: Dante considered Rainoart so valiant that he included him, paired with Guillaume, in the fifth circle of heaven in the *Paradiso*, along with Joshua, Judas Maccabaeus, Godfrey of Bouillon, Roland, and Charlemagne. This military sainthood confirms the completeness of the giant's integration into the *corpus Christianum*.

The incongruity of a giant as proper knight is the source of much burlesque humor in *Aliscans*. At his baptism, Rainoart is suddenly thirsty and drains the holy water from the font. Angry with William, he leaps into a ship, determined to lead the Saracens against Orange; the threat of reversion into monstrosity is quickly undercut as Rainoart realizes that he does not know how to sail the craft and is pitched headlong into the sea. When Rainoart decides that to become a true chevalier he must be able to ride a steed, he climbs onto a horse's saddle but mounts facing the animal's posterior. He frightens the horse into a sudden gallop. After praying that he will not fall and contorting his features into various grotesque expressions, he tumbles ungracefully to the ground. Grasping the horse's tail and dragged along the earth, he makes a fist and knocks the mount down with a single blow. William and his men find the scene vastly entertaining. In their comic excess, the giant's flailing limbs validate the chivalric ascesis that produces a well-trained body, as well as a dominance over those other bodies (such as horses) on which knights rely for their full chivalric identity. *Aliscans* brims with physical humor that invites the audience to laugh at the ridiculous corporeality of the giant, a performance that works only to the extent that it elicits an identification with its spectacle. Romance ordinarily represents the progress toward stable embodiment, toward perfect masculine-chivalric identity, with equal measures of reverence and anxiety. Rainoart reveals that the *corps morcelé* as the body out of control is also richly comedic. Rabelais before Rabelais: comic giants clearly existed before Gargantua and Pantagruel delighted audiences with their somatic antics and playful indulgence.

Even as the encounter with the giant is written in a humorous, rather than horrific, mode, the same exclusions and distortions that the romance gigantomachia enacts obtain in this chanson. Sexuality is evacuated from the male corpus, returning only after the business of war has been accomplished. Rainoart is revealed to be a virgin at the close of the narrative, and the audience is invited to watch as "he and his wife fulfill their desires" and engender a son (8489). The maternal body is introduced only to vanish. The nameless wife of the giant dies within a couplet because her child is so large that he must be ripped from her womb. Besides a few good and chaste women such as Vivien and Guiborc, the text offers only disappearing mothers and monstrous feminine bodies. The giantess Flohart, perhaps the model for Barrok in *The Sowdon of Baylon,* is a "mad, dirty, old woman" who sweeps through William's army with a scythe. Foul smoke bellows from her mouth, her flesh radiates a disgusting smell, and Rainoart immediately links his sister's filth with sexual pollution (6530). Her threat is phallic, transgressive of gender. She attempts to slice away the club that Rainoart loves so much that he "kisses and fondles" the weapon, praising God for its continued, identity-giving presence (6580). Violence against Flohart "gives Rainoart real pleasure" (6551), for he knows that enjoyment is found in desexualized male-male relations and not in the obscenities of copulation that the female body is here made to represent. In both the comic mode of *Aliscans* and the tragic mode of the Alliterative *Morte Arthure,* women and their bodies suffer an identical, monstrous fate.

Rainoart as Christian hero expands the cultural role of the medieval giant to include enjoyment that is not always obscene, laughter that is not always cruel. In becoming William's protégé, he teaches the hero as much as his mentor instructs him: after all, were it not for the giant, William would fail a second time in battle at Aliscans. Comic giants like Rainoart undercut the mythic autonomy of the chivalric subject by suggesting that, the cult of the hero aside, identity is a contingent phenomenon that does not depend on residence in a single, self-sufficient body, but rather occurs *between* bodies, in a process of constant communication and exchange.

The folklorist and semiotician Susan Stewart writes reverently of the processional giants of the Middle Ages that "in both statuary and living form, the gigantic appeared as a symbol of surplus and licentiousness, of overabundance and unlimited consumption" (*On Longing,* 80). Following Mikhail Bakhtin's explication of the carnivalesque giant, she explains that "festivals of the giants were accompanied by feasting, drinking, and parodying of official institutions" (81). Yet as Walter Stephens points out, like Bakhtin, Stewart "runs afoul of the historical evidence" (*Giants in Those Days,* 37). Processional giants to be paraded through cities at times of holiday were a late development; the earliest references I have been able to find for England involve the ceremonies of welcome staged in London for Henry V. Further, as Stephens insists, these effigies are invariably produced by official sources and can hardly be said to represent the carnivalesque opposition of a "people's culture of laughter" to sober and oppositional authority. As the Carl of Carlisle and the Green Knight make clear, giants are always bound up in "official" ideologies, if only because the manufacture of texts and images is nearly always controlled by those already invested in keeping such ideologies in circulation. Further, as Shepherdson and Zizek argue, enjoyment and authority are not incommensurable. Rainoart's merry disposition ensured that he became a world-class hero, familiar from England to Italy. He was eventually joined in the comic pantheon of giants by Ascopart, a particularly English sibling who was destined to become something like a "processional giant," or at least a town mascot.

Embodiment as Intersubjectivity

It is never filiations which are important, but alliances. . . . An animal is defined less by its genus, its species, its organs, and its functions, than by the assemblages into which it enters.
— Gilles Deleuze and Claire Parnet, *Dialogues*, 69.

A popular film by one of the most populist of directors, John Hughes, explores the situational comedy that arises when an uptight perfectionist (Steve Martin) and a slovenly but happy-go-lucky salesman (John Candy) are forced to share a series of misadventures as they make their way home for the holidays. *Planes, Trains, and Automobiles* maps a trajectory of becoming for both men's bodies: one learns that his self-regulation has produced an anticonsumerist self that, in comedy, can only be laughable; the other discovers that his boundless indulgence in food, drink, and pleasure might be an inherent good but needs to find a limit if he is to find a stable place in the social network. That the disciplined body should be slim and the unruly form excessively corpulent is no surprise: it's the same "odd-couple" pairing familiar from such pop culture icons as Abbot and Costello, Laurel and Hardy, Felix Unger and Oscar Madison. This combination is ancient and invokes the mythology of the giant. The pairing of John Candy with Steve Martin is only a twentieth-century version of the coupling of Rainoart to William.

Medieval England had its native version of the "odd couple," with a similarly energetic bodily dynamic that renders identity an intersubjective, even intercorporeal process. The giant Ascopart ineptly serves a young hero struggling to establish his chivalric singularity in the popular romance *Bevis of Hampton*. Like *Guy of Warwick*, *Bevis* was originally composed in Anglo-Norman but adapted into English as the prestige language shifted. Because of its widespread appeal, the work was also eventually translated into Welsh, Irish, Dutch, Italian, Yiddish, Romanian, and Russian. In 1338 Robert Mannyng listed Bevis as an Arthurian knight in the *Story of England*, blurring the line once more between history and romance. In a further reification, effigies of Bevis and Ascopart were carved at Southampton (the "Hamtoune" of the story), in the Bar Gate. That the moment from the romance chosen for memorialization at the entrance into the town should be Bevis paired with his giant squire is revealing. *Bevis of Hampton* owes its enduring popularity as much to Ascopart as it does to its plucky and earnest protagonist, even though the giant figures prominently in comparatively little of the sprawling narrative.

Just as he is about to be decapitated by Bevis, Ascopart is spared at the intercession of Josian, a virtuous Saracen who is the love interest of the story and a model of fully successful Christian integration. In contrast, the giant's very name figures a resistance to incorporation. According to both *Mandeville's Travels* and *The Sowdon of Babylon*, "Ascopart" is a proper noun that designates "a desert people of the Near East" (*Middle English Dictionary*). Ascopart attacks Bevis in a comic rewriting of the topos of the giant's club stroke that misses; he loses his balance and topples to the ground. This inability of his body to maintain equilibrium is his defining characteristic. Ascopart is always about to tumble and fall into something else, metaphorically or physically. He acknowledges his difference from the other giants of romance tradition when he confides to his new master that he was driven from his hometown for being too small:

[I] was idrive out of me toun;
Al for þat ich was so lite,
Everi man me wolde smite;
Ich was so lite & so meruȝ
Everi man me cleped dweruȝ. (2522–26)

[I was driven out of my town; because I am so small, everyone used to hit me. I was so small and delicate that they all called me "dwarf."]

Something simultaneously comic and touching animates the passage. Giants, Ascopart reveals, are not an *absolute* category of monstrousness but a *relational* one.[37] Ascopart is a dwarf among his own kind, but once he lives among humans, he finds himself in a completely different category of identity: "And now icham in þis londe, / I-woxe mor, ich vnderstonde, / And strengere" [And now that I am in this land, as I see it, I've grown greater and stronger] (2527–29).

The giant is an exile from his native country, ostracized against his will from his family and social place. Ascopart's history exactly parallels that of Bevis. As the romance opens, Guy, earl of Southampton, is slain by his treacherous wife's lover. Bevis, Guy's young son, is sold by his mother to pirates, who in turn present him to the king of Armenia.[38] When he encounters the giant, Bevis is hastening to England to reclaim his lost title and the identity long denied him. Ascopart has been sent by the wicked king Garcy to break apart the family that Bevis is intent on founding with his beloved Josian. The giant represents a force directed toward the fragmentation of community, but at the same time, this monster is himself a victim of that lost sense of belonging. Perhaps for this reason he agrees at his defeat to become the knight's obedient page, to accept integration into the bodily system of socialized meaning that he had intended to destroy.

Ascopart immediately assists Josian against those Saracens with whom he was formerly allied, winning Bevis's trust. At Josian's christening, an enormous font is constructed for the giant. When the bishop attempts to baptize him, he leaps away and cries: "Prest, wiltow me drenche? / þe deuel 3eve þe helle pine, / Icham to meche to be cristine!" [Priest, are you going to drown me? The devil give you hell's pain, I am too big to be Christian!] (2594–96). The strange mixture of the monstrous and the human that coinhabit Ascopart's resolutely hybrid body imbues the situations in which he finds himself with their humorous dissonance. Without a measure of human qualities, he would resist an investment of identification, and without a portion of his essential gigantism, he would not be the incongruous page who never succeeds in getting things quite right. Ascopart's hybridity figures a category resistance even in his incorporation into the Christian chivalric milieu, but here the audience laughs rather than grows anxious—although as Freud insisted in his writing on jokes and the unconscious, laughter and terror are not nearly as distinct as they appear but are two related discharges of a single fleshly tension.

Through Ascopart's undisciplined body, the narrative generates an abundance of mirth, manipulating the bodies of its audience to the pleasures of visceral response. Ascopart bursts out of towers too small to hold him, rows across a lake in a fishing boat that awkwardly contains his bulk, lifts a horse and its rider up from the battlefield and carries them through the clamor to his master. The giant conjoins powerful masculine fantasies of omnipotence, domination, and ebullient sensuality to an undercutting lack of precise somatic control. One episode in particular is revealing of this boisterous psychosomatic dynamic. While Bevis is conducting a martial campaign in England, he leaves Ascopart in Germany as Josian's protector. Earl Miles of Cologne falls in love with her and forges a letter from Bevis commanding the giant to rendezvous at a distant tower. The page is immured the moment he arrives. Josian murders the lecherous Miles when he forcibly weds and attempts to have sex with her. The people of Cologne are about to burn her alive when Ascopart notices the rising smoke. The monster shatters the walls that enclose him and rescues his ward just as catastrophe is about to erupt.

The vigorous episode replays almost exactly a scene from Chrétien de Troyes's earlier romance *Le Chevalier de la charrette*, in which Lancelot has been tricked through a false letter into imprisonment in a remote tower. A wicked nobleman has likewise concocted this scheme so that he can enjoy the body of the woman whom the knight is devoted to protecting.[39] Whereas Lancelot's body dwindles into an emaciated fraction of its former robustness during his long captivity, so that he must rely on a damsel riding an inglorious mule to liberate him, Ascopart bursts through the wall of his stone prison the instant he realizes his failure. Ascopart is always on the verge of trouble, always about to cause some catastrophe because the immensity of his flesh and the magnitude of his heroism do not fully correspond; but Ascopart's special charm is his ability to avoid these disasters by breaking at the last minute through those limitations that prevent him from being a knight, that arrest his development at the status of eternal, incongruous page.

Ascopart may triumph where Lancelot fails, but whereas Lancelot enjoys a full sexuality in his relation to the queen, the giant is bound to his master and his master's wife by a servitude that forecloses erotic performance. Yet this submission to the will of the hero is constructed as the deepest kind of love, a sexuality that exists outside of the sex act. It is puzzling, then, that Ascopart eventually betrays Bevis by kidnapping Josian shortly after she gives birth to twin sons. This heartless deed is performed at the direction of the Saracen king Yvor, who pulls Ascopart back into the monstrousness from which he had emerged under Bevis's tutelage. The narrator's rather tepid excuse for this sudden infidelity is simply that Ascopart "was falle in pouerte, / For whan a man is in pouerte falle, / He haþ fewe frendes wiþ alle" [was fallen into poverty, and when a man falls into poverty, he finds he has few friends] (3592–94). Quickly thereafter follows the giant's death at the hands of the good steward Saber, the servant who since Bevis's birth has embodied the ideals of manly submission to the heroic corpus. Perhaps Ascopart's true identity as monster has simply reasserted itself, for all of Bevis's humanizing influence. Perhaps his words at his baptism are all too true: "Icham to meche to be cristine!" Like Caliban, Ascopart may be of a nature nurture cannot transform, a body that illustrates the ultimate incompatibility of the chivalric subject with that which it defines itself against. Or it could be that having outlived his comic utility, the giant has unbelievably been turned to treachery as a plot expedient, a quick exit from a story now interested in other things.

More likely, Ascopart departs because at the point of his vanishing, Bevis has made his primary relationship domestic and familial rather than martial and homosocial, a sea change in the erotics of his private life announced by the arrival of his twin progeny. A space no longer exists in the narrative for this mismatched and therefore attractive male-male, "odd couple" relationship. The sidekick giant dies and takes with him a world of homosocial bonding — of playful dominance and submission, of two male bodies testing the limits of their self-identity by explor-

175

ing the process of their own embodiment. Homosomatic alliance becomes part of a progress narrative, aligned with "childish things" that must quickly be put away as the hero matures into full adulthood.[40] Bevis becomes a father and starts directing his desire exclusively toward family and marriage, toward what today is called institutionalized heterosexuality. Ascopart abruptly vanishes, unmourned, taking with him the whole world of same-sex relationality.

Ascopart in his relation to Bevis is similar to Galehaut, *fils de la Belle Geanesse*, who was likewise tied by desire to Lancelot.[41] In the *Prose Lancelot*, Galehaut dies of longing for the hero, who is so busy trying to please Guenevere that his stalwart companion's demise long goes ungrieved. Like Achilles and Patroclus, Orestes and Pylades, Amis and Amile, Aeneas and Achates, or Brutus and Corineus, Lancelot and Galehaut are an inseparable pair of men whose relationship is based on one's willing embrace of the other's dominating heroic glory. This act of submission is depicted as the highest ideal of manly love. It is also often disrupted when the more powerful partner takes a lover and introduces a *physical* sexuality into the narrative. When the hero chooses heterosexual orthodoxy, the beloved companion vanishes from the story.

Ascopart's exuberant presence in *Sir Bevis of Hampton* marks a midpoint for the romance giant: hovering at the edges of integration (serving as a page, becoming the source of celebratory humor), but ultimately marginalized and dismissed (unwilling to be baptized, reverting to his wicked ways, his originary gigantism). Tellingly, the author of the romance did not make Sir Bevis himself slay Ascopart, assigning the task to one of the knight's minions. To have Bevis and Ascopart engage in a final combat would invoke the long tradition of self-definition within disidentification that was always at work in the gigantomachia—and, with the change in the giant's use here, is a dialectical model suddenly insufficient. Bevis's act of assertion was to allow Ascopart to live, to acknowledge the extimacy of Ascopart's excessive and insufficiently disciplined body, its foundational presence in the construction of his selfhood.

In the giant-hero pairs that Rainoart and William, Ascopart and Bevis, represent, embodiment works as an *intersubjective* process. The hero instructs the giant how to body forth chivalric masculinity. At the same time, the giant teaches the hero that this process is never perfected, that something within the body is always too big to be captured in the limited subjective field of romance idealism. Embodiment never occurs for one subject alone but is a relational process caught up within a wide cultural matrix. Rainoart and Ascopart display the joyful ways in which gender identity is always incomplete, because the limits of the body do not stop at the skin; the heroic individual, despite every protestation to the contrary, relies for his meaning-in-being on a network of relations that includes both the human and the inhuman. Susan Crane has observed that medieval romance, "importantly informed by chivalric ideology," depicts a process "in which the subject both instantiates collectivity and responds to it by shaping the requirements of collective identity" (*Gender and Romance*, 33). The giants Rainoart and Ascopart push Crane's intriguing insight further and declare that identity is actively invested in, and borne by, the world of people and partial objects that surround any particular body. *Aliscans* opens with William's failure in battle against the Saracens; it is only after he has led his giant companion through the long process of containing his drives and desires within a chivalric circuit that William is able to return to that same field and, with the help of transformed Rainoart, vanquish the army that had earlier humiliated him. The progress narrative written across the giant's flesh culminates in William's public victory over the bodies of his foes, suggesting an interdependence of identity between the hero and his devoted monster. Likewise, every failing of the giant Ascopart is a movement of Bevis toward his final triumph as national hero; the giant's body falters so that the hero's embodiment becomes more perfect. Stalking the great dragon of Cologne, Ascopart flees in terror when he hears the monster's dreadful voice. The incompatibility of the giant's frame and mouse's heart is laughable. Bevis perseveres, so that he will become a secular version of Saint George. He endures an alchemical change to his body as the dragon's poison transmutes him into a leper and then suffers a second transmutation as water touched by a virgin rejuvenates his wretched form (2803–910). This fight against the dragon is the pivotal moment in the construction of Bevis as a national hero. The episode cites not only the dragon fights of Lancelot and Wade but, more importantly, Guy of Warwick's fight against "a dragoun in Norþ-Homberlande" (2608), as well as Saint George's banishing of a dragon to make the land safe for English nationhood. By performing both the actions of a foundational saint and the labors of Guy, his chief competitor for the title of national hero—just as Guy earlier performed that same saintly performance to solidify his own heroic authority—Bevis's identity is reified and expanded through placement within a long history. At the same time as Ascopart joins forces with these figures of history to illustrate the intersubjectivity of identity, the historicity of "self-making," the giant teaches Bevis that a body not produced through surveillant discipline and interior regulation must become comic, a spectacle for public disavowal. Ascopart bodies forth all that Bevis cannot be and carries it away for him, screaming in absurd, impossible fear.

Giants are figures of sublime dread, but also of boundless comedy and complex enjoyment, a fact Rabelais knew well. The medieval giant could be an object-cause of both desire and joy, especially when his wild corporeality is being transfigured by a hero who forms an alliance with him. Guillaume d'Orange had his giant squire Rainoart, who—when he left his life as a temperamental kitchen slave and learned to ride a horse, wield a sword, and feel at home in his own body—was assigned by Dante a space in the fifth circle of paradise, the arena of Christian heroes. Bevis of Hampton likewise taught his giant page Ascopart the relationship between proper embodiment and proper chivalry; this murderous and rapinous pagan eventually found himself the town mascot of Southampton. Both heroic apotheoses reveal a gesture toward enlarged, intersubjective identities at work in the reception of the narratives in which they figure: a transnational Christian male identity for Dante's Rainoart, consonant with the macrocosmic sweep of the poem; and a communal, bourgeois identity for Southampton's Ascopart, in every way appropriate for a town in search of a history under which to organize its present sense of its importance, its present sense of self.

Embodiment as a *process* depends, for its success, on intersubjective relations, on other bodies to bear for the subject the burdens of a multiple, fragmented selfhood. This "circuit of flows" is seen most clearly in the mythology that constructs marriage or courtly love as a mingling of two identities into a single body. An even more complex vision of intercorporeality, however, is offered by those romances that explore the "hero and his buddy" topos, especially when the buddy is a giant, a body in pieces that resists any totalization into a self-contained whole. Comedy arises as the giant's body is transformed from a fragmentary and dangerous physicality into a "miniaturized" system, a harmonious microcosm, a "successful" individual. That this training has a deeply homoerotic component is suggested by the giant Galehaut's moving love for Lancelot: when his hero loses himself in desire for Guenevere, Galehaut dies of a broken heart.

The Exorbitance of Desire

It is important to emphasize that although heterosexuality operates in part through the stabilization of gender norms, gender designates a dense site of significations that contain and exceed the heterosexual matrix.
—Judith Butler, *Bodies That Matter*, 238

Let me teach you this about my heart.
—Galehaut to Lancelot, *Prose Lancelot*

To return for a moment to a contemporary counterpart to the bodily dynamics of *Bevis of Hampton*, the film *Planes, Trains, and Automobiles* insists that identity occurs across bodies as much as within them. Its plot outwardly celebrates family and heterosexuality. Its protagonists suffer their impossible misadventures as they attempt to return to Chicago to celebrate Thanskgiving at home. Yet most of the film involves the two men's attempts to establish a balanced domesticity that excludes their wives. Not only do they occupy together the many vehicles of the title, but they often share the same hotel room, and the same bed. A key scene opens as they peacefully sleep, cuddling each other and dreamily repeating the names of their absent spouses. They awaken to find themselves locked in a strange embrace. "Where is your hand?" asks the fastidious character. "Between two pillows," the slovenly giant murmurs drowsily. "Those aren't two pillows!" The men jump out of bed instantly, nervously, and re-heterosexualize themselves by talking too enthusiastically about baseball. The comedy of "odd-couple" pairings arises through a homoeroticism that is invoked at the same moment it is disavowed, enjoyed just as it is safely dismissed. In this final section, I will suggest that this intersubjective flow of desire in romance exceeds containment in the pairing of the giant's body with the hero's frame. This exorbitance begins to function less as a precise, systematizable phenomenon, like *extimité,* and starts to resemble the postmodern identity category *queer.*

Although Rainoart and Ascopart are trained into the proper contours of chivalric masculinity, neither ultimately coincides with the subject position of his mentor. Something in the nature of their bodies resists incorporation into a wholly human frame of reference—resists, in fact, any static structuration at all. Ascopart betrays his master; Rainoart never learns the grace that signals fully successful embodiment. Neither giant comprehends what it means to be *confortable dans sa peau,* at home in one's body, because neither is able to materialize precisely those limits that precipitate an "individual" from the intersubjective network. If Ascopart and Rainoart figure the giant who is the intimate stranger at the heart of the romance knight, they also suggest that embodiment is a never-final process in which one body forms a circuit with another, losing its autonomy through a touch that is surprising, disturbing, and alluring. Read back from the "perfect" body of the chivalric hero, the giant is simply the body under process; divorced from teleology, however, the giant is the nontotalized body in its pure potentiality, the site where everything that exceeds containment in the chivalric matrix becomes possible again. The giant suggests that there is more to human corporeality than any reduction into systematicity (psychoanalytic, historical, biological) can measure. Primal monster lurking at every origin, the giant declares that identity is something larger and more multiple than residing as a lonely individual in some merely human frame.

In other words, the giant insists that because desire is caught up in, and dispersed throughout, a mobile network of bodies, objects, temporalities, and subjectivities, identity is always larger than any singular body that would circumscribe its trajectory. Proper identities can be culturally constructed and socially promulgated, but they do not always manage to capture desire within their limited contours. It may well be, for example, that the bond of intimacy that unites hero to giant is something in excess of mutual friendship. The giant's body is always an overly sexual body, as his repeated connection to promiscuous incubi attests. What has not yet been remarked, however, is the way in which the giant's hypersexuality becomes increased in romance through his racial alterity. Like their evil counterparts, Rainoart and Ascopart are Saracens—that is, Muslims. As John Boswell has demonstrated, medieval polemic characterized Saracen bodies as exorbitantly erotic: adulterers, polygamists, sodomites. Guibert of Nogent declared that Saracens were not satisfied with possessing numerous wives but also were "sullied by uncleanliness with men," and Jacques de Vitry claimed that Muhammad had "popularized the vice of sodomy among his people, who sexually abuse not only both genders but even animals."[42] In the Western medieval imaginary, the Saracen is characterized by a voluptuous physicality that "normal" heterosexuality fails to contain. His voracious desire alights indiscriminately upon a multitude of bodies, violating the regulation of difference by ignoring the "natural" constraints of gender, species, and race. How much more excessive, then, must be the sexualized body of the Saracen *giant.*

Extimité has been glossed throughout this book as "external intimacy" or "intimate alterity." This strangely foreign, disturbingly familiar site could be pushed out from its embedment in Lacanian psychoanalytic theory and be allied with what the term *queer* has come to signify within postmodern identity theory. A site that is perturbing, disruptive, and at the same time *attractive,* the queer functions as both secret inside and forbidden exterior to all that is straight and normal. The disavowed progeny of abjection and heteronormativity, the queer designates a supposedly "unlivable" space, and yet the production of this impossible realm marks a foundational moment for the identities that attempt to exclude it. The queer can thus become a contestatory point of resistance to systemization, as well as a powerful site from which to deconstruct dominant ideologies: "In contrast to the stabilizing categories of identity politics, the term 'queer' would resist nominalization, functioning as an adjective, adverb, even verb, stressing epistemology rather than ontology" (Burger, "Queer Chaucer," 156). Jonathan Dollimore describes the queer's gendered effects as repeatedly unsettling "the very opposition between the dominant and the subordinate" and labels it "sexual dissidence" (*Sexual Dissidence,* 21). Carolyn Dinshaw gives the queer an ontologically unruly definition:

> Queerness works by contiguity and displacement, knocking signifiers loose, ungrounding bodies, making them strange; it works in this way to provoke perceptual shifts and subsequent corporeal response in those touched. . . . It makes people stop and look at what they have been taking as natural, and it provokes inquiry into the ways that "natural" has been produced by particular discursive matrices of heteronormativity. ("Chaucer's Queer Touches/A Queer Touches Chaucer," 76–77)

Something in the queer prevents its full reintegration into whatever matrix of identity it arises to challenge with its perversity, its excess, its defiant joy. Its "disillusioning" force is certainly an "insistent reminder... of heterosexual incompleteness" (Dinshaw, "Chaucer's Queer Touches," 92), but it is also something bigger: the discomfiting limit of any circumscriptive system (of space, of time, of identity) that parcels the world into discrete phenomena and impossibly immobile categories.[43]

The queer involves something more than an erotics of homosexual desire, but — as the beauty of Galehaut's passion demonstrates — it certainly includes same-sex longing. From their first meeting, Lancelot and Galehaut share a bond of intimacy. When Lancelot convinces his *amis* (friend, beloved) to surrender his army to Arthur as an act of friendship, he is moved to tears of joy as the giant fulfills the request, and murmurs, "Blessed Lord God, who can be worthy of this?"[44] Galehaut so loves Lancelot that he arranges for the knight's secret tryst with Guenevere. Even though Galehaut knows this relationship will isolate him from the body to which he seeks proximity, he is willing to embrace a position at the margins of a coherent identity so that Lancelot's joy will in some measure be his own. It is not precisely possible to say why Galehaut acts as he does; there is something in his self-abnegation that makes him all the more forceful as a presence but prevents his exact location within the heterosexual cultural matrix that the bodies around him enact.

Unlike the describable, almost quantifiable phenomenon of extimacy, Ascopart, Rainoart, and Galehaut are not wholly reducible to structural effects within the identity systems in which they arise. Galehaut is more than a "stain of enjoyment" who functions in the text as a support for its normalizing apparatus of gender; if those reductive mechanics held true, he would not die so alone, so brokenhearted, and so invested with the passions of the reader, who has been invited to share with him his excluded subject position. Galehaut's death is among the most affecting episodes of the long *Lancelot-Grail* cycle. Convinced by misleading evidence that his beloved Lancelot has committed suicide, Galehaut refuses to eat or drink. Monks warn him that "if he died as a result, his soul would be damned" (*Lancelot*, 3.106), but he perseveres in his movement toward a forbidden destiny. His last, painful days on earth are spent gazing fondly at Lancelot's shield, the metonym of the absent and identity-giving body of his beloved. Galehaut out-Lancelots Lancelot, whose every attempt to achieve immortality by dying for love is ingloriously botched. In making this assertion, I do not intend to repeat uncritically the all too frequent conjoining of the queer, the tragic, and the death bound.[45] Although *Lancelot* itself to some degree makes this conflation, perhaps as a reluctant way of containing the queer's power to unsettle, it is undermined in advance by the proleptic section "The Nobility of Galehaut" (Micha 1.1, Lacy 3.72). Galehaut's eventual demise is announced just as he is first united with Lancelot, but only to make certain that the audience realizes that his impending fate is undeserved; that his passion for Lancelot is "a love greater than loyal companionship alone could make a man feel for someone outside of his family"; and that although Galehaut could have been greater than Arthur had he so chosen, his choice to "make bold to love good knights" is—despite the inability of other men to understand that choice, despite the fact that this makes him culturally incoherent outside of his relationship to Lancelot—an ennobling action. Lancelot's passionate reaction to Galehaut's self-starvation later ensures that his friend's death will be received as neither natural nor inevitable, that the possibility of a non-foreclosed queer cultural space is at least temporarily entertained as a textual, and perhaps cultural, good.

Kept ignorant of Galehaut's self-sacrifice by Guenevere, Lancelot wanders to a chapel where a beautiful casket is guarded by five knights. Its inscription is a stunning rebuke to his obliviousness, to his inability to see beyond the relationship he enjoys with the queen and notice that his identity is caught in other circuits of desire. Etched in the huge casket are the words "HERE LIES GALEHAUT THE SON OF THE GIANTESS, THE LORD OF THE DISTANT ISLES, WHO DIED FOR THE LOVE OF LANCELOT" (Micha 2.44, Lacy 4.120). The knight faints at this declaration of Galehaut's love, at the eternal inscription of his *amis* under Lancelot's name. Galehaut died of the very lovesickness (*mal d'amors*) from which Lancelot once suffered, which Galehaut introduced his beloved to Guenevere in order to assuage. Lancelot's perseverance proves that it is easy to live for love; Galehaut goes further and suggests that the truest passion embraces its trajectory of becoming even as it curves into the realm of the unlivable, the incoherent, the abjected—into an immortality beyond the limits of the body.[46]

Lancelot attempts to integrate his friend back into a normative structure of meaning by interring the corpse at Joyous Guard/Dolorous Guard, where Galehaut will lie beside the hero's future grave and that of Guenevere. Yet this extimate figure inserted between the two lovers retains its queer power, even in the supposed immobility of death. There is something more to Galehaut than can easily be absorbed through obsequies and other public rituals, something that "exceed[s] the heterosexual matrix"—something that acts like an "insistent reminder...of heterosexual incompleteness," but also of heroic insufficiency, of the limits and failings and sad exclusions enacted through chivalric embodiment. With three sweet kisses on the mouth, Galehaut is interred by Lancelot within a monument described as "the most splendid tomb in the world,... made for King Narbaduc, who was the author of the law upheld by the Saracens after Mohammed" (Micha 2.50, Lacy 4.121). A holy object to pagans, the tomb is not wrought from the all too human materials of silver and gold but is "crafted entirely of precious stones joined together so subtly" that it seems no "mortal man could have made such work." Beatiful and alien, strange body at the heart of a familiar architecture, the exorbitant tomb stands as an eternally resistant reminder of Galehaut's intimate alterity.

Galehaut haunts with the force of his desire Lancelot's subjectivity. This giant figures the failures of symbolization, the part of the system that cannot be folded back into its functioning and be made to undergird its structures of cultural signification. Galehaut, who loved Lancelot so much that he died for him, figures another way of being in the world that escapes reduction into the limited human frame within which most romances close. The giant's queer corporeality is the absolute guarantee that no human body is reducible simply to the system of identity through which it is rendered culturally legible. Since the body is always in motion, always in the process of becoming, there always remains some exorbitance that cannot be held captive in structure, in explication, in the "final" resting place of a lonely grave.

Transhistoricity

s I finish writing this book about the life of the giant in medieval
England, I am haunted by a very American television commercial for an imported automobile, a four-wheel-drive sport utility
vehicle manufactured in Japan. The giant in this advertisement is an im-
mensely fat white man, middle-aged and balding, dressed in an expensive dark suit—visual shorthand for Evil Corporate Culture incarnate.
With the self-absorbed glee of a nasty child, the giant strolls over an expansive green landscape, plopping down the skyscrapers he carries in his
arms like toys. A city springs to life around the monster: ominous buildings, ugly bridges, clogged roadways, and a multitude of traffic signs commanding NO, STOP, DO NOT. A vehicle appears, driven by a smiling man
who blithely ignores the new roads and the new rules. The car follows
an unpaved path through what remains of the original fields. Enraged,
the giant attempts to crush the errant vehicle underfoot, but the man in
his machine is too swift. The commercial closes as the man escapes forever the constricted, commanding space of the giant's gray city for the
green freedom of the countryside. A disembodied voice commands the
viewer to buy an Isuzu Trooper.

The advertisement interests me because it transforms the medieval
giant into a monster for the late 1990s. The subject of the commercial's
address would seem to be those men who define themselves against corporate America, with its restrictive rules and barrage of inflexible commands; yet the vehicle's most likely consumer is a wealthy business-
man with a family in search of a safe but prestigious means of travel.
"Feel freedom, buy this car!": the imperatives that the advertisement
visually and verbally conveys are very much a part of the world its narrative appears to reject, the world from which its product seemingly offers
an escape. The Isuzu commercial offers as its site of enjoyment the defeat of the prohibitive giant (the car and its driver achieve an unfettered,
bucolic bliss), then folds that enjoyment back into itself to induce regulated consumption. The giant is simultaneously disavowed and heeded,
abjected and interiorized. An image of rebelliousness, saturated with desire, is sold to make palatable a certain restrictive conformity as well as
a late-twentieth-century construction of masculinity (responsible paterfamilias, successful corporate manager, and unbroken sixties-style rebel

all in one—as if the incompatibility among these roles could be overcome through the purchase of a specific make of car).

This recent advertisement reminds us whence the giant derives his transhistorical power of fascination. Because he conjoins enjoyment and prohibition in culturally transformable ways, because he seems fully exterior to masculine self-identity at the same time as he performs his identity-giving work at the heart of embodied subjectivity, the giant returns. Just as in the nation-building legends of Brutus, there is no place for women in this modern redaction of the gigantomachia: the vehicle is driven by a man and pursued by a man; the other seats in the car are empty. The myth of the giant has been reconfigured across time while remaining structurally unchanged, performing the same violences, the same abjections, the same masculinist interpellations. That Old English elegy and exegesis, chronicles of Britain's mythic past, numerous medieval romances, a variety of manuscript illustrations, Chaucer, and contemporary television can find their common ground in the vast body of a monster indicates that the premodern might, as its name indicates, be wholly alien to what is now called the postmodern; and yet for all its disturbing alterity, the medieval intimately endures. *Extimité* suggests that temporality itself works rather differently from what historicist accounts of the past have led us to believe: the past is always with us, active and engaged, as dangerous as it is enticing, as violent as it is compelling, as unassimilable as it is familiar.

Notes

Introduction

1. Henri Bresc, "Les Temps des Géants," 246. All translations in this book are my own unless otherwise attributed.

2. See Jacques-Alain Miller, "Extimité," 74–87, and Charles Shepherdson, "The Intimate Alterity of the Real," 4. Both Miller and Shepherdson describe *extimité* as a phenomenon that occurs during the process of symbolization, as a "formal effect" of the transformation of the real of the world into a system of law and language. Dylan Evans (*An Introductory Dictionary of Lacanian Psychoanalysis*) describes extimacy as the psychoanalytic problematization of the opposition between inside and outside, related to the excentricity of the Lacanian unconscious and the subject (58–59).

3. Grendel's mother and the giantess Barrok (*The Sowdon of Babylon*) are two of the very few English examples. Modern giantesses are no more abundant; even a film such as *Attack of the Fifty Foot Woman* relies on the traditional masculine gendering of the giant's body to make its misogynistic point about the supposed dangers of feminine agency and desire.

4. See John Block Friedman's magisterial *The Monstrous Races in Medieval Art and Thought*; Rudolf Wittkower, "Marvels of the East"; Norman Smith, "Loathly Births off Nature,"; Richard Bernheimer, *The Wild Man in the Middle Ages*; Jean Céard, *La Nature et les prodiges*; Mary Campbell, *The Witness and the Other World*. Friedman treats the giant at greatest length, but as "monstrous race," the giant is no more remarkable than the fantastic bodies of the creatures who fly, hop, and otherwise perform their somatic deviance around him.

5. The English word "monster" and its cognates in the romance languages derive from Latin *monnstrum*, a divine portent, usually of misfortune. Augustine followed Cicero's example in *De divinatione* (I.xlii.93) and connected the Latin noun to the verb *monstrare*, "to show, to reveal" (*De civitate dei*, XXI.8). Isidore of Seville, following the example of Varo (*De lingua latina*), derived *monstrum* from *monere*, "to warn" (Norman Smith, "Loathly Births off Nature," 3).

6. On containment strategies for "extraordinary bodies," see Rosemarie Thompson's introduction to *Freakery*, 1–19.

7. The second chapter of *The Monstrous Races* is entitled "A Measure of Man" and gives a brief cultural history of the "prejudice" of the classical and medieval world "concerning alien peoples" (32). White describes "the technique of ostensive self-definition by negation" in "The Forms of Wildness," in *Tropics of Discourse*, 151–52. Le Goff argues that in the monsters that the medieval West thought to populate the Indian Ocean's shores, "a poor and limited world formed for itself an extravagant combinatoric dream" that "freed [it] from repression" ("The Medieval West and the Indian Ocean," in *Time, Work, and Culture in the Middle Ages*, 197, 195).

8. Quotation from Stephens, page 2, argument about medieval giants presented fully in 58–97.

9. Even here, though, Stephens overstates the case. In theological writing, giants were ordinarily seen as unremittingly evil, as Stephens insists, but important exceptions exist. Robert Kaske has shown how the giant of the Vulgate translation of Psalm 18:6 ("Exsultavit ut gigas ad currendam viam") was often glossed as Christ, "the *deus-homo,* of double nature and so aptly signified as a giant in the psalm" (*"Gigas* the Giant in *Piers Plowman,* 180) — a gloss that would be impossible if Stephens's estimation of the giant's cultural valence were universally true.

10. See Bernheimer, *The Wild Man in the Middle Ages;* Hayden White, "The Forms of Wildness: The Archaeology of an Idea" and "The Noble Savage Theme as Fetish," in *Tropics of Discourse,* 150–96; and Louise Olga Fradenburg, "The Wild Knight," in *City, Marriage, Tournament,* 225–43 (quotation from 236).

11. Lacan's description of the ex-centricity of the Other in Seminar 7, p. 71.

12. See my "Monster Culture (Seven Theses)," 5. This is not to say that no family resemblance unites the two modes of vampirism; indeed, both are conjoined by locating the site of their enjoyment in homoeroticism, masochism, and an exploration of the limits of the body.

13. Fradenburg and Freccero formulate the aim of such a "transhistorical" project well when applied to the construction of sexual identity; see "Caxton, Foucault, and the Pleasures of History," xix.

14. Elizabeth Grosz, *Volatile Bodies: Toward a Corporeal Feminism,* 160. Grosz is the best contemporary theorist of embodied subjectivity, although it often seems that she is posing her questions to classical philosophy, as if the Middle Ages contained no intervening challenges.

1. The Ruins of Identity

1. W. P. Ker, *The Dark Ages,* 252–53; cited in Tolkein, *"Beowulf:* The Monsters and the Critics," 9.

2. Tolkien's use of Christian allegory is far more complex than that of later, more reductive readings of medieval literature. Tolkien argues that the poem's power derives from its admixture of Latin piety with northern marvels: "At this point new Scripture and old tradition are ignited," forming a "universal tragedy of man" that Clare A. Lees has critiqued well in its gendered specificity ("Men and *Beowulf,*" 130–35).

3. The bibliography on monstrousness in Old English texts is too long to reproduce here, but see, most recently, Andy Orchard, *Pride and Prodigies: Studies in the Monsters of the "Beowulf"-Manuscript.*

4. Cotton Tiberius Bv is a hybrid version of *Wonders,* written in Latin and Old English; it has been reproduced in an excellent facsimile (*An Eleventh-Century Anglo-Saxon Miscellany*). An Old English version of *Wonders* is bound with *Beowulf* in Cotton Vitellius Axv. Recent and thorough discussions of *Wonders of the East* may be found in Campbell, *Witness and the Other World,* 47–86, and Orchard, *Pride and Prodigies,* 175–203.

5. See Nicholas Howe, *Migration and Myth-Making in Anglo-Saxon England,* and Sarah Foot, "The Making of Angelcynn."

6. Old English contains four nouns carrying the modern signification of "giant": *ent, eten, eoten,* and *gigant; þyrs* could also be used, but it has the wider denotation of "large monster" (Alexandra Hennessey Olsen, " 'Thurs' and 'Thyrs' "). The etymology of most of these words is unclear, though *eten* may be related to *etan* ("to eat"), and *eoten* is probably cognate with Old Norse *jotunn;* compare even the formulaic phrase for "race of giants" (*iotna ætt* in the *Edda* and *eotena cyn* in *Beowulf*). *Gigant* is taken directly from the oblique forms of Latin *gigas. Ent* is by far the most common designation. The glossary in Ælfric's *Grammar* supplies *ent* for Latin *gigas* ("Additional Glosses to the Glossary in Ælfric's *Grammar,*" *Dictionary of Old English* transcript), and Aldhelm provides it for *ciclopum* ("Ænigmata," in *Anecdota Oxiensia: Old English Glosses, Chiefly Unpublished*).

Any discussion of the Anglo-Saxon conception of the giant is necessarily indebted to a triad of scholarly works: Oliver F. Emerson, "Legends of Cain, Especially in Old and Middle English"; R. E. Kaske, "The *Eotenas* in *Beowulf*"; and Kaske, "*Beowulf* and the Book of Enoch." I acknowledge them at the outset because the influence of their writing is pervasive in what follows.

7. The discussion that follows is based in large part on the giants of the following texts: *Edda, die Lieder des Codex regius nebst verwandten Denkmälern*, ed. Gustav Neckel and Hans Kuhn; *Edda Snorra Sturlusonar*, ed. Finnur Jónsson; *Fornaldar Sögur Norðurlanda*, ed. Guðni Jónsson; *Islendinga Sögur*, ed. Guðni Jónsson; and John R. Broderius, *The Giant in Germanic Tradition*.

8. The primordial cow Audumla creates Buri, whose son Bor marries the giantess Bestla; their sons are Odin, Vili, and Vé, who in turn slay the world-giant Ymir and begin the war of the gods against the giants, a kind of civil war.

9. Quotations are from the edition by R. F. Leslie; translation by Michael Alexander, *The Earliest English Poems*, with some slight modifications.

10. All modern English translations are from Howell D. Chickering Jr., *Beowulf, a Dual-Language Edition*, unless otherwise noted; Old English from Klaeber's edition.

11. On abjection and the construction of a zone of uninhabitability, see Judith Butler, *Bodies That Matter*, 3.

12. *Beowulf*, 1679 and 1562, respectively.

13. To cite one familiar example, an unnamed hill giant builds a stone citadel safe from the attacks of Jotunheim for the Aesir to inhabit in the popular tale told in the *Gylfaginning* of Snorri Sturluson (XLII) and perhaps mentioned in the older Poetic *Edda* (but see J. Harris, "The Master Builder Tale in Snorri and Two Sagas").

14. "The Mirror Stage as Formative of the Function of the I," in *Écrits*, 1–7.

15. "Aggressivity in Psychoanalysis," in *Écrits*, 11. Lacan lists these images as "castration, mutilation, dismemberment, dislocation, evisceration, devouring, bursting open of the body" (11).

16. Lacan insists that topographical metaphors for the unconscious are misleading (Seminar on *The Purloined Letter*), though he will continue to use topographical language and schematics throughout his writing.

17. The quotation is from Wallace Stevens, "The Auroras of Autumn," in *Collected Poems*, 414 — another poetic meditation on loss, homelessness, and the fragility of identity.

18. Slavoj Zizek, *Looking Awry*, 112. Zizek argues the psychoanalytic structure of nostalgia at greater length than I have space to account for here.

19. "See "The Signification of the Phallus," in *Écrits*, 284, and "The Agency of the Letter in the Unconscious, or Reason since Freud," in *Écrits*, 148.

20. "But we must insist that *jouissance* is forbidden to him who speaks as such, although it can only be said between the lines for whoever is subject of the Law, since the Law is grounded in its prohibition. Indeed, the Law appears to be giving the order, '*Jouis!*,' to which the subject can only reply '*J'ouis*' (I hear), the *jouissance* being no more than understood." Lacan, "The Subversion of the Subject and the Dialectic of Desire in the Freudian Unconscious," in *Écrits*, 319.

21. That this fullness is never more than a retroactive fantasy is clear from the fact that no subject exists *until* this entry into language; the plenitudinous past that the subject creates is a back-formation, a projection into an inaccessible time of a present desire. For the same reason, the identifications of the mirror stage are not so clearly differentiated from this second set; Lacan describes the three orders (imaginary, symbolic, real) as entwined within a Borromean knot rather than as stages of a bodily progress.

22. See Zizek, *Looking Awry*, where he writes, "The point is . . . to acknowledge that part of enjoyment is lost from the very beginning, that it is immediately impossible, and not concentrated 'somewhere else,' in the place from which the agent of prohibition speaks. . . .

It is precisely this dependence of the Oedipal father—the agency of symbolic law guaranteeing order and reconciliation—on the perverse figure of the Father-of-Enjoyment that explains why Lacan prefers to write *perversion* as *père-version*, i.e., the version of the father. Far from acting only as a symbolic agent, restraining pre-oedipal 'polymorphous perversity,' subjugating it to the genital law, the 'version of,' or turn toward, the father is the most radical perversion of all" (24–25).

23. Here the third pun inherent in Lacan's *nom-du-père* becomes evident: *les non-dupes errent*, exactly caught in the English phrase "the non-duped err." Because fantasy materializes identity and history—because fantasy is not some dreamy mist that gets in the way of seeing reality "as it really is" but instead that which solidifies the ground beneath one's feet—there is no way to "do without fantasy," to stop positing myths of origin such as the two fathers. "Those in the know are lost": to think that one has gained distance on this fantasy is another way of participating in it, of allowing it to make real the world.

24. Bede, for example, worried endlessly about the proper dating of Easter and the variations between Roman and regional liturgical practice. On the engendering of the medieval category *Christianitas* as a foundational category and the violence to difference that its institution enacts, see Biddick, "Genders, Bodies, Borders," 390, 392–93, 402–9. On the creation and sustenance of the "identity of a given ideological field beyond all possible variations of its positive content," see Zizek, *Sublime Object*, 87–129 (quotation from 87).

25. Thus, when both Bede and Alcuin gloss the meaning of *gigantes*, they characterize the monster as a large body endowed with excess physicality: "Gigantes dicit homines immensis corporibus editos ac potestate nimia preditos" (Bede, *Libri quatuor in principium Genesis*, 100); "homines immenso corpore . . . moribus inconditi" (Alcuin, *Interrogationes et Responsiones in Genesin* XCVI, PL 100 c.526). Orchard treats both passages in *Pride and Prodigies*, 78–79.

26. *King Alfred's Old English Version of Boethius' "De Consolatione Philosophiae"* (ed. Walter John Sedgefield), 115–16. A portion of the quotation appears in Oliver Emerson, "Legends of Cain," who points out that the Old English poetical version of the *Metres of Boethius* contains a similar gloss in its translation of the same verses (908).

27. PL 82, c.314. Augustine makes a similar statement in his *Confessions*, 1.xvii (27). Cf. the explanation of idolatry found in the Book of Wisdom (Sapientia 14:14–20).

28. The writer(s) of Wisdom no doubt knew the Greek myth of the gigantomachia, recorded as early as 600 B.C.E. on vase paintings and frequently allegorized in poetry and literature thereafter. Anglo-Saxon England would have known the myth from the Roman fascination with its political symbolism. Vergil refers to the storming of Olympus twice (*Georgics*, 1.277–83; *Aeneid*, 6.578–84), and Ovid related the myth at length in his *Metamorphoses* (1.128–62).

29. There are, in fact, two brief references connecting giants to pagan deities in the Eastern church: Justin Martyr's *Apologia* (1.190) and *The Instructions of Commodius* (chap. 3). It is likely that this tradition and the Old English one were separate, both arising directly from independent knowledge of the Book of Enoch and its giants.

30. *Homilies for Unspecified Occasions* (ed. Napier, 1883), no. 42, p. 144. The reference is taken from Healey, *Microfiche Concordance to Old English.*

31. Translated by Ælfric from the Vulgate (*gigantes erant super terram in diebus illis*— giants were on the earth in those days) in the course of a sermon; Bosworth, *Anglo-Saxon Dictionary*, 252.

32. For a detailed argument of this point, see David L. Clark, "Monstrosity, Illegibility, Denegation: *The Martyrology* after de Man."

33. Josephus (*Antiquities*), Augustine (*De civitate dei*), Orosius, and Isidore (*Etymologiae*) all mention the architect Nimrod.

34. *De civitate dei* 16.4, ed. Hoffmann, p. 134; cited by Dean ("The World Grown Old," 565), who also points out that Peter Comestor later interpreted Nimrod as a hunter of men.

35. History repeats itself: "Probably the observation of vast temple ruins elicited this theological explanation [for the abandoned city] by those to whom this culture was alien." *The New English Bible with the Apocrypha*, 11 n. 9. The translation quoted is likewise from this edition; I have used this version rather than the Vulgate because it better gives the passage its folkloric feel.

36. "The World Grown Old," 565. Dean provides an excellent overview of the appearances of Nimrod in Middle English literature, including a reference to the legend that Nimrod built the Tower because he suffered from hydrophobia and was afraid of another giant-destroying Flood (566). The encyclopedic Hereford mappamundi (1290) depicts dog-headed giants near Babylon, where the rubric announces "Nimrod the giant built it," but connecting Nimrod to the giants began to grow rather rare by the thirteenth century. Even though Augustine, Hrabanus Maurus, and Peter Comestor all asserted that Nimrod had been a giant, theological interest in his gigantic nature dwindled as the days of Anglo-Saxon England and its cultural mania for giants came to a close.

37. A. Napier, *Wulfstan*, 105; quoted by Menner, *The Poetical Dialogues of Solomon and Saturn*, 122 (where it is wrongly attributed to Ælfric). For an informed discussion on the abundant Old English variations of Nimrod's name, see Menner, 124.

38. The MS has *cames*, a reading that seems to be a confusion of Cain and Cham. A derivation from Cham is more logical, but descent from Cain fits the thematic associations better. It seems likely that an original reading of Cain was later imperfectly emended.

39. It might be useful here to distinguish the Freudian *unheimlich* from Lacanian *extimité*. Whereas extimacy is a phenomenon of structuration (related to the ex-centricity of an excluded something), the uncanny is mainly an aesthetic experience and primarily *affective*. The uncanny is caused by the return of the repressed and so has a way of warping temporality; extimacy is not an experience but a description of a structural state that may have various affects connected to it, but such affects are secondary to the phenomenon itself. See Elizabeth Wright, *Feminism and Psychoanalysis*, 436–40.

40. The use of the word *comitatus* (a Latin term, from Tacitus) to describe the organization of Germanic tribes of later periods has been questioned; I use it here in the loosest possible way, as an equivalent to the term "Männerbund." See Joseph Harris, "Love and Death in the *Männerbund*: An Essay with Special Reference to the *Bjarkamál* and *The Battle of Maldon*," 77–114.

41. What the invasion of Heorot would seem from the monster's point of view is well conveyed by *Grettis saga*, in which the hero is rightfully mistaken for a troll as he bursts into a house and kills its inhabitants (ed. Jónsson, 130–31).

42. Cf. Avitus 4.88–93 ("*De diluvio mundi*"): "Nor is it lawful to utter from what seed they were sprung. As to their mother, men spoke of an origin common to all [of the giants]; why this offspring, whence the fathers, mystery shrouds from disclosing" (in *Monumenta Germaniae Historica, Auctores Antiquissimi* [Berlin, 1883]; cited by Kaske, "*Eotenas*," 304).

43. Abjection might be thought of as a specifically gendered kind of *extimité*, and the same kind of structural effect, even though Kristeva never makes that connection herself. The problem with Kristeva's formulation of abjection is one that many feminist critics have pointed out as a problem in her work as a whole: the maternal and the feminine are problematically conflated.

44. Orchard traces the interrelation of dragon and hero well in *Pride and Prodigies*, 29–30.

45. Zizek, *Sublime Object*, 135. On the relation of *das Ding* to originary fantasies and medieval studies, see Margherita, *Romance of Origins*, 153–61.

46. That the author of the *Liber monstrorum* knew some version of the Beowulf tradition is indicated by a reference to *Higlacus, rex Getarum* (Hygelac, king of the Geats). Orchard offers a thorough discussion of the relation of the *Liber* to Beowulf, as well as an edition of the Latin text (*Pride and Prodigies*, 86–115, 254–317).

2. Monstrous Origin

1. F. W. Fairholt, *Gog and Magog*, 28–29. Although out of date, Fairholt's account is the best gathering of material about the Guildhall giants.

2. Or, as Monika Otter has written, medieval "history is not reality, not a sequence of events, but a means of 'recognizing' past facts. In medieval uses of *historia*, the semantic elements of cognition and of truth outweigh the semantic element of 'pastness'" (*Inventiones*, 9).

3. Latin text from Wright's edition, English translation from Thorpe (sometimes slightly modified to make it more literal).

4. Tracing British descent from Brutus was not Geoffrey's innovation (as the ninth-century pseudo-Nennian *Historia Brittonum* makes clear). Geoffrey is responsible for giving the myth of Brutus's paternity a form powerful enough to become history.

5. Otter writes that the prophecy "prepares and legitimizes Brutus's appropriation of Britain" in terms of a "manifest destiny" to which even the giants contribute: they are "nonhuman creatures whose very nature disqualifies them from having a serious moral or legal claim to the land" (*Inventiones*, 73).

6. The first signal, I would argue, that women in the *Historia*—even divine women—are problematic in their relation to this narrative of origin, so that for the most part, feminine bodies are relentlessly found wanting or otherwise abjected from meaning in the text. Margherita considers this foundational disavowal at length in *Romance of Origins*.

7. James Dean writes that medieval theologians broke the antediluvian age into five stages: "Original Sin, fratricide, development of the city, technocracy, illicit sexuality and giants, and empire" ("The World Grown Old," 549). Geoffrey is rewriting the Genesis palimpsest by thematically associating the Trojans with God's purging flood, thus glorifying the displacing empire and the new age that commences at its introduction.

8. The Anakim reappear with a similar function in the Book of Deuteronomy, this time in a divine declaration of national superiority (Deut. 9:1–2). Because they are impediments to the Israelite expansion, the Anakim necessarily become enemies of their God and hence are defined by their fallen state. Once this opposition is set in motion, their displacement becomes a divine punishment for a sinful existence (Deut. 9:4). For the Middle Ages, these lines are direct proof of the evil nature of the giants. That each appearance of these *gigantes* (whether before the Flood or after) is followed by their destruction only adds to the impression of their moral insufficiency. Cf. Deut. 2:10–11, 20–21.

9. Giraldus Cambrensis tells a related but abbreviated story of victory over aboriginal giants in Ireland; see *The History and Topography of Ireland*, 94.

10. That is, as Geoffrey's Trojans found what will become the Celtic nation of Britain, they write in reverse the "actual" history of the island, in which the Celts were displaced by colonizing Germanic tribes. Geoffrey monsterizes the "Saxons" at every turn, even uniting them with Saracens as Mordred ruins Arthur's empire. This monsterization was no doubt attractive to the Anglo-Norman rulers of the island, bolstering their claim to political and cultural superiority.

11. Geoffrey describes Corineus as "dux corineus ... qui si cum aliquo gigante congressum faceret ilico obruebat eum acsi cum puero contenderet" (10). The connection between Corineus and the slaying of giants is present from the start, probably in imitation of the biblical David.

12. For the significance of "crooked Greek" to Geoffrey's linguistic background, see T. D. Crawford, "On the Linguistic Competence of Geoffrey of Monmouth."

13. Cf. Gabrielle Spiegel: "Historical writing is a powerful vehicle for the expression of ideological assertion, for it is able to address the historical issues so crucially at stake and to lend to ideology the authority and prestige of the past, all the while dissimulating its status *as* ideology under the guise of a mere accounting of 'what was'" (*Romancing the Past*, 2).

14. In fact there are two giants in this section of the *Historia*. Retho of Mount Arvaius, the second Arthurian giant, is mentioned only in comparison to the giant of Mont Saint Michel. Retho had demanded Arthur's beard to add to a cloak woven from a collection of king's beards; they dueled when Arthur refused. To reestablish the inverted paradigm, the victorious British king shaved Retho, an act of humiliation and subjugation, a clipping away of masculinity and of subversive wildness. Retho and the unnamed Spanish giant were conflated in later romance tradition, so that in the *Alliterative Morte Arthure*, Arthur fights a horrible composite of both.

15. Knight sees a political significance in the giant episode, reading the battle against the giant as a setting-right of a humiliating episode from Henry I's life (*Arthurian Literature and Society*, 58–59).

16. This lack of a proper name was a conscious authorial decision; Gogmagog and Retho have their proper names elsewhere in the *Historia*. Wace was disturbed by this lack when he translated the work into French, and he christened the giant Dinabuc.

17. If history must be materialized, that does not mean that it is not also the product of *sedimentation*, the accumulation through time of repeated materializations (Butler: "The power of discourse to materialize its effects is thus consonant with the power of discourse to circumscribe the domain of intelligibility," *Bodies That Matter*, 187). That is to say, I am not arguing that history is infinitely malleable, that *any* narrativization of history can be thought. Because history is received into a present that is itself a sedimented product of that history, its fragments can be arranged only in a limited number of ways that leave little room for a voluntarist notion of unbounded agency. Powerful versions of history are those, like Geoffrey's, that narrativize the past in a way that resonates strongly within the discursive regime of the world into which they are received.

18. Reynolds, "Medieval 'Origines Gentium' and the Community of the Realm," 377.

19. See Flint, "The *Historia Regum Britanniae* of Geoffrey of Monmouth: Parody and Its Purpose" (which argues that the *Historia* parodies Henry of Huntingdon and William of Malmesbury), and Patterson, *Negotiating the Past*, 201–2. Lesley Johnson touches on the theme in "Return to Albion" (4), and Wright argues against Flint in his edition of the *Historia* (xix).

20. There are too many murders in the *Historia* to catalog here, but one example will suffice: Morvidus, son of Danius by his mistress, becomes king of Britain and fights off an invasion of marauding Moriani. He kills the prisoners one by one by his own hand, and when he is too exhausted to slaughter any more, he has the remainder skinned alive and then burnt. An evil monster suddenly appears, and he fights her; she "rushed at him with her jaws wide open and swallowed him up as though he had been a puny fish" (102). Another king, Mempricius, "abandoned himself to the vice of sodomy, preferring unnatural lust to normal passion" (78). Mordred's treachery is the worst of the *Historia*'s many illustrations of the sin.

21. Patterson, *Negotiating the Past*, 201. See also 180: "Anglo-Norman history was throughout disfigured by internecine and generational violence."

22. This low regard no doubt had much to do with the fact that Henry II had become "retroactively" Geoffrey's patron, promulgating his work in Latin and in Wace's translation after his death, whereas the competing histories were allied with the Cistercians, perennial enemies of Henry.

23. On the difficulty of recovering an "original" political intention in the *Historia*, see Hanning, *Vision of History*, 14–41.

24. On the barrenness of adulterous queens in later romance tradition, see Peggy McCracken, "The Body Politic and the Queen's Adulterous Body in French Romance," and my review of *Feminist Approaches to the Body in Medieval Literature*.

25. See Carol J. Clover, "Regardless of Sex." According to Clover, thirteen of the "founding fathers" of Iceland were women (366).

26. Margherita's observation about "literary epics" is apt: "Literary epics constitute a kind of communal fantasy of paternal origins, a fantasy of which the erasure or abjection

of the maternal or feminine origin is an essential component.... 'father Aeneas' can be established as the paternal progenitor of the Roman State only against the claims of Juno and the various other *matres* who continually threaten the patriarchal agenda" (*Romance of Origins*, 129).

27. I use Carroll and Tuve's somewhat antiquated designation to distinguish this work from the other versions of the *Short Metrical Chronicle*, none of which contain the Albina story. My quotations are from Zettl's EETS edition.

28. In fact, most English versions of the story call the princess Albin. I have used the Latinized form Albina throughout for the sake of consistency, since I will be examining French and Latin versions of the story as well.

29. For contextualization of Albina as a "founding mother," see Danielle Regnier-Bohler, "Figures féminines et imaginaire généalogique: étude comparée de quelques récits brefs."

30. For dilation (*dilatio*) as a rhetorical figure specific to the female body and text, and to its containment, see Patricia Parker, *Literary Fat Ladies*, 8–35.

31. The best example of the *Prose Brut* version of the Albina story is found in MS Douce 323, on which the following discussion is based; quotations are from Brie's EETS edition. To my knowledge, the Albina myth appears in English only twice more. Thomas Bek of Castleford's *Chronicle of England* (c. 1327) has an Albina prologue derived from an Anglo-Norman exemplar similar to MS BL Cotton Cleopatra D.ix. John Hardyng co-opted the Albina story in his fifteenth-century chronicle defense of England's right to rule over Scotland, but even in the service of his nationalistic argument, the outline of the story was not changed significantly.

32. Quoted in Friedman, *Monstrous Races*, 124. This allegorization of the giant's body is commonplace in the bestiaries; for example, the author of the Westminster Bestiary writes that pygmies stand for humility, cynocephali for irascibility, giants simply for pride.

33. Ecclesiasticus (the Book of Jesus, son of Sirach) 16:8. The Book of Baruch contains the most famous apocryphal reference to the giants, transforming them into a terse fable of transgression and divine punishment (Bar. 3:26–28; the passage was also familiar in the Middle Ages from the quotation by Augustine of the Vetus Latina translation, *De civitate dei*, 15.23).

34. "Gigas diaboli typum expressit, qui superbo appetitu culmen celsitudinis appetivit" (*Etymologiae*, PL 83.103). Gregory explicates the body of the giant as an allegory for pride at great length in *Moralia in Iob* XVII.xxi.30–31, PL 76.25, as does Bernadus Silvestris, *Commentum super sex libros Eneidos Virgilii*, 101.

35. The entire allegory of this episode is succinctly summarized in the fifteenth-century *Ovide Moralisé en Prose*, a terse retelling of the *Ovide Moralisé* (53). Cf. the same episode in *The Vulgate Commentary on Ovid's "Metamorphoses."*

36. Another analogue of the Albina myth is classical. The murder or attempted murder of the husbands is an adaptation of a Greek myth familiar throughout the Middle Ages. Ovid, Horace, Servius, and Hyginus wrote of the Danaides, the fifty daughters of King Danaus of Argos. When these daughters were forced to marry fifty cousins against both their will and that of their father, Danaus presented them with golden daggers as a wedding present. All except the youngest, Hypermnestra, murdered their bridegrooms on their wedding night.

37. Explication and emendation began even before the relation of the Septuagint version's *angeloi* (which appears instead of *filii dei*) to the Watchers of the Book of Enoch and to the Hebrew Bible tradition of giants, and they were later carried on by influential Jewish commentators such as Josephus (*Antiquities*) and Philo of Alexandria (*De gigantibus*). From these writers, a growing scholarly inheritance passed through the early Christian exegetes Origen, Eusebius, John Chrysostom, Justin Martyr (who wrote at some length on the angels who "transgressed their appointment, and were captivated by the love of women"), and Augustine.

38. Although this particular interpretation had been in circulation at least as early as the time of Julius Africanus (died c. 240), it was not codified until its inclusion in the *City of God.*

39. "God's sons took men's daughters, meaning that the sons of Seth took the daughters of Cain and begot giants. . . . And it may be that incubi, such fiends that lay with women in the likeness of men, engendered giants, whose greatness of heart [i.e., pride] corresponds to their hugeness of body."

40. Joan Cadden has persuasively demonstrated that it is best to conceptualize medieval medical thinking in terms of its internal debates and lack of a single reductive model; see *Meanings of Sex Difference,* esp. 117–30. See also E. Jane Burns, *Bodytalk,* 71–106.

41. In this way, Albina is an example of what Burns calls a "woman talking back." Analyzing the female figures of fabliaux, Burns argues that even if these women are constructed by and through a misogynistic male imaginary, and even though their "voices do not represent what women might say or how they might say it," nonetheless they do show that "women could have a say," that "access to subjectivity and the authority that accompanies it" is the site of struggle more than of simple denial (*Bodytalk,* 59).

42. *The Chronicle of John Harding,* ed. H. Ellis (London, 1812), 26; cited by Lesley Johnson, "Return to Albion," 38.

43. Ellmann, introduction to *Psychoanalytic Literary Criticism,* 16. Medieval grammarians likewise connected the rules of grammar to the laws of sexuality; see John Boswell, *Christianity, Social Tolerance, and Homosexuality,* 381–89; Elizabeth Pittenger, "Explicit Ink," 228.

44. Jacques Lacan, "The Function and Field of Speech and Language in Psychoanalysis," in *Écrits,* 66. Cf. Ellman, *Psychoanalytic Literary Criticism,* 16.

45. See Derrida's critique of this muddled originary moment in "Structure, Sign, and Play in the Discourses of the Human Sciences." Further on Lévi-Strauss and the inadequate invention of family, see "Becoming and Unbecoming," Cohen and Wheeler's introduction to *Becoming Male in the Middle Ages.*

46. For Irigaray, the only way out from this impasse is through strategic mimesis; see *This Sex Which Is Not One,* 8. Elizabeth Grosz comes to a similar conclusion about the exteriority of lesbian sexuality to a language capable only of describing *male* sexuality in "Rethinking Queer Subjectivity," in *Space, Time, and Perversion,* 207–27.

47. Even if language is constitutive of reality, that reality is not impervious to challenge and reconfiguration. The great strength of Lacanian psychoanalysis is that it provides a systematic way of thinking through how such rupture occurs. Unlike the synchronic, "frozen" social field of structuralism, Lacan insists that there is always something excluded from a given reality (a something he calls the Real), which haunts its borders and may erupt in a trauma that (according to Zizek) can alter the master signifier under which reality is produced. Language is powerfully productive but is neither impervious nor autonomous.

48. Alain de Lille, *Plaint of Nature,* trans. James J. Sheridan, pr. 9, 215–16. The passage is well explicated by Elizabeth Pittenger in "Explicit Ink," 232–33. See also John Alford, "The Grammatical Metaphor," and Jan Ziolkowski, *Alan of Lille's Grammar of Sex.* On the ways in which "grammar, the basic discipline of the early medieval language arts, served to ground a world view expressed in social institutions," see R. Howard Bloch, *Etymologies and Genealogies,* 30–91 (quotation from 64).

49. On the relation of activity and passivity to sexuality in Alain, see the denunciation of sodomy in meter 1, 67–69, and pr. 4, 136–37; as well as Steven Kruger, "Claiming the Pardoner," 127–28.

50. Cf. R. Howard Bloch on the Genesis narrative, *Etymologies,* 9–10.

51. Parker, *Literary Fat Ladies,* 188. Stella Georgoudi examines the origin of this widespread modern myth in "Creating a Myth of Matriarchy," 449–63; see also Louis Montrose, "Shaping Fantasies," 68.

52. See "Constructing Albion's Past: An Annotated Edition of *De origine gigantum*," which contains an edition of the Latin version of the story, as well as a detailed introduction (quotation from p. 51). On the cultural significance of translation of the vernacular into Latin, see also Rita Copeland, *Rhetoric, Hermeneutics, and Translation in the Middle Ages*, 104.

3. The Body in Pieces

1. See Clover, *Men, Women, and Chain Saws*, esp. 21–64.

2. And so a recent television news magazine (*Hard Copy*) ran a story about a man in Detroit who saved all of his money to buy a suit of armor. After work every day, he dresses up and preaches the virtues of chivalry (which he interprets mainly as fidelity to one's spouse) in front of shopping malls around the city.

3. *Epic of Gilgamesh*, trans. N. K. Sanders, 83–85. The goddess Ishtar immediately falls in love with him, although Gilgamesh's fidelity continues to be to his male friend Enkidu.

4. "Medusa's Head," in *Standard Edition of the Complete Psychological Works of Sigmund Freud*, vol. 18.

5. "How Culhwch Won Olwen," in *The Mabinogion*, ed. and trans. Jeffrey Gantz, 134–76. Knight reads the narrative against nascent British ideology in *Arthurian Literature and Society*, 1–35. The term *mabinogi* is similar to Latin *infantia* or French *enfances:* a story about the boyhood of a hero, a coming-of-age tale. Such narratives often describe their protagonist's struggle to assert his sexual identity against a forbidding father figure.

6. Decapitation scenes are richly complicated in Celtic literature. The Irish *Fled Bricrennd* (*Bricriu's Feast*), of the Cuchulainn cycle, describes the uncanny reattachment of a giant's severed head and both invokes and reinvents all the accumulated expectancies behind such rituals. The decapitations in *Culhwch* and *Fled Bricrennd* have romance analogues in *Le Livre de Caradoc, La Mule sanz frain, Hunbaut, Sir Gawain and the Green Knight, Sir Gawain and the Carl of Carlisle,* and *The Turk and Gawain*.

7. The words, used to describe the sublime effect of Kafka's *The Trial* on its readers, belong to Slavoj Zizek, in *Looking Awry*, 151. Enjoyment is sticky because no matter how much one tries to extricate oneself from it, one becomes further entrapped in its web; as Lacan pointed out, even the renunciation of enjoyment paradoxically produces a surplus of that very thing.

8. This literary moment seems to have resonated powerfully as early as the Second Temple period, when the Jael-Sissera story (in which a Hebrew woman drives a tent spike through the head of a Canaanite leader [Judges 3:17–5:31]) was reworked as the apocryphal tale of Judith, in which Holofernes is decapitated and his head displayed to the enemy he leads.

9. See also the summary of the episode in Sirach 47, where the religious subtext has become the main text.

10. On beheading as a means of appropriating an enemy's power, see Stahl, *Histoire de la décapitation*. Guillaume Vrelant's illustration of the gigantomachia (Bibliothèque Royale Albert 1er, Brussels, MS 9243 f.49v; see chapter 2) captures the public nature of the spectacle well. Arthur and the giant fight on an island in a choppy sea, and the violated nurse watches from nearby. The battle is observed by an encampment of twenty-three knights on shore, and four more in a ship.

11. Camille, *Image on the Edge*, 62–65 (quotation from 63–64). Camille reproduces a wonderful illustrated capital from a MS of Josephus's *Antiquities* in which Cain murders Abel below a giant figure that devours the letter entwining the scene.

12. On the relation of the mouth to the grotesque body of the giant, Bakhtin writes, "All the main organs and areas, as well as all the basic acts of the grotesque body, are pictured and developed around the central image of the gaping jaws, ... a wide entrance leading into the depths of the body.... The bodily depths are fertile; the old dies in them, and

the new is born in abundance.... [The grotesque body] swallows and generates, gives and takes" (*Rabelais and His World*, 339). Bakhtin is referring to the mirthful body of Pantagruel; his words take on quite a different resonance when transposed to horrific giants such as Geoffrey's.

13. *Bodytalk*, 54; see 31–70 for her full argument.

14. See Edward Fichtner, "The Etymology of *Goliard*," and James Westfall Thompson, "The Origin of the Word *Goliardi*."

15. *Sceleratissimus inuisi nominis gigas*: the giant's name [*nomen*] is *invisus*, an adjective with the figurative meaning of "detested" and the literal signification of "unseen."

16. "The multitude of 'floating signifiers,' of proto-ideological elements, is structured into a unified field through the intervention of a certain 'nodal point' (the Lacanian *point de capiton* ['upholstery button']) which 'quilts' them, stops their sliding and fixes their meaning.... But this enchainment is possible only on condition that a certain signifier — the Lacanian 'One' — 'quilts' the whole field and, by embodying it, effectuates its identity" (Zizek, *Sublime Object*, 87–88).

17. Karl Marx, *Capital*, 63. Zizek explains further: " 'Being-king' is an effect of the network of social relations between a 'king' and his 'subjects'; but — and here is the fetishistic misrecognition — to the participants of this social bond, the relationship appears necessarily in an inverse form: they think that they are subjects giving the king royal treatment because the king is already in himself, outside the relation to his subjects, a king" (*Sublime Object*, 25). The observation that "identity is finally in the gift of the community" is from Susan Crane, *Gender and Romance*, 29.

18. "Instance" is Lacan's translation of Freud's *Instanz* and covers a range of meanings from "agency" to "acting upon" to "insistence." See "The Agency [*l'instance*] of the Letter in the Unconscious, or Reason since Freud," in *Écrits*, 146–78.

19. See Lillian Herlands Hornstein in Severs, *Manual of the Writings in Middle English*, vol. 1, 124.

20. The phrase is from Jauss, *Toward an Aesthetic of Reception*, 19.

21. On the staging of sexually charged coming-of-age scenes in romance, see Robert Stein's "Desire, Social Reproduction, and Marie's *Guigemar*," which traces the production and regulation of desire in such narratives. Stein argues as well for an erosion in romance of the opposition between public and private (enacted in Marie through a frame-breaking *surplus*).

22. Cf. my "Armour of an Alienating Identity": "Heroic masculinity is performative: a gendered identity that derives from feats of arms (or 'feats of arms and love'), it is always to be proven in movement (wandering, errantry) through the world" (15).

23. Another variation of this scene takes place in the didactic poem *Roland and Vernagu*, found in the Auchinleck MS. Here the protagonist fights a Saracen giant, and when he sees that his opponent is growing tired, he allows him to sleep. The giant snores loudly, so Roland places a stone pillow under his head. The monster is so taken by this act of kindness that he asks Roland all about Christianity. The battle resumes on the next day, this time in more pronounced religious terms, and the giant is ultimately slain.

24. See Geoffrey Abbot, *Lords of the Scaffold*, 12.

25. The idea was famously advanced by Georges Duby in "Dans la France du Nord-Ouest au XIIe siècle: les 'Jeunes' dans la société aristocratique" and, although frequently expanded, has never been fully replaced; in the words of Jean-Charles Huchet, "La naissance de la littérature romanesque... ne saurait se penser indépenamment du désir d'intégration sociale de la fraction défavorisée de la chevalerie que G. Duby a appelée les *juvenes*, les 'jeunes' " (*Le Roman médiéval*, 32). Crane contrasts the French environment with England's more stable system (*Insular Romance*, 89–91), but as the quotations from Peter of Blois will show, knightly disorder was a tremendous problem on both sides of the channel.

26. Petrus of Blois, *Epistolae* 94, PL 207 cols. 294 (1904). The letter is quoted, translated, and examined at length in Bumke, *Courtly Culture*, 311–12. The best recent treat-

ment of the letter is C. Stephen Jaeger, "Courtliness and Social Change." Jaeger points out that the letter must not be seen as offering in any simple way the reality of knightly existence at the time, which no doubt lies in the tension between such polemic against contemporary knighthood and "idealizing literature" and its heroic code — each of which requires the other to exist (293–95).

27. *Le Dialogue de Placides et Timéo, ou Li Secrés as Philosophes,* ed. C. Thomasset, 389–91. See Lecouteux, 223–24, who writes of the condemnation of the *ordo militum* by the church: "Ces accusations, notamment celle de *superbia* — par ailleurs crime essentiel des géants depuis les origines—, apparentent les chevaliers aux géants: comme eux, ce sont des prédateurs. Est-ce bien étonnant? Non, quand on sait qu'un géant [Nemrod] est le 'créateur' de la chevalerie" (223). Cf. Thomasset: "Parmi les candidats au titre de créateur de la chevalerie arrive à la première place un personnage universellement connu au Moyen Age, le géant biblique Nemrod.... il faut concevoir Nemrod comme un *bâtisseur* et comme le créateur du *système d'imposition féodale....* Très légitiment, les clercs se démarquent de ceux qui répandent le sang et, pendant trois siècles, Nemrod, fidèle à sa vocation biblique de chasseur sanguinaire, a été la représentation du chevalier" (*Commentaire,* 215–16).

28. Along these lines, Albrecht Classen argues that the giant in Hartmann von Aue's translation of *Yvain, Iwein,* represents "the other self of Iwein," in whose body he is "cleansed" of the "shortcomings" of his knighthood ("Monsters, Devils, Giants," 107).

29. *PL* 207:296A. For a fuller discussion of the passage see Jaeger, "Courtliness and Social Change," 291, 307. Jaeger observes that Peter's letter is ultimately not an objective antidote to the idealism of romance, but an advocate of its transformative, interventionist project.

30. Patterson, *Chaucer and the Subject of History,* 176. Patterson provides the most recent contextualization of the long history of argument over what cultural function medieval chivalry served, from Huizinga to Keen. Patterson argues that it was a "form of class consciousness," the insufficiency of which authors such as Chaucer were quick to perceive, leading to a "crisis of chivalric identity"; see *Subject,* 165–79. As should be clear from my own argument, I am in substantial agreement with Patterson, although with the important qualification that chivalry is to be seen as a gendered mode of behavior that is *always* in crisis, and whose power derives from that crisis of internal contradiction itself.

31. Keen, *Chivalry,* 194.

32. See Bumke, 318, and Larry Benson, "The Tournament."

33. Robert the Monk wrote that the Saracens "circumcise the Christians, and the blood of circumcision they either spread upon the altars or pour into the bases of the baptismal font. When they wish to torture men by a base death, they perforate their navels, and dragging forth the extremity of the intestines, bind it to a stake; then with flogging they lead the victim around until, the viscera having gushed forth, the victim falls prostrate upon the ground" (*Historia Hierosolymitana,* cited by Dana C. Munro, *Medieval Civilization,* 5–6). The best discussion of the Saracen threat to the integrity of the corpus Christianus is Michael Uebel, "Unthinking the Monster."

34. Richard's cannibalism of Saracen enemies is a frequent motif of the romance *Richard Coeur de Lion;* see *Der Mittelenglische Versroman über "Richard Löwenherz,"* ed. Karl Brunner.

35. Johan Huizinga, *The Waning of the Middle Ages,* 69.

36. A traditional psychoanalytic critic might argue that in contradistinction to Lacan's and Marx's notions of ideology, Huizinga insists on a cynical distance between this "mask" and self-identity. Slavoj Zizek, following Peter Sloterdijk, insists that this distance is exactly what is required for identification to take effect: "Cynical distance is just one way — one of many ways — to blind ourselves to the structuring power of ideological fantasy: even if we do not take things seriously, even if we keep an ironical distance, *we are still doing them*" (*Sublime Object,* 32–33; see also 28–32).

37. See Le Goff, "Head or Heart?" for the quotation and a complete explication of the medieval metaphorical resonance of *caput*. For a parodic rendering of the same body-as-society structure ("The Ass's Will"), see Bakhtin, *Rabelais and His World*, 351.

38. On this point compare Patterson, *Chaucer and the Subject of History*, 172, 174.

39. Slavoj Zizek writes persuasively of the ways in which such internal contradiction is necessary to subjectivization; see "Re-visioning 'Lacanian' Social Criticism," 16.

40. *Etymologiae* 11.25, *PL* 82 col. 400. Cited in Le Goff, "Head or Heart?" 22. Of heads used as ornamentation in twelfth-century churches, Camille writes, "The idea of placing grinning demons and other reforms, mostly heads, along the upper walls as supports for other remembers, is deep-rooted in ancient history; in the North it is related to the Celtic custom of worshipping decapitated heads. The body was, after all, the first human building; the corpse literally became the dwelling-place from where the spirits of evil could be expelled. The human head, the most basic of human images, is also the most dangerous, and its apotropaic use, along with the evil eye, was widespread in pre-modern culture" (*Image on the Edge*, 72).

41. Louis Réau collects some of the most important examples (*Iconographie de l'art chrétien*, vol. 2, pt. 1, 260–63). Christ's temptations in the desert and his defeat of the devil is in itself another coming-of-age, this time to the full realization of divinity rather than heroism; just as the encounter with the giant is the center of the identity mechanics of romance, a struggle against desert demons was the definitional struggle in the hagiography of the eremetic saints, as in Athanasius's *Vita Antonii*.

42. As Walsh points out, "Golias" and "familia Goliae" were familiar terms for "socially undesirable characters" by the Carolingian period (and in the twelfth and thirteenth centuries were terms used to describe *vagantes* wandering Northern Europe), but the "versifying" Golias did not appear until 1140 to 1150 ("'Golias' and Goliardic Poetry," 2, 6). Although the "alleged headquarters" of Golias are in France, Goliardic writing can be connected to the numerous students from England studying in Paris and Chartres (Walsh, 4).

43. See *Moralia in Iob* XVII.xxi.30–31, *PL* LXXVI, 25.

44. For more detailed information on the Goliards, see James H. Hanford, "The Progenitors of Golias"; F. J. E. Raby, *A History of Latin Secular Poetry in the Middle Ages*, vol. 2, 171–235; and P. G. Walsh, "'Golias' and Goliardic Poetry."

45. See Fewster, *Traditionality*, 89–92, who analyzes the episode brilliantly.

46. All of my quotations from the edition of Zupitza, Auchinleck (fourteenth-century) version.

47. See Mehl, The *Middle English Romances*, 221; Fewster, *Traditionality and Genre*, 45–46.

48. Guy is fighting for Jonas, whose sons are held hostage by Triamour; Triamour's son killed the sultan's son and started all the trouble. Fewster writes, "While this episode is an exercise in models of correct heroic behaviour, it also uses the analogy to Guy's own act of son-killing: he is both external and central, judge and judged" (91).

49. As Crane points out, it would be wrong to see Guy's embrace of a saintly identity at this point as anything but a reinvention of, or "secular corrective" to, hagiography: "Rather than isolating him from society, Guy's pilgrim identity replenishes his knightly identity" (*Insular Romance*, 112–13).

50. Fewster chronicles the metamorphosis of the feature of landscape called "Gibbeclyf" in 1279 to "Guyclif" in 1530—a transformation much assisted by Richard Beauchamp's placing a statue of Guy there to localize and harness the power of the romance narrative (113).

51. The armor is enormous and is displayed next to a 120-gallon vessel called Guy's Porridge Pot and the rib of a gigantic cow that he is supposed to have slain. The idea that the heroes of old were larger and heartier (more like giants) than present-day, dwindled man is an ancient one (Augustine arrived at the idea through Pliny). The pot is actually a garrison crock, and the armor is horse armor; both date from the sixteenth century (although material remains of Guy have been on display since long before that date). See Lee, "Guy of Warwick," 830–31, and Timmins, *History of Warwickshire*, 17–19.

52. Loomis, *Medieval Romance*, 132; it is impossible to know whether the painting was medieval, since the only reference was made in 1824.

53. See the edition of Hales and Furnivall in *Bishop Percy's Folio Manuscript*, vol. 2, 509–49.

54. The volume is actually composed of two distinct MSS bound together in the sixteenth century; the first contains the romances. See Mills, *Lybeaus*, 1.

55. The romance is bound with both in Lambeth Palace MS 306, one of the best versions; medical prescriptions likewise are found in Biblioteca Nazionale (Naples) MS XII B.29, which also contains *Beves* and *Isumbras*.

56. See Edwards and Pearsall, "The Manuscripts of the Major English Poetic Texts," 257–58.

57. Patterson ("What Man Artow?") explores both the necessity and the limits of romance identification through "Sir Thopas," which "represents, in diminutive and parodic form, attributes and values that are central to the 'comedye' of *The Canterbury Tales*" (123; see also 171–75). On Chaucer's vast debt to romance, further see D. S. Brewer, "The Relationship of Chaucer to the English and European Traditions," and Alan T. Gaylord, "The Moment of *Sir Thopas*."

58. Zizek, *Enjoy Your Symptom*, 22. See also "Re-visioning 'Lacanian' Social Criticism," 17.

59. See Fewster, 108 n. 21. My discussion of Guy relies on Fewster's excellent discussion of the materialization of Guy's history in *Traditionality and Genre*, 104–28.

60. A reality already expanding by the time of the Auchinleck MS, where the section of *Guy of Warwick* that treats Reynbron is made into a separate romance.

4. The Giant of Self-Figuration

1. Bynum, *The Resurrection of the Body*, 320–29. This paragraph summarizes 322–24.

2. See Pearsall, "The Development of Middle English Romance," 91.

3. The coherence of these six tales has been previously suggested, although not with much conviction; see, for example, Paul F. Baum, *Chaucer: A Critical Appreciation*, 74–84; Donald R. Howard, *The Idea of the Canterbury Tales*, 271–88; Emerson Brown Jr., "Fragment VII of Chaucer's *Canterbury Tales* and the 'Mental Climate of the Fourteenth Century.'"

4. "General Prologue," 751, 756. All citations from *The Riverside Chaucer*, ed. Larry Benson.

5. Vis-à-vis "The Shipman's Tale," this latrine becomes the newly shrunken space of capital, of Jewish "foul usure and lucre of vileynye" (491). Bodily functions are reduced from the sexual to the excretive, with a corresponding debasement of capital gains.

6. Walter W. Skeat, *The Complete Works of Geoffrey Chaucer*, vol. 5, 183.

7. John Burrow, "Sir Thopas: An Agony in Three Fits," 61.

8. "The text is devoid of glosses, not least because in the early manuscripts there is no room for any: we tend to think of *Sir Thopas*, on the model of recent editions, as a *narrow* poem, but in Ellesmere, Hengwrt, Gg.4.27, and Dd.4.24 — four of the seven earliest manuscripts — and in some others, it sprawls right across the page, threatening to fall off the right-hand side of the folio altogether" (Helen Cooper, *Oxford Guides to Chaucer*, 300).

9. Lee Patterson, "'What Man Artow?': Authorial Self-Definition in *The Tale of Sir Thopas* and *The Tale of Melibee*," 149.

10. At the end of the tale, as the widow who owns the farm and all her animals are chasing the fox that carries Chauntecleer in his mouth, the commotion is likened to the noise made by "Jackke Straw and his meynee" when "they wolden any Flemyng kille." Jack Straw was one of the leaders of the Rising.

11. R. L. Chapman famously argued that these lines were spoken "in a piping falsetto"; see "*The Shipman's Tale* Was Meant for the Shipman," 5. Derek Pearsall labels Chapman's interpretation "a little desperate": *The Canterbury Tales*, 5.

12. Gilles Deleuze and Félix Guattari, *Anti-Oedipus: Capitalism and Schizophrenia*, 292. They continue, "We have difficulty understanding what principles psychoanalysis uses to support its conception of desire, when it maintains that the libido must be desexualized or even sublimated in order to proceed to the sexual investments.... The truth is that sexuality is everywhere" (292–93).

13. If sex and money are the prescribed telos of desire in this tale, that only proves Deleuze and Guattari's corollary assertion that "*social production is purely and simply desiring production itself under determinate conditions.* We maintain that the social field is immediately invested by desire, that it is the historically determined product of desire, and that the libido has no need of any mediation or sublimation, any psychic operation, in order to invade and invest the productive forces and relations of production. *There is only desire and the social, and nothing else*" (*Anti-Oedipus*, 29). Desire is gigantic in its potential investment in "all possible worlds"; desire is dwarfish in its allowed articulation through the stranglehold of conjugal and mercantile relations (two versions of a single systematicity glued together by the same social/narratival coding).

14. The name at once recalls that of a famous romance giant, Amoraunt; and "Olifant" is also the name of Roland's great horn in the *Chanson de Roland* (1702), comically invoked here.

15. Laura Hibbard Loomis collects the relevant analogues in "Sir Thopas," in *Sources and Analogues of Chaucer's Canterbury Tales*, ed. W. F. Bryan and Germaine Dempster, 486–559.

16. See *Gender and Romance in Chaucer's "Canterbury Tales,"* where Susan Crane observes that "The hero of romance is constituted so fundamentally by his culture that he resembles the postmodern subject more closely than the Lockean individual. Self-definition involves recognizing and accepting the social component of personal identity" (17; see also 31–38, on the postmodern subject and the utility of Foucault's *Discipline and Punish*).

17. The monster's aristocratic title is intriguing but not unparalleled; Robert Mannyng of Brunne identifies the monster who leads the aboriginal giants of England against Brutus and his men as "Sir Gogmagog," apparently because he is the strongest of his kind (*Chronicle*, 1777).

18. When I read a version of this chapter at New Chaucer Society (Los Angeles, 1996), Lorraine K. Stock suggested to me that this overuse of "pryke" is not just (as several critics have argued) erotic, but autoerotic: Thopas is trapped in a world so circumscribed that even his sexuality circulates only around his own body.

19. Laura Hibbard Loomis ("Sir Thopas and David and Goliath") argues that Chaucer "perceived to the full the jocose effect of transferring the famous 'fel staf-slynge' and making the giant chase with it the well-armed 'Child.' The episode becomes a climax, not of heroism, but of absurdity" (312).

20. On the limitations of Lacan's ideas of sexuation, see Butler's brilliantly challenging chapter "The Lesbian Phallus," in *Bodies That Matter*, 57–91.

21. See Cooper, *Oxford Guides to Chaucer*, 307.

22. See, for example, *Sir Landevale*, 508–14, where the fairy mistress articulates the full conditions of their "dern loue."

23. Tryamour keeps her magical powers but loses her narrative ones. As Crane observes, she is reduced at the moment of her exposure to "a mere surface, a body whose only gestures are to reveal itself (riding into the court and removing her mantle) or conceal itself (blinding Guenevere and then departing)" (*Gender and Romance*, 158).

24. *English Medieval Lapidaries*, ed. Evans and Serjeantson, EETS 190 (1933) 19, 106, 122.

25. "We might best think of the literal action of the poem as describing not so much a Flemish bourgeois pretending to be a chivalric hero as a boy dressing up as a knight, as common an activity among medieval boys as among their modern counterparts, whose liberal parents sadly observe their offsprings' seemingly ineradicable need to play war" ("What Man Artow?" 129–30).

26. I am arguing not that children are in any way presexual or asexual, but that a rhetoric of innocence surrounds medieval and modern children because it is socially necessary to keep childhood a desexualized space. The quotation from Bartholomew the Englishman is found in *On the Properties of Things: John Trevisa's Translation of Bartholomaeus Anglicus, De proprietatibus rerum*, ed. M. C. Seymour et al. (Oxford: Clarendon Press, 1975), 1. 300; cited by Patterson, "What Man Artow?" 165.

27. *Hurd's Letters on Chivalry and Romance*, ed. Edith J. Morley (1765; London, 1922); cited by Loomis in *Sources and Analogues*, 486.

28. "Innocuous innocence" is not the redundant phrase it may at first glance seem. Chaucer has made this point in "The Prioress's Tale," where the "litel clergeon" destroys a whole community of Jews via his relentless innocence, via what Sedgwick calls "the epistemological privilege of unknowing" ("Privilege of Unknowing: Diderot's *The Nun*," in *Tendencies*, 23–51). This strategic power of ignorance Sedgwick specifically connects to the deployment of sexuality.

29. In fact, Mannyng was translating Wace's French *Brut*, but it is clear that he also had a copy of Geoffrey's Latin *Historia* in front of him as he worked (*Chronicle*, ed. Idelle Sullens, 53). Although Chaucer may not have known Mannyng's *Chronicle*, he was certainly familiar with some version of the legendary history of Britain that it contained.

30. On this point, especially cf. Crane, *Gender and Romance*, 114–15.

31. See Crane, "The Writing Lesson of 1381," 202, 207–12.

32. See Derek Pearsall, "Interpretative Models for the Peasants' Revolt," 65–66.

33. No evidence exists that would date "The Tale of Sir Thopas"; it is certain, however, that it found its place in fragment 7 well after 1380.

34. The closed (sealed) letters sent by the king are recorded on these parchment sheets; a clerk would have copied her deed onto the back of one of these rolls. The original release has vanished. Cannon argues that it "was presumably written—and certainly signed and sealed—on May 1, 1380, when it probably passed for good into Chaucer's possession, and then, ultimately, into oblivion" (*"Raptus* in the Chaumpaigne Release and a Newly Discovered Document concerning the Life of Geoffrey Chaucer," 90).

35. *Chaucer Life-Records*, ed. Martin M. Crow and Clair C. Olson (Oxford, 1966), 343; Cannon, *"Raptus,"* 74. I have reproduced Cannon's translations throughout for consistency's sake, since it is upon his understanding of the documents that my argument depends.

36. For the text of the documents see *Chaucer Life-Records*, 344–45.

37. "A deliberate revision, a revision, moreover, that had as its main effect the elimination of the noun *raptus* from the language of the release" (Cannon, *"Raptus,"* 92).

38. In her tongue-in-cheek version of secular history, the elves, faeries, and incubi have been chased away by the friars, who continue to perform the monsters' sexual misdeeds ("Wife of Bath's Tale," 879–80). Further on elves and "Thopas" see Patterson, "What Man Artow?" 131–32 (who writes that elves are "persistently invested with a powerfully sexual valence"); Crane, *Gender and Romance*, 114–15; and on elves more generally, C. S. Lewis, *The Discarded Image*, 122–38.

39. Patterson ("What Man Artow?" 132 n. 52) surveys the literature on the subject, as well as the desexualizing counterargument offered by Greene and Arsdale; he concludes that it "is impossible to ignore the *Tale's* edge of sexual innuendo."

40. The name is rather mysterious even here, for it does not figure at all in the Anglo-Norman version of the story.

41. See Loomis in *Sources and Analogues*, 487. The encounter against the giant in *Guy*, Loomis states, is the seminal rendition of the gigantomachia for all of Middle English romance (531 n. 1; "Sir Thopas and David and Goliath," 311 n. 1); further, she argues that Chaucer knew the version of *Guy* in the Auchinleck MS, from which I have been quoting.

42. *Leman* is exactly the word Thopas uses to describe his elf-queen. *The Riverside Chaucer* notes that the word's primary meaning is "mistress," and it is used "by the mature Chaucer only in contexts degraded morally or socially or both" (920 n. 788).

5. The Body Hybrid

1. "Fils de chien," *Minuit*, no. 7 (January 1974). The story is retold in Deleuze and Guattari, *A Thousand Plateaus* (258–59) and further explicated by Brian Massumi in *A User's Guide to Capitalism and Schizophrenia: Deviations from Deleuze and Guattari*, 93.

2. See John Block Friedman, *The Monstrous Races*, 72–75; Walter Stephens, *Giants in Those Days*, 43–52; and David Gordon White, *Myths of the Dog-Man*, 34–42.

3. Friedman writes that "giants placed near paradise, dog-headed or otherwise, suggest the story of the fallen angels copulating with the 'daughters of men' and producing a race of giants" (84). A second group of cynocephali occupy the North of the Hereford map, probably following Adam of Bremen's relocation of the monstrous races to Scandinavia.

4. The romance exists in two manuscripts, National Library of Scotland Advocates 19.3.1 and British Library Royal 17.B.43. The latter is generally held to be the superior version, and I have relied on it throughout in the edition of Maldwyn Mills. The Middle English romance retells the French *Robert le diable* story, but with important differences; see L. Loomis, *Medieval Romance in England*, 49–57; Mortimer J. Donovan in J. Burke Severs, ed., *A Manual of the Writings in Middle English, 1050–1500*, vol. 1, 141–42; and Shirley Marchalonis, "*Sir Gowther:* The Process of a Romance," 14–29. The romance is traditionally dated c. 1400.

5. The Name of the Father is the illusory coherence sutured around a name that binds the symbolic into a genealogical identity system with individuated, historical, familial subjects. Its nearest equivalent in the Middle Ages is the ancestral title (e.g., "duke of Gloucester") in its mythy existence outside of particular bearers. On ancestral romance and the ubiquity of family crisis, see Susan Crane, who is critical of the idea that these works should be attached in their genesis to specific families, even if they were adopted as legitimating history later (*Insular Romance*, 16–17).

6. Margaret Robson argues that the romance "could be said, from some points of view," to be Gowther's mother's story; it is disturbing, then, that the maternal should so quickly become a vanishing point in the narrative. Fathers abound; by Robson's count, Gowther has five ("Animal Magic: Moral Regeneration in Sir Gowther," 140, 146).

7. On the complex history of this biblical passage, see Nicholas Kiessling, *The Incubus in Medieval Literature*; James Dean, "The World Grown Old and Genesis in Middle English Historical Writings," 548–68; and Stephens, *Giants in Those Days*, 76–84. On medieval incubi, see Augustine, *De civitate dei*, 15.23 (PL 41.468); Thomas Aquinas, *Quaestiones de potentia Dei*, 6, "De miraculis," 8, *Opera omnia and Summa theologiae* 1.51.3.6; Kiessling, *Incubus*; and Andrea Hopkins, *The Sinful Knights*, 165–68. Hopkins's book contains a useful and thorough discussion of Gowther and the mythology of the incubus.

8. This localizing movement finds its best expression in the Royal MS, which conflates Gowther and "Seynt Gotlake" [St. Guthlac], the heroic hermit who fought legions of airy spirits (fiends, demons, perhaps even incubi) and founded the abbey of Croyland. E. M. Bradstock argues that there is little continuity between the two "saints" ("The Penitential Pattern in *Sir Gowther*," 6), but I disagree: both fight for a coherent identity versus a fiend or legions of fiends that represent a dangerous multiplicity of becomings and desires.

I label identity romances such as *Gowther* "familial" simply because their scope tends to be limited to discovering the ways in which intersubjectivity configures personal identities, rather than (say) proving how manifest destinies dictate national histories through exceptional bodies, such as those of heroes. The familial in romance tends to exist as an exterior, idealized fantasy space that pulls the hero through and out of the "real" horror of actual family space: for example, the knight Gregorius is the offspring of brother-sister incest who unknowingly marries his own mother but turns out well in the end (Hartmann von Aue, *Gregorius*).

9. That this resistance is posed specifically against the maternal is suggested by the fact that in the Middle Ages, breast milk was believed to be a transformation of the mother's menstrual blood; see Shulamith Shahar, *Childhood in the Middle Ages*, 77–83.

10. See especially *Anti-Oedipus*, but also *A Thousand Plateaus*. The translator's note to *L'anti-Oedipe* explains "Oedipus" well: "The term Oedipus ... refers, for instance, not only to the Greek myth of Oedipus and to the Oedipus complex as defined by classical psychoanalysis, but also to Oedipal mechanisms, processes, and structures" (3). Or, as Massumi summarized in the earlier quotation, Oedipus stands for "phallocentrism, molar personhood itself."

11. Oedipus, argue Deleuze and Guattari, produces "a definable and differentiable ego in relation to parental images serving as co-ordinates (mother, father). There we have a triangulation that implies in its essence a constituent prohibition, and that conditions the differentiation between persons....But a strange sort of reasoning leads one to conclude that, since it is forbidden, that very thing was desired. In reality, global persons—even the very form of persons—do not exist prior to the prohibitions that weigh on them and constitute them, any more than they exist prior to the triangulation into which they enter" (*Anti-Oedipus*, 70–71).

12. It is unclear to me, for example, how Oedipus would function in the early Germanic sex/gender system described by Carol J. Clover in "Regardless of Sex: Men, Women, and Power in Early Northern Europe." If Clover is correct, the binary active/passive was employed with minimal regard to anatomy, eliminating the "destiny" from Freud's historically specific equation.

13. My remarks derive from Slavoj Zizek's analysis in *Looking Awry*, 107–22. Cf. the similar but more physicalized moment in Chaucer's "The Merchant's Tale" ("And sodeynly anon this Damyan / Gan pulled up the smok, and in he throng," 2352–53).

14. Dorothy S. McCoy uses the various versions of the Robert the Devil story to gauge differences in attitude toward human sexuality, and she resists such a generalized, theological reading of Gowther ("From Celibacy to Sexuality," 29–39). I am arguing that it is necessary to read through the monster here, rather than dismissing it as an "external," extraneous evil: the fiend embodies in inverted form the transcendent principle of Original Sin *as* embodiment.

15. This fantasy of transcendence is connected, therefore, to Brutus's foundational repudiation of the feminine as mere *materia* and his installation of a regime of "pure" language that, despite its universalizing thrust, is strongly gendered masculine. See chapter 2.

16. A good idea of what Deleuze and Guattari mean by molar (and its relation to "personal" bodies) is conveyed by Steven Shaviro: "The relations of power in our society ... select and organize the singularities of an anarchic, molecular sexuality, subject them to the laws of morality and the signifier, arrange them hierarchically, distribute them around a statistical norm, and finally construct heterosexuality as a majoritarian standard or as a transcendent model" (*The Cinematic Body*, 71).

17. Deleuze and Guattari speak of dogs as Oedipal animals in *A Thousand Plateaus*, 28–29, 240, 248; see Massumi, 179.

18. See Friedman, 61–69, and C. Meredith Jones, "The Conventional Saracen of the Songs of Geste."

19. The best discussion of the Vézelay Tympanum and its relation to the cynocephali is Friedman, 77–79. See also Wittkower, "Marvels of the East," 176.

20. "The average, plodding, medieval English romance writer, quite ignorant of the classics, took his material ready-made from the French and knew little and cared less about the superior ethics, learning, and civilization of Islam....The Crusades had never become a national movement in England as they had in France, with its Mediterranean seaboard, and the majority of writers in the fourteenth century knew precious little about them and still less about Islam" (Beatrice White, "Saracens and Crusaders: From Fact to Allegory," 178).

21. *Kyng Alisaunder,* ed. G. V. Smithers, 1932–36. The Middle English romance (c. 1330) is based on the Anglo-Norman *Roman de Toute Chevalrie,* but the Alexandrine material dates at least as far back as pseudo-Callisthenes (before fourth century A.D.) and was popular in myriad versions throughout the Middle Ages; see Andrew Runni Anderson, *Alexander's Gate, Gog and Magog, and the Inclosed Nations,* and George Carry, *The Medieval Alexander.* On the cynocephali's lack of humanity as a function of inarticulateness, Vincent of Beauvais writes that their "very barking shows they were more beasts than men" (*Speculum Quadriplex sive Speculum Maius,* 4.34).

22. *Der mittelenglische Versroman über "Richard Löwenherz,"* ed. Karl Brunner.

23. Beatrice White treats the episode at length, 186–91.

24. Jacobus de Voragine, *Legenda Aurea Vulgo Historia Lombardica Dicta,* ed. Th. Graesse, 430; *Acta Sanctorum Iulii,* v. 6, 146. Other Western versions of his hagiography include Ratramnus of Corbie, *Epistola de Cynocephalis* (*PL* 121, cols. 1153–56) and prose and verse accounts by Walter of Speyer, "Vita et Passio Sancti Christopher Martyris" and "Passio Sancti a Beatissimi Martyris Cristofori Rithmice Conposita." My reading of the legend is informed by Stephens, Friedman, and David Gordon White.

25. The reasons for this conflation are complex, but a spur to this admixture was that beginning with Ctesias, the description of giants is almost always followed by the cynocephali in lists of the monstrous races; see, for example, Isidore of Seville, *Etymologiae,* 11.3.1–3.

26. Donna Crawford contrasts the violence against the Saracens with Gowther's earlier aggression against nurses and nuns, finding in the former a rejection of the diabolical; but we may as well call this rewriting of violence a rejection of the *paternal.* See "Gronyng wyth grysly wounde," 45.

27. Bynum has written of the difference between theologic and mystical expressions of desire: "However much the theologians of the thirteenth century might define blessedness as the stilling of desire, spiritual writers came increasingly to treat love as a longing that cannot be satiated or filled, magnifying itself forever as each increase of joy further stimulates need" (*Resurrection of the Body,* 329). The same duality is at work in romance and accounts for the difference between Yvain and Lancelot, or Gowther and Guy of Warwick.

28. The status of *Sir Gowther* itself as a kind of interstitial monster, a hybrid of romance and saint's life, has caused much critical anxiety; see especially E. M. Bradstock, "Sir Gowther: Secular Hagiography or Hagiographical Romance or Neither?" 26–47. Perhaps the best descriptor for *Gowther* is, simply, a cynocephalic (i.e. irreducibly hybrid) narrative.

29. Eve Kosofsky Sedgwick, "Nationalisms and Sexualities: As Opposed to What?" in *Tendencies,* 143–53.

30. On Lacan and Christianity, see (for example) Judith Butler, *Bodies That Matter,* 56; Franco Rella, *The Myth of the Other: Lacan, Deleuze, Foucault, Bataille,* trans. Nelson Moe, 21; and especially Alexandre Leupin, *Barbarolexis,* 12–14.

31. Elizabeth Grosz, "A Thousand Tiny Sexes: Feminism and Rhizomatics," 193–94. Grosz argues that Deleuze and Guattari's work is useful to feminists as a way to reconceive bodies "outside of the binary polarizations imposed on the body by the mind/body, nature/culture, subject/object, and interior/exterior oppositions" (194).

32. Joan Cadden's work is especially important here. *Meanings of Sex Difference in the Middle Ages* argues that although medievals had numerous totalizing models of the body to choose from (including Galen's), medieval medical thinking is remarkable for its unsystematized interrogations: "What emerges is not a grand synthetic scheme … but rather a cluster of gender-related notions, sometimes competing, sometimes mutually reinforcing; sometimes permissive, sometimes constraining; sometimes consistent, sometimes ad hoc" (9–10). Thus Thomas Laqueur's limitation in reducing all medical thought to a one-sex model; see *Making Sex: Body and Gender from the Greeks to Freud,* and Gail Kern Paster, *The Body Embarrassed: Drama and the Discipline of Shame in Early Modern England.*

33. See B. White, "Saracens and Crusaders," 188.

6. Exorbitance

1. *The Amazing Colossal Man* is therefore an ancestor of the wild man described by Bernheimer, and a predecessor of the mythologized wild man of the "men's movement" of the late eighties and early nineties. Inspired by writers such as Robert Bly, this philosophy of manhood encouraged its adherents to discover the untamed, noble savage within, mainly by taking to the woods and beating drums with other men. Although laudable in some of its aims (most notably in its insistence that men explore the fragility of their own identities and be accountable for this self-knowledge), the men's movement predictably blamed feminism for the crisis it saw in contemporary masculinity, unconsciously allying itself via abjection of femininity with the misogyny inherent in (for example) medieval chivalry.

2. A messenger of some marauding Saracens, the giant in *King Horn* bursts into the Irish court with ominous words for the king, whom the incognito Horn is presently serving. He arrives on Christmas Day — along with Pentecost, a traditional time for the intrusion of unearthly challengers in romance.

3. "I believe that he was half a giant on the earth, but at any rate I declare him to be the biggest of men," 140–41. The linguistic complexities of these lines are discussed at length by Tolkien, Gordon, and Davis in their note to the passage (80).

4. On *Sir Gawain* as a poem about absent narratives more generally, see Elizabeth Scala, "The Wanting Words of *Sir Gawain and the Green Knight*," especially 314–17.

5. See, for example, Margherita's reading of the poem in *Romance of Origins* (129–51) and Sheila Fisher, "Taken Men and Token Women."

6. On the negative value of *commercium* within the poem, see R. A. Shoaf, *The Poem as Green Girdle*.

7. The giant Estragot in *The Sowdon of Babylon*, for example, has a boar's head atop a vast, black body.

8. See chapter 3 for a complete discussion of *Sir Eglamour* in relation to the romance encounter against the giant.

9. A third parallel is also offered by *Eglamour*, which culminates in a quest for a dragon in which the hero is wounded but successful — much like Gawain's ultimate fate.

10. On the application of the anthropological idea of liminality to the Middle Ages, see Bynum, *Fragmentation and Redemption*, 30.

11. Brenda Webster points out the significance of the holy day in "Golpe por golpe." Gayle Margherita ties circumcision to the theme of the poem in *Romance of Origins*, 141.

12. Likewise in the *Livre de Caradoc* the beheaded challenger is biologically the hero's father, and the game is of discovered paternity.

13. Building on Kristeva's work on abjection, Margherita argues that this revelation works to connect the narrative back to a disavowed maternal origin in Morgan le Fay; see *Romance of Origins*, 141–51.

14. On "the melancholia of gender identification," see Judith Butler, *Gender Trouble*, 57–65, from where I have taken the phrase.

15. Freud, *The Ego and the Id*, trans. Joan Riviere (New York: Norton, 1960), 19; quoted in Butler, *Gender Trouble*, 58, where she adds the gloss, "Strictly speaking, the giving up of the object is not a negation of the cathexis, but its internalization and, hence, preservation" (62).

16. Quotation from James Goldstein in "Medieval Masculinities" (Cohen, "The Armour of an Alienating Identity," 11).

17. The twinning of Arthur with monstrousness is perhaps already present in Geoffrey's *Historia*, especially in the narration of Arthur's birth and the ways in which it recalls the birth of giants: Merlin, the son of an incubus, uses his magic to allow Uther to likewise act like an incubus, impregnating a woman in the specious form of her husband. For a consideration of the defects of heroism in the poem and its relation to the biblical David story, see R. A. Shoaf, "The Alliterative *Morte Arthure:* The Story of Britain's David."

18. "The king's two bodies" is Ernst Kantorowicz's famous formulation (*The King's Two Bodies: A Study in Medieval Political Theology*); see also Vance Smith, "Body Doubles," a recent meditation on the concept's gendered implications.

19. *Morte Arthure: A Critical Edition*, ed. Mary Hamel, 3152–57.

20. The text twice refers to Barrok as the wife of "Astrogot" rather than Alagolafre, but it is clear that she attacks Charlemagne and his men in retaliation for their slaying of Alagolafre, who, like Barrok and her children, is living at Mantrible. The giant Estragot is slain so early in the story (at the gates of Rome) that it is unlikely he should reappear here.

21. All quotations from "'*Syre Gawene and the Carle of Carelyle*': An Edition," ed. Robert W. Ackerman, unless otherwise noted.

22. "The yard mentioned here may well be an ell of forty-five inches rather than the more modern lineal unit. If so, the giant would have a breadth of more than seven feet and . . . a height of almost thirty-four feet" (Ackerman's note, 29). The ramifications of such immense height are here, as in other romances, not given much consideration.

23. Thomas Hahn observes that "the bed temptation enacts a crude but unmistakable demonstration of Sir Gawain's courteous respect for the Carle and for his proprietary rights over his wife and household" (*Sir Gawain: Eleven Romances and Tales*, 82).

24. The beheading episode has been omitted from the Porkington MS account, perhaps due to the loss of a folio from the scribe's manuscript, or perhaps because of a change of copyist that occurs at about this point. The episode is supplied from the Percy Folio version.

25. Bakhtin, *Rabelais and His World*, 317. The quotation applies, of course, only to the body prior to the conclusion of the romance, when it may (like Gowther's sacred corpse) become an immutable form that renders its previous plasticity all the more intriguing.

26. Charles Shepherdson, "History and the Real: Foucault with Lacan," 47.

27. "The Turke and Sir Gawain," in *Sir Gawain: Eleven Romances and Tales*, ed. Thomas Hahn, 337–58; quotation from lines 132–33. Welles, in the original *Manual of Writings in Middle English*, wrote that the story is "connected with traditions current in the Isle of Man . . . which was long held to be inhabited by giants and to contain underground dwellings of wonderful magnificence" (59).

28. *The Turk and Gawain, The Carle of Carlisle, Guy and Colbrand*, and *Guy and Amaraunt* are bound together in the Percy Folio, indicating a great interest in giants for one late compositor.

29. Hahn points out that the Turk as "emblem of festive exoticism" appeared in civic pageants in Gloucester; he is also a familiar figure from the mummings, medieval folk plays (352).

30. Stephens's research on biblical giants is impeccable, so that chapter 2 of *Giants in Those Days* ("*In Diebus Illis*: Giants, History, and Theology") is the best available work on the subject. On English traditions of giants, however, his research is full of gaps. He relies too heavily on Susan Stewart, who relies too heavily on Fairholt's amateurish and out-of-date investigations. For the Albina myth, for example, he cites a chapbook cited at secondhand by Fairholt and at thirdhand by Stewart.

31. The story originates in the *chansons de geste Balan* (twelfth century, lost and known only through Philippe Mouské's summary of 1243) and *Fierabras* (c. 1170). *The Sowdon of Babylon* is derived from the latter in a rather complex way; it contains one of the Middle English versions of Fierabras's conversion. See Smyser in Severs, 80–87.

32. *Otuel and Roland* preserves the episode in English.

33. I am grateful to Richard Chisholm for sharing with me his research on Rainoart.

34. *Aliscans*, 3160. Translation quoted from the edition of Joan Ferrante.

35. Literally, "Rainoart of the yoke." The wooden *tinel* is meant to be a kind of club, and he uses this weapon until Guiborc presents him with a sword, signaling that his indoctrination into chivalry is complete: "Il reçoit une epée, abandonne une arme de rustre

ou de vilain et s'élève ainsi au rang de chevalier" (Lecouteux, "Harpin de la Montagne [*Yvain*, v. 3770 et ss.]," 220).

36. Friedman treats the King of Tars episode at length in *Monstrous Races,* where he also provides the example of "a Tartar king who produces a child by his Christian concubine which is black on the left side of its body and white on the right. Once the child is baptized the blackness disappears" (65).

37. Jacques de Vitry wrote that "just as we consider Pygmies to be dwarfs, so they consider us to be giants.... And in the land of the Giants, who are larger than we are, we would be considered dwarfs" (quoted by Friedman in *Monstrous Races,* 163–64). On the "situational monstrosity" of giants, see Anne Lake Prescott, "The Odd Couple: Gargantua and Tom Thumb," 75.

38. Again in this text, the feminine body is aligned with the disavowed maternal. Bevis's mother, the daughter of the king of Scotland, detests her husband Guy because of his great age and bestows her favors upon Devoun of Armenia. She then plots Guy's death, sending him into a forest to be ambushed by Devoun (circumstances that recall the demise of William Rufus). When Bevis calls her a whore, his mother orders her steward to kill him. A high point of the narrative occurs when she tumbles from a tower and breaks her neck, bodily punishment for her bodily crimes.

39. *Lancelot, or The Knight of the Cart (Le Chevalier de la charrette),* ed. William W. Kibler, 6092–6695.

40. "When I was a child, I spake as a child, I understood as a child, I thought as a child; but when I became a man, I put away childish things" (1 Cor. 13:10). On homosexuality and bisexuality reduced to a phase within a heterosexual progress narrative, see Marjorie Garber, *Vice Versa,* 306–16.

41. Although his stature is not as excessive as that of other romance giants, Galehaut—as "son of the beautiful giantess" and inheritor of a paternal tradition of monstrous violence—is physically taller than any other knight, as well as exceptional in his strength and martial cunning. He enters the narrative by challenging Arthur and almost succeeds in annexing Camelot to his own dominions, but Lancelot teaches Galehaut to embrace a properly subordinate place under the aegis of Arthurian monarchy. On the brief critical history of the *amor* between Lancelot and Galehaut, see Hyatte, "Recoding Ideal Male Friendship," 505–7; on the inadequacy of Hyatte's decidedly unqueer reading, see Burns, "Refashioning Courtly Love," 130.

42. Boswell, *Christianity, Social Tolerance, and Homosexuality,* 280–81.

43. Recent work by Claire Sponsler and Robert Clark applies queer theory to race as well as sexuality in the Middle Ages; Dinshaw's unexamined limitation is in applying queerness exclusively against heteronormativity (that is, against sexual difference outside of its overlap with other differences). An excellent examination of "queer" in contemporary American culture that emphasizes the importance of ethnicity to the construction of sexual alterity is Robert McRuer, *The Queer Renaissance;* see 25–29 for a definition of queer very close to that advanced by Burger and Dinshaw ("a fluid and disruptive identity openly constructed and reconstructed in innumerable *pockets* of power," 27).

44. "Biax sire Diex, qui porra ce deservir?" French quotations of the *Prose Lancelot* from Alexandre Micha's edition (here, 52a, 69); translation from the edition produced under the general editorship of Norris J. Lacy (here, 2.52).

45. On the folding of homosexual desire (especially male homosexual desire) into a structuration by death, see Butler, "Sexual Inversions," esp. 346. Galehaut's desire is not, of course, *simply* homosexual (in which case it would cease to be so queer): the giant, for example, also loves the Lady of Malohaut. As Hyatte observes, "Throughout the romance the nature of Galehout and Lancelot's *amistié/amor* is ambiguous, as it is homosexual and heterosexual at one and the same time" ("Recoding Male Friendship," 506). More to the point, Galehaut's desire is as exorbitant to either of these contemporary categories of sexuality as it is to medieval ones.

46. And so when the sorrowing Lancelot attempts to impale himself on his sword ("He told himself that now he would be too wicked if he did not in turn die for Galehaut"), he is immediately distracted by a messenger from Guenevere. The Lady of Malohaut, on the other hand, *does* die of grief, her dead body another reminder of the violence even the queerest of man-giant relations does to the excluded feminine.

Bibliography

✣

Abbreviations

ANTS   Anglo-Norman Text Society
CFMA   Classiques français du moyen âge
EETS   Early English Text Society
  OS   Original Series
  ES   Extra Series
  SS   Supplementary Series
PL   Patralogia Latina, ed. J. P. Migne
SATF   Société des anciens textes français

Primary Sources

Acta Sanctorum Iulii. Antwerp, 1729. Reprint, Brussels: Culture et Civilisation, 1970.

Ælfric. *Sermones Catholici.* Ed. Benjamin Thorpe. New York: Johnson Reprint Corp., 1971.

Alain de Lille. *Plaint of Nature.* Trans. James J. Sheridan. Toronto: Pontifical Institute of Medieval Studies, 1980.

Alexander, Michael, trans. *The Earliest English Poems.* London: Penguin Books, 1977.

"Alexander's Letter to Aristotle." In *Three Old English Prose Texts in MS Cotton Vitellius A xv,* ed. Stanley Rypins. EETS-OS 161 (1924).

Alfred the Great. *King Alfred's Old English Version of Boethius' "De Consolatione Philosophiae."* Ed. Walter John Sedgefield. Oxford: Clarendon Press, 1899.

———. *King Alfred's Orosius.* Ed. Henry Sweet. EETS 79 (1883).

Alighieri, Dante. *The Inferno.* Trans. John Ciardi. New York: New American Library, 1982.

Aliscans, chanson de geste. Ed. M. M. F. Guessard and A. de Montaiglon. Paris: A. Franck, 1870.

———. In *Guillaume d'Orange: Four Twelfth-Century Epics,* trans. Joan M. Ferrante, 197–279. New York and London: Columbia University Press, 1974.

Amis and Amiloun. Ed. MacEdward Leach. EETS-OS 203 (1937).

Amys e Amillyoun. Ed. Hideka Fukui. ANTS, Plain Texts Series 7. London: ANTS, 1990.

Andrew of Wyntoun. *Original Chronicle.* Ed. F. J. Amours. Edinburgh: Scottish Text Society, 1903–1914.

Der anglonormannische Boeve de Haumtone. Ed. Albert Stimming. Bibliotheca normannica 7. Halle: Niemeyer, 1899.

An Anonymous Short English Metrical Chronicle. Ed. Ewald Zettl. EETS-OS 196 (1935).

Apollodorus. *The Library.* Ed. Sir James George Frazer. New York: Loeb Classical Library/ G. P. Putnam's Sons, 1921.

Augustine. *Sancti Aurelii Augustini de Civitate Dei.* Ed. Bernardus Dombart and Alphonsus Kalb. Corpus Christianorum, Series Latina 47–48. Turnhout: Brepols, 1955.

———. *The City of God.* Trans. W. M. Green. Cambridge: Loeb Classical Library/Harvard University Press, 1972.

Bede. *The Ecclesiastical History of the English People*. Ed. Judith McClure and Roger Collins. Oxford: Oxford University Press, 1994.

Beowulf. Ed. Fr. Klaeber. Lexington, Mass.: D. C. Heath, 1950.

Beowulf: A Dual-Language Edition. Trans. Howell D. Chickering Jr. New York: Anchor Books, 1977.

Bernardus Silvestris. *Commentary on the First Six Books of Virgil's "Aeneid."* Trans. Earl G. Schreiber and Thomas E. Maresca. Lincoln: University of Nebraska Press, 1979.

Biblia Sacra (Iuxta Vulgatam Versionem). Ed. Bonifatio Fischer et al. Stuttgart: Deutsche Bibelgesellschaft, 1983.

The Boke of Duke Huon of Bordeux, done into English by Sir John Bourchier. Part 1, ed. S. L. Lee. EETS-ES 40 (1882).

The Book of Enoch, or I Enoch. Trans. R. H. Charles. Oxford: Clarendon Press, 1912.

The Brut, or The Chronicles of England. Ed. Friedrich W. D. Brie. EETS 131 (1906; reprint, 1960).

Burke, Edmund. *A Philosophical Enquiry into the Origin of Our Ideas of the Sublime and Beautiful*. Ed. J. T. Boulton. London: Routledge and Kegan Paul, 1958.

Chaucer, Geoffrey. *The Canterbury Tales: A Facsimile and Transcription of the Hengwrt Manuscript, with Variants from the Ellesmere Manuscript*. Ed. Paul G. Ruggiers. Norman: University of Oklahoma Press, 1979.

——. *The Complete Works of Geoffrey Chaucer*. Ed. Walter W. Skeat. 6 vols. Oxford: Oxford University Press, 1894.

——. *The Ellesmere Manuscript of Chaucer's Canterbury Tales: A Working Facsimile*. Ed. Ralph Hanna III. Cambridge: D. S. Brewer, 1990.

——. *The Riverside Chaucer*. Ed. Larry D. Benson. 3d ed. Boston: Houghton Mifflin Company, 1987.

Chaucer Life-Records. Ed. Martin M. Crow and Clair C. Olson. Oxford, 1966.

Chestre, Thomas. "Sir Launfal." In *Middle English Metrical Romances*, ed. Walter Hoyt French and Charles Brockway Hale. New York: Prentice-Hall, 1930.

——. *Lybeaus Desconus*. Ed. Maldwyn Mills. EETS-OS 261 (1969).

Chrétien de Troyes. *The Knight with the Lion, or Yvain (Le Chevalier au lion)*. Ed. and trans. William W. Kibler. New York: Garland Publishing, 1985.

——. *Lancelot, or The Knight of the Cart (Le Chevalier de la Charrete)*. Ed. and trans. William W. Kibler. New York: Garland Publishing, 1981.

Cleanness. Ed. Israel Gollancz, trans. Derek S. Brewer. Cambridge: D. S. Brewer, 1974.

"Constructing Albion's Past: An Annotated Edition of *De origine gigantum*." Ed. James P. Carley and Julia Crick. *Arthurian Literature* 13 (1995): 41–114.

Coulson, Frank Thomas. *A Study of the Vulgate Commentary on Ovid's "Metamorphoses" and a Critical Edition of the Glosses to Book One*. Ottawa: National Library of Canada, 1982. Canadian Theses on Microfiche, 1985.

Ctesias. *La Perse, L'Inde: Les sommaires de Photius*. Trans. R. Henry. Collection Lebègue, 7th ser., 84. Brussels: J. Lebègue, 1947.

Cursor Mundi. Part 2, ed. Richard Morris. EETS-OS 59 (1875).

Cynewulf. *Elene*. Ed. P. O. E. Gradon. Exeter: University of Exeter, 1977.

Des Grantz Geanz: An Anglo-Norman Poem. Ed. Georgine E. Brereton. Oxford: Society for the Study of Mediaeval Languages and Literature/Basil Blackwell Publishing, 1937.

Edda, die Lieder des Codex regius nebst verwandten Denkmälern. Ed. Gustav Neckel and Hans Kuhn. Heidelberg, 1962.

Edda Snorra Sturlusonar. Ed. Finnur Jónsson. Copenhagen, 1931.

The Epic of Gilgamesh. Trans. N. K. Sanders. London: Penguin Books, 1972.

Fornaldar Sögur Norðurlanda. Ed. Guðni Jónsson. Reykjavik, 1959.

Froissart, Jean. *Chronicles*. Trans. Geoffrey Brereton. Harmondsworth: Penguin Books, 1968.

——. *Chroniques*. Ed. Siméon Luce, Gaston Raynaud, and Albert Mirot. 14 vols. Paris: Reynouard, 1869–1967.

Geoffrey of Monmouth. *The "Historia Regum Britannie" of Geoffrey of Monmouth.* Ed. Neil Wright. Cambridge: D. S. Brewer, 1984.

———. *The Historia Regum Britanniae of Geoffrey of Monmouth.* Ed. Actom Griscom and R. E. Jones. Geneva: Slatkine Reprints, 1977.

———. *The History of the Kings of Britain.* Trans. Lewis Thorpe. London: Penguin Books, 1966.

Giraldus Cambrensis. *Topographia Hibernae (The History and Topography of Ireland).* Trans. John J. O'Meara. Atlantic Highlands, N.J.: Humanities Press, 1982.

Grettis saga Asmundarsonar. Ed. Guðni Jónsson. Reykjavik: Íslenzk Fornrit, 1936.

Hesiod. *Theogony.* Trans. Norman O. Brown. Indianapolis: Bobbs-Merrill, 1953.

Higden, Ralph. *Polychronicon Ranulphi Higden monachi Cestrensis, Together with the English Translations of John Trevisa and of an Unknown Writer of the Fifteenth Century.* Ed. Joseph Rawson. Nendeln, Liechtenstein: Kraus Reprints, 1964.

Homer. *The Odyssey.* Ed. A. T. Murray. Cambridge: Loeb Classical Library/Harvard University Press, 1953.

———. *The Odyssey.* Trans. Robert Fitzgerald. Garden City, N.Y.: Anchor Books/Doubleday, 1963.

Islendinga Sögur. Ed. Guðni Jónsson. Reykjavik, 1968.

Isumbras. In *The Thornton Romances.* Ed. James Orchard Halliwell. London: Camden Society, 1844.

Jacobus de Voragine. *Legenda Aurea Vulgo Historia Lombardica Dicta.* Ed. Th. Graesse. 3d ed. 1890. Reprint, Osnabrück: Otto Zeller, 1965.

Jacques de Vitry. *Historia Orientalis.* Meisenheim am Glan, 1971.

John of Salisbury. *Policraticus: Of the Frivolities of Courtiers and the Footprints of Philosophers.* Ed. and trans. Cary J. Nederman. Cambridge: Cambridge University Press, 1990.

"King Horn." In *Middle English Metrical Romances,* ed. Walter Hoyt French and Charles Brockway Hale. New York: Prentice-Hall, 1930.

Kyng Alisaunder. Ed. G. V. Smithers. EETS-OS 227, 237 (1952, 1957).

Lancelot do Lac: The Non-Cyclic Old French Prose Romance. Ed. Elspeth Kennedy. 2 vols. Oxford: Clarendon Press, 1980.

Lancelot-Grail: The Old French Arthurian Vulgate and Post-Vulgate in Translation. 5 vols. Ed. Norris J. Lacy. New York: Garland Publishing, 1993–1996.

Lancelot: Roman en prose du XIIIe siecle. Ed. Alexandre Micha. Geneva: Droz, 1982.

The Mabinogion. Ed. and trans. Jeffrey Gantz. London: Penguin Books, 1976.

Malory, Sir Thomas. *The Works of Sir Thomas Malory.* Ed. Eugène Vinaver. 2d ed. Oxford: Oxford University Press, 1981.

Mandeville's Travels. Ed. P. Hamelius. EETS-OS 153–54 (1923).

Mannyng, Robert, of Brunne. *The Chronicle.* Ed. Idelle Sullens. *Medieval and Renaissance Texts and Studies,* vol. 153. Binghamton, N.Y.: Binghamton University, 1996.

Marie de France. *Les Lais de Marie de France.* Ed. Jean Rychner. CFMA 93. Paris: Champion, 1983.

The Middle English Genesis and Exodus. Ed. Olof Arngart. Lund, Gleerup, 1968.

Morte Arthure: A Critical Edition. Ed. Mary Hamel. New York: Garland Publishing, 1984.

Napier, R. H., ed. *Anecdota Oxiensia: Old English Glosses, Chiefly Unpublished.* Oxford: Clarendon Press, 1900. Reprint, New York: AMS Press, n.d.

The New English Bible with the Apocrypha. Oxford Study Edition. New York: Oxford University Press, 1976.

Ovid, Publius Naso. *Metamorphoses.* Ed. G. P. Goold. Cambridge: Loeb Classical Library/Harvard University Press, 1984.

Ovide moralisé: Poème du commencement du quatorzième siècle. Ed. C. de Boer. Amsterdam: Johannes Müller, 1915.

Pálsson, Hermann, and Paul Edwards, trans. *Seven Viking Romances.* New York and London: Penguin Books, 1987.

Paulus Deaconus [Paul the Deacon]. *History of the Langobards.* Trans. William Dudley Foulke. Philadelphia: Department of History of the University of Pennsylvania, 1907.

The Pearl Poems: An Omnibus Edition. Vol. 1, *"Pearl" and "Cleanness,"* ed. William Vantuono. New York: Garland Publishing, 1984.

Perceval of Galles. In *The Thornton Romances,* ed. James Orchard Halliwell. London: Camden Society, 1844.

The Percy Folio. *Bishop Percy's Folio Manuscript: Ballads and Romances.* Ed. John W. Hales and Frederick J. Furnivall. 3 vols. London: Trubner, 1868. Reprint, Detroit: Singing Tree Press, 1968.

Pliny the Elder. *Natural History.* Trans. H. Rackham. Cambridge: Loeb Classical Library/Harvard University Press, 1969.

The Poetic Edda. Trans. Lee M. Hollander. 2d ed. Austin: University of Texas Press, 1962.

The Poetical Dialogues of Solomon and Saturn. Ed. Robert J. Menner. Modern Language Association of America Monograph Series 13. New York: MLA, 1941.

The Quest for the Holy Grail. Trans. Pauline Matarasso. New York and London: Penguin Books, 1969.

[Richard Coeur de Lion.] *Der Mittelenglische Versroman über "Richard Löwenherz."* Ed. Karl Brunner. Wien and Leipzig: Wilhelm Braumüller, 1913.

"Roland and Vernagu." In *The English Charlemagne Romances, Part 6,* ed. Sidney J. H. Herrtage. EETS-ES 39 (1882).

The Romance of Guy of Warwick: The First or Fourteenth-Century Version. Ed. Julius Zupitza. EETS-ES 42, 49, 59 (1883, 1887, 1891).

The Romance of Sir Beves of Hamtoun. Ed. Eugen Kölbing. EETS-ES 46, 48, 65 (1885, 1886, 1894).

The Ruin. In *The Exeter Book,* ed. George Philip Krapp and Elliott Van Kirk Dobbie. Vol. 3 of *The Anglo-Saxon Poetic Records, A Collective Edition.* New York: Columbia University Press, 1936.

The Seafarer. In *The Exeter Book,* ed. George Philip Krapp and Elliott Van Kirk Dobbie. Vol. 3 of *The Anglo-Saxon Poetic Records, A Collective Edition.* New York: Columbia University Press, 1936.

Sir Degaré. In *Middle English Metrical Romances,* ed. Walter Hoyt French and Charles Brockway Hale. New York: Prentice-Hall, 1930.

Sir Degrevant. In *The Thornton Romances,* ed. James Orchard Halliwell. London: Camden Society, 1844.

Sir Eglamour of Artois. In *The Thornton Romances,* ed. James Orchard Halliwell. London: Camden Society, 1844.

"Sir Gawain and the Carl of Carlisle." In *Syr Gawayne: A Collection of Ancient Romance-Poems, by Scottish and English Authors, Relating to That Celebrated Knight of the Round Table,* ed. Sir Frederic Madden. Bannatyne Club Publ. 61. London: Richard and John E. Taylor, 1839.

Sir Gawain and the Green Knight. Ed. Norman Davis. 2d ed. Oxford: Oxford University Press, 1967.

Sir Gawain: Eleven Romances and Tales. Ed. Thomas Hahn. Kalamazoo: Medieval Institute Publications, 1995.

Sir Gowther. In *Six Middle English Romances,* ed. Maldwyn Mills, 148–68. Rutland, Vt.: Everyman's Library/Charles E. Tuttle, 1988.

Sir Landevale. In *Sir Launfal,* ed. A. J. Bliss. Edinburgh and London: Nelson's Medieval and Renaissance Library, 1960.

"Sir Perceval of Galles." In *Middle English Metrical Romances,* ed. Walter Hoyt French and Charles Brockway Hale. New York: Prentice-Hall, 1930.

The Sowdone of Babylone. Ed. Emil Hausknecht. EETS-ES 38 (1891).

Speculum Gy de Warewyke. Ed. Georgina Lea Morrill. EETS-ES 65 (1898).

Sturluson, Snorri. *The Prose Edda.* Trans. Arthur Gilchrist Brodeur. New York: American-Scandinavian Foundation, 1967.

"'*Syre Gawene and the Carle of Carelyle*': An Edition." Ed. Robert W. Ackerman. *The University of Michigan Contributions in Modern Philology* 8 (April 1947).

Thomas. *The Romance of Horn.* Ed. Mildred K. Pope and T. B. W. Reid. 2 vols. ANTS 9–10, 12–13. Oxford: Basil Blackwell, 1955, 1964.

Thomas of Erceldoune. Ed. Murray. EETS 61 (1875).

Torrent of Portyngale. Ed. E. Adam. EETS-ES 51 (1887, 1973).

The Travels of Marco Polo the Venetian. Ed. and rev. Manuel Klamroff, trans. William Marsden. New York: Liveright Publishing, 1953.

The Travels of Marco Polo. Ed. and trans. Ronald Latham. London: Penguin, 1958.

"Two Manuscripts of the Middle English *Anonymous Riming Chronicle.*" Ed. Marion Crane Carroll and Rosemond Tuve. *PMLA* 46 (1931): 115–54.

Vergil, Publius Maro. *Virgil* [Collected Works]. Ed. H. Rushton Fairclough. Cambridge: Loeb Classical Library/Harvard University Press, 1973.

Vincent of Beauvais. *Speculum Quadriplex sive Speculum Maius.* Douai, 1624. Reprint, Graz: Akademische Druck, 1964–1965).

Von Aue, Hartmann. *Gregorius: Bilingual Edition.* Ed. and trans. Sheema Zeben Buehne. New York: F. Ungar, 1966.

Wace. *Le Roman de Brut de Wace.* Ed. Ivor Arnold. 2 vols. Paris: Société des Anciens Textes Français, 1938–1940.

Walter of Speyer. "Passio Sancti ac Beatissimi Martyris Cristofori Rithmice Conposita." In *Poetae Latini Aevi Carolini: Monumenta Germaniae Historica.* Vol. 4, sec. 2. Berlin, 1964.

———. "Vita et Passio Sancti Christopher Martyris." In *Poetarvm Latinorvm Medii Aevii: Monumenta Germaniae Historica,* ed. Karl Strecker and Gabriel Silagi. Vol. 5, sec. 1. Leipzig: 1937–1939. Reprint, Munich, 1978.

The Wanderer. Ed. R. F. Leslie. Manchester: Manchester University Press, 1966.

The Wars of Alexander. Ed. Walter W. Skeat. EETS-ES 47.

Wonders of the East. In *An Eleventh-Century Anglo-Saxon Miscellany,* ed. Patrick McGurk, Ann Knock, et al. Early English Texts in Facsimile 21. Baltimore: Johns Hopkins University Press, 1985.

Wonders of the East. In *Three Old English Prose Texts in MS. Cotton Vitellius A xv.* EETS-OS 161 (1924).

Ywain and Gawain. Ed. Albert B. Friedman and Norman T. Harrington. EETS 254 (1964, for 1963).

Secondary Sources

Abbot, Geoffrey. *Lords of the Scaffold: A History of the Executioner.* New York: St. Martin's Press, 1991.

Acker, Kathy. *In Memoriam to Identity.* New York: Pantheon Books, 1990.

Aers, David. *Community, Gender, and Individual Identity: English Writing, 1360–1430.* London and New York: Routledge, 1988.

Ahrendt, Ernst Herwig. *Der Riese in der mittelhochdeutschen Epik.* Güstrow: Carl Michael, 1923.

Alfano, Christine. "The Issue of Feminine Monstrosity: A Reevaluation of Grendel's Mother." *Comitatus* (1993): 1–16.

Alford, John. "The Grammatical Metaphor: A Survey of Its Use in the Middle Ages." *Speculum* 57 (1982): 728–60.

Allen, John L. "Lands of Myth, Waters of Wonder: The Place of the Imagination in the History of Geographical Exploration." In *Geographies of the Mind: Essays in Historical Geosophy,* ed. David Lowenthal and Martyn J. Bowden, 41–62. Oxford: Oxford University Press, 1976).

Anderson, Andrew Runni. *Alexander's Gate, Gog and Magog, and the Inclosed Nations.* Cambridge: Medieval Academy of America, 1932.

Ashe, Geoffrey. *The Discovery of King Arthur*. London: Guild Publishing, 1985.

Auerbach, Erich. *Mimesis: The Representation of Reality in Western Literature*. Trans. Willard R. Trask. Princeton, N.J.: Princeton University Press, 1953.

Bachelard, Gaston. *La Poétique de l'espace*. Paris: Presses Universitaires de France, 1958.

———. *The Poetics of Space*. Trans. Maria Jolas. Boston: Beacon Press, 1969. Reprint, 1994.

Baker, Steven. *Picturing the Beast: Animals, Identity, and Representation*. Manchester: Manchester University Press, 1993.

Bakhtin, Mikhail M. *The Dialogic Imagination: Four Essays*. Trans. Caryl Emerson and Michael Holquist. Austin: University of Texas Press, 1981.

———. *Rabelais and His World*. Trans. Hélène Iswolsky. Bloomington: Indiana University Press, 1984.

Baldwin, John W. "Five Discourses on Desire: Sexuality and Gender in Northern France around 1200." *Speculum* 66 (1991): 797–819.

Bandy, Stephen C. "Cain, Grendel, and the Giants of Beowulf." *Papers on Language and Literature* 9 (1973): 235–49.

Barber, Richard. *The Knight and Chivalry*. 2d ed. Ipswich: Boydell, 1974.

Bartra, Roger. *Wild Men in the Looking Glass: The Mythic Origins of European Otherness*. Trans. Carl T. Berrisford. Ann Arbor: University of Michigan Press, 1994.

Baswell, Christopher. "Talking Back to the Text: Marginal Voices in Medieval Secular Literature." In *The Uses of Manuscripts in Literary Studies*, ed. Charlotte Cook Morse, Penelope Reed Doob, and Marjorie Curry Woods, 121–60. Kalamazoo, Mich.: Medieval Institute Publications, 1992.

Baum, Paull F. *Chaucer: A Critical Appreciation*. Durham: Duke University Press, 1958.

Baumgartner, Emmanuèle. "Géants et Chevaliers." In *The Spirit of the Court: Selected Proceedings of the Fourth Congress of the International Courtly Literature Society*, ed. Glyn S. Burgess and Robert A. Taylor, 9–22. Cambridge: D. S. Brewer, 1985.

Bechman, Roland. *Trees and Man: The Forest in the Middle Ages*. Trans. Katharyn Dunham. New York: Paragon House, 1990.

Beecher, W. J. "Giant." In *A Dictionary of the Bible, Dealing with Its Language, Literature, and Contents*. Vol. 2, ed. James Hastings, 166–68. New York: Charles Scribner's Sons, 1899.

Bennett, Helen. "The Female Mourner at Beowulf's Funeral: Filling in the Blanks/Hearing the Spaces." *Exemplaria* 4, no. 1 (1992): 35–50.

Bennett, Judith. "Medievalism and Feminism." *Speculum* 68, no. 2 (1993): 309–31.

Benson, Larry D. *Art and Tradition in "Sir Gawain and the Green Knight."* New Brunswick, N.J.: Rutgers University Press, 1965.

———. "The Pagan Coloring of Beowulf." In *Old English Poetry: 15 Essays*, ed. Robert P. Creed, 193–213. Providence, R.I.: Brown University Press, 1967.

———. "The Tournament in the Romances of Chrétien de Troyes and *L'Histoire de Guillaume Le Maréchal*." In *Chivalric Literature: Essays on Relations between Literature and Life in the Later Middle Ages*, ed. Larry D. Benson and John Leyerle, 1–24. Kalamazoo, Mich.: Medieval Institute Publications, 1980.

Bergstrom, Janet. "Androids and Androgyny." In *Close Encounters: Film, Feminism, and Science Fiction*, ed. Constance Penley, Elisabeth Lyon, Lynn Spigel, and Janet Bergstrom, 33–60. Minneapolis: University of Minnesota Press, 1991.

Bernheimer, Richard. *The Wild Man in the Middle Ages: A Study in Art, Sentiment, and Demonology*. Cambridge: Harvard University Press, 1952. Reprint, 1970.

Berrong, Richard M. *Rabelais and Bakhtin: Popular Culture in "Gargantua" and "Pantagruel."* (Lincoln: University of Nebraska Press, 1986.

Bettelheim, Bruno. *Symbolic Wounds: Puberty Rites and the Envious Male*. New York: Collier Books, 1968.

Bewell, Alan. "An Issue of Monstrous Desire: Frankenstein and Obstetrics." *The Yale Journal of Criticism* 2 (1988): 105–28.

Biddick, Kathleen. "Genders, Bodies, Borders: Technologies of the Visible." *Speculum* 68 (1993): 389–418.

Birns, Nicholas. "The Trojan Myth: Postmodern Reverberations." *Exemplaria* 5 (1993): 45–78.

Bloch, Marc. *La Société féodale.* 2 vols. Paris: 1939–1940.

———. *Feudal Society.* Trans. L. A. Manyon. 2 vols. Chicago: University of Chicago Press, 1961.

Bloch, R. Howard. *Etymologies and Genealogies: A Literary Anthropology of the French Middle Ages.* Chicago: University of Chicago Press, 1983.

———. "Medieval Misogyny: Woman as Riot." In *Misogyny, Misandry, and Misanthropy,* ed. R. Howard Bloch and Francis Ferguson. Los Angeles: University of California Press, 1989.

Boberg, Inger M. "Ogres." In *Motif-Index of Early Icelandic Literature.* Copenhagen: Munksgaard, 1966.

Bonheim, Helmut. "The Acromegalic in Chrétien's *Yvain.*" *French Studies: A Quarterly Review* 44 (1990): 1–9.

Borch-Jacobsen, Mikkel. *Lacan: The Absolute Master.* Trans. Douglas Brick. Stanford: Stanford University Press, 1991.

Boren, James H. "Narrative Design in the Alliterative *Morte Arthure.*" *PQ* 56 (1977): 310–19.

Borst, Arno, ed. *Das Rittertum im Mittelalter.* Darmstadt: Wissenschaftliche Gesellschaft, 1982.

Boswell, John. *Christianity, Social Tolerance, and Homosexuality: Gay People in Western Europe from the Beginning of the Christian Era to the Fourteenth Century.* (Chicago: University of Chicago Press, 1980.

Bosworth, Joseph. *An Anglo-Saxon Dictionary: Based on the Manuscript Collections of the Late Joseph Bosworth.* Ed. and enlarged by T. Northcote Toller. London: Oxford University Press, 1898. Reprint, 1964.

Bowie, Malcolm. *Lacan.* Cambridge: Harvard University Press, 1991.

Bradstock, E. M. "The Penitential Pattern in *Sir Gowther.*" *Parergon* 20 (1978): 3–10.

———. "Sir Gowther: Secular Hagiography or Hagiographical Romance or Neither?" *AUMLA: Journal of the Australasian Universities Language and Literature Association* 59 (1983): 26–47.

Bresc, Henri. "Les Temps des Géants." In *Temps, Memoire, Tradition au Moyen Age,* ed. Bernard Guillemain, 243–66. Aix-en-Provence: Pubs. Univ. de Provence, 1983.

Brewer, D. S. "The Relationship of Chaucer to the English and European Traditions." In *Chaucer and the Chaucerians,* ed. D. S. Brewer, 1–38. Tuscaloosa: University of Alabama Press, 1966.

Briggs, Katherine M. *The Faeries in English Tradition and Literature.* Chicago: University of Chicago Press, 1967.

Broderius, John R. *The Giant in Germanic Tradition.* Ph.D. diss., University of Chicago, 1932. Private edition, distributed by the University of Chicago Libraries.

Brooke, Christopher. "Geoffrey of Monmouth as Historian." In *Church and Government in the Middle Ages,* ed. Christopher Brooke, 77–91. Cambridge: Cambridge University Press, 1976.

Brown, Emerson, Jr. "Fragment VII of Chaucer's *Canterbury Tales* and the 'Mental Climate of the Fourteenth Century.'" In *Traditions and Innovations: Essays on British Literature of the Middle Ages and Renaissance,* ed. David G. Allen and Robert A. White, 50–58. Newark: University of Delaware Press, 1990.

Brown, Peter. "Bodies and Minds: Sexuality and Renunciation in Early Christianity." In *Before Sexuality: The Construction of Erotic Experience in the Ancient Greek World,* ed. David M. Halperin, John J. Winkler, and Froma Zeitlin, 479–93. Princeton, N.J.: Princeton University Press, 1990.

Bruce, James Douglas. *The Evolution of Arthurian Romance.* 2 vols. Gloucester, Mass.: Johns Hopkins Press, 1958.

Bryan, William F., and Germaine Dempster, eds. *Sources and Analogues of Chaucer's "Canterbury Tales."* New York: Humanities Press, 1958.

Bullough, Vern L. "On Being Male in the Middle Ages." In *Medieval Masculinities: Regarding Men in the Middle Ages,* ed. Clare A. Lees, 31–45. Minneapolis: University of Minnesota Press, 1994.

Bumke, Joachim. *Courtly Culture: Literature and Society in the High Middle Ages.* Trans. Thomas Dunlap. Berkeley: University of California Press, 1991.

Burger, Glenn. "Kissing the Pardoner." *PMLA* 107 (1992): 1143–56.

———. "Queer Chaucer." *English Studies in Canada* 20, no. 2 (1994): 153–70.

———. "Erotic Discipline...Or 'Tee Hee, I Like My Boys to Be Girls': Inventing with the Body in Chaucer's *Miller's Tale.*" In *Becoming Male in the Middle Ages,* ed. Jeffrey Jerome Cohen and Bonnie Wheeler, 245–60. New York: Garland Publishing, 1997.

Burns, E. Jane. *Bodytalk: When Women Speak in Old French Literature.* Philadelphia: University of Pennsylvania Press, 1993.

———. "Refashioning Courtly Love: Lancelot as Ladies' Man or Lady/Man?" In *Constructing Medieval Sexuality,* ed. Karma Lochrie, Peggy McCracken, and James A. Schultz, 111–34. Minneapolis: University of Minnesota Press, 1997.

Burrow, John. "Sir Thopas: An Agony in Three Fits." In *Essays in Medieval Literature,* 61–65. Oxford: Clarendon Press, 1984.

Butler, Judith. *Gender Trouble: Feminism and the Subversion of Identity.* New York: Routledge, 1990.

———. "Sexual Inversions." In *Discourses of Sexuality: From Aristotle to AIDS,* ed. Domna C. Stanton, 344–61. Ann Arbor: University of Michigan Press, 1992.

———. *Bodies That Matter: On the Discursive Limits of "Sex."* New York: Routledge, 1993.

Bynum, Caroline Walker. *Fragmentation and Redemption: Essays on Gender and the Human Body in Medieval Religion.* New York: Zone Books, 1991.

———. *The Resurrection of the Body in Western Christianity, 200–1336.* New York: Columbia University Press, 1995.

Cadden, Joan. *Meanings of Sex Difference in the Middle Ages: Medicine, Science, and Culture.* Cambridge: Cambridge University Press, 1993.

Calin, William. *The French Tradition and the Literature of Medieval England.* Toronto: University of Toronto Press, 1994.

Camille, Michael. *Image on the Edge: The Margins of Medieval Art.* Cambridge: Harvard University Press, 1992.

Campbell, Mary. *The Witness and the Other World: Exotic European Travel Writing, 400–1600.* Ithaca: Cornell University Press, 1988.

Cannon, Christopher. "*Raptus* in the Chaumpaigne Release and a Newly Discovered Document concerning the Life of Geoffrey Chaucer." *Speculum* 68 (1993): 74–94.

Carry, George. *The Medieval Alexander.* Cambridge: Cambridge University Press, 1956.

Carter, M. L. "The Psychological Symbolism of the Magic Fountain and the Giant Herdsman in *Yvain.*" *Mythlore: A Journal of J. R. R. Tolkien, C. S. Lewis, Charles Williams, General Fantasy, and Mythic Studies* 11 (1985).

Céard, Jean. *La Nature et les prodiges.* Geneva: Droz, 1977.

———. "La Querelle des géants et la jeunesse du monde." *Journal of Medieval and Renaissance Studies* 8 (1978): 37–76.

Cervantes. *Don Quixote.* Trans. J. M. Cohen. Harmondsworth: Penguin Books, 1950.

Chambers, R. W. *Beowulf: An Introduction.* 3d ed., with supplement by C. L. Wrenn. Cambridge: Cambridge University Press, 1963.

Chapman, R. L. "*The Shipman's Tale* Was Meant for the Shipman." *Modern Language Notes* 71 (1956): 4–5.

Charpentier, Louis. *Les Géants et le mystère des origines.* 1969. Reprint, Paris: Editions J'ai Lu, 1975.

Chênerie, Marie-Luce. "L'aventure du chevalier enferré, ses suites et le thème des géants dans le *Lancelot.*" In *Approches du Lancelot en Prose,* ed. Jean Dufournet, 59–100. Genève-Paris: Editions Slatkine, 1984.

Chisholm, Richard. "Rainoart, a Forgotten Saint in Dante's Paradise." Unpublished paper.

Cixous, Hélène, and Catherine Clément. *The Newly Born Woman.* Trans. Betsy Wing. Minneapolis: University of Minnesota Press, 1986.

Clark, David L. "Monstrosity, Illegibility, Denegation: *The Martyrology* after de Man." In *Monster Theory: Reading Culture,* ed. Jeffrey Jerome Cohen, 40–71. Minneapolis: University of Minnesota Press, 1996.

Classen, Albrecht. "Monsters, Devils, Giants, and Other Creatures: 'The Other' in Medieval Narratives and Epics, with Special Emphasis on Middle High German Literature." In *Canon and Canon Transgression in Medieval German Literature,* ed. Albrecht Classen, 83–121. Göppingen: Kümmerle Verlag, 1993.

Clover, Carol J. *Men, Women, and Chain Saws: Gender in the Modern Horror Film.* Princeton, N. J.: Princeton University Press, 1992.

———. "Regardless of Sex: Men, Women, and Power in Early Northern Europe." *Speculum* 68 (1993): 363–87.

Coates, Paul. *The Double and the Other: Identity as Ideology in Post-Romantic Fiction.* London: Macmillan Press, 1988.

———. *The Gorgon's Gaze.* (Cambridge: Cambridge University Press, 1991.

Cohen, Jeffrey Jerome. "The Limits of Knowing: Monsters and the Regulation of Medieval Popular Culture." *Medieval Folklore* 3 (1994): 1–37.

———. "Review of *Feminist Approaches to the Body in Medieval Literature.*" *Bryn Mawr Medieval Review,* 6 April 1994.

———. "The Armour of an Alienating Identity." *Arthuriana* 6, no. 4 (1996): 1–24. Published in hypertext as "Medieval Masculinities: Heroism, Sanctity, and Gender." *Interscripta* (1993, 1995) http://www.georgetown.edu/labyrinth/e-center/interscripta/mm.html.

———. "Monster Culture (Seven Theses)." In *Monster Theory: Reading Culture,* ed. Jeffrey Jerome Cohen, 3–25. Minneapolis: University of Minnesota Press, 1996.

Cooper, Helen. *Oxford Guides to Chaucer: The Canterbury Tales.* 2d ed. Oxford: Oxford University Press, 1996.

Copeland, Rita. *Rhetoric, Hermeneutics, and Translation in the Middle Ages.* Cambridge: Cambridge University Press, 1991.

Coulson, Frank Thomas. *A Study of the Vulgate Commentary on Ovid's "Metamorphoses" and a Critical Edition of the Glosses to Book One.* Ottawa: National Library of Canada, 1982; Canadian Theses on Microfiche, 1985.

Crane, R. S. "The Vogue of Guy of Warwick from the Close of the Middle Ages to the Romantic Revival." *PMLA* 30 (1915): 125–94.

Crane, Susan. *Insular Romance: Politics, Faith, and Culture in Anglo-Norman and Middle English Literature.* Berkeley: University of California Press, 1986.

———. "The Writing Lesson of 1381." In *Chaucer's England: Literature in Historical Context,* ed. Barbara A. Hanawalt, 201–21. Minneapolis: University of Minnesota Press, 1992.

———. *Gender and Romance in Chaucer's "Canterbury Tales."* Princeton, N.J.: Princeton University Press, 1994.

Crawford, Donna. " 'Gronyng wyth grysly wounde': Injury in Five Middle English Breton Lays." In *Readings in Medieval English Romance,* ed. Carol M. Meale, 35–52. Cambridge: D. S. Brewer, 1994.

Crawford, T. D. "On the Linguistic Competence of Geoffrey of Monmouth." *Medium Aevum* 51 (1982): 152–62.

Crimp, Douglas. "The Boys in My Bedroom." In *The Lesbian and Gay Studies Reader,* ed. Henry Abelove et al., 344–49. New York: Routledge, 1993.

Curley, Michael J. *Geoffrey of Monmouth*. New York: Twayne Publishers/Macmillan Publishing Company, 1994.

Darré, René. *Géants d'hier et d'aujourdhui*. Arras: Imprimerie de la Nouvelle Société Anonyme du Pas-de-Calais, 1944.

Davidson, H. R. Ellis. *Myths and Symbols in Pagan Europe*. Syracuse, N.Y.: Syracuse University Press, 1988.

Dean, James. "The World Grown Old and Genesis in Middle English Historical Writings." *Speculum* 57, no. 3 (1982): 548–68.

De Beauvoir, Simone. *The Second Sex*. Trans. H. M. Parshley. New York: Bantam Books, 1964.

De Lauretis, Teresa. "Queer Theory: Lesbian and Gay Sexualities—An Introduction." *Differences* 3, no. 2 (1991): iii–xviii.

Deleuze, Gilles, and Félix Guattari. *L'anti-Oedipe: Capitalisme et Schizophrénie*. Paris: Les Editions de Minuit, 1972. Trans. Robert Hurley, Mark Seem, and Helen R. Lane as *Anti-Oedipus: Capitalism and Schizophrenia*. Minneapolis: University of Minnesota Press, 1983.

———. *Mille plateaux, v. 2 de Capitalisme et Schizophrénie*. Paris: Les Editions de Minuit, 1980. Trans. Brian Massumi as *A Thousand Plateaus: Capitalism and Schizophrenia*. Minneapolis: University of Minnesota Press, 1987.

Deleuze, Gilles, and Claire Parnet. *Dialogues*. Trans. Hugh Tomlinson and Barbara Habberjam. New York: Columbia University Press, 1977.

Deloach, Charles. *Giants: A Reference Guide from History, the Bible, and Recorded Legend*. Metuchen, N.J.: Scarecrow Press, 1995.

Derrida, Jacques. "Structure, Sign, and Play in the Discourse of the Human Sciences." In *Writing and Difference*, trans. Alan Bass, 278–93. Chicago: University of Chicago Press, 1978.

Dinshaw, Carolyn. *Chaucer's Sexual Poetics*. Madison: University of Wisconsin Press, 1989.

———. "A Kiss Is Just a Kiss: Heterosexuality and Its Consolations in *Sir Gawain and the Green Knight*." *Diacritics* 24, no. 2 (1994): 205–26.

———. "Chaucer's Queer Touches/A Queer Touches Chaucer." *Exemplaria* 7, no. 1 (1995): 75–92.

Dollimore, Jonathan. *Sexual Dissidence: Augustine to Wilde, Freud to Foucault*. Oxford: Clarendon Press, 1991.

Dragonetti, Roger. *La Vie de la lettre en Moyen Age (Le Conte du Graal)*. Paris: Seuil, 1980.

Duby, Georges. "Dans la France du Nord-Ouest au XIIᵉ siècle: les 'Jeunes' dans la société aristocratique." *Annales* 19 (1964): 835–46.

———. *The Chivalrous Society*. Trans. Cynthia Postan. Berkeley: University of California Press, 1977.

———. *Medieval Marriage*. Baltimore: Johns Hopkins University Press, 1978.

———. "The Culture of the Knightly Class: Audience and Patronage." In *Renaissance and Renewal in the Twelfth Century*, ed. Robert L. Benson and Giles Constable, 248–62. Cambridge: Harvard University Press, 1982.

Dundes, Alan. "Earth Diver: Creation of the Mythopoeic Male." *American Anthropologist* 64 (1962).

Dunton-Downer, Leslie. "Wolf Man." In *Becoming Male in the Middle Ages*, ed. Jeffrey Jerome Cohen and Bonnie Wheeler, 203–18. New York: Garland Publishing, 1997.

Edwards, A. S. G., and Derek Pearsall. "The Manuscripts of the Major English Poetic Texts." In *Book Production and Publishing in Britain, 1375–1475*, ed. J. J. Griffiths and Derek Pearsall, 257–78. Cambridge: Cambridge University Press, 1989.

Ellmann, Maud. *Psychoanalytic Literary Criticism*. New York: Longman Publishing, 1994.

Emerson, Oliver F. "Legends of Cain, Especially in Old and Middle English." *PMLA* 21 (1906): 831–929.

Evans, Dylan. *An Introductory Dictionary of Lacanian Psychoanalysis*. New York: Routledge, 1996.

Fairholt, F. W. *Gog and Magog, the Giants in Guildhall: Their Real and Legendary History, with an Account of Other Civic Giants, at Home and Abroad.* London: John Camden Hotten, 1859.

Fewster, Carol. *Traditionality and Genre in Middle English Romance.* Cambridge: D. S. Brewer, 1987.

Fichtner, Edward G. "The Etymology of *Goliard.*" *Neophilologus* 51 (1967): 230–37.

Finlayson, John. "Arthur and the Giant of St. Michael's Mount." *Medium Aevum* 33 (1964): 112–20.

Fisher, Sheila. "Taken Men and Token Women in *Sir Gawain and the Green Knight.*" In *Seeking the Woman in Late Medieval and Renaissance Writings: Essays in Feminist Contextual Criticism,* ed. Sheila Fisher and Jane E. Halley, 71–105. Knoxville: University of Tennessee Press, 1989.

Flint, Valerie I. J. "The *Historia Regum Britanniae* of Geoffrey of Monmouth: Parody and Its Purpose. A Suggestion." *Speculum* 54 (1979): 447–68.

Foot, Sarah. "The Making of Angelcynn: English Identity before the Norman Conquest." *Transactions of the Royal Historical Society* 6 (1996): 25–49.

Foucault, Michel. *Discipline and Punish: The Birth of the Prison.* Trans. Alan Sheridan. New York, Pantheon Books, 1977.

———. *The History of Sexuality, Volume 1: An Introduction.* New York: Vintage Books/ Random House, 1978.

———. "The Subject and Power." In *Michel Foucault: Beyond Structuralism and Hermeneutics,* ed. Hubert L. Dreyfus and Paul Rabinow, 208–26. Chicago: University of Chicago Press, 1983.

———. "Nietzsche, Genealogy, History." In *The Foucault Reader,* ed. Paul Rabinow, 76–97. New York: Pantheon Books, 1984.

———. *The Order of Things: An Archaeology of the Human Sciences.* New York: Vintage Books, 1994.

Fradenburg, Louise Olga. *City, Marriage, Tournament: Arts of Rule in Late Medieval Scotland.* Madison: University of Wisconsin Press, 1991.

———. " 'Be Not Far from Me': Psychoanalysis, Medieval Studies, and the Subject of Religion." *Exemplaria* 7, no. 1 (1995): 41–54.

Fradenburg, Louise Olga, and Carla Freccero. "Caxton, Foucault, and the Pleasures of History." In *Premodern Sexualities,* ed. Louise Fradenburg and Carla Freccero, xiii–xxiv. New York: Routledge, 1996.

Frank, Roberta. "The Beowulf Poet's Sense of History." In *The Wisdom of Poetry: Essays in Early English Literature in Honor of Morton W. Bloomfield,* ed. Larry Benson and Siegfried Wenzel, 53–65. Kalamazoo, Mich.: Medieval Institute, 1982.

Frantzen, Allen J. *Desire for Origins: New Language, Old English, and Teaching the Tradition.* New Brunswick, N.J.: Rutgers University Press, 1990.

Freud, Sigmund. *The Standard Edition of the Complete Psychological Works of Sigmund Freud.* Trans. under the general editorship of James Strachey. London: Hogarth Press, 1986.

Friedman, John Block. *The Monstrous Races in Medieval Art and Thought.* Cambridge: Harvard University Press, 1981.

Fry, Donald K. "Polyphemus in Iceland." *The Fourteenth Century, Acta* 4 (1977): 65–86.

Ganim, John. "Medieval Literature as Monster: The Grotesque before and after Bakhtin." *Exemplaria* 7, no. 1 (1995): 27–40.

Garber, Marjorie. *Shakespeare's Ghost Writers: Literature as Uncanny Causality.* New York: Methuen, 1987.

———. *Vested Interests: Cross-Dressing and Cultural Anxiety.* New York: HarperCollins, 1993.

———. *Vice Versa: Bisexuality and the Erotics of Everyday Life.* New York: Simon and Schuster, 1995.

Gaunt, Simon. *Gender and Genre in Medieval French Literature.* Cambridge: Cambridge University Press, 1995.

Gaylord, Alan. "Chaucer's Dainty 'Dogerel': The 'Elvyssh' Prosody of *Sir Thopas.*" *Studies in the Age of Chaucer* 1 (1979): 84–104.

———. "The Moment of *Sir Thopas:* Toward a New Look at Chaucer's Language." *Chaucer Review* 16 (1981–1982): 311–29.

———. "The 'Miracle' of Sir Thopas." *Studies in the Age of Chaucer* 6 (1984): 65–84.

Georgoudi, Stella. "Creating a Myth of Matriarchy." In *A History of Women in the West,* vol. 1, ed. Pauline Pantel, trans. Arthur Goldhammer, 449–63. Cambridge: Harvard University Press, 1992.

Gransden, A. *Historical Writing in England c. 550–c. 1307.* London: Routledge and Kegan Paul, 1974.

———. *Historical Writing in England c. 1307 to the Early 16th Century.* London: Routledge and Kegan Paul, 1982.

Grosz, Elizabeth. "A Thousand Tiny Sexes: Feminism and Rhizomatics." In *Gilles Deleuze and Theater of Philosophy,* ed. Constantin V. Boundas and Dorothea Olkowski, 187–210. New York: Routledge, 1994.

———. *Volatile Bodies: Toward a Corporeal Feminism.* Bloomington: Indiana University Press, 1994.

———. *Space, Time, and Perversion.* New York: Routledge, 1995.

Hallissy, Margaret. *Venomous Woman.* Westport, Conn.: Greenwood Press, 1987.

Hanford, James H. "The Progenitors of Golias." *Speculum* 1 (1926): 38–58.

Hanks, D. Thomas, Jr. "Malory's Way with His Source for 'The Giant of Saint Michael's Mount': Style and Characterization." *Arthurian Interpretations* 4 (1990): 24–34.

Hanning, Robert W. *The Vision of History in Early Britain: From Gildas to Geoffrey of Monmouth.* New York: Columbia University Press, 1966.

Hansen, Elaine Tuttle. *Chaucer and the Fictions of Gender.* Berkeley: University of California Press, 1992.

Haraway, Donna J. *Simians, Cyborgs, and Women: The Reinvention of Nature.* New York: Routledge, 1991.

Harf-Lancner, Laurence. *Les fées au Moyen Age.* Paris: Chapion, 1984.

———. "Le Roman de Mélusine et le Roman de Geoffrey à la Grande Dent." *Bibliothèque d'Humanisme et Renaissance* 50 (1988): 349–66.

Harris, Joseph. "The Masterbuilder Tale in Snorri's *Edda* and Two Sagas." *Arkiv for Nordisk Filologi* 91 (1976): 66–101.

———. "Love and Death in the *Männerbund:* An Essay with Special Reference to the *Bjarkamál* and *The Battle of Maldon.*" In *Heroic Poetry in the Anglo-Saxon Period: Studies in Honor of Jess B. Bessinger, Jr.,* 77–114. Kalamazoo, Mich.: Medieval Institute Publications, 1993.

Healey, Antonette di Paolo, and Richard L. Venezky. *A Microfiche Concordance to Old English Microform.* Newark: University of Delaware, 1980.

Hegel, G. W. F. *Hegel's Recollection.* Trans. D. Ph. Verene. Albany: State University of New York Press, 1985.

Heng, Geraldine. "Feminine Knots and the Other *Sir Gawain and the Green Knight.*" *PMLA* (1991) 500–14.

———. "A Woman Wants: The Lady, Gawain, and the Forms of Seduction." *The Yale Journal of Criticism* (1992) 101–34.

Hirsch, David A. Hedrich. "Liberty, Equality, Monstrosity: Revolutionizing the Family in Mary Shelley's *Frankenstein.*" In *Monster Theory: Reading Culture,* ed. Jeffrey Jerome Cohen, 115–40. Minneapolis: University of Minnesota Press, 1996.

Hopkins, Andrea. *The Sinful Knights: A Study of Middle English Penitential Romance.* Oxford: Clarendon Press, 1990.

Howard, Donald R. *The Idea of the Canterbury Tales.* Berkeley: University of California Press, 1976.

———. *Chaucer: His Life, His Works, His World.* New York: E. P. Dutton, 1987.

Howe, Nicholas. *Migration and Mythmaking in Anglo-Saxon England.* New Haven: Yale University Press, 1989.

Huchet, Jean-Charles. *Littérature Médiévale et Psychoanalyse: Pour une Clinique Littéraire.* Paris: Presses Universitaires de France, 1990.

———. *Le Roman Occitan Médiéval.* Paris: Presses Universitaires de France, 1991.

Huet, Marie-Hélène. "Living Images: Monstrosity and Representation." *Representations* 4 (1983): 73–87.

———. *Monstrous Imagination.* Cambridge: Harvard University Press, 1993.

Huizinga, Johan. *The Waning of the Middle Ages.* Trans. F. Hopman. New York: St. Martin's Press, 1924. Reprint, 1984.

Hyatte, Reginald. "Recoding Ideal Male Friendship as *Fine Amour* in the *Prose Lancelot.*" *Neophilologus* 75 (1991): 505–18.

Irigaray, Luce. *This Sex Which Is Not One.* Trans. Catherine Porter. Ithaca: Cornell University Press, 1985.

Jaeger, C. Stephen. *The Origins of Courtliness: Civilizing Trends and the Formation of Courtly Ideals, 939–1210.* Philadelphia: University of Pennsylvania Press, 1985.

———. "Courtliness and Social Change." In *Cultures of Power: Lordship, Status, and Process in Twelfth-Century Europe,* ed. Thomas N. Bisson, 287–309. Philadelphia: University of Pennsylvania Press, 1995.

Janson, H. W. *Apes and Ape Lore in the Middle Ages and Renaissance.* London: The Warburg Institute/University of London, 1952.

Jauss, Johann. *Toward an Aesthetic of Reception.* Trans. Timothy Bahti. Minneapolis: University of Minnesota Press, 1982.

Johnson, Lesley. "Return to Albion." *Arthurian Literature* 13 (1995): 19–40.

Jones, C. Meredith. "The Conventional Saracen of the Songs of Geste." *PMLA* 17 (1942): 201–25.

Jones-Davies, M. T. *Monstres et prodiges au temps de la Renaissance.* Paris: Touzot, 1980.

Kafka, Franz. *Selected Short Stories of Franz Kafka.* Trans. Willa and Edwin Muir. New York: Modern Library, 1952.

Kantorowicz, Ernst. *The King's Two Bodies: A Study in Medieval Political Theology.* Princeton, N.J.: Princeton University Press, 1957.

Kappler, Claude. *Monstres, demons et merveilles à la fin du Moyen Age.* Paris: Payot, 1980.

Kaske, R. E. "*Gigas* the Giant in *Piers Plowman.*" *Journal of English and Germanic Philology* 56, no. 2 (1957).

———. "*Sapientia et Fortitudo* as the Controlling Theme of *Beowulf.*" *Studies in Philology* 15 (1958): 423–56.

———. "The *Eotanas* in *Beowulf.*" In *Old English Poetry: Fifteen Essays,* ed. Robert P. Creed, 285–310. Providence, R.I.: Brown University Press, 1967.

———. "*Beowulf* and the Book of Enoch." *Speculum* 46, no. 3 (1971): 421–31.

Kay, Sarah. *The Chansons de Geste in the Age of Romance: Political Fictions.* Oxford: Clarendon Press, 1995.

Keen, Maurice. *Chivalry.* New Haven: Yale University Press, 1984.

Kennedy, Edward Donald. "Chronicles and Other Historical Writing." In *A Manual of the Writings in Middle English, 1050–1500,* vol. 8, ed. Albert E. Hartung. New Haven: Connecticut Academy of Arts and Sciences, 1989.

Kennedy, Elspeth. *Lancelot and the Grail: A Study of the Prose "Lancelot."* Oxford: Clarendon Press, 1986.

Kiessling, Nicholas. *The Incubus in English Literature: Provenance and Progeny.* N.l.: Washington State University Press, 1977.

Knapp, Peggy A. "Alienated Majesty: Grendel and Its Pretexts." *The Centennial Review* 32, no. 1 (1988): 1–18.

Knight, Stephen. *Arthurian Literature and Society.* London: Macmillan, 1983.

Kristeva, Julia. *Powers of Horror: An Essay on Abjection.* Trans. Leon S. Roudiez. New York: Columbia University Press, 1982.

———. *Strangers to Ourselves.* New York: Columbia University Press, 1992.

Kruger, Steven F. "The Bodies of Jews in the Late Middle Ages." In *The Idea of Medieval Literature: New Essays on Chaucer and Medieval Culture in Honor of Donald R.*

Howard, ed. James Dean and Christian Zacher, 301–23. Newark: University of Delaware Press, 1993.

———. "Claiming the Pardoner: Toward a Gay Reading of Chaucer's Pardoner's Tale." *Exemplaria* 6, no. 1 (1994): 115–39.

———. "Becoming Christian, Becoming Male?" In *Becoming Male in the Middle Ages*, ed. Jeffrey Jerome Cohen and Bonnie Wheeler, 21–41. New York: Garland Publishing, 1997.

Lacan, Jacques. *Écrits*. Selections trans. Alan Sheridan. Paris: Editions du Seuil, 1970; New York: W. W. Norton, 1977.

———. *The Four Fundamental Concepts of Psycho-Analysis*. Ed. Jacques-Alain Miller, trans. Alan Sheridan. New York: W. W. Norton, 1981.

———. *The Seminar, Book II: The Ego in Freud's Theory and in the Technique of Psychoanalysis, 1954–55*, Trans. Sylvana Tomaselli, notes by John Forrester. New York: Norton, 1988.

———. *The Seminar, Book VII: The Ethics of Psychoanalysis*. Trans. Dennis Porter. London: Routledge, 1992.

Langer, Karl. *Wachstum des Menslichen Skeletes mit Bezug auf den Riesen*. Denkschriften der Kaiserlichen Akademie der Wissenschaften, Mathematisch-Naturwissenschaftliche Classe 31. Vienna, 1872.

Langfors, Arthur. "'L'Anglais qui couve' dans l'imagination populaire au Moyen Age." In *Mélanges de philologie romane et de littérature médiévale offerts à Ernest Hoepffner*, 89–94. Paris: Publications de la Faculté des Lettres de l'Université de Strasbourg, 1949.

Laplanche, Jean. *Life and Death in Psychoanalysis*. Trans. Jeffrey Mehlman. Baltimore: Johns Hopkins University Press, 1976.

Laqueur, Thomas. *Making Sex: Body and Gender from the Greeks to Freud*. Cambridge: Harvard University Press, 1990.

Lecouteux, Claude. *Les Monstres dans la littérature allemande du moyen âge: Contribution à l'étude du merveilleux médiévale*. 3 vols. Göppingen: Kümmerle, 1982.

———. "Harpin de la Montaigne *(Yvain, v. 3770 et ss.)*." *Cahiers de Civilisation Medievale (Xe–XIIe Siecles)* 30 (1987): 219–25.

Lee, Sidney. "Guy of Warwick." In *Dictionary of National Biography*, vol. 8, ed. Leslie Stephen and Sidney Lee, 829–31. London: Smith, Elder, 1908.

Lees, Clare. "Men and *Beowulf*." In *Medieval Masculinities: Regarding Men in the Middle Ages*, ed. Clare A. Lees, 129–48. Minneapolis: University of Minnesota Press, 1994.

Le Goff, Jacques. *Time, Work, and Culture in the Middle Ages*. Trans. Arthur Goldhammer. Chicago: University of Chicago Press, 1980.

———. "Head or Heart? The Political Use of Body Metaphors in the Middle Ages." Trans. Patricia Ranum, in *Fragments for a History of the Body*, vol. 3, ed. Michel Feher, with Ramona Naddaff and Nadia Tazi, 12–26. New York: Zone Books, 1989.

Leicester, H. Marshall. *The Disenchanted Self*. Berkeley: University of California Press, 1990.

Leupin, Alexandre. *Barbarolexis: Medieval Writing and Sexuality*. Trans. Kate M. Cooper. Cambridge: Harvard University Press, 1989.

Lévi-Strauss, Claude. *The Elementary Structures of Kinship*. Trans. James Harle Bell, John Richard von Sturmer, and Rodney Needham. Boston: Beacon Press, 1969.

Lewis, C. S. *The Discarded Image*. Cambridge: Cambridge University Press, 1964.

Lomperis, Linda. "Unruly Bodies and Ruling Practices: Chaucer's *Physician's Tale* as Socially Symbolic Act." In *Feminist Approaches to the Body in Medieval Literature*, ed. Linda Lomperis and Sarah Stanbury, 21–37. Philadelphia: University of Pennsylvania Press, 1993.

———. "Bodies That Matter in the Court of Late Medieval England and in Chaucer's *Miller's Tale*." *Romanic Review* 86, no. 2 (1995): 243–64.

Loomis, Laura A. Hibbard. "Sir Thopas and David and Goliath." *Modern Language Notes* 51 (1936): 311–13.

———. *Medieval Romance in England: A Study of the Sources and Analogues of the Non-cyclic Metrical Romances.* New York: Burt Franklin, 1963.

Loomis, Roger Sherman. "Edward I, Arthurian Enthusiast." *Speculum* 33 (1958): 242–55.

———, ed. *Arthurian Literature in the Middle Ages: A Collaborative History.* Oxford: Clarendon Press, 1959.

MacRitchie, David. "Giants." In *Encyclopaedia of Religion and Ethics,* vol. 6, ed. James Hastings, 189–93. New York: Charles Scribner's Sons, 1899.

Mann, Jill. "Price and Value in *Sir Gawain and the Green Knight.*" *Essays in Criticism* 36 (1986): 298–318.

Marchalonis, Shirley. "*Sir Gowther:* The Process of a Romance." *The Chaucer Review* 6 (1971): 14–29.

Margherita, Gayle. *The Romance of Origins: Language and Sexual Difference in Middle English Literature.* Philadelphia: University of Pennsylvania Press, 1994.

Massumi, Brian. *A User's Guide to Capitalism and Schizophrenia: Deviations from Deleuze and Guattari.* Cambridge: MIT Press, 1992.

McAlpine, Monica E. "The Pardoner's Homosexuality and How It Matters." *PMLA* 95 (1980): 8–22.

McCoy, Dorothy. "From Celibacy to Sexuality: An Examination of Some Medieval and Early Renaissance Versions of the Story of Robert the Devil." In *Human Sexuality in the Middle Ages and Renaissance,* ed. Douglas Radcliff-Umstead, 23–39. Pittsburgh: Center for Medieval and Renaissance Studies of the University of Pittsburgh, 1978.

McCracken, Peggy. "The Body Politic and the Queen's Adulterous Body in French Romance." In *Feminist Approaches to the Body in Medieval Literature,* ed. Linda Lomperis and Sarah Stanbury, 38–64. Philadelphia: University of Pennsylvania Press, 1993.

McKisack, May. *The Fourteenth Century (1307–1399).* Vol. 5 of *The Oxford History of England.* Oxford: Clarendon Press, 1959.

McRuer, Robert. *The Queer Renaissance: Contemporary American Literature and the Reinvention of Lesbian and Gay Identities.* New York: New York University Press, 1997.

Mehl, Dieter. *The Middle English Romances of the Thirteenth and Fourteenth Centuries.* New York: Barnes and Noble, 1969.

Mellinkoff, Ruth. "Cain's Monstrous Progeny in Beowulf: Part 1, Noachic Tradition." *Anglo-Saxon England* 8 (1979): 143–62. "Part 2, Post-diluvian Survival." *Anglo-Saxon England* 9 (1981): 183–97.

Miller, Jacques-Alain. "Extimité." In *Lacanian Theory of Discourse: Subject, Structure, and Society,* ed. Mark Bracher, Marshall Alcorn, Jr., et al., 74–87. New York: New York University Press, 1994.

Miller, Madeliene S., and J. Lane Miller. *Black's Bible Dictionary.* London: A. and C. Black, 1973.

Montrose, Louis Adrian. " 'Shaping Fantasies': Figurations of Gender and Power in Elizabethan Culture." *Representations* 1, no. 2 (1983): 61–94.

Motz, Lotte. "The Rulers of the Mountain." *The Mankind Quarterly* 20 (1979–1980): 393–416.

———. "Giantesses and Their Names." *Fruhmittelalterliche Studien* 15 (1981): 495–511.

———. "Giants in Folklore and Mythology: A New Approach." *Folklore* 93 (1982): 70–84.

———. "Gods and Demons of the Wilderness: A Study in Norse Tradition." *Arkiv för nordisk filologi* 99 (1984): 175–86.

———. "Trolls and Aesir." *Indogermanische Forschugen* 89 (1984): 180–95.

———. "The Families of Giants." *Arkiv för nordisk filologi* 102 (1987): 216–36.

———. "Old Icelandic Giants and Their Names." *Fruhmittelalterliche Studien* 21 (1987): 295–317.

———. "The Storm of the Troll Women." *Maal og Minne* 1–2 (1988): 31–41.

Muir, Lynette R. *Literature and Society in Medieval France: The Mirror and the Image, 1100–1500.* London: Macmillan, 1985.

Munro, Dana C. *Medieval Civilization: Selected Studies from European Authors.* New York: Century, 1910.

Newman, Karen. " 'And Wash the Ethiop White': Femininity and the Monstrous in Othello." In *Shakespeare Reproduced: The Text in History and Ideology,* ed. Jean E. Howard and Marion F. O'Connor, 142–62. New York: Methuen, 1987.

Olsen, Alexandra Hennessey. " 'Thirs' and 'Thyrs': Giants and the Date of *Beowulf.*" In *Geardagum* 6 (1984): 35–42.

Orchard, Andy. *Pride and Prodigies: Studies in the Monsters of the "Beowulf"-Manuscript.* Cambridge: D. S. Brewer, 1995.

Otter, Monika. *Inventiones: Fiction and Referentiality in Twelfth-Century English Historical Writing.* Chapel Hill and London: University of North Carolina Press, 1996.

Overing, Gillian R., and Marijane Osborn. *Landscape of Desire: Partial Stories of the Medieval Scandinavian World.* Minneapolis: University of Minnesota Press, 1994.

Painter, Sidney. *French Chivalry: Chivalric Ideas and Practices in Medieval France.* Ithaca: Cornell University Press, 1967.

Pallister, Janis L. "Giants." In *Mythic and Fabulous Creatures: A Source Book and Reference Guide,* ed. Malcolm South. Westport, Conn.: Greenwood Press, 1987.

Parker, Patricia. *Literary Fat Ladies: Rhetoric, Gender, Property.* New York: Methuen, 1987.

Paster, Gail Kern. *The Body Embarrassed: Drama and the Discipline of Shame in Early Modern England.* Ithaca: Cornell University Press, 1993.

Patterson, Lee. *Negotiating the Past: The Historical Understanding of Medieval Literature.* Madison: University of Wisconsin Press, 1987.

———. " 'What Man Artow?': Authorial Self-Definition in *The Tale of Sir Thopas* and *The Tale of Melibee.*" *Studies in the Age of Chaucer* 11 (1989): 117–75.

———. *Chaucer and the Subject of History.* Madison: University of Wisconsin Press, 1991.

Pearsall, Derek. "The Development of Middle English Romance." *Medieval Studies* 27 (1965): 91–116.

———. *Old English and Middle English Poetry: The Routledge History of English Poetry.* Vol. 1. London: Routledge and Kegan Paul, 1977.

———. *The Canterbury Tales.* London: George Allen and Unwin, 1985.

———. "Interpretive Models for the Peasants' Revolt." In *Hermeneutics and Medieval Culture,* ed. Patrick J. Gallacher and Helen Damico, 63–70. Albany: SUNY Press, 1989.

———. *The Life of Geoffrey Chaucer: A Critical Biography.* Oxford, U.K., and Cambridge, Mass.: Blackwell, 1992.

Peters, Edward. *Torture.* Oxford: Blackwell, 1985.

Pittenger, Elizabeth. "Explicit Ink." In *Premodern Sexualities,* ed. Louise Fradenburg and Carla Freccero, 223–42. New York: Routledge, 1996.

Prescott, Anne Lake. "The Odd Couple: Gargantua and Tom Thumb." In *Monster Theory: Reading Culture,* ed. Jeffrey Jerome Cohen, 75–91. Minneapolis: University of Minnesota Press, 1996.

Putter, Ad. *"Sir Gawain and the Green Knight" and French Romance.* Oxford: Clarendon Press, 1995.

Raby, F. J. E. *A History of Secular Latin Poetry in the Middle Ages.* 2d ed. Oxford: Clarendon Press, 1957.

Ramsey, Lee C. *Chivalric Romances: Popular Literature in Medieval England.* Bloomington: Indiana University Press, 1983.

Réau, Louis. *Iconographie de l'art chrétien.* Paris: Presses Universitaires de France, 1957.

Redpath, H. A. "Og." In *A Dictionary of the Bible, Dealing with Its Language, Literature, and Contents,* vol. 3, ed. James Hastings, 590. New York: Charles Scribner's Sons, 1899.

Regnier-Bohler, Danielle. "Figures féminines et imaginaire généalogique: étude comparée de quelques récits brefs." In *Le récit bref au moyen âge: Actes du colloque d'Amiens, 1979,* 73–95. Paris: Universite de Picardie, 1980.

Rella, Franco. *The Myth of the Other: Lacan, Deleuze, Foucault, Bataille.* Trans. Nelson Moe. Washington, D.C.: Maisonneuve Press, 1994.

Reynolds, Susan. "Medieval 'Origines Gentium' and the Community of the Realm." *History* 68 (1983): 375–90.

Rigaud, J. *Le Monstrueux dans la litterature et la pensée anglaises.* Aix: Presses de l'Universitie de Provence, 1985.

Rigg, A. G. "Golias and Other Pseudonyms." *Studi medievali,* 3d ser., 18 (1977).

Robson, Margaret. "Animal Magic: Moral Regeneration in Sir Gowther." *The Yearbook of English Studies* 22 (1992): 140–53.

Rowland, Beryl. *Animals with Human Faces: A Guide to Animal Symbolism.* Knoxville: University of Tennessee Press, 1973.

Roy, Bruno. "En marge du monde connu: les races de monstres." In *Aspects de la marginalité au Moyen Age,* ed. Guy-H. Allard. Quebec: Les Éditions de l'Aurore, 1975.

Rubin, Gayle. "The Traffic in Women: Notes on the 'Political Economy' of Sex." In *Toward an Anthropology of Women,* ed. Rayna R. Reiter, 157–210. New York: Monthly Review Press, 1975.

Rubin, Miri. "The Body, Whole and Vulnerable, in Fifteenth Century England." In *Bodies and Disciplines: Intersections of Literature and History in Fifteenth-Century England,* ed. Barbara A. Hanawalt and David Wallace, 19–28. Minneapolis: University of Minnesota Press, 1996.

Ruch, Lisa M. "The Legendary Story of Albina and Her Sisters: Its Role in the Medieval Chronicle Tradition." Unpublished paper, 27th International Congress on Medieval Studies, Kalamazoo, 8 May 1992.

Salecl, Renata. "Love Me, Love My Dog." Unpublished conference paper, Association for the Psychoanalysis of Culture and Society, November 1996.

Salecl, Renata, and Slavoj Zizek, eds. *Gaze and Voice as Love Objects.* Durham: Duke University Press, 1996.

Scala, Elizabeth. "The Wanting Words of *Sir Gawain and the Green Knight:* Narrative Past, Present and Absent." *Exemplaria* 6, no. 2 (1994): 305–38.

———. "Canacee and the Chaucer Canon: Incest and Other Unnarratables." *The Chaucer Review* 30, no. 1 (1995): 15–39.

Scott, W. "Giants (Greek and Roman)." *Encyclopaedia of Religion and Ethics.* Vol. 6, ed. James Hastings, 193–97. New York: Charles Scribner's Sons, 1899.

Sedgwick, Eve. *Between Men: English Literature and Homosocial Desire.* New York: Columbia University Press, 1985.

———. *Tendencies.* Durham: Duke University Press, 1993.

Severs, J. Burke, general editor. *A Manual of the Writings in Middle English, 1050–1500.* New Haven: Connecticut Academy of Arts and Sciences, 1967.

Shahar, Shulamith. *Childhood in the Middle Ages.* London: Routledge, 1991.

Shaviro, Steven. *The Cinematic Body.* Minneapolis: University of Minnesota Press, 1993.

Shepherdson, Charles. "History and the Real: Foucault with Lacan." *Postmodern Culture* 5, no. 2 (1995).

———. "The Intimate Alterity of the Real: A Response to Reader Commentary on 'History and the Real.'" *Postmodern Culture* 6, no. 3 (1996).

Shoaf, R. A. "The Alliterative *Morte Arthure:* The Story of Britain's David." *JEGP* 81, no. 2 (1982): 204–26.

———. *The Poem as Green Girdle: "Commercium" in "Sir Gawain and the Green Knight."* Gainesville: University Press of Florida, 1984.

———. "Literary Theory, Medieval Studies, and the Crisis of Difference." In *Reorientations: Critical Theories and Pedagogies,* ed. Bruce Henricksen and Thais E. Morgan, 77–92. Urbana and Chicago: University of Illinois Press, 1990.

Smith, Norman. "Loathly Births off Nature: A Study of the Portentous Monster in the Sixteenth Century." Ph.D. diss., University of Illinois at Urbana-Champaign, 1978.

Smith, Vance. "Body Doubles: Producing the Masculine *Corpus.*" In *Becoming Male in the Middle Ages,* ed. Jeffrey Jerome Cohen and Bonnie Wheeler, 3–19. New York: Garland Publishing, 1997.

Sources and Analogues of Chaucer's Canterbury Tales, ed. W. F. Bryan and Germaine Dempster. New York: Humanities Press, 1958.

Spence, Lewis. *The Minor Traditions of British Mythology.* London: Rider, 1948.

Spiegel Gabrielle. "Genealogy: Form and Function in Medieval Historical Narrative." *History and Theory* 22 (1983): 43–53.

———. "Social Change and Literary Language: The Textualization of the Past in Thirteenth-Century Old French Historiography." *Journal of Medieval and Renaissance Studies* 17 (1987): 129–48.

———. "History, Historicism, and the Social Logic of the Text in the Middle Ages." *Speculum* 65 (1990): 59–86.

———. *Romancing the Past: The Rise of Vernacular Prose Historiography in Thirteenth-Century France.* Berkeley: University of California Press, 1993.

Stahl, Paul-Henri. *Histoire de la décapitation.* Paris: Presses Universitaires de France, 1986.

Stanbury, Sarah. *Seeing the Gawain-Poet: Description and the Act of Perception.* Philadelphia: University of Pennsylvania Press, 1991.

———. "Feminist Masterplots: The Gaze on the Body of Pearl's Dead Girl." In *Feminist Approaches to the Body in Medieval Literature,* ed. Linda Lomperis and Sarah Stanbury, 96–115. Philadelphia: University of Pennsylvania Press, 1993.

———. "The Body and the City in Pearl." *Representations* 48 (1994): 30–47.

Stein, Robert. "Desire, Social Reproduction, and Marie's *Guigemar*." In *In Quest of Marie de France, a Twelfth-Century Poet,* ed. Chantal A. Maréchal, 280–94. Lewiston, N.Y.: Edwin Mellen, 1992.

Stephens, Walter. *Giants in Those Days: Folklore, Ancient History, and Nationalism.* Lincoln: University of Nebraska Press, 1989.

Stevens, Wallace. *The Collected Poems of Wallace Stevens.* New York: Vintage Books, 1982.

Stewart, Susan. *On Longing: Narratives of the Miniature, the Gigantic, the Souvenir, the Collection.* Baltimore: Johns Hopkins University Press, 1984.

Strohm, Paul. *Social Chaucer.* Cambridge: Harvard University Press, 1989.

Stuard, Susan Mosher. "Burdens of Matrimony: Husbanding and Gender in Medieval Italy." In *Medieval Masculinities: Regarding Men in the Middle Ages,* ed. Clare A. Lees, 61–72. Minneapolis: University of Minnesota Press, 1994.

Thomasset, Claude. *Commentaire du "Dialogue de Placides et Timéo."* Geneva: Librairie Droz, 1982.

Thompson, James Westfall. "The Origin of the Word *Goliardi*." *Studies in Philology* 20 (1923): 83–98.

Thompson, Rosemarie, ed. *Freakery: Cultural Spectacles of the Extraordinary Body.* New York: New York University Press, 1996.

Timmins, Samuel. *A History of Warwickshire.* London: E. Stock, 1889.

Tolkien, J. R .R. "*Beowulf*: The Monsters and the Critics." In *The Proceedings of the British Academy,* vol. 22. London: Oxford University Press, 1936, 1960.

Uebel, Michael. "Unthinking the Monster: Twelfth-Century Responses to Saracen Alterity." In *Monster Theory: Reading Culture,* ed. Jeffrey Jerome Cohen, 264–91. Minneapolis: University of Minnesota Press, 1996.

Vale, Juliet. *Edward III and Chivalry: Chivalric Society and Its Context, 1270–1350.* Woodbridge: Boydell, 1982.

Vale, Malcolm. *War and Chivalry: Warfare and Aristocratic Culture in England, France, and Burgundy at the End of the Middle Ages.* London: Duckworth, 1981.

Walsh, P. G. " 'Golias' and Goliardic Poetry." *Medium Aevum* 52 (1983): 1–9.

Webster, Brenda. "Golpe por golpe: Una nueva interpretacíon de *Sir Gawain and the Green Knight*." In *Mythopoeis: Literatura, Totalidad, Ideología,* ed. Joan Ramón Resina. Anthropos, n.d.

Wells, John Edwin. *A Manual of Writings in Middle English, 1050–1400.* New Haven: Connecticut Academy of Arts and Sciences, 1916.

White, Beatrice. "Saracens and Crusaders: From Fact to Allegory." In *Medieval Literature and Civilization: Studies in Memory of G. N. Garmonsway*, ed. D. A. Pearsall and R. A. Waldron, 170–91. London: Athlone Press of the University of London, 1969.

White, David Gordon. *Myths of the Dog-Man*. Chicago: University of Chicago Press, 1991.

White, Hayden. *Tropics of Discourse: Essays in Cultural Criticism*. Baltimore: Johns Hopkins University Press, 1978.

Wittkower, Rudolf. "Marvels of the East: A Study in the History of Monsters." *The Journal of the Warburg and Courtland Institutes* 5 (1942): 159–97.

Wright, Elizabeth. *Feminism and Psychoanalysis: A Critical Dictionary*. Cambridge: Blackwell, 1993.

Ziolkowski, Jan. *Alan of Lille's Grammar of Sex*. Cambridge: Medieval Academy, 1985.

Zizek, Slavoj. *The Sublime Object of Ideology*. London and New York: Verso, 1989.

————. *For They Know Not What They Do*. London and New York: Verso, 1991.

————. *Enjoy Your Symptom! Jacques Lacan in Hollywood and Out*. New York and London: Routledge, 1992.

————. *Looking Awry: An Introduction to Jacques Lacan through Popular Culture*. Cambridge: MIT Press, 1992.

————. *Tarrying with the Negative*. Durham: Duke University Press, 1993.

————. "Re-visioning 'Lacanian' Social Criticism: The Law and Its Obscene Double." *JPCS: The Journal for the Psychoanalysis of Culture and Society* 1, no. 1 (spring 1996): 15–25.

Index

✥

MEDIEVAL CULTURES

Jeffrey Jerome Cohen is associate professor of English and human sciences at George Washington University. He is the editor of *Becoming Male in the Middle Ages* and *Monster Theory* (Minnesota, 1996).